The
Recording
Studio
Handbook

The Recording Studio Handbook

John M. Woram

Editor, **db Magazine**
President, **Woram Audio Associates**

With an Introduction by Norman H. Crowhurst

ELAR Publishing Company, Inc.
Plainview, New York 11803

First Edition

ELAR Publishing Company, Inc.
Plainview, New York 11803

Copyright © 1981

Printed in the United States of America
Library of Congress Catalog Number 76-6250
ISBN 0-914130-01-3

Fifth Printing

to Christina Marie

Contents

Introduction

Human beings come in types. At one extreme we find the artistic individualists. The other end of the spectrum is occupied by "coldly logical" non-persons. Engineers tend toward the latter end of the spectrum, although if an engineer is to "break new ground," by doing something that has not been done before, he needs a certain amount of creativity.

However, people who work in studios with audio, at whatever stage in the overall production of listenable program material, are not just engineers. They are a somewhat special "breed of cat." In fact, they are so special that they really belong to a different era.

My acquaintanceship with John Woram, who authored this book, came about because both of us are columnists for the same professional magazine, *db, The Sound Engineering Magazine.* In some issues, our columns give the impression that we must have collaborated, but in fact that is never possible, mainly because we live on opposite sides of the continent. The way our columns often seem to corroborate each other arises simply because what we have to say is apparently something that needs saying just then.

Each of us achieved our respective degree of success, because we had something of that "special breed" quality that our vocation needs. The author devotes the whole of his book to the specifics of that vocation, so perhaps it would be appropriate for me to comment briefly on why such "cats" seem to be so rare.

The reason is exemplified in a type of question that is often directed to both of us: "How did you learn to do what you do?" The way the questioner asks this, we could imagine the same person asking Thomas Edison, "How did you learn to invent the electric light bulb?"

His manner of asking suggests that Thomas Alva might have been wandering past the book stalls down Main Street, when one particular paperback caught his eye: "How to Invent the Electric Light Bulb."

So he bought the book, went home, and invented it! To even the most brainwashed product of our modern "educational system," the absurdity of such a suggestion should be apparent.

Yet such a questioner often asks us for information that would help him to make a gold record, for example. How is a gold record made? Quite often a second or third gold record may result from repeating the formula that was successful in making the first. But how does one hit upon that magic formula for the first time?

Hollywood-type stories often imply that the answer has something to do with meeting the right person at the right time. That may play its part. But meeting the right promotion man at the right moment would scarcely, on its own, sell a million records. The recording itself must have something. And our questioner seems to be asking, "Where or how do you find that something that makes it gold record material?"

We often see books advertised, with such titles as , "How to Make a Million Dollars on a Shoe String." The book usually has nothing to tell us that we did not already know. So we finally conclude that the book was its author's way of making his own million dollars! (It's the old story about taking enough suckers.)

In our vocation, the secret of success rests in creativity. Technology, in recent years, has been a big help, simply because by making so many new things available, so fast, it has opened the door for creativity to bloom. But unfortunately, too few people seem possessed of that quality, today.

One of the real grandfathers of our art was Harvey Fletcher, of Fletcher-Munson curve fame. We have often heard him tell about "how they did it." What amazes us is not so much how they did it, as what they did it with! They had virtually none of our modern precision equipment. Almost everything used for their research experiments had to be made from scratch.

When we say "from scratch," today's engineer just does not know what that means. Today's cake baker will call it a "scratch cake," if he has to add water, and perhaps milk, to the ready mix, before he puts it in the oven. Back in Harvey Fletcher's day, the cake baker would have had to harvest his own grain and grind his own flour, before he would have anything to bake!

Some old timers say the modern generation is spoiled, because everything is done for them. Maybe that is true, but we feel envious: not because so much is done for today's generation, but because they have so much available that we never had.

So, John's book is not a "Cookbook of Success." It is based on his years of experience in recording and teaching. It does tell you much of what you need to know, and provides the right emphasis, to enable you to develop the capability that will carry you to success. But, in the real world, nobody hands out success on a silver platter. You must develop your own "smarts," using the talents with which you were born. You will find John's book a real help in doing just that, provided you are prepared to do your part.

Norman H. Crowhurst
Dallas, Oregon, 1976

Preface

Now that this little opus is at last finished, I'm told I have to write a preface to explain why it was started in the first place.

Well, if you must know, it all started when I realized that after some fifteen years of hanging around the recording studio, it would be a cinch to jot down all I had learned. That notion lasted about a week. After some fifteen years of hanging around, it was amazing to discover just how much I had *really* learned. It turned out to be not much at all. Certainly not enough for a book. A pamphlet maybe, but never a book. But the editor didn't think a pamphlet was a terribly clever idea, especially when my contract said "book." Besides, he argued, there are a lot of people around who could use either a refresher course on what they were doing, or an introduction to what they would like to be doing, once they got the chance.

So, I spent the last two years trying to figure out what it was that I had been doing over the previous fifteen. What, for example, is the difference between echo and reverberation? Does a limiter compress, or a compressor limit? Do noise reduction systems really work? Do hit records come from cardioid microphones? Which speaker tells what's really on the tape? What *is* really on the tape?

Apparently I wasn't the only one who had trouble with these questions. As I did my research, it was comforting to discover how many of my colleagues were either uncertain of, or had forgotten, the answers. So that I wouldn't forget again, I wrote it all down. All 80,000 words, but who's counting?

I suppose a few words about the manner of presentation wouldn't hurt. When writing about anything, some sort of background knowledge must be taken for granted. For instance, one can't talk about the mixdown session (Chapter 18) without first knowing a little something about the recording session (Chapter 17). But that means some familiarity with equalizers (Chapter 7), compressors (Chapter 6), and other signal processing devices. But you can't process a signal if you can't hear it (Chapter 5), and you can't hear it unless you've put up a microphone (Chapters 3 and 4). So, the book begins with microphones, and eventually concludes with the mixdown session.

Section I is more or less a prelude—a collection of those various little bits of odds and ends that have been explained to death elsewhere. The treatment here is reasonably brief—hopefully just enough to help the reader to wrestle through the rest of the book.

As far as possible, no term is introduced ahead of its time, so you don't have to know all about Chapter 7 in order to make sense out of Chapter 6. However, there are a few exceptions here and there. Equalization is introduced in Chapter 7, but not before it has made premature entrances in two earlier chapters. We first hear about it in the Chapter 2 coverage of the equal loudness contours. And again it surfaces for a moment in Chapter 5 under the guise of room equalization.

In both places, the word *equalization* is all but unavoidable in discussing the subject at hand, and I trust the reader will not be put off by this. To put the equalization chapter at the front of the book would have created many more serious problems, expecially for the student.

The section on tape and tape recorders posed some organizational problems. For example, should bias be discussed along with magnetic tape, or with the tape recorder? The former requires the bias, while the latter delivers it, and one must really talk about both the tape and the tape recorder in any discussion of bias. So, it seemed reasonable to discuss bias twice; the theory in the chapter on tape—the application in the chapter on alignment.

The reader may wonder about the conspicuous absence, throughout the text, of references to what is reverently known as, "the Literature," that is, the mountain of already published information from which every author begs, borrows and steals. I've left out these obligatory footnotes, references and quotations for a few reasons which strike me as reasonable, if not academically defensible;

1. More often than not, my interpretation of "the Literature" bears little resemblance to "t.L." itself.
2. I don't wish to imply, however indirectly, that my conclusions are in any way endorsed by those who have gone before.
3. No intelligent burglar would dream of publicizing the house from which he has been stealing.

However, there is a bibliography in the Appendix which lists various books, journals, magazine articles and papers which have crossed my path over the years. Most, if not all, have contributed in one way or another to the writing of this text. The serious student is urged to attack this mountain of information for himself and to draw his own conclusions. Where this book agrees with what has gone before, the previous author deserves full credit. Where it does not, I didn't agree, or what is more likely, didn't understand what was being said, and so came up with my own version, which you find here.

To conclude, I'm certainly glad it's done, and doubt that I shall ever do it again (unless of course, I am asked). If you get half as much out of reading this as I did writing it, I shall be well rewarded. That, and the royalties.

John M. Woram
Rockville Centre,
New York
June, 1976

Section I
THE BASICS

Introduction

In subsequent sections of this book, it has been assumed that the reader has at least a nodding acquaintance with the basics. That is, a general understanding of the decibel, and a fair idea of the nature of sound. However, this section has been prepared for those who need a little refresher course in some of these first principles of recording.

I suspect the average recording studio reader will not necessarily be enthralled by a dissertation on the physics of sound waves, but would rather get to the point, and then be off to more interesting aspects of recording science. With that in mind, this section has been prepared to cover as briefly as possible the basic minimum requirements.

Too many engineering books assume that the technician must know all about atomic structure if he is to be trusted to replace a transistor. For those who seek that sort of background information, the shelves are already bulging with high school and college level texts.

The presentation here will no doubt enrage academicians who stumble across this book by accident. But this was not written for (or by) one who already knows all there is to know. Such people are advised to put the book down quickly, and go on to more learned reading wherever they may find it.

Section I is not the most interesting part of the whole book. But it may be required reading in order to make the most sense out of the other sections with a minimum of grief.

CHAPTER 1

The Decibel

The decibel (abbreviated dB) is popularly understood to be the unit with which sound levels are measured. For example, we read that a jet aircraft at takeoff creates a noise of 130 dB, or that in the countryside on a quiet day the ambient noise level may be about 30 dB.

These and other sounds, whether pleasantly musical or just plain noisy, may be measured with a sound level meter. On the meter, 0 dB corresponds, not to absolute silence, but to the **threshold of hearing** – that is, the lowest sound pressure level that an average listener with good hearing can detect. This **zero reference level** corresponds to a sound pressure of 0.0002 dynes/cm^2. In terms of intensity, this is equal to 0.000000000001 watts/meter^2. The sound level meter itself will be described in greater detail in the next chapter.

Even a reasonably silent environment will contain a certain amount of background noise, so we may find that in an apparently quiet room the sound level is about 30 dB. In other words, the ambient noise level is 30 dB greater than our zero reference level.

Now it may be noted that the meter readings on a studio tape recorder or recording console are not necessarily related to the sound level in the room. Even with the monitor system turned off, the meters will still move if a signal is being recorded. In fact, varying the listening level has no effect whatever on these meter readings. Furthermore, typical readings of, say, +3 or -10, suggest that we are making measurements above or below some point other than the zero reference level just described.

Actually, there are two measuring systems in which the decibel is used. The first is as a measure of acoustic power – the sound of falling leaves or of roaring engines. These sounds are all louder than the threshold of hearing, and here the decibel tells us just how loud they are. Figure 1-1 lists typical sound levels for various environments.

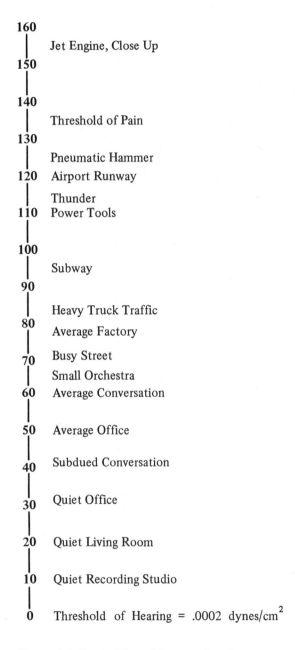

dB	
160	
	Jet Engine, Close Up
150	
140	
	Threshold of Pain
130	
	Pneumatic Hammer
120	Airport Runway
	Thunder
110	Power Tools
100	
	Subway
90	
	Heavy Truck Traffic
80	Average Factory
70	Busy Street
	Small Orchestra
60	Average Conversation
50	Average Office
40	Subdued Conversation
30	Quiet Office
20	Quiet Living Room
10	Quiet Recording Studio
0	Threshold of Hearing = .0002 dynes/cm^2

Figure 1-1. Typical Sound Pressure Levels

The other decibel tells us something about electrical power, or in most studio applications, voltage. In the case of power measurements, whether acoustical or electrical, the formula is the same:

$$NdB = 10 \log [P/P_r]$$

NdB = Number of decibels
P = The power being measured
P_r = A reference power level

In the case of sound, the reference level, P_r, corresponds as noted to the pressure produced by a sound at the threshold of hearing. Depending on the measuring system in use, the same zero reference level may be expressed in microbars, dynes/cm^2, or newtons/m^2. The relationship between systems is:

$$0 \text{ dB} = 0.0002 \text{ microbars} = 0.0002 \text{ dynes/cm}^2 = 0.00002 \text{ newtons/m}^2$$
$$= .000000000001 \text{ watts/m}^2$$

Therefore, 1 microbar = 1 dyne/cm^2 = 0.1 newton/m^2
   or: 10 microbars = 10 dynes/cm^2 = 1 newton/m^2

In electrical measurements, a more appropriate reference level will be chosen later in the chapter.

Logarithms

From the formula, we see that the decibel is defined in terms of logarithms (abbreviated log). Therefore, some comprehension of the mathematical significance of the log is essential to an understanding of the decibel. The reader who is completely familiar with logs may

Problems	Answers
1 =	1, or, 10^0
10 =	10, or, 10^1
10 x 10 =	100, or, 10^2
10 x 10 x 10 =	1,000, or, 10^3
10 x 10 x 10 x 10 =	10,000, or, 10^4
10 x 10 x 10 x 10 x 10 =	100,000, or, 10^x (x=5)

Figure 1-2. A Few Simple Multiplication Problems Solved.

wish to skip ahead. Others may also wish to do so, but should avoid the temptation.

In Figure 1-2, several very simple multiplication problems are solved. To the right of each answer, there appears a shorthand notation, consisting of the number 10 followed by a superscript. In mathematics, this superscript is known as an exponent, and to help us realize its significance, we may say that an exponent indicates how many times the number, 1, is to be multiplied by 10. In the last problem, the exponent, x, is equal to 5, and is read as, "ten, raised to the fifth power," or simply, "ten to the fifth."

The fact that $10^0 = 1$ may be difficult to understand. It may help to understand that 10^0 is *not* 1 multiplied by 0; rather, it indicates that the 1 is not to be multiplied by 10 at all, and so it remains simply, 1. This explanation may not please the mathematicians, but it will enable us to get on with our introduction to the decibel with a minimum of pain.

We should also note that numbers less than 1 can be represented by powers of ten. For example:

$$0.1 = 10^{-1}$$
$$0.01 = 10^{-2}$$
$$0.001 = 10^{-3}$$

In fractional form, $0.001 = 1/1,000$ or, $1/10^3$. So, we may say that $0.001 = 1/10^3 = 10^{-3}$. In other words, a power of ten in the denominator of a fraction may be moved to the numerator, simply by changing the sign, in this case from plus to minus.

Often, a difficult fraction may be simplified by following this procedure. For example:

$$\frac{3,200,000}{.004} = \frac{32 \times 10^5}{4 \times 10^{-3}} = \frac{32 \times 10^5 \times 10^3}{4} = \frac{32 \times 10^{5+3}}{4} = \frac{32 \times 10^8}{4} = 8 \times 10^8$$

Note that when powers of ten are to be multiplied, the exponents are merely added to find the product ($10^5 \times 10^3 = 10^{(5+3)} = 10^8$). Likewise, division may be accomplished by subtracting the exponents ($10^5 \div 10^3 = 10^{(5-3)} = 10^2$). The significance of this operation will be appreciated later in solving power and voltage equations in terms of decibels. For now, we may realize that cumbersome numbers become less so when converted to powers of ten. For example, the sound intensity at the threshold of hearing, stated earlier as

0.000000000001 watts/m² becomes simply 10^{-12} watts/m². A number such as 0.0000025 may be rewritten as 2.5×10^{-6}, or if it is more convenient, 25×10^{-7}.

Now, if $1 = 10^{0}$, and $10 = 10^{1}$, it stands to reason that we should be able to represent any number between 1 and 10 by 10^{x}, with x equal to some value between 0 and 1. To find the value for x in a problem such as $3 = 10^{x}$, we will call this exponent a logarithm, and offer the following explanation:

The logarithm of a number is that power to which 10 must be raised (not multiplied) to equal the number.

The statement may appear to contradict what was just said about multiplying 1 by 10 a number of times. To help resolve the apparent contradiction, we may note that although the number 10 may indeed be simply multiplied by itself, say four times for example, ($10^{4} = 1 \times 10 \times 10 \times 10 \times 10 = 10,000$), it is no simple matter to do the same thing 4.7 times. Yet, if $10^{4} = 10,000$, and $10^{5} = 100,000$, surely there must be a value for $10^{4.7}$.

To find the answer, something beyond simple multiplication is required. Returning to our sample problem, $3 = 10^{x}$, we may say that the log of 3 is x. The actual calculation of this, or any other log, is an involved calculation appreciated only by mathematicians, and the working recording engineer need not concern himself with the process, since tables of logarithms are readily available, with a simplified version given here, as Figure 1-3. However it is important to understand the significance of the log, so that calculation of decibels will be clearly understood.

By studying the table of logs, we may notice several important characteristics of logs, which are really extensions of what was just pointed out about multiplying and dividing exponents. Since a log *is* an exponent:

When numbers are multiplied, the log of the product is equal to the sum of the logs of the numbers.

$$
\begin{aligned}
\log (4 \times 5) &= \log 4 + \log 5 \\
\log 20 &= \log 4 + \log 5 \\
1.301 &= 0.602 + 0.699 \\
1.301 &= 1.301
\end{aligned}
$$

Number	Log	Number	Log	Number	Log
1	0.000	10	1.000	100	2.000
2	0.301	20	1.301	200	2.301
3	0.477	30	1.477	300	2.477
4	0.602	40	1.602	400	2.602
5	0.699	50	1.699	500	2.699
6	0.778	60	1.778	600	2.778
7	0.845	70	1.845	700	2.845
8	0.903	80	1.903	800	2.903
9	0.954	90	1.954	900	2.954
10	1.000	100	2.000	1,000	3.000

Figure 1-3. A Simple Table of Logarithms.
(A more complete Table of Logarithms is given in the Appendix)

When numbers are divided, the log of the quotient is equal to the difference of the logs of the numbers.

$$\log (800/20) = \log 800 - \log 20$$
$$\log 40 = \log 800 - \log 20$$
$$1.602 = 2.903 - 1.301$$
$$1.602 = 1.602$$

A final point: note that when any number is doubled, the log increases by a constant amount; 0.301. When a number is multiplied by 10, its log increases by 1, and when a number is squared, its log is doubled.

Acoustic Power Measurements

If we know that a jet aircraft produces a sound intensity of 10 watts/m^2, we may calculate the decibel level from the formula:

$$N_{dB} = 10 \log \frac{P}{P_{ref}} = 10 \log \frac{10^1}{10^{-12}} = 10 \log 10^{(1+12)} = 10 \log 10^{13} = 10 \times 13 = 130 \text{ dB}$$

$$P = 10 \text{ watts/m}^2$$
$$P_{ref} = 10^{-12} \text{ watts/m}^2 \text{ (threshold of hearing)}$$

The jet noise is therefore 130 dB above the threshold of hearing, or 10^{13} times as intense. Now although this certainly isn't anybody's idea of quiet, we probably wouldn't think of a jet plane being 10,000,000,000,000 times as loud as the threshold of hearing. Indeed, we may be surprised to realize that our ears are capable of responding to such an incredibly wide range of intensities.

The decibel notation makes these wide intensity ranges a little more manageable, and, pretty much follows the psychoacoustical properties of the ear. For example, if one jet aircraft produces 130 dB, what sort of acoustic horror awaits us in the presence of two such noises? Certainly, two jets will seem louder than one, but not by as much as one might expect. The listener will probably note that the noise level has increased somewhat, but certainly it is nowhere near twice as loud as before.

Note that if one jet produces 10 watts/m^2, two would produce 20 watts/m^2. Or,

$$N_{dB} = 10 \log \frac{20}{10^{-12}} = 10 \log \frac{2 \times 10^1}{10^{-12}} = 10 \log [2 \times 10^{13}] =$$

$$10 [\log 2 + \log 10^{13}] = 10 [0.301 + 13] = 10 [13.301] = 133.01 \text{ dB}$$

In other words, the two aircraft produce a racket that is only 3 dB above the noise of one of them. This 3 dB value rather accurately parallels the listener's subjective impression of the increase in level. In fact, if we returned to a more normal monitoring environment and listened to a musical program, and were then instructed to turn up the volume control until the program was "twice as loud," the measured sound pressure level would likely be about ten times greater than before. Of course, this is merely an approximation, since the conception of change in listening level will vary somewhat from one person to another.

Electrical Power Measurements

In any electrical circuit, a certain amount of power is dissipated. For example, the power dissipated in a resistor may be found from the formula, $P = E^2/R$ or $P = I^2 R$. Therefore, if we know the value of the resistance, and either the current, I, flowing through it or the voltage, E, across it, we may calculate the power. If the power then increases, we may calculate the difference in terms of decibels by

35

comparing the new power with the old. For example, if the power dissipated in a resistor increases from 0.5 watts to 10 watts, the increase in decibels is found from the log of the ratio of the two powers, with the first value, 0.5 watts, used as the reference level.

$$N_{dB} = 10 \log \frac{P}{P_{ref}} = 10 \log \frac{10}{0.5} = 10 \log 20 = 10 \times 1.301 = 13.01 \text{ dB}$$

If we had wished, instead, to calculate a decrease in dissipated power, the reference power would simply be placed in the numerator, and a negative sign would appear in the answer, to indicate a power loss.

In the recording studio, it is more convenient to work with voltage levels. This presents no problem, since power ratings are usually found only after the voltage has been measured anyway. And, since we invariably make all our measurements across the same resistance value, it may be eliminated from our calculations in the following manner.

Consider two different power values, P_a and P_b. Comparing them in terms of dB, $N_{dB} = 10 \log P_a/P_b$. But, since $P = E^2/R$, we may rewrite the formulas as: $10 \log \dfrac{E_a{}^2/R_a}{E_b{}^2/R_b}$. Since the value of the resistance does not change, $R_a = R_b$, and the formula may be simplified to $10 \log E_a{}^2/E_b{}^2$, or to $20 \log E_a/E_b$. Now if we measure the voltage across the resistance at, say 6 volts, and later increase it to 12 volts, the dB increase is,

$$N_{dB} = 20 \log \frac{12}{6} = 20 \log 2 = 20 \times 0.301 = 6.02 \text{ dB}$$

Note that whereas a doubling of power gave us an increase of 3 dB, a voltage doubling yields a 6 dB gain.

As in the case of acoustic power measurements, there is a standard zero reference level. Although this zero reference level represents an extremely low value (the threshold of hearing), in the studio it is more convenient to use an electrical zero reference level equivalent to the voltage found across a resistance in a typical operating condition. Then, we may compare other voltages and note that they are so many decibels above or below our zero reference standard.

The dBm

The voltage drop across a 600 ohm resistor through which 1 milli-

watt of power is being dissipated is our standard studio zero reference level. Via the formula, $P = E^2/R$, we may discover that the
zero reference voltage is 0.775 volts. Actually, the meters in the
studio are voltmeters, but they are calibrated in decibels to enable us
to make the kind of measurements that are most suited to audio
signals. Although the range of voltages is nowhere near as great as the
sound intensity variations cited earlier, the dB scale is still a most
practical measuring system. Over the years, there have been other
standard reference levels used. And so, to clarify the fact that our
decibel measurements are made relative to 1 milliwatt across 600
ohms, the notation, dBm, is used. The m refers to the milliwatt reference power level.

Many regular voltmeters will also show a dB scale (Figure 1-4A) and
upon inspection of the meter face, we may verify that 0 dB = 0.775
volts. However, it should be remembered that these dB scales are not
dBm unless the measurements are being made across a 600 ohm line.
Studio meters are usually permanently wired across the proper circuit values, but when using a bench-type voltmeter, there is no
reason to suppose that all measurements are being made across 600
ohms. Of course, the voltage scale is accurate regardless of the resistance across which the measurement is being made, but if we were
making our measurements across a 1,200 ohm resistor, we would
have to use the following formula to determine the actual dBm value:

$$NdB_m = 10 \log \frac{E^2/R}{E^2_{ref}/R_{ref}}$$

When R_{ref} is less than R, the formula may be rewritten as;

$$NdB_m = 20 \log E/E_{ref} - 10 \log R/R_{ref}$$

E_{ref} and R_{ref} are the values of our standard zero reference level;
0.775 volts and 600 ohms. E is the voltage across the nonstandard
resistance, and R is the value of that nonstandard resistance.

If we read an apparent 0 dBm (0.775 volts) across 1,200 ohms, the
actual dBm value would be:

$$20 \log E/E_{ref} - 10 \log R/R_{ref} = 20 \log (0.775/0.775) -$$
$$10 \log (1,200/600) = 20 \log 1 - 10 \log 2 = 20 \times 0 - 10 \times 0.301 =$$
$$-3.01 \text{ dBm} = \textit{actual value in dBm}$$

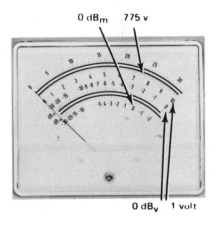

Figure 1-4A. A meter with both
voltage and dB scales.
The dB level is the sum of the meter
reading, plus the dB value printed
next to the rotary switch pointer.
(Waveforms 520-A.)

Figure 1-4B. A voltmeter with two
dB scales:
   0 dBm = .775 volts (for use on
                600 ohm lines)
   0 dBV = 1 volt (for other dB
              measurements not
              referenced to
              1 mw/600 ohms).
(Sennheiser RV55)
[Sennheiser photo]

We may verify this by comparing the power dissipated across the
zero reference standard with that dissipated across the 1,200 ohm
resistance.

$$P = E^2/R = (0.775)^2/600 = 1 \text{ milliwatt}$$
$$\text{(in the zero reference standard)}$$
$$P = E^2/R = (0.775)^2/1{,}200 = 0.5 \text{ milliwatt}$$
$$\text{(in the 1,200 ohm resistance)}$$

Since the power across the 1,200 ohm resistance is half the reference power, the decibel value is down 3 dB, which confirms our
previous calculation.

The dBV (1 volt reference level)

Decibel measurements are often made under conditions where a

600 ohm/1 milliwatt reference is inconvenient. For example, a certain acoustic pressure in front of a microphone may create an output level of -55 dBV.

The dBV nomenclature indicates a zero reference level of 1 volt. If the microphone's output voltage is 0.0005 volts, its dBV output is:

$$N \text{ dBV} = -20 \log (1/0.0005) = -20 \log 2,000 =$$
$$-20 \times 3.301 = -66.02 \text{ dBV}$$

Microphone output levels are discussed in greater detail in Chapter 3.

The dBV (0.775 volt reference level)

Some confusion arises from the fact that dBV measurements are also frequently made with respect to a 0.775 volt reference level. Since 0.775 volts corresponds to 0 dBm, many voltmeters are calibrated so that 0.775 volts and 0 dB line up on the meter face, as shown in Figure 1-4A. Such meter faces generally contain the legend, "1mW., 600 ohms," reminding the user that the scale measures dBm *only* across a 600 ohm line.

But since the meter is so often used under other circuit conditions, where the line impedance remains constant, though not at 600 ohms, there is little point in referring every reading back to a dBm value. In fact, in some cases the impedance of the circuit being measured may be unknown, making it impossible to calculate the actual dBm values.

And so, the meter scale is simply read directly. Although readings thus made are not dBm, the arithmetic difference between any readings will be the same as if they were both converted to dBm via the formula given earlier.

This type of measurement is usually given in dBV, and the zero reference voltage may or may not be clearly specified. Generally, the nature of the measurement gives some clue as to the probable zero reference of 0.775 or 1 volt.

Figure 1-4B shows a meter face containing both dB scales; 0 dBV = 1 volt, and 0 dBV = 0.775 volts.

Sample Problem

An amplifier is rated at 100 watts, ±3 dB. What is the actual range of output powers that would meet this specification?

Given, P_{out} = 100 watts, first solve for $P_{-3\,dB}$, the power at "-3 dB".

1) $NdB = 10 \log P_{out}/P_{-3dB} = 10\,(\log P_{out} - \log P_{-3dB}) = 3\,dB$
2) $\quad\quad 10 \log P_{-3dB} = 10 \log P_{out} - 3\,dB = 10 \log 100 - 3 =$
   $\quad\quad 10 \times 2 - 3 = 17$
3) $\quad\quad \log P_{-3dB} = 17/10 = 1.7$
4) $P_{-3dB} = 10^{1.7\,*} = 50$ watts

*Since the exponent, 1.7, lies between 1 and 2, the answer must lie between 10^1 and 10^2. That is, between 10 and 100. The actual number is found in the Log Table (Column N), next to the logarithm that is closest to 0.7 (=.6990). Therefore, N = 50.
(If the exponent had been 2.7, the number would have been 500).

Now, solve for P_{+3dB}, the power at +3 dB.

$$Ndb = 10 \log P_{+3dB}/P_{out} = 200 \text{ watts}$$

Therefore, an amplifier that is rated at 100 watts, ±3 dB, may have an output power anywhere between 50 and 200 watts.

The Volume Indicator

So far, we have talked about studio meters in terms of decibels. However, when audio signals are being measured, the proper unit of measurement is usually the volume unit, or VU.

The decibel has been defined as a ratio of powers, or perhaps voltages. As long as we are measuring a constant level, such as a 1,000 Hz reference level tone, we may express the reading in dBm.

On the other hand, an audio signal has a constantly changing level. Occasional peaks may be far above the average signal level, yet they do not contribute much to the listener's sensation of program loudness, for the ear has a tendency to average the fluctuating program level in evaluating its subjective loudness. Thus, a program with a fairly constant, though moderate, level will be considered much louder than a low-level program with some recurring high-level peaks.

Equating this to the meter, we may note that a regular bench type voltmeter does a poor job of responding to the rapid level changes of an audio program. The meter ballistics are such that it is accurate only on steady-state tones. For audio measurements, a different meter movement has been designed. This is known as the volume indicator, and it is calibrated in volume units, or VU. When measuring steady-state tones, the volume indicator readings will correspond to those seen on a regular dBm-calibrated voltmeter, yet on program measurements, the volume indicator will read somewhere between the average and peak values of the complex audio waveform. Volume indicator ballistics are designed so that the meter scale movement approximates the response of the ear; thus the meter does not register instantaneous peaks above the average level. If the peaks are frequent, the meter will read somewhat higher than the average level, yet still below the actual peak level.

The volume indicator's correspondence with the listener's subjective impression of loudness makes it a valuable recording tool. However it should be clearly understood that actual recorded levels are consistently higher than the meter readings. For example, the maximum-to-average ratio of program levels may be such that the volume indicator reads, say, +2. But the instantaneous level that causes that +2 reading may be +10 dBm or greater. Therefore, the reading should always be interpreted as +2 VU, not +2 dBm.

Both in practice and in the literature there is a tendency to refer to audio program measurements in decibels. Although there is surely little real danger in honoring this custom, the recording engineer should understand the difference between the decibel and the volume unit. The difference is particularly significant when high-level peaks are causing distortion, while the meter reading displays an apparently conservative recording level.

The Peak Reading Meter

The peak reading meter is more responsive to actual program peaks. Its ballistics are such that it will more accurately track the attacks of sudden high-level transient peaks. But since these peaks may be over just as suddenly as they occur, the movement is usually tailored to provide a more gradual fall-off, lest the rapid up and down movement be too fast for the eye to see.

Although many engineers use the loudness-related volume indicator, the peak reading meter gives a more accurate indication of what is actually being recorded. Since magnetic tape, as well as amplifiers, may be overloaded (and therefore distorted), by sudden bursts of high-level energy, some engineers prefer the peak reading meter, since it is more reliable in alerting the operator to potentially troublesome peaks that may escape the notice of the ear. Of course, a distorted amplifier will certainly be heard, but if the distortion takes the form of tape overload, it may not be noticed until the tape is played back later.

As noted earlier, the volume indicator and peak reading meter will read substantially the same on a sustained level program. However, with a program containing a significant number of high-level transients (for example, drums, tambourines, etc.) the peak reading meter may indicate levels 10 dBm or more above the volume indicator.

Since the peak reading meter is *not* a volume indicator, it is correct to read it in decibels, rather than volume units.

The Decibel or Volume Unit in Equipment Specifications

In reading other chapters of this book, continuing reference is made to the decibel (dBm), with little or no further mention of the volume unit (VU). For example, we may read that a tape saturates at +10 dBm, or that an equalizer supplies a 6 dBm cut at 3,000 Hz. Since the effects of these variables are so often observed on volume indicators, it may seem contradictory to discuss them in terms of decibels.

Although the volume unit is a measure of a complex audio waveform, for ease of measurement a steady tone is invariably used to determine equalizer performance or tape saturation. Therefore, the dBm becomes the correct unit of measurement.

As an example, consider an equalizer set to give a boost at 1,000 Hz of +3. When the equalizer is inserted, it might be expected that 1,000 Hz tones will now be higher by three volume units. However, if the 1,000 Hz tone is in the form of a sharp transient, the volume indicator may show little or no increase in reading, for the reasons discussed earlier. On the other hand, a sustained 1,000 Hz tone will be three volume units higher than before. Therefore, since the meter's response to the equalization change remains dependent on the nature of the program, it cannot be stated with certainty that a boost of +3 will always produce an increase of 3 VU. Consequently, these variables are specified in dBm, taking into account the steady-state conditions under which the measurements or calibrations were made.

Studio and Broadcast Reference Levels

Up until now, we have been talking about a zero reference level equal to 1 mW of power dissipated across a 600 ohm resistor. This value has no inherent significance—it is merely a mathematically convenient reference point.

However, the assignment of handy reference points is one thing, and the design of efficient meter movements is quite another. Early on, it was found that due to the vagaries of meter construction, it was difficult to build a meter movement that would satisfactorily register 0 dBm (or 0 VU). Such a meter would have an impedance of less than 4,000 ohms, and would therefore load the circuit it was supposed to be measuring, causing misleading readings.

To negate the loading effect of the meter movement, a series resistor (empirically valued at 3,600 ohms) was inserted in the meter circuit. But now, although the meter no longer affected the circuit being measured, the presence of the series resistor caused the meter to read about 4 dBm too low, when measuring an actual 0 dBm. With the 3,600 ohm resistor in the meter circuit, when the meter did read 0 dBm, the level would actually be +4 dBm.

Rather than re-define the zero reference level, it was considered expedient to leave 0 dBm at 1 mW across 600 ohms, with the understanding that 4 dBm above this value would correspond to a zero meter reading.

Most, if not all, recording studio equipment now adheres to this 0 VU = +4 dBm convention. However, the broadcast and telephone industries commonly go one step further and define a zero reference of +8 dBm. This takes into account the higher output levels required for telephone lines, which play such an important part in broadcasting.

As may be noted in Figure 1-5, a standard volume indicator's meter face reads from -20 to +3. Therefore, if 0 VU = +4 dBm, the meter is capable of reading levels up to +3 VU = +7 dBm. For broadcast applications, an additional 4 dBm of attenuation is placed in the meter circuit, so that 0 VU = +8 dBm. Now, a meter reading of +3 VU signifies +11 dBm.

Because of these conflicting zero reference levels, there is often some confusion about differences—if any—in recorded levels between studio and broadcast tape recorders. It often comes as a sur-

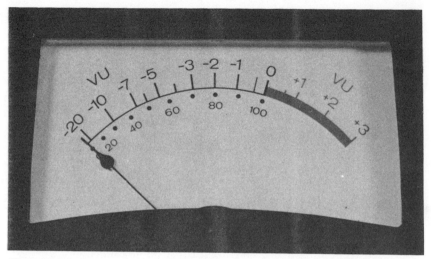

Figure 1-5A. A typical volume indicator, calibrated in volume units (VU). (API 561A)

Figure 1-5B. A peak program meter using light-emitting diodes as level indicators.
(Quad/8 PK-14) [Quad/8 photo]

Figure 1-5C. A similar meter in a vertical format.
(Quad/8 PK-16) [Quad/8 photo]

Figure 1-5D. Two examples of peak reading meters. The meters on the left contain 69 L.E.D.'s, arranged in a vertical column. In the right hand meters, a moving beam of light indicates the peak program level. (NTP 177-700 & NTP 177-210)

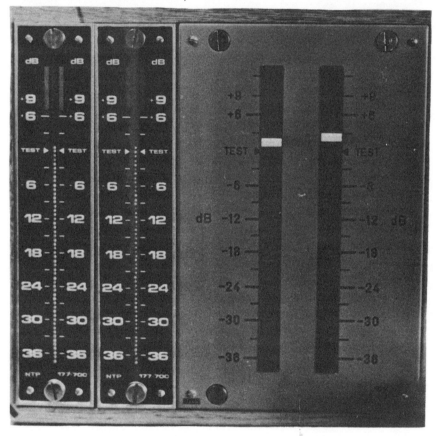

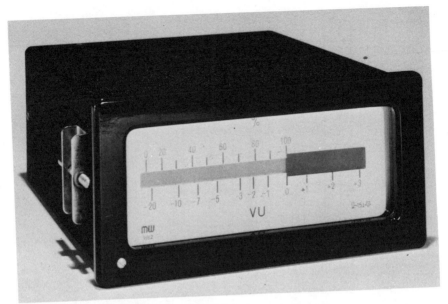

*Figure 1-5E. A VU meter with moving light beam indication.
(Gotham LBV) [Gotham Audio photo]*

prise to learn that there is actually *no* difference in recorded level, regardless of what level (+4, +8, or whatever) has been defined as a zero reference.

For example, a standard test tape is used to align all machines, whether used in broadcast or recording studio work. The output level control is rotated until the meter reads zero. Depending on the machine's meter circuit, this zero will indicate an output level of either +4 dBm or +8 dBm. Nevertheless, the input level — in this case from the test tape — remains the same. Consequently, when the machines are placed in the record mode, the same input level applied to both machines will cause identical meter readings.

Of course, if the actual output levels are compared, the broadcast machine will be louder. But this is because its playback amplifier has been turned up to +8, rather than +4. In either case, the input level, and therefore the level recorded on the tape, remains the same.

Figure 1-5F. A novel approach to the problem of reading 16 or more meters at once. The video monitor displays a moving vertical bar for each metered channel. (Audio Designs 560 Vue-Scan) [Audio Designs photo]

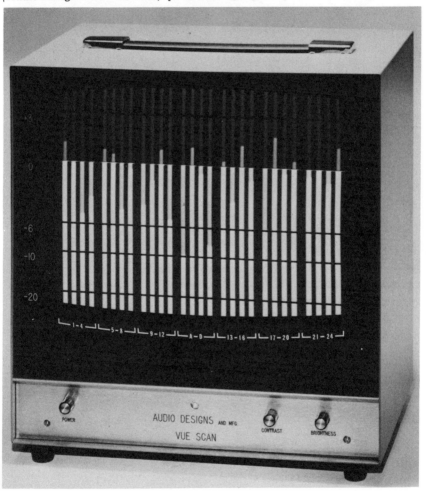

Figure 1-5G. On this console, two types of meters may be seen. On the right, the traditional VU meters. On the left, 24 segmented light display meters, switchable between VU and peak reading. (MCI JH 416LM Console) [MCI photo]

CHAPTER 2

Sound

Sound and Vibration

Simply stated, sounds are produced by mechanical vibrations. A vibrating object disturbs the molecules of air surrounding it, causing periodic variations in the air pressure. As the object vibrates back and forth, the pressure becomes alternately more, and then less, dense. These pressure variations radiate away from the object, eventually reaching the listener's ear, creating the sensation we know as sound.

The classic example of a vibrating object is a taut length of string, which may be set into vibratory motion by striking it, (as in the piano), plucking it (guitar), or drawing a bow across it (violin). The rate of vibration is a function of the tension applied to the string, as well as its length. In wind or brass instruments, the vibration is that of a column of air, and the vibration rate is regulated by changing the length of the air column, usually by opening and closing valves or keys.

Frequency and Range of Musical Instruments

When we say that a tone has a frequency of say, 440 hertz (abbr. Hz), we mean that the device producing the tone is vibrating back and forth 440 times each second. Musical instruments may of course produce a wide range of frequencies, and a chart of typical frequency ranges for various instruments is given in Figure 2-1. Note that the chart gives no information about the relative amplitude of the frequencies produced by the instruments. In most cases, the musician may vary the amplitude of each note played according to his taste.

Dynamic Range

The dynamic range of an instrument is a measure of the span between the quietest and loudest sounds it is capable of producing.

49

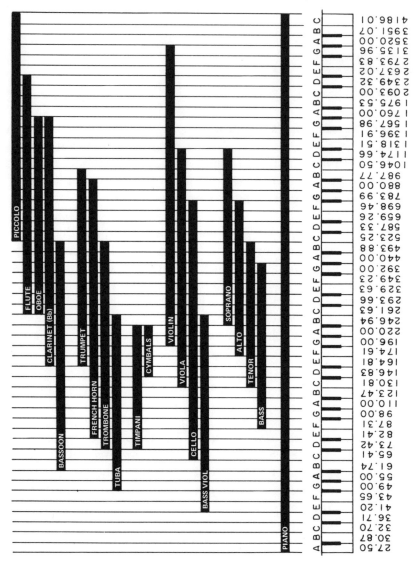

Figure 2-1. The frequency range of various musical instruments.

Subjective terms such as pianissimo (very quiet), mezzoforte (moderately loud), and fortissimo (very loud) are used to describe the relative intensity of the note produced.

The dynamic range of the human voice is quite broad—from a pianissimo whisper to a fortissimo shout—while that of the harpsichord is practically zero, since each of its strings is plucked with the same amount of force, regardless of the strength with which the keys are struck. In fact, the harpsichord's successor, the pianoforte, got its name in recognition of its wide dynamic range capability, as compared to its predecessor.

Frequency Response and Dynamic Range of Audio Equipment

Of course, vague terms such as piano and forte cannot be used to describe audio equipment. Although the equipment must be able to reproduce the dynamic range of whatever musical program is passing through it, its performance is evaluated in terms of frequency response. The frequency response of a device is a measure of its relative amplitude at various frequencies within its range. Presumably, an amplifier will have a "flat" frequency response, so that if it supplies a gain of say, 10 dB, all frequencies will be boosted by 10 dB (plus or minus whatever dB tolerance is specified).

In addition to a flat frequency response, an amplifier should not alter the dynamic range of the signal passing through it. However, this is not always possible, since the dynamic range capabilities of an audio system sometimes are exceeded by very wide dynamic range programs. This will be discussed in greater detail in the chapter on compressors, limiters and expanders (Chapter 8).

Figure 2-2. An amplifier with a "flat" frequency response between 40 Hz and 10,000 Hz and a bandwidth from 20 Hz to 20,000 Hz.

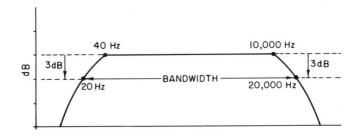

Amplifier Bandwidth

The bandwidth of an amplifier, or any other audio device, is the interval between the lowest and highest frequencies that are no more than 3 dB down in level. Figure 2-2 shows the frequency response of an amplifier with a flat response between 40 Hz and 10,000 Hz, and a 20 Hz to 20,000 Hz bandwidth. Note that the amplifier also passes frequencies below 20 Hz and above 20,000 Hz, but these are considered as being outside the amplifier's bandwidth, since they are attenuated by more than 3 dB.

Frequency Response and Logarithms

As mentioned earlier, the listener's subjective response to loudness varies logarithmically. In a similar manner, our perception of the interval between any two frequencies depends on the relative location of those frequencies within the audio bandwidth. To a musician, a 220 Hz interval between the two tones of 220 Hz and 440 Hz is recognized as an octave (abbr. 8va). However, the same 220 Hz interval between 440 Hz and 660 Hz would be—in musical terms—a perfect fifth. An octave above 440 Hz would be 880 Hz. Therefore, we may define an octave as:

Octave: The interval between any two frequencies,
f_1 *and* f_2, *when* $f_2 = 2f_1$.

By observation, we see that as the frequency of f_1 increases, the arithmetic frequency interval within the octave grows larger. Yet to the ear, any octave interval "sounds" the same as any other. This indicates that the ear's response to frequency is likewise logarithmic.

Log Paper

If frequency response measurements are drawn on standard graph paper, as shown in Figure 2-3A, it will be seen that each successive octave requires twice as much space as the one preceding it, for the reasons just described. A more satisfactory arrangement would allot an equal space to each octave, thus compensating for the ear's logarithmic response to frequency.

Log paper is used for this purpose, and may be prepared as shown in Figure 2-3B. Four equally spaced intervals, a-d, are drawn along

TWO METHODS OF REPRESENTING
FREQUENCY RESPONSE GRAPHICALLY

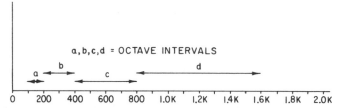

Figure 2-3A. When standard graph paper is used for frequency response data, each octave uses more space than the one preceding it.

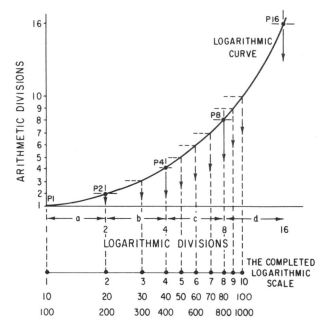

Figure 2-3B. A method of producing a logarithmic scale, so that each octave uses an equal amount of space.

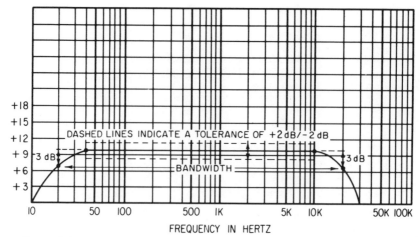

Figure 2-4. The frequency response of Figure 2-2, re-drawn on logarithmic scale paper.

the horizontal axis. The beginning of each interval is numerically labelled at twice the one before it (1, 2, 4, 8, 16).

The vertical axis is a simple arithmetic progression (1, 2, 3, 4,... 16). Points are placed on the graph (P_1, P_2, P_4, P_8, P_{16}) at the intersections of lines drawn from corresponding numbers on both axes. (1-1, 2-2, 4-4, 8-8, 16-16). A curve is drawn connecting the points. Now, lines from points 1 through 10 on the arithmetic axis are drawn to the curve, and then down (dashed lines) to complete the logarithmic scale. The 10 points on the logarithmic scale are labelled 1 through 10. Or, they may be labelled 10-100, 100-1,000, etc. If the scale is repeated several times (Figure 2-4) it may be seen that every octave now takes the same amount of space, regardless of its frequency interval.

The dB scale (vertical) is not drawn logarithmically, since the dB itself takes into account the logarithmic sensitivity of the ear to loudness.

The Human Voice

Like the musical instrument and the audio amplifier, the human voice may be analyzed in terms of frequency, amplitude and bandwidth. Speech sounds are of course quite complex, and are not generally thought of as having a recognizable musical pitch. Some have deeper voices than others, but people do not speak in musical "keys", since every spoken word produces energy at a great many frequencies simultaneously.

When the voice is analyzed, its "frequency response" is usually shown as an energy distribution curve, as in Figure 2-5. The curves show the relative amount of acoustic energy present at each frequency in a typical voice.

Sibilant sounds; s, z, sh, zh, produce a surprisingly large concentration of high frequency/high level acoustic energy. Although the listener may not be distracted by an occasional sibilant peak, an amplifier may be driven into distortion, producing an unpleasant "spitty" sound if corrective measures are not taken. These too will be discussed in greater detail in Chapter 8.

Wavelength of Sound in Air

As the vibrations from a musical instrument are transmitted through the air, we may calculate the physical length of one complete alternation of air pressure and call this the wavelength of that particular frequency. If we attach a pen to a vibrating object, and slide a piece of paper past, the line traced will be a graphical representation of the vibration. If the vibration produces a pure tone; that is, a single frequency with no harmonics or overtones, the graph is

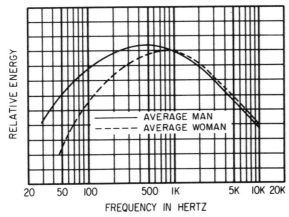

Figure 2-5. Energy distribution curves for typical speaking voices.

called a **sine wave**. In Figure 2-6, a sine wave is being produced by a tuning fork. If the paper were moving at the speed of sound, the physical length required for one complete oscillation to be drawn on the paper would correspond to the wavelength of the sine wave being measured. Since this is of course impractical, we may simply calculate the wavelength (abbr. λ) as:

$$\lambda = \frac{V}{F}$$

λ = wavelength, in feet (per cycle)
V = velocity of sound, in feet/second
F = frequency, in Hertz (cycles/second)

From the formula, we see that wavelength is dependent not only on frequency, but on the velocity of sound in air. This has been computed to be 1,087 feet/second at a temperature of 32° F., and increases about 1.1 feet/second for each degree increase in temperature. Therefore it is convenient in most cases to round off the velocity to 1,100 feet/second and say that a frequency of 100 Hz has a wavelength of 1,100/100, or 11 feet. If the temperature changes, the velocity — and therefore the wavelength — does too, but not by any significant amount.

Wavelength On Tape

On the other hand, when any frequency is to be recorded on tape, the velocity is by no means as constant as the speed of sound in air. Most tape recorders are capable of running at several speeds, and so its velocity may be halved, or doubled, depending on the speed selected. In Figure 2-6, the amount of paper taken up by one complete cycle depends on the speed at which the paper moves. Obviously, the slower the paper travels past the tuning fork, the less distance is used for each cycle, or, the smaller is the wavelength. And so it is with magnetic tape as it travels past the record head. If a 1,000 Hz sine wave is recorded and then played back at the same speed, each recorded cycle will last one thousandth of a second, and will be spread over whatever amount of tape passed the record head during that interval.

But later on, there would be no way to determine the frequency of the original sine wave *unless* we knew the tape speed at which the recording had been made. On playback, the frequency heard will depend on the speed at which the tape is moving. For example, at half

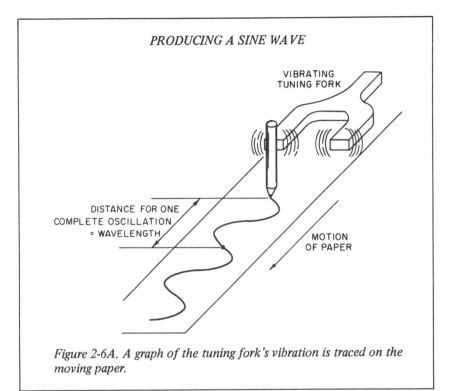

PRODUCING A SINE WAVE

VIBRATING
TUNING FORK

DISTANCE FOR ONE
COMPLETE OSCILLATION
= WAVELENGTH

MOTION
OF PAPER

Figure 2-6A. A graph of the tuning fork's vibration is traced on the moving paper.

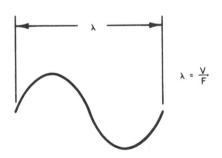

$$\lambda = \frac{V}{F}$$

$\lambda = V/F$ $\lambda =$ Wavelength, in feet (per cycle)
$V =$ Velocity of sound, in feet/second
$F =$ Frequency of sound, in hertz (cycles/second)

Figure 2-6B. One cycle of a sine wave.

speed, each cycle of a sine wave that was originally 1,000 Hz will now take *two* thousandths of a second to pass the playback head, and the output will appear to be a 500 Hz tone. The recorded wavelength remains unchanged, yet the frequency heard has dropped a full octave. Of course, an actual musical program played back at the wrong speed would be painfully obvious, but for the moment we are concerned with sine waves only. A sine wave with a recorded wavelength of one thousandth of an inch (1 mil) may produce the following frequencies:

> 7,500 Hz at a tape speed of 7½ in/sec.
> 15,000 Hz at a tape speed of 15 in/sec.
> 30,000 Hz at a tape speed of 30 in/sec.

In evaluating the performance of a tape recorder, references to playback frequency response are invariably made, since our primary concern is, how well does the machine reproduce the audio bandwidth? However, the playback head is actually responding to the wavelength on tape, and the frequency response depends on the "wavelength response" of the playback head, and the tape speed (velocity) selected.

When the tape speed is doubled, each wavelength now represents twice the original frequency, and the machine appears to have an extended high frequency response.

Diffraction

When a sound wave travels past an obstacle, a portion of the wave bends around the obstacle and moves off at an angle to the original straight line path. The phenomenon recalls the popular high school physics demonstration in which a beam of white light is made to pass through a prism, where it is dispersed into a rainbow of colors.

White light is a composite of energy of many different wavelengths, and as it passes through the prism, each wavelength—with its characteristic color—is refracted at a different angle.

Now while energy passing through an object is refracted, when it travels past the object, it is diffracted. In either case, the result is the same; some of the energy is re-routed in a different direction, and the angle of deflection depends on the wavelength of the energy wave.

In the recording studio, diffraction is an important consideration.

A long wavelength (low frequency) may be bent (diffracted) almost completely around an obstacle in its path, while short wavelengths (high frequencies) are diffracted scarcely at all. Therefore, a listener (or microphone) in the shadow of the obstacle will hear a frequency-distorted version of the original sound wave.

Sound and Hearing

In the chapter on decibels, we learned that the ear may regularly encounter sound pressure levels between a very few dB and somewhat more than 100 dB. 0 dB was defined as the threshold of hearing. Here, it should be pointed out that the actual sound pressure level at the threshold of hearing varies considerably, depending on the frequency of the sound. Actually, the ear is highly sensitive to frequencies between 3,000 and 4,000 Hz, and less sensitive to lower and higher frequencies.

For example, if a 3,500 Hz tone is heard at the threshold of hearing, the sound pressure level will be 0 dB (10^{-12} watts/M^2) as stated before. But, if the frequency of the tone is changed to 350 Hz, the sound pressure level may have to be raised about 17 dB above this reference level, in order for the average listener to detect the signal. At 35 Hz, the sound pressure level may have to be raised more than 50 dB in order for the signal to be heard.

Equal Loudness Contours

Therefore, our threshold of hearing is by no means constant over the entire range of audible frequencies.

Figure 2-7A is a graph of equal loudness contours. The dashed line indicates the average listener's perception of equal loudness for frequencies determined to be at the threshold of hearing. As noted, low frequencies must be boosted considerably in sound pressure level in order to be heard, and frequencies above the maximum sensitivity area of 3,000 to 4,000 Hz must also be boosted, though not to the same extent.

Notice that the various contours are labelled in Phons, ranging from 0 to 130, and that at 1,000 Hz, the Phon rating corresponds to the sound pressure level in decibels. The Phon is a measure of "equal loudness". If we first listen to a 1,000 Hz tone, measured at say, 50 dB sound pressure level, and then adjust another tone so that it appears to be just as loud, both tones are considered to have a loud-

THE EQUAL LOUDNESS
CONTOURS DEVELOPED BY
FLETCHER-MUNSON

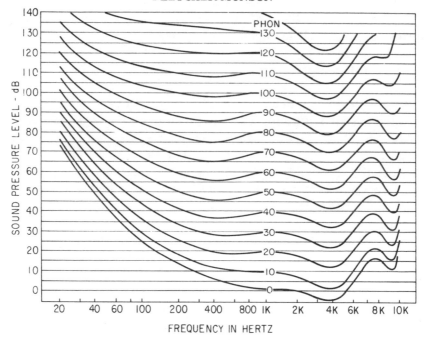

Figure 2-7A. The contours illustrate the ear's relative sensitivity at various sound pressure levels.

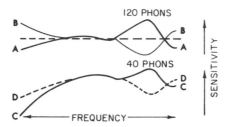

Figure 2-7B. The 120 and 40 Phon contours, inverted to compare the ear's relative sensitivity at these two listening levels.
A. The 120 Phon contour. Note the ear's extreme sensitivity in the 3,500 Hz area.
B. Equalization required to achieve an apparently flat frequency response (dashed line) at a 120 Phon listening level.
C. The 40 Phon contour. Note the sharper fall-off in sensitivity at low frequencies.
D. The apparent frequency response at 40 Phons, as a result of the equalization that was added when listening at 120 Phons. Note the deficient bass response and the lack of "presence" at 3,500 Hz.

ness level of 50 Phons, even though the measured sound pressure level of the second tone differs from the 50 dB level of the 1,000 Hz standard.

Notice that although the equal loudness contours each follow the same general direction, there are significant differences in the ear's relative sensitivity at differing listening levels. Sensitivity is always greatest in the 3,000 to 4,000 Hz region, and falls off as the frequency is lowered. However, in the 30 to 100 Phon range, there is again some increase in sensitivity as the frequency falls from 1,000 Hz to about 450 Hz, and then sensitivity again decreases until at the low end of the frequency spectrum, the ear is at its least sensitive point.

The equal loudness contours are often referred to as Fletcher-Munson curves, named after the two men who did early research in this area.

The implications of the equal loudness contours should be clearly understood by every recording engineer. As the loudness level is changed, the ear's frequency response is significantly altered. Therefore, a frequency balance that is satisfactory at one listening level may not be so at another.

Many engineers prefer a loud monitoring level, claiming it allows them to hear everything clearly. Later, when the level is reduced, there is inevitably some disappointment with the apparent lack of bass. Here, the equal loudness contours are working against the engineer.

For example, from Figure 2-7A we see that at 120 Phons, the ear is 15 dB more sensitive to 3,500 Hz, compared with 1,000 Hz. Below 1,000 Hz, the ear's sensitivity is uniform to about 200 Hz and then sensitivity falls off gradually.

At 40 Phons, there is only a 7 dB sensitivity difference between 1,000 Hz and 3,500 Hz, and below 300 Hz, the sensitivity decreases rapidly.

So, if a recording is balanced at 120 Phons, and then played back at 40 Phons, the bass will invariably sound weaker, and there may be lack of "presence" in the 3,500 Hz area if these frequencies were attenuated earlier as a reaction to the ear's extreme sensitivity to them at 120 Phons.

The situation may be clarified somewhat if we invert the 120 and 40 Phon contours, as shown in Figure 2-7B. The curves now depict a graph of the ear's relative frequency response at 40 and 120 Phons. Now, imagine that we added some equalization while listening at 120

Phons, in order to create the apparently flat frequency response shown by the dashed line. If we now observe the effect of this equalization on the 40 Phon contour, we arrive at the unsatisfactory frequency response shown as curve "D".

The low frequency response has apparently fallen off, and there is also a pronounced fall-off in the 3,000 to 4,000 Hz range.

It is an oversimplification to state that recordings should be monitored at the same loudness level at which they will be heard later on. Obviously, the engineer has no control over the record buyer's listening habits, and cannot predict the level at which he will choose to listen to the record.

However, the equal loudness contours do suggest that if studio monitoring levels are kept on the conservative side, there will be less disappointment later on. If the proper amount of bass is heard at low monitoring levels, any subsequent level increase will bring with it an apparent bass boost. Generally, this is to be preferred over the opposite condition, where the bass apparently decreases from the ideal point as the level is dropped.

The Sound Level Meter

Although the recording engineer is concerned with the decibel primarily in terms of electrical power or voltage ratios, some understanding of the sound level meter is essential to good engineering practice.

Basically, a sound level meter consists of a microphone, an amplifier, and a meter calibrated in decibels. However, such a device may not be created simply by connecting any available microphone, amplifier and meter. In addition to a specially calibrated microphone, the sound level meter will contain several filters and "weighting" networks.

The filter networks allow the meter to respond to sound energy within various narrow bandwidths. For example, if the filter network was set at 1,000 Hz, sound, (or noise) containing 1,000 Hz components could be measured, while the meter would be comparatively insensitive over the rest of the audio spectrum. This tunable feature allows the engineer to determine the frequency band which is contributing the greatest energy to the overall sound or noise level. (Figure 2-8 is a photo of a Sound Level Meter).

Figure 2-8. A Sound Level Meter.
(Bruel & Kjaer 2206)
[Bruel & Kjaer photo]

Weighting Networks

In addition to the filters just described, the sound level meter may contain additional filters, called weighting networks. These weighting networks correspond to the ear's varying sensitivity at different loudness levels.

As just described and shown by the Fletcher-Munson curves in Figure 2-7A, the ear is less sensitive to extreme high and low frequencies at lower listening levels. Therefore, at lower listening levels, noise in the low and high frequency regions would of course be less objectionable than the same amount of noise in the mid frequency area.

The "A" and "B" weighting networks are filters which correspond to the sensitivity of the ear at listening levels of 40 and 70 Phons, respectively. When making measurements at these levels, the insertion of the appropriate weighting network will therefore give a meter reading that is pretty much in accordance with what the listener subjectively hears.

Although noise level measurements of recording studio equipment are commonly made on a standard voltmeter, an "A" weighting net-

AN "A" WEIGHTED
FILTER NETWORK

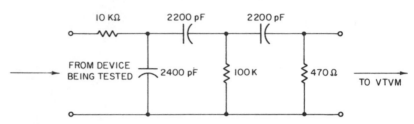

Figure 2-9A. Schematic. The network produces a 4 dB insertion loss.

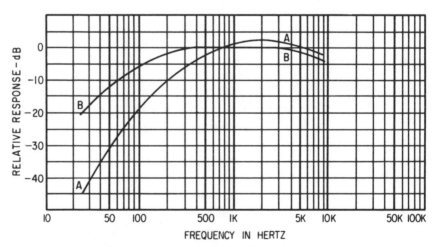

Figure 2-9B. The "A" and "B" weighting curves.

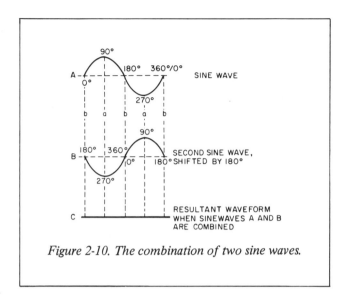

Figure 2-10. The combination of two sine waves.

work is often inserted just before the meter input so that, as in sound level measurements, the reading conforms to the subjective impression that the noise would make at low listening levels. Accordingly, noise level specifications are frequently quoted at so many decibels, dBA. Or the level may be quoted in dBm, with the notation, "A Weighting". An "A" weighting network is shown in Figure 2-9A and the "A" and "B" weighting curves are drawn in Figure 2-9B.

Phase and Coherence

In Figure 2-10A, various points along a sine wave are marked off in degrees. A second sine wave is drawn in Figure 2-10B. Although the two are of course identical in wave shape, we may say that the second one has been shifted by 180° due to its relative position with respect to the first sine wave.

Notice that as one sine wave reaches positive maximum amplitude, the other reaches negative maximum (points "a"). Both sine waves pass through zero amplitude at the same time (points "b"). If the two waves are combined graphically, (Figure 2-10C), the resultant wave form will be a straight line, indicating zero amplitude. Since the

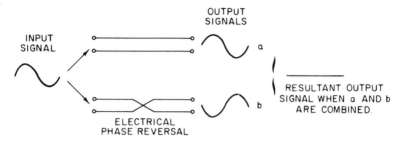

Figure 2-11. The effect of an electrical phase reversal.

waves are at all times equal in amplitude and opposite in polarity, they have cancelled each other out.

A similar condition will occur electrically if audio signals of equal amplitude and opposite polarity are combined. This might happen to an audio signal that is passing through two different signal paths, if there is a wiring reversal in one of the paths. As shown in Figure 2-11, when the two are eventually combined, any signal common to both of them is cancelled out. The signals are said to be electrically out of phase.

An acoustic phase cancellation might occur if two microphones are positioned in such a way that one receives a positive pressure wave at the same time the other receives a negative one, as shown in Figure 2-12. This is a very real problem, which will be discussed in greater detail in the chapter on microphone applications.

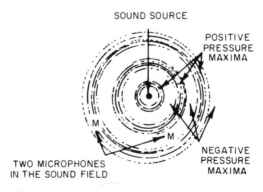

Figure 2-12. The acoustic phase reversal between the two microphones will cause a cancellation if their outputs are combined.

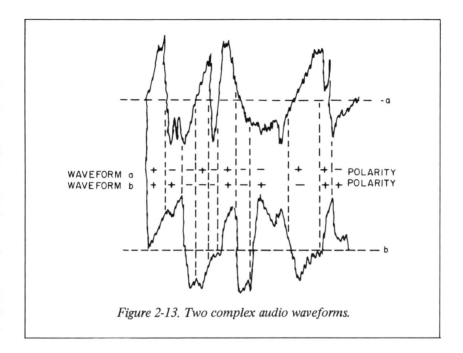

WAVEFORM a   + |− |−|−+|− + |−|− | + |+|− POLARITY
WAVEFORM b   + |+|−|−|−| + |−|− + | − |+|+ POLARITY

Figure 2-13. Two complex audio waveforms.

Of course, actual program waveforms are considerably more complex than sine waves, and the relationship of one to another cannot really be measured as precisely as two sine waves of the same frequency. Phase relationships become meaningless, and about all that can be said for the two waveforms shown in Figure 2-13 is that sometimes they are of the same polarity (+, + or −, −) and other times they are not (+, − or −, +). Even when the polarities are opposite, the waveforms do not cancel out, since their amplitudes are usually unequal.

During those intervals when the waveforms are of the same polarity, they are said to be "coherent"; when the polarities are opposite, the waveforms are incoherent. When the same signal is applied to two signal paths, they are totally coherent since, regardless of the complexity of the waveforms, they are of course identical. But if one of the paths contains an electrical phase reversal, the two signals become totally incoherent since they are at all times identical in amplitude yet opposite in polarity. As with the sine waves shifted by 180°, the totally incoherent waveforms will cancel out if combined.

Signals from two different sources, say a guitar and piano, will display a random coherence, since there is no signal component common to both signals. An electrical phase reversal will have no effect on an eventual combination of the signals. However, if a signal from a center placed soloist is common to both sources, the phase reversal will cause it to cancel out when the signals are combined.

The Cathode Ray Oscilloscope.

The cathode ray oscilloscope is an effective monitor of phase and coherency information.

If a sine wave is applied to the scope's Y AXIS input, a vertical line will be seen, as in Figure 2-14A. If the signal is instead applied to the X AXIS input, a horizontal line will be seen, as in Figure 2-14B. In both cases, the length of the line is an indication of the amplitude of the applied signal.

If the sine wave is applied, in phase to both scope inputs, a diagonal line will be seen, as shown in Figure 2-14C. The angle of the line will indicate the relative amplitudes of the signal at both inputs. If the amplitudes are equal, the line will appear at a 45° angle, as seen in Figure 2-14C. If the amplitudes are unequal, the angle will change towards the vertical or horizontal axis, depending on which amplitude is greatest.

If there is an electrical phase reversal in one of the lines, the slope of the diagonal line will be reversed. (Figure 2-14D). The visual display is a clear indication of the phase reversal, which might otherwise escape notice.

If complex audio waveforms are applied to both scope inputs, the coherent component will tend to produce a diagonal display in the in-phase direction, while the incoherent component will tend toward an out-of-phase display. The net resultant pattern will resemble those patterns shown in Figures 2-14E, F, G. The general diagonal orientation of the display indicates the amount of coherency. As before, a totally coherent signal (same program applied to both inputs) will produce a diagonal line that moves in the direction shown in Figure 2-14C, while a totally incoherent program will resemble Figure 2-14D.

Most stereo programs contain a signal component that is common to both left and right. This is the center channel information which is heard equally from both speakers. Depending on the relative level of this center channel component, the scope pattern will take on an in-phase orientation, as in Figure 2-14E. However, if an accidental phase reversal has occurred, the general orientation will be reversed, as in Figure 2-14G. This visual display will warn the engineer of a potentially troublesome condition which should be traced and cor-

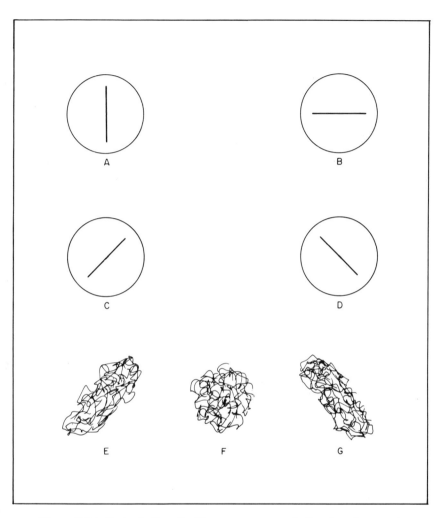

Figure 2-14. Cathode Ray Oscilloscope patterns, indicating phase and coherence between two signals.

A. Signal applied to Y axis input only (generally signifies left track of a stereo program.)

B. Signal applied to X axis input only (generally signifies right track.)

C. Same signal applied to both inputs.

D. Same signal applied to both inputs, but with a phase reversal in one input line.

E. Stereo signal with a strong coherent component, resulting in an "in-phase" orientation.

F. Stereo signal with random coherency, resulting in a circular pattern with no noticeable diagonal orientation.

G. Stereo signal with a strong incoherent component, resulting in an "out-of-phase" orientation.

rected.

An accidental phase reversal—whether due to an improperly wired cable or an acoustic condition in the studio—may be difficult or impossible to detect by ear alone. In fact, it may actually enhance the sound by giving it a more spacious feeling. However, later on when the signals are combined, the signals may cancel out almost completely. Therefore, the use of an oscilloscope as a visual monitor while recording cannot be overemphasized.

Section II
TRANSDUCERS: MICROPHONES AND LOUDSPEAKERS

Introduction

Transducer: *1. Any device whereby the energy of one power system may be transferred to another system, whether of the same or a different type. 2. A microphone or loudspeaker.*

Modern recording studio practice is a curious mixture of art and science. The engineer who can describe the operating parameters of every transistor in the studio may yet be content to describe his favorite drum microphone as "crisp." While demanding less than a small fraction of a percent distortion from an equalizer, he may not even care about the sensitivity rating of a new microphone, providing it sounds "right" to him.

As for monitor speakers, he's apt to be more concerned with similar subjective value judgments than with rated efficiency, radiation angles, and so forth.

Needless to say, these subjective terms aren't much help to the beginner who is trying hard to learn more about the science of recording; yet it is difficult, or impossible, to avoid such descriptions of transducers in the recording studio.

Perhaps the avoidance of more precise terminology is a necessary function of the transducing processes in the signal path from musical instrument to listener. Along the way, many subtle changes take place. The microphone converts acoustic energy into mechanical, then electrical, energy. The loudspeaker reverses the process. At the end of the chain, the listener's ear converts acoustic energy into brain waves, and he forms a subjective opinion about what he hears. Even in the control room, the listener is several generations away from the actual musical event, and is actually evaluating the performance of the transducing system as well as the music.

Personal taste, upbringing, and the generation gap are a very few of the factors that influence our musical taste and perception, and these variables all come into play when we evaluate what we hear in the control room. Another engineer will have another opinion—just as subjective—about the same reproduced sound. One may prefer microphone "A," while another likes microphone "B." If the monitor system is changed, opinions may change with it. And under almost no conditions will there be unanimous agreement as to what sounds "right."

Since microphones are easily changed — while speakers are not — the listener tends sometimes to ignore the role of the speaker in his evaluation of the microphone. Yet a change in speakers will certainly influence one's preference in microphones.

Given the subjectivity of music, and the inter-dependence of one transducer on the other, definitive statements — especially on microphone technique — cannot easily be made. Nevertheless, a basic understanding of the more scientific aspects of both transducing systems will help the engineer develop his own personal recording technique.

Chapter 3 covers the basics of microphone theory, while Chapter 4 discusses some of the more general microphone techniques, which may be adapted or modified to suit the demands of everyday studio practice. Chapter 5 concludes the section with a description of the loudspeaker and the enclosure in which it is placed, and also considers the interface between the speaker and the listening room.

Microphone Design

At the heart of any microphone is its diaphragm, where acoustical energy is converted into an electrical signal as the diaphragm vibrates in response to the impinging sound wave. Microphones are commonly classified according to the manner in which this energy conversion takes place, and a description of the most popular classifications of studio microphones, Dynamic and Condenser, follows.

DYNAMIC MICROPHONES

Microphones in which an electrical signal is produced by the motion of a conductor within a magnetic field are classified as dynamic microphones.

Dynamic Moving Coil Microphones

In this type of microphone, a coil of wire is attached to the rear of the diaphragm, and the coil is suspended within a magnetic field, as shown in Figure 3-1. As the diaphragm vibrates, so does the coil, and the magnetic field induces a voltage within the coil. The voltage is the electrical equivalent of the acoustical energy that caused the diaphragm to vibrate.

Dynamic Ribbon Microphones

In this type of dynamic microphone, a thin corrugated sheet, or "ribbon" of metal foil takes the place of the diaphragm/moving coil combination. The ribbon is suspended within a magnetic field, and a small voltage is induced as the ribbon vibrates to and fro. The corrugations lend some structural strength to the ribbon which, in early designs, was quite delicate. Modern ribbon microphones, however, are well-suited to studio use, and may be just as sturdy as their moving coil counterparts. A typical ribbon microphone is illustrated in

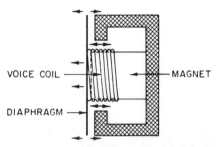

Figure 3-1. Cross-sectional sketch of a dynamic moving coil microphone.

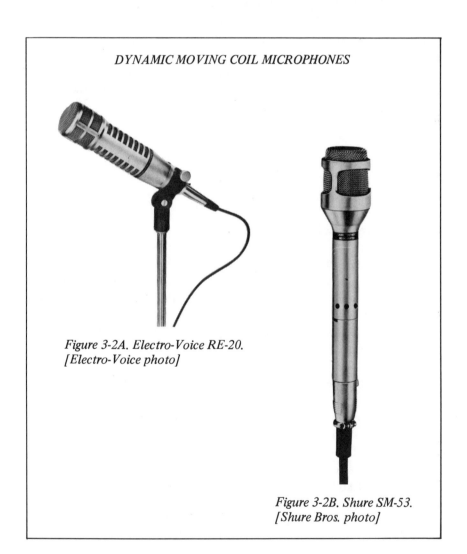

DYNAMIC MOVING COIL MICROPHONES

Figure 3-2A. Electro-Voice RE-20.
[Electro-Voice photo]

Figure 3-2B. Shure SM-53.
[Shure Bros. photo]

Figure 3-3. Note that the ribbon microphone contains a built-in output transformer. The impedance of the ribbon is quite small, usually on the order of a fraction of an ohm. Therefore, a transformer is required to raise the microphone's output impedance to a usable value. (Note: A possible source of confusion is the common studio practice of referring to moving coil microphones as "dynamics" while ribbons, which are also dynamic, are known simply as "ribbons.")

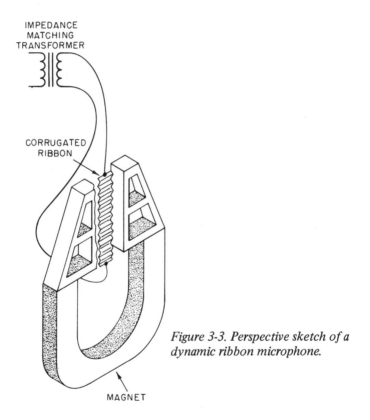

IMPEDANCE
MATCHING
TRANSFORMER

CORRUGATED
RIBBON

Figure 3-3. Perspective sketch of a dynamic ribbon microphone.

MAGNET

CONDENSER MICROPHONES

In the condenser microphone, the diaphragm is actually one of the plates of a condenser. (Although in other branches of electronics the condenser is now known as a capacitor, here the term condenser remains in popular usage.) As the condenser microphone's diaphragm vibrates, the spacing between it and a stationary back plate

DYNAMIC RIBBON MICROPHONES

Figure 3-4A. A rugged studio
ribbon microphone. (Shure SM-33)
[Shure Bros. photo]

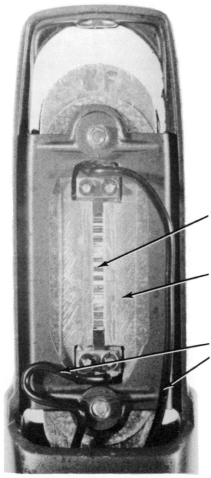

Corrugated
Ribbon

Magnet

Signal Leads

Figure 3-4B. Close-up of a ribbon
microphone, with the protective
covers removed. (Shure 300)

varies, producing a varying capacitance. A signal voltage is thus derived, in conjunction with a pre-amplifier built into the microphone's case. The preamplifier is required since the capacitor's output and impedance must be converted to microphone level values.

Of course, the preamplifier requires a power supply, and this is usually mounted externally, due to its physical bulk. The power supply furnishes a polarizing voltage to the condenser/diaphragm, as well as supplying the necessary voltages for the tubes or transistors within the microphone's preamplifier. Figure 3-5 illustrates the built-in preamplifiers in several condensor microphones.

Electret Condenser Microphones

Electret condenser microphones utilize a condenser/diaphragm that has been permanently polarized by the manufacturer. Consequently, the diaphragm does not require an external voltage source, although a power supply is still needed for the transistors in the preamplifier.

Condenser Microphone Power Supplies

Like any preamplifier, the one within the microphone requires a power supply, as noted above. In the case of tube type condenser microphones, the power supply will furnish filament voltages, as well as a polarizing voltage to the diaphragm. As shown in Figure 3-6A, the cable between the microphone and the power supply contains extra conductors to supply the microphone with the voltages required.

Condenser Microphone Phantom Power Supplies

Many modern condenser microphones employ so-called phantom power supply circuits, in which both the audio and the d.c. supply voltage travel within the same conductors. The phantom circuit greatly simplifies recording set-ups, since now the engineer need not set up a separate power supply for each condenser microphone he wishes to use. In a studio properly equipped with a phantom power supply system, condenser and other microphones may be quickly interchanged before or during a recording session. The condenser microphone will automatically draw the required power as soon as it is plugged in, while the other microphones will in no way be affected by the phantom power supply.

*SEVERAL EXAMPLES OF CONDENSER MICROPHONES,
SHOWING THE BUILT-IN PREAMPLIFIERS*

Figure 3-5A. Neumann U-67. [Gotham Audio photo]

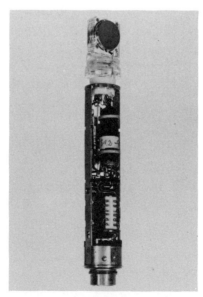

*Figure 3-5B. Neumann KM-56.
[Gotham Audio photo]*

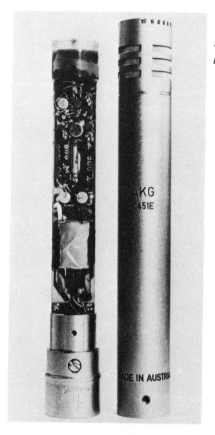

*Figure 3-5C. AKG C 451E.
[AKG photo]*

Condenser Plates

Metal Foil   Ceramic
Protective Casing   Diaphragm   Back Plate

*Figure 3-5D. AKG C 451E capsule
detail. [AKG photo]*

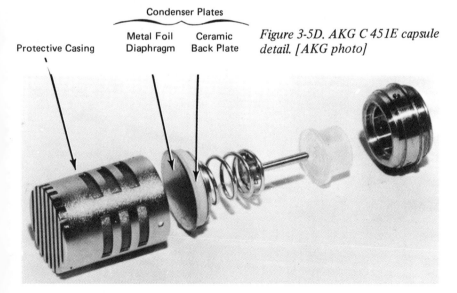

THE CONDENSER MICROPHONE POWER SUPPLY

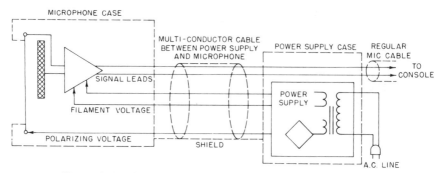

Figure 3-6A. Simplified schematic of a condenser microphone system showing external power supply and multi-conductor cable to microphone.

Figure 3-6B. A power supply for a tube type condenser microphone.

TWO METHODS OF SUPPLYING PHANTOM POWERING
TO CONDENSER MICROPHONES

Figure 3-7A. The phantom powering system is wired to the center tap of the console's input transformer.

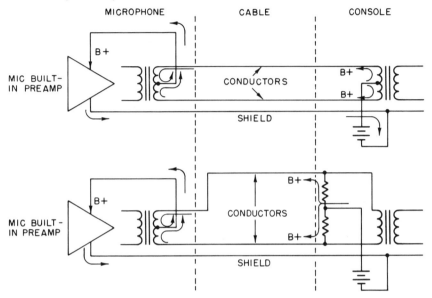

Figure 3-7B. An artificial center tap is created with two matched resistors.

If the recording console uses center-tapped microphone input transformers, the required positive supply voltage may be applied as shown in Figure 3-7A. Since transformers do not pass d.c. from one winding to another, the only path for the supply voltage is through *both* conductors in the microphone cable, back towards the microphone. Within the microphone, another transformer—also center-tapped—passes the supply voltage to the preamplifier as shown.

In modifying a console for phantom powering, it is a common practice to create an artificial center tap with two matched resistors, as shown in Figure 3-7B. Note that in either application of phantom powering, the microphone cable's shield is attached to the negative side of the power supply. Thus it becomes doubly important that all microphone cables have their shields well-connected at both ends of the cable. The shield must now provide a d.c. path back to the power supply, as well as fulfilling its primary purpose of shielding the signal leads against noise. Although a slight interruption in the shield may not make the cable unusable with dynamic microphones, it will prevent a phantom powered microphone from properly functioning. Microphone cables are discussed in some detail at the end of this chapter (Balanced and Unbalanced Lines).

A phantom power supply system will not necessarily replace all of the individual condenser power supplies within any given studio. Power requirements vary from one microphone manufacturer to another and may not always be compatible. And, of course, vacuum tube condenser microphones will still require filament voltage, which is not available through phantom powering.

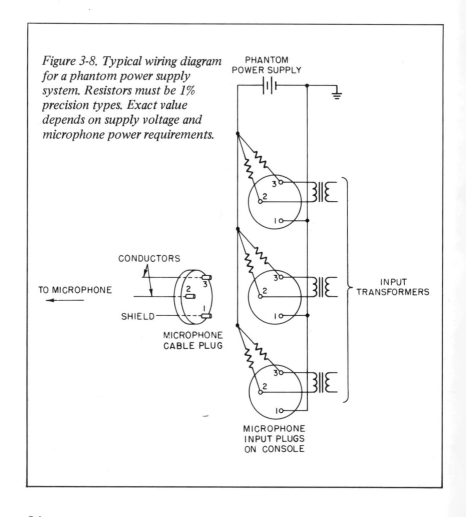

Figure 3-8. Typical wiring diagram for a phantom power supply system. Resistors must be 1% precision types. Exact value depends on supply voltage and microphone power requirements.

ACOUSTICAL SPECIFICATIONS

Directional Characteristics of Microphones

In any normal listening situation, we generally prefer to face the source of sound which interests us. In fact, sounds originating directly in front of us (called **on-axis signal**) may often be clearly heard despite the presence of loud distracting sounds in the surrounding, but off-axis, area. It seems that our brain allows us some flexibility in focusing on what it is we wish to hear, and with concentration we may be able to tune out other distracting sounds. But this ability is greatly influenced by the relative direction from which the sound arrives. We find that we invariably attempt to face in the general direction of the sound to which we are listening. For example, consider a concert performance by a large orchestra. A listener in the theatre audience might have little trouble concentrating on a particular instrument within the ensemble, and a reasonable amount of distraction (air conditioning noises, outside traffic, and such) would be all but unheard, due to the listener's ability to concentrate on the music.

On the other hand, a single microphone in the audience will hear, and pass along, *every* sound occurring within its range, without regard for the musical importance of one sound over another. Obviously, the microphone does not enjoy the listener's ability to concentrate on the music alone. If a recording were made in this manner, the microphone will transmit both music and noise with equal facility, as shown in Figure 3-9A.

Later on, lacking the visual cues which help the brain to concentrate, the listener will find it difficult or impossible to sort out the music from the noise, or to concentrate on some instrument which he may have clearly heard during the actual performance.

And, needless to say, the recording engineer will have no control whatever over anything but the overall recorded level of the total ensemble. A dramatic improvement in perspective, if not control, may be realized by employing two microphones in an attempt to more closely simulate the effect of listening via two ears. Yet two microphones have no more "brain power" than one, and some attempt must be made to separate – for the microphone's benefit – those sounds that are to be recorded from those that are not desired. To accomplish this, we might put the microphones very close to the sound source of interest (Figure 3-9B), so that all other sounds are,

THE EFFECTS OF MICROPHONE PLACEMENT

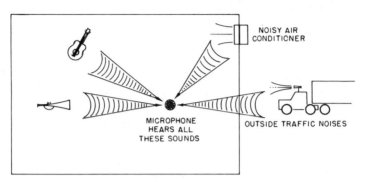

Figure 3-9A. A microphone in the middle of the room hears both wanted and unwanted sounds.

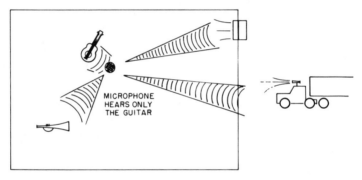

Figure 3-9B. A microphone placed very close-up hears the instrument directly in front of it, and most other sounds are considerably attenuated.

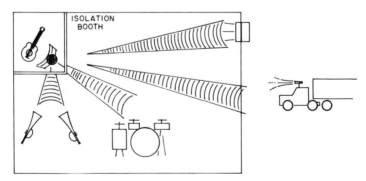

Figure 3-9C. In very noisy rooms, the isolation booth helps shield the microphone from unwanted sounds.

from the microphone's point of view, drowned out by the sheer volume of the close-up instrument or voice.

Even the most unwanted of noises—if very loud or quite close to one ear—will mask all other sounds, regardless of the listener's interest in them. Likewise, a microphone placed quite close to a musical instrument (or noise) simply will not hear much of anything else, wanted or not. This means that several microphones may be required to cover a large group, or even a small ensemble, if each microphone is placed close to an instrument, or group of instruments.

In the case of a severe noise problem—and here "noise" may even mean the sound of other musical instruments—we may place certain instruments in isolation booths (Figure 3-9C) to acoustically protect them from being drowned out by other, much louder, sound sources.

Another approach takes into consideration the actual design of the microphone. In any typical recording application, the microphone is no doubt placed so that wanted sounds arrive on-axis; that is, from directly in front of the microphone. Presumably, unwanted sounds are off to the side or in the rear (off-axis).

A certain degree of insensitivity to these unwanted sounds may be designed into the microphone. Of course it should be kept in mind that the microphone's insensitivity has nothing to do with whether a sound is wanted or not, but is strictly a function of the angle from which the sound arrives.

Directional Sensitivity: Omni-, Bi-, Uni-Directional Microphones

According to its design, a microphone may be classified as omni-, bi-, or uni-directional, with these terms referring to the type of directional sensitivity that has been built in. A brief description of each type follows.

Omni-Directional (Pressure) Microphones

A microphone that is equally sensitive to all sound sources, regardless of their relative direction, is known as an omni-directional microphone. Basically, the microphone consists of a diaphragm and a sealed enclosure, as shown in Figure 3-10. It is often referred to as a pressure microphone, since it responds to instantaneous variations in air pressure, caused by the sound wave in the vicinity of the diaphragm. Since the microphone has no way of determining the location of the sound source causing the pressure variation, it responds

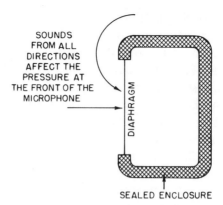

Figure 3-10. The omni-directional microphone.

with equal sensitivity to sounds (or rather, pressure variations) coming from all directions; hence the name omni-directional.

The microphone approximates the directional characteristics of the ear, which is likewise an omni-directional transducer. In the case of the ear, the head itself is somewhat of an acoustical obstruction to sounds arriving from certain off-axis locations. High frequencies in particular are better heard by the ear closest to the source producing them.

In a similar manner, the case of a physically large microphone may somewhat obstruct rear-originating sounds, causing a slight decrease in sensitivity—again most apparent at high frequencies.

Bi-Directional (Pressure Gradient) Microphones

The bi-directional microphone is equally sensitive to sounds originating directly in front (0°) or directly behind it (180°). It is least sensitive to sounds arriving from the sides (90° and 270°). The bi-directional characteristic is generally realized by leaving both sides of the diaphragm exposed, as shown in Figure 3-11. Thus, sounds may impinge upon either the front or the rear of the diaphragm. This type of microphone is often referred to as a pressure gradient microphone, since the movement of the diaphragm is in response to the pressure gradient—that is, the difference in acoustic pressure between the front and rear of the diaphragm. Side-originating sounds reach both front and rear at the same time and intensity, creating a net pressure

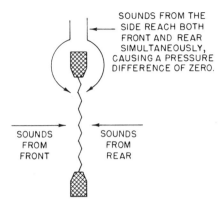

Figure 3-11. The bi-directional microphone.

gradient, or difference, of zero, thus explaining why this type of microphone is so highly insensitive at 90° and 270°.

An important aspect of the bi-directional microphone is the electrical phase reversal between its front and rear. To understand the significance of this, consider an instantaneous positive pressure wave striking the diaphragm. If the wave arrives from in front of the microphone, the diaphragm moves towards the rear, and a positive voltage is produced. If the same instantaneous positive pressure was to simultaneously strike the *rear* of another bi-directional microphone, its diaphragm would move in the same relative direction (that is, away from the pressure wave) but this would be toward the *front* of this microphone. Consequently, a negative voltage would be produced.

Although either voltage would constitute a usable audio signal, their equal and opposite polarities would cause a complete cancellation if the outputs were combined. In like manner, a complex audio signal that simultaneously reached the front and rear of two bi-directional microphones would be severely attenuated when the outputs of these microphones were combined, either while recording, or later on during a mixdown session.

Therefore, when bi-directional microphones are used, it is important to take into consideration this phase reversal and to make sure that no signal source is located between the rear of the bi-directional microphone and the front of another microphone, whether bi-directional or not. In practice, the attenuation is rarely total, especially if the individual frequency responses of the microphones are dissimilar.

Characteristically, the combined output signal may sound thin or generally distorted in frequency response, as the two frequency responses combine subtractively.

Uni-Directional (Phase Shift) Microphones

A uni-directional microphone is most sensitive to sounds originating directly in front of it, that is, at 0°, or on axis. If the microphone is slowly rotated through 360°, while its diaphragm remains at a constant distance from the sound source, its output level will gradually decrease, until the microphone is facing directly away from the sound source (180°). As the microphone continues to be rotated from 180° to 360°, (or 0°), its output level will gradually increase again.

The fall-off in sensitivity at the rear is generally the result of one, or a series, of side- or rear-entry ports, as shown in Figures 3-12 and 3-13. The ports are so arranged that rear-originating sounds may reach the diaphragm by two paths: 1) around the microphone to the front (p_1) and, 2) through an entry port to the rear of the diaphragm (p_2). If the two paths are of equal length, (with therefore no phase shift), the pressure on both sides of the diaphragm will be the same, causing no "pressure gradient," and hence no output voltage. On the other hand, sounds arriving from the front (p_3) must travel an extra distance to reach the rear of the diaphragm (p_4). The phase shift caused by the difference in path lengths p_3 and p_4 causes a reinforcement of on-axis signals.

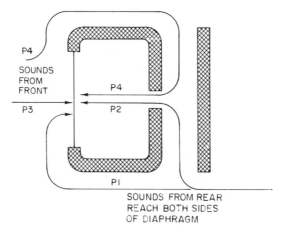

Figure 3-12. The uni-directional microphone.

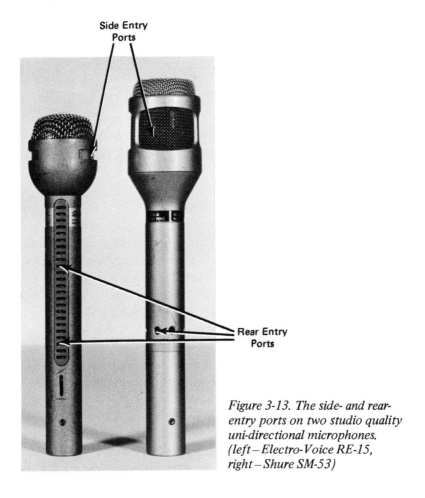

Figure 3-13. The side- and rear-entry ports on two studio quality uni-directional microphones. (left – Electro-Voice RE-15, right – Shure SM-53)

MICROPHONE POLAR PATTERNS

A polar pattern is simply a graph of a microphone's relative sensitivity to sounds originating at various locations around it. Polar patterns for omni-, bi-, and uni-directional microphones are shown in Figures 3-14A,B,C. In each case, the heavy line is the polar pattern itself, while the concentric circles indicate 5 dB increments of sensitivity.

The Omni-Directional Polar Pattern

The omni-directional polar pattern is simply a circle, indicating that the microphone is equally sensitive to sounds, regardless of the direction from which they arrive. In practice, the omni-directional microphone is apt to be slightly less sensitive to rear-originating sounds since – as mentioned earlier – the microphone's case may serve as somewhat of an acoustical barrier. The effect is noted by the slight flattening of the polar pattern in the vicinity of 180°, as shown in Figure 3-14A. Note that here, the pattern almost touches the concentric circle marked 5 dB. This means that the microphone being measured is actually almost 5 dB less sensitive to rear-originating sounds.

The Bi-Directional (Figure-8) Polar Pattern

The bi-directional polar pattern (Figure 3-14B) illustrates this microphone's equal sensitivity to front- and rear-originating sounds, as well as its relative insensitivity to sounds originating at 90° and 270°. The bi-directional microphone is popularly known as a Figure-8 micorphone, due to the characteristic shape of its polar pattern.

The Uni-directional (Cardioid) Polar Pattern

Note that the uni-directional polar pattern drawn in Figure 3-14C crosses the concentric circle marked 5 dB at about 100°, and at the rear (180°) just touches the 20 dB circle. This means that sounds originating at these locations will be attenuated by 5 dB and 20 dB respectively as compared to the same sound originating on-axis (0°).

It is important to realize that the practical uni-directional microphone is certainly not totally deaf to 180° off-axis sounds. These sounds are merely attenuated by a certain number of dB, as the polar pattern indicates. Due to the heart-like shape of the polar pattern, the uni-directional microphone is popularly known as a cardioid microphone.

The Super- and Hyper-Cardioid Polar Patterns

Somewhere between the double lobe pattern of the Figure-8 microphone and the single lobed cardioid, a series of intermediate patterns may be drawn in which the rear lobe of the Figure-8 pattern gets progressively smaller, while the front lobe takes on a cardioid shape. Although many of these patterns are merely mathematical models, several of them may be found in studio quality microphones.

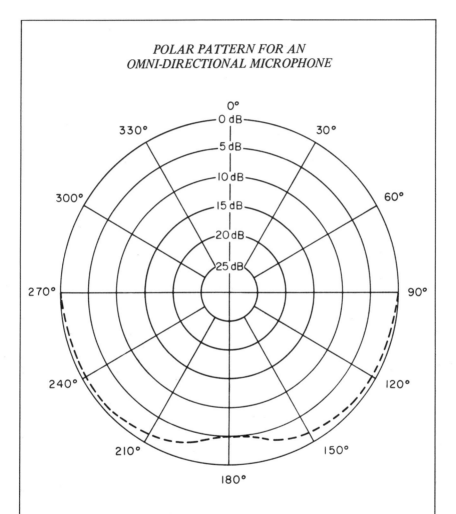

Figure 3-14A. The omni-directional polar pattern. The dashed line indicates a slight loss of sensitivity in the rear.

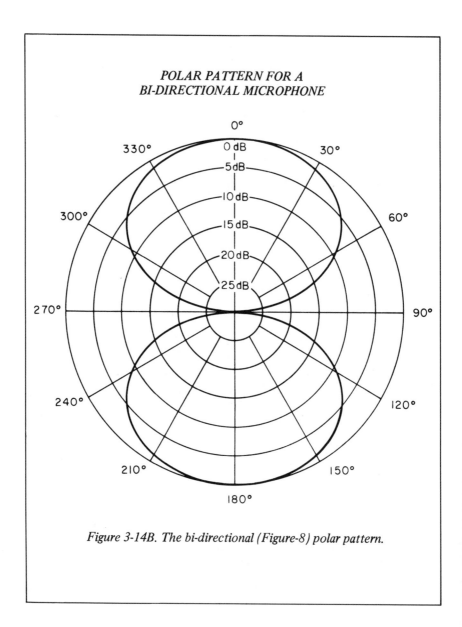

Figure 3-14B. The bi-directional (Figure-8) polar pattern.

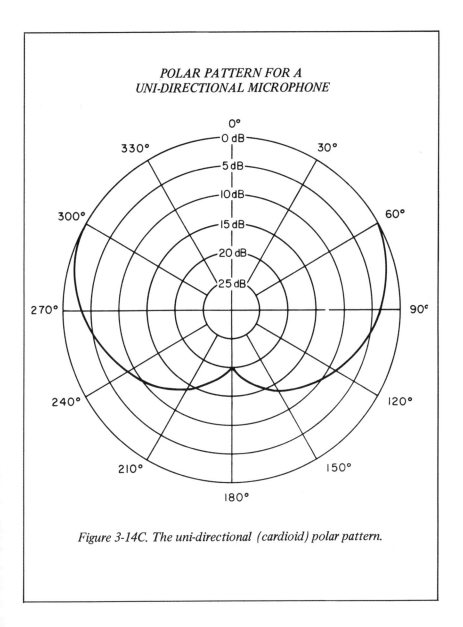

Figure 3-14C. The uni-directional (cardioid) polar pattern.

The so-called super-cardioid pattern, as shown in Figure 3-15A, is often found in high quality directional microphones. In Figure 3-15B, the super-cardioid pattern is overlaid on a regular cardioid pattern. From the illustration, it will be seen that the super-cardioid is more sensitive in the rear, but somewhat less sensitive at the sides than the cardioid. In addition, the super-cardioid has two areas of minimum sensitivity, at about 150° and 210°.

The hyper-cardioid pattern is somewhat less sensitive at the sides than the super-cardioid, and has a larger rear lobe, as shown in Figure 3-16.

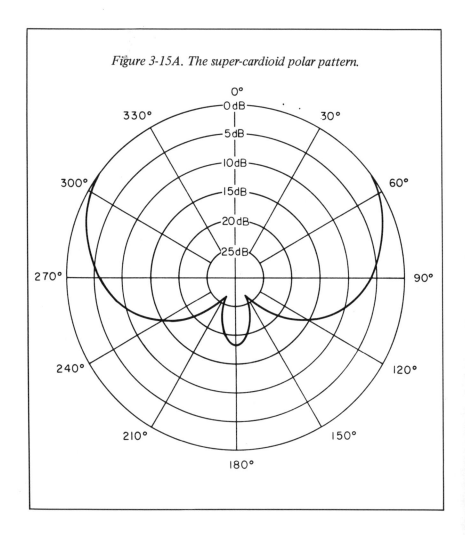

Figure 3-15A. The super-cardioid polar pattern.

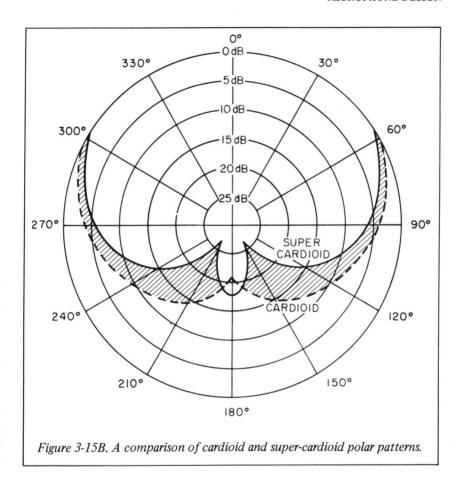

Figure 3-15B. A comparison of cardioid and super-cardioid polar patterns.

The Cottage Loaf Polar Pattern

Although the term "cottage loaf" is rarely heard in American recording studios, it is widely used by the British Broadcasting System to describe super- and hyper-cardioid polar pattern microphones.

The Ultra-Directional (Shot-Gun) Polar Pattern

The polar pattern for highly directional microphones generally resembles a flattened-out front lobe, with a series of very small rear lobes, as shown in Figure 3-17A. This microphone is not often used in recording studios, but may be a valuable tool on remote sessions when it is impossible to place cardioid or other microphones close to

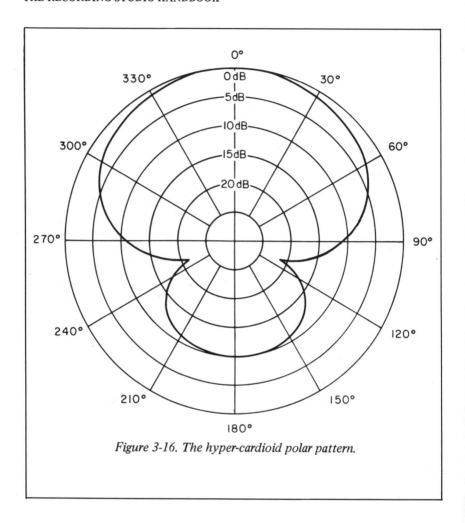

Figure 3-16. The hyper-cardioid polar pattern.

the performers. It is also widely used in television studios, when the microphone must be kept well out of camera range.

The microphones are popularly known as shot-gun microphones, due to their appearance.

MICROPHONES WITH MORE THAN ONE POLAR PATTERN

Dual Diaphragm Microphones

A frequently seen design in condenser microphones utilizes two diaphragms, in order to provide the user with a choice of polar patterns. The dual diaphragm design takes advantage of the fact that

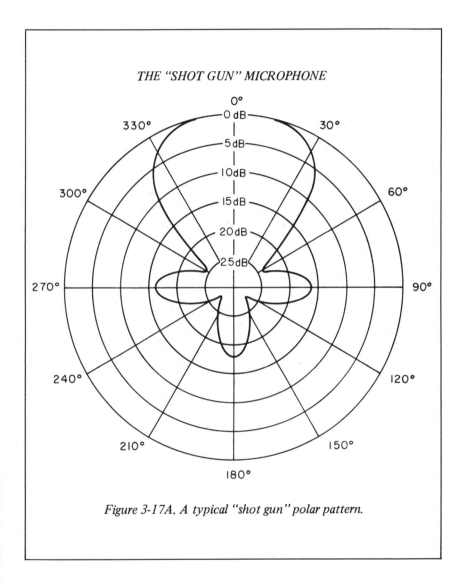

THE "SHOT GUN" MICROPHONE

Figure 3-17A. A typical "shot gun" polar pattern.

THE "SHOT GUN" MICROPHONE

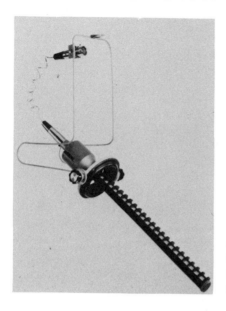

*Figure 3-17B. A modern
ultra-directional microphone.
(Electro-Voice DL-42)
[Electro-Voice photo]*

two cardioid patterns may be combined to produce either a bi-directional or an omni-directional pattern. Figure 3-18 is a simplified illustration of a dual diaphragm condenser microphone system. Note that the diaphragms, D_1 and D_2, are on either side of a common center plate. Each diaphragm used alone will provide a cardioid polar pattern. With the pattern selector switch in position 1, only one diaphragm, D_1, is in use, and the microphone functions as a simple cardioid microphone. In position 2, the second diaphragm, D_2, is also energized, and the two cardioid patterns combine to produce the omni-directional polar pattern, seen in Figure 3-19A. In position 3, the polarity of diaphragm D_2 is reversed: the opposing polarities cause a cancellation in the areas where the cardioid patterns overlap. The result is a bi-directional pattern, as shown in Figure 3-19B.

When the pattern switch is in position 4, the second diaphragm is still negatively polarized, yet the resistor, R, drops the polarizing voltage somewhat. Consequently, although D_2 still yields a cardioid pattern, it is somewhat smaller than the D_1 pattern, and their combination yields the intermediate pattern shown in Figure 3-19C. The size of the rear lobe depends on the actual value of R. By observation, we may realize that if R=0, the pattern would be fully bi-directional—the equivalent of the pattern switch being in position 3. And if R=∞ (open circuit), the pattern becomes cardioid again, since the

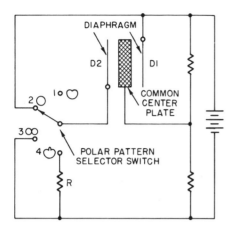

Figure 3-18. A dual diaphragm condenser microphone.
Position 1. Cardioid pattern.
Position 2. Omni-directional pattern.
Position 3. Bi-directional pattern.
Position 4. Intermediate (hyper- or super-cardioid) pattern.

THE EFFECTS OF VARIOUS COMBINATIONS OF TWO CARDIOID POLAR PATTERNS

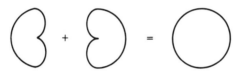

Figure 3-19A. Two cardioid patterns, added to create an omni-directional polar pattern.

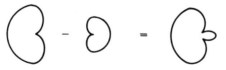

Figure 3-19B. Two cardioid patterns, subtracted to create a bi-directional polar pattern.

Figure 3-19C. Two unequal cardioid patterns, subtracted to create a super-cardioid pattern.

second diaphragm is once more out of the circuit.

In some multi-pattern condenser microphone systems, the pattern switch is replaced by a potentiometer, allowing a variable polarizing voltage to be supplied to the rear diaphragm. In this way, the microphone's polar pattern is continuously variable from full bi-directional to omni-directional, with infinite intermediate patterns. Often, the continuously variable potentiometer is located at the microphone's power supply, allowing changes in the polar pattern without the necessity of going to the microphone itself to do so. This may be a great convenience, when the microphone is located high in the air, at the end of a long boom.

Figure 3-20 shows both the four position pattern switch built into a microphone, and a continuously variable pattern control that is externally located.

Multi-Pattern Single Diaphragm Microphones

In another version of the multi-pattern microphone, variations in polar pattern are realized by altering the enclosure surrounding the diaphragm. An omni-directional microphone utilizes a sealed enclosure in order to function as a pressure-operated device, as described earlier and shown in Figure 3-10. In the multi-pattern single diaphragm microphone, a mechanical linkage opens the rear of the enclosure to expose the rear of the diaphragm when bi-directional operation is required. For uni-directional operation, the same mechanical linkage opens side-entry ports, similar to those shown earlier in Figure 3-12.

A simplified drawing of the multi-pattern single diaphragm microphone is shown in Figure 3-21.

Dual Pattern (Pressure/Pressure Gradient) Microphones

Just as two cardioid patterns may be combined to produce other patterns, a bi-directional and an omni-directional pattern may be combined to produce a cardioid pattern. A typical example is a pressure gradient ribbon microphone, in which an additional pressure-operated moving coil diaphragm has been installed. The ribbon supplies a typical pressure gradient pattern (Figure-8). However, when the moving coil output is also switched on, its omni-directional pattern combines with the Figure-8 to produce a cardioid pattern.

VARIABLE POLAR PATTERN CONTROLS

Figure 3-20A. A dual diaphragm condenser microphone with built-in four position polar pattern switch. (AKG C-412) [AKG photo]

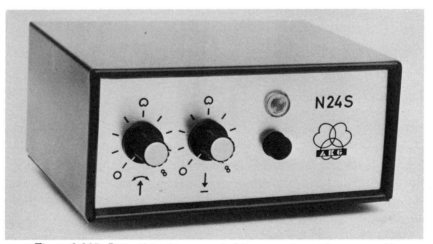

Figure 3-20B. Potentiometers mounted in a separate enclosure provide continuously variable polar patterns. (AKG S24) [AKG photo]

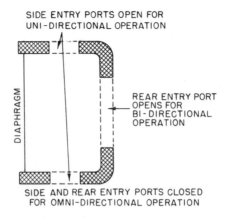

SIDE ENTRY PORTS OPEN FOR
UNI-DIRECTIONAL OPERATION

DIAPHRAGM

REAR ENTRY PORT
OPENS FOR
BI-DIRECTIONAL
OPERATION

SIDE AND REAR ENTRY PORTS CLOSED
FOR OMNI-DIRECTIONAL OPERATION

Figure 3-21. A multi-pattern, single diaphragm microphone.

Single Pattern Dual Diaphragm Microphones

In some microphones, two diaphragms are used—one for low frequencies and the other for high frequencies—just as many loudspeakers utilize two drivers—a woofer and a tweeter—to cover the complete audio spectrum. This type of microphone is illustrated in Figure 3-22. The high frequency system is physically small, with a rear-entry port quite close to the diaphragm. The design maintains a good cardioid pattern at high frequencies.

In the example shown, the low frequency system is designed for optimum performance below 800 Hz, and the microphone contains a 400 Hz crossover network separating the two systems.

MEASURING POLAR RESPONSE

The Anechoic Chamber

In practice, a microphone's polar response is measured by rotating the microphone through 360°, while keeping the sound source fixed, both in level and location. The microphone is set up so that as it rotates, its diaphragm remains at a constant distance from the sound source, as shown in Figure 3-23. The measurements are made within an anechoic chamber, so there will be no reflections from nearby surfaces to influence the off-axis response.

The many reflections within any studio will alter the microphone's apparent polar response, but there is no way to predict

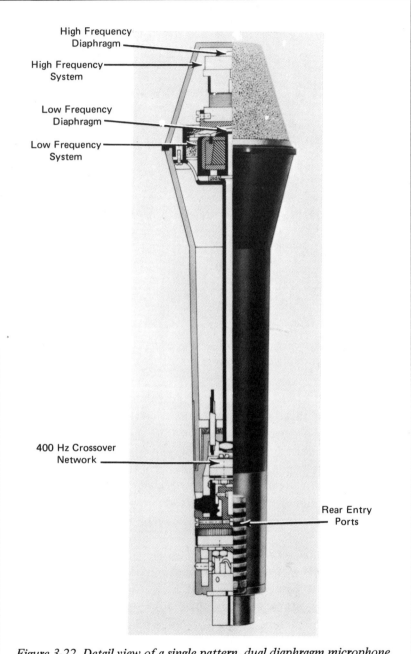

High Frequency
Diaphragm

High Frequency
System

Low Frequency
Diaphragm

Low Frequency
System

400 Hz Crossover
Network

Rear Entry
Ports

*Figure 3-22. Detail view of a single pattern, dual diaphragm microphone.
(AKG D-202E) [AKG photo]*

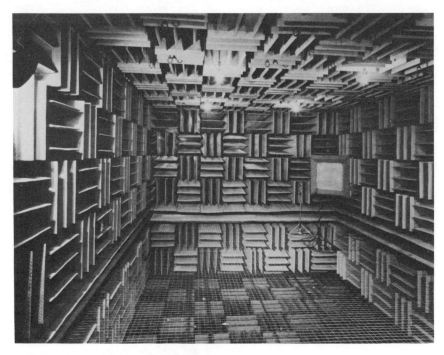

Figure 3-23. A large anechoic chamber. The wedges on all surfaces eliminate virtually all reflections within the room.

the net effect of these reflections, which will vary from one studio to another, or at different locations within the same studio. In fact the engineer will take into account the varying reflective conditions within his studio when he determines the best locations for certain instruments, or the exact placement of a particular microphone in front of an instrument. Relatively dead areas may be favored for drum sets, while a more live section may be used to advantage for strings.

In any case, the reflection-free anechoic chamber serves as a re-peatable standard measuring condition, enabling the engineer to compare the ideal polar responses of many different microphones. The recording engineer can study these polar responses and predict, with reasonable accuracy, the performance he may expect within his own studio.

Although polar patterns are drawn in two dimensions, as an artis-tic—and measuring—convenience, it should be understood that the patterns are actually three-dimensional, as shown in Figure 3-24.

*THREE-DIMENSIONAL
REPRESENTATIONS OF
MICROPHONE
POLAR PATTERNS*

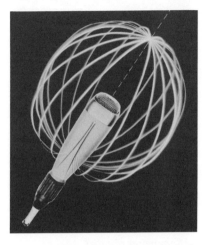

*Figure 3-24A. The omni-directional
polar pattern.*

*Figure 3-24B. The bi-directional
(Figure-8) polar pattern.*

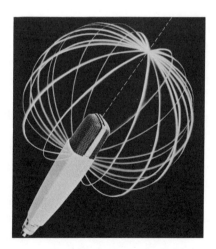

*Figure 3-24C. The uni-directional
(cardioid) polar pattern.*

THREE-DIMENSIONAL REPRESENTATIONS OF
MICROPHONE POLAR PATTERNS

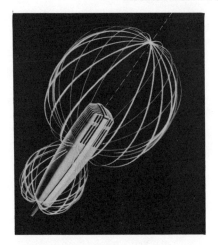

Figure 3-24D. The uni-directional
(super-cardioid) polar pattern.

Figure 3-24E. The ultra-directional
("shot gun") polar pattern.
[Sennheiser photos]

Off-Axis Frequency Response

So far, our examples of polar responses have shown single line patterns, thereby implying that at off-axis locations, the microphone is equally insensitive to *all* sounds, regardless of frequency. In practice, this is often not the case, especially with inexpensive cardioid microphones.

For a more accurate indication of the microphone's off-axis response, a polar pattern should be drawn at each of several frequencies, as shown in Figure 3-25A. From these patterns, we may draw graphs of the microphone's frequency response at various off-axis angles, as shown in Figure 3-25B.

These response curves indicate that although the microphone performs satisfactorily with respect to on-axis sound, its off-axis response is quite irregular. The condition is known as **off-axis coloration**, so-called because of the distorted, or colored, frequency responses.

Off axis coloration may take the form of an unpleasant muddy sound, since the microphone's high frequency response usually falls off much more than the lower frequencies. At some increase in

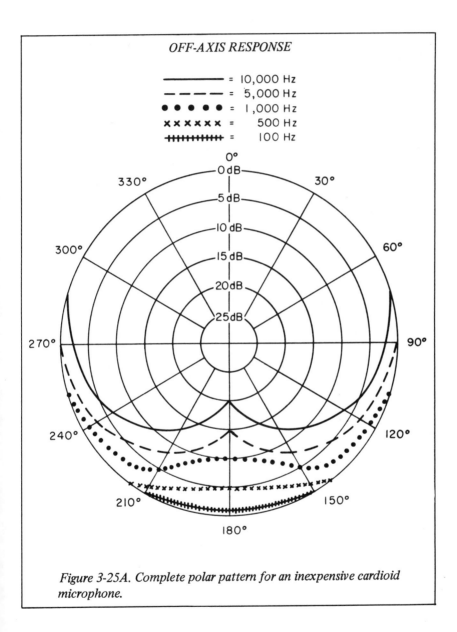

Figure 3-25A. Complete polar pattern for an inexpensive cardioid microphone.

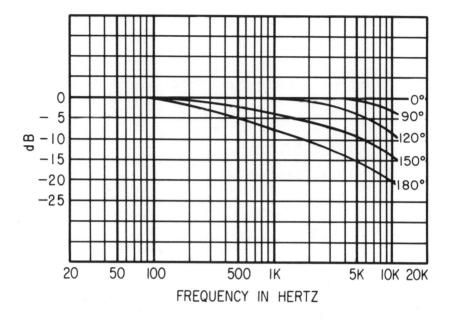

Figure 3-25B. Frequency response at various angles for an inexpensive cardioid microphone.

design complexity, and therefore cost, some or most of this frequency coloration may be designed out. However, it should be kept in mind that omni-directional microphones do not have this inherent defect. As noted earlier, a large omni-directional microphone may show some attenuation of high frequencies arriving from the rear, if the microphone case itself acts as an acoustical obstruction. However in most practical applications this slight fall-off may be ignored, while a cardioid with severe off-axis coloration may not be disregarded.

Proximity Effect

Another characteristic of many cardioid microphones is called the **proximity effect**; an increase in bass response as the microphone is moved closer to the sound source. The condition is illustrated in Figure 3-26, where on-axis response at various microphone-to-source distances is shown. Notice that as the distance decreases, the bass response rises considerably. This rising bass *may* be beneficial in achieving a more robust sound on a voice; however, the slightest

PROXIMITY EFFECT

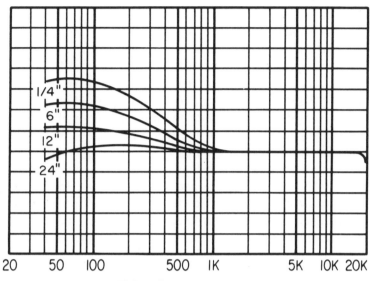

FREQUENCY IN HERTZ

Figure 3-26A. Typical proximity effects at various working distances.

Figure 3-26B. A switchable bass roll-off filter to minimize the proximity effect. (Electro-Voice RE-20)

movement of the singer, or announcer, towards or away from the microphone, will change the overall frequency response, often noticeably. Especially in hand-held applications, the working distance is continually changing, and a microphone without proximity effect, such as an omni-directional type or a better and more expensive cardioid, may be required. Even when the microphone is stand-mounted close to, say, an acoustic guitar, the variations in bass response may be noticeable as the guitarist moves about while playing, however slightly. On the other hand, when the microphone is placed in front of a stationary guitar amplifier, the working distance may be varied to achieve the desired bass response.

Some cardioid microphones have a built-in switchable low frequency roll-off filter to counteract the proximity effect. The filter restores the low end response to normal at some specified close-in working distance. At greater distances, the filter should be switched out, since its fixed low end attenuation is now unnecessarily rolling off the microphone's normal low end response.

Off-Axis Response and Proximity Effect in Dual Diaphragm Microphones

As just noted, off-axis coloration and proximity effects are largely a function of the design limitations of a cardioid microphone. Microphones with other polar patterns are usually free of these characteristics. However, if these other patterns are produced by combining two cardioid patterns, as in the dual diaphragm microphone described earlier, and illustrated in Figures 3-18 and 3-19, the inherent limitations of the cardioid pattern will be present even when other patterns have been selected.

On the other hand, if the other patterns are derived from a single diaphragm microphone (Figure 3-21), the off-axis coloration and proximity effect of the cardioid pattern should not be found in non-cardioid positions of the pattern selector switch.

ELECTRICAL SPECIFICATIONS

Microphone Impedance

For professional studio use, low impedance microphones are practically an industry standard. Although high impedance microphones are not necessarily inferior in themselves, the long cable lengths required in most studio applications prohibit their use.

To understand why, an equivalent circuit for a microphone connected to a console input is drawn in Figure 3-27. Note that R_M and R_L are in series with the source voltage, E. Therefore, if R_M is much smaller than R_L, most of the generated voltage will appear across the console input; that is, R_L. C represents the typical capacitance of any microphone cable; the longer the cable, the greater the capacitance. Now, as frequency increases, this capacitance lowers the impedance of the cable/console combination. Since the microphone's impedance remains constant, the voltage across C (and consequently across R_L), falls off as the frequency rises, since more and more of the total voltage is dropped across R_M.

With a high impedance microphone, this fall-off of high frequencies will be quite noticeable within the audio bandwidth, unless cable lengths — and therefore, capacitance — are kept to an absolute minimum. On the other hand, a low impedance microphone will allow the use of cable runs of several hundred feet with no adverse effects on the frequency response. Although the cable capacitance remains the same, the microphone's relatively low impedance keeps the high frequency roll-off well above the audio bandwidth, where its effect is of no consequence.

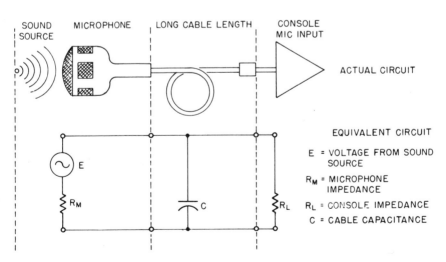

Figure 3-27. The equivalent circuit of a microphone connected to a console input.

Microphone Sensitivity: Voltage and Power Ratings

A microphone's sensitivity rating tells the user something about its relative efficiency in converting acoustic energy to electrical energy. Sensitivity is usually expressed in dB below a specified reference level, and two types of ratings are commonly used: 1) the open circuit voltage rating, and 2) the maximum power rating.

Open Circuit Voltage Rating

In this type of rating, either the microphone is not connected to any input, or the input impedance to which it is connected is some twenty times higher in impedance than the microphone itself, which is effectively an open circuit. The reference sound pressure is 1 microbar (1 $dyne/cm^2$), and the zero reference level is 1 volt. In other words, if a sound pressure of 1 microbar resulted in a 1 volt output, the microphone's sensitivity would be 0 dB. In practice, much lower output voltages are produced, and typical open circuit voltage ratings are on the order of -85 to -35 dB. To prevent confusion with other rating methods, the sensitivity specification should clearly indicate the reference used. For example, a -60 dB sensitivity measured under the method just described should be written as -60 dB (re: 1 volt per microbar).

Maximum Power Rating

With this type of rating, the microphone is connected to a load, R_L, that is equal to the microphone's internal impedance, and the sensitivity is specified in terms of power rather than voltage. Here, the sound pressure reference is 10 microbars, and the zero reference power level is 1 milliwatt. Under these condtions, if the microphone delivers 10^{-6} milliwatts to R_L, its sensitivity would be

$$NdB = -10 \log (1 \text{ milliwatt}/10^{-6} \text{ milliwatts}) = -10 \log 10^6 = -10 \times 6$$
$$= -60 \text{ dB (re: 10 microbars/1 milliwatt)}$$

Balanced and Unbalanced Lines

A balanced line is one which uses two conductors plus a shield, while an unbalanced line contains only one conductor, with the shield serving as the second conductor. Figure 3-28 shows both types

114

of lines, as well as typical balanced and unbalanced circuits.

An important advantage of the balanced line is that any unwanted noise signals in the area through which the line is placed will be picked up equally by both conductors, and will cancel out. In the unbalanced line, the noise voltage will travel down the single conductor, and be transmitted to the next stage of the circuit.

Providing the audio signal is of sufficiently high level, the noise signal may not be heard, especially if the unbalanced line is reasonably short. But as noted before, microphone lines are apt to be quite long, and signal levels are very low. Consequently, the slightest noise or hum induced in the microphone line may become almost as loud as the microphone's output signal. For this reason, balanced lines are an absolute necessity between a microphone and the recording console.

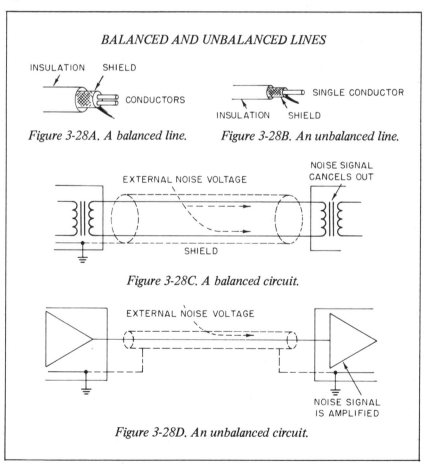

BALANCED AND UNBALANCED LINES

Figure 3-28A. A balanced line.

Figure 3-28B. An unbalanced line.

Figure 3-28C. A balanced circuit.

Figure 3-28D. An unbalanced circuit.

Microphone Plugs

Practically all professional microphones use a three pin output plug, with Pin No. 1 used as shield and the output signal appearing across Pins No. 2 and No. 3. A positive pressure at the diaphragm produces a positive voltage at Pin No. 2 with respect to Pin No. 3. However, this convention is by no means a standard, and some European manufacturers may use either Pin No. 2 or No. 3 as shield.

Before putting a microphone into service, it is important to verify the relative polarity of the output pins, so that phase reversals are avoided. It is good practice to designate one microphone as the studio standard and compare all new microphones with it. This may be done quickly by mixing the outputs of the standard and the new microphone, and listening to the combination. If the combination produces a lower output level, or a frequency-distorted signal, there is a phase reversal which must be corrected. In most cases, the microphone plug can be rewired if necessary. If this is not possible, a short adapter cable should be permanently attached to the non-standard microphone.

Before designating a certain microphone as the studio standard, make sure that it is not itself non-standard. This will prevent having to rewire practically every new addition in the future.

SOME CAUSES OF DISTORTION:
Overload, Wind, Vibrations

Dynamic Microphone Overload

For all practical purposes, it is almost impossible to produce a sound pressure level that will overload a professional quality moving coil microphone. Older ribbon microphones may be overloaded – and actually damaged – by very high sound pressure levels, but more recent versions should be able to withstand most sound levels found in the studio.

However, a very high microphone output level may overload the microphone preamplifier in the recording console. Many consoles contain a sensitivity switch that allows the engineer to insert ten or more dB of attenuation in the microphone line, to protect against this type of overload. In cases where such facility is not built-in, an attenuation pad may be inserted in the microphone line when required. Figure 3-29 shows a commercially available attenuation pad, and also gives resistance values for 10 and 20 dB attenuation.

AN "IN-LINE" ATTENUATION PAD

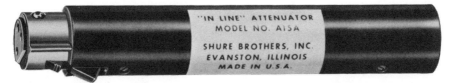

Figure 3-29A. A commercially available microphone line attenuator. (Shure A-15A) [Shure Bros. photo]

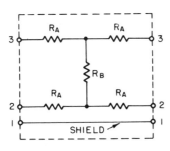

Figure 3-29B. Circuit values for a microphone line attenuator.
For 10 dB attenuation,
R_a = 56 ohms, R_b = 150 ohms
For 20 dB attenuation,
R_a = 82 ohms, R_b = 39 ohms
(Caution – this type of attenuator must not be used with a phantom powered condenser microphone, since it will interfere with the voltage being supplied to the microphone.)

Condenser Microphone Overload

In a condenser microphone, the voltage produced at the condenser/diaphragm may be – in the case of very high sound pressure levels – sufficient to overload the microphone's own built-in preamplifier. Attenuation facilities at the console will be of no use, since the overload occurs within the microphone itself. To protect the microphone against overload, many condenser microphones have a built-in pad that inserts 10 to 20 dB of attenuation between the diaphragm and the preamplifier. Figure 3-30A illustrates a microphone with a switchable 20 dB pad. Figure 3-30B shows another arrangement, in which a 10 to 20 dB accessory pad may be inserted between the diaphragm capsule and the preamplifier when required.

Wind Noises

Although a microphone's diaphragm must, of course, vibrate in order for it to produce an output voltage, some care must be taken

117

BUILT-IN AND PLUG-IN MICROPHONE PADS

Figure 3-30B. An accessory
attenuation pad, inserted between a
condenser microphone's diaphragm
capsule and preamplifier.
(Schoeps MK-24) [Schoeps photo]

Figure 3-30A. A condenser
microphone with a built-in 20 dB
pad. (AKG C-412) [AKG photo]

to prevent certain unwanted vibrations from distorting the signal output. For example, a stream of air blown across a microphone would certainly create an unpleasantly distracting noise as the diaphragm was set into vibration by the wind. Although this is hardly likely within the recording studio, a close-up voice often produces an occasional shock wave that distorts the microphone's output. In particular, words containing "p," "t," and "b" may create an objectionable pop due to the movement of air across the diaphragm. Pressure gradient microphones (cardioid and figure-8 patterns) are particularly susceptible, since the pressure differential between the front and back of the diaphragm is considerable. On the other hand, a pressure microphone (omni-directional pattern) is sealed in the rear, so the sound wave — although loud — is less likely to create a distortion-producing pressure differential.

Wind Screens

To minimize these noises, a wind screen, or pop filter, may be placed over the microphone. The wind screen is made from an open-pore acoustical foam material that does not affect the microphone's sensitivity. On the other hand, the screen does prevent puffs of wind from striking the diaphragm. When a wind screen is used on a microphone with rear-entry ports, it is important to shield these entrances too, so that the pressure differential is reduced, rather than accentuated. Figure 3-31 illustrates several microphones protected by wind screens.

In addition to its primary function, the wind screen protects against moisture and dust particles reaching the diaphragm. Especially in close-up vocal pickups, it is a good idea to use a wind screen as a matter of routine. The screen may be rinsed out frequently to remove accumulated dust and grime. Needless to say, it would be much more difficult and time-consuming to periodically clean the diaphragm itself.

Vibration Noises

Most studio structures are susceptible to at least some building vibration, particularly in heavy traffic metropolitan areas. Even when the vibrations are inaudible to the listener in the studio, they may be transmitted via the microphone stand to the microphone, creating an audible rumble over the control room monitor speakers. In the case

MICROPHONE WINDSCREENS

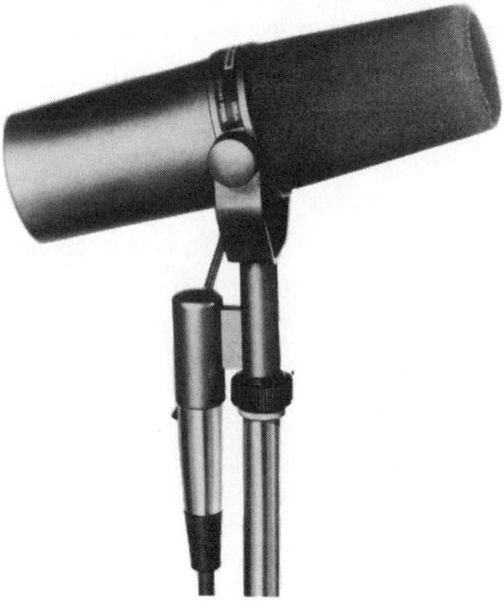

Figure 3-31A. A dynamic
microphone with a built-in
windscreen.
(Shure SM-7) [Shure Bros. photo]

Figure 3-31C. An accessory
windscreen placed over a condenser
microphone. Note the cut-out to
permit access to the polar pattern
selector switch. (Neumann U-67
microphone)
[Gotham Audio photo]

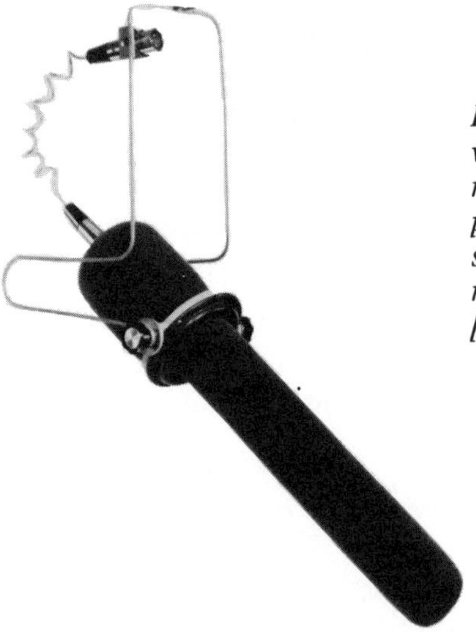

Figure 3-31B. An ultra-directional microphone, completely protected by
windscreens. (The same microphone is seen in Figure 3-17B without the
windscreen.) (Electro-Voice DL-42) [Electro-Voice photo]

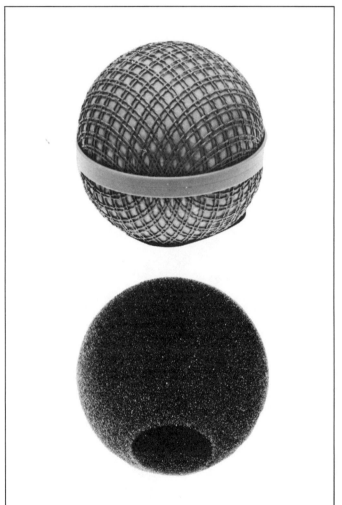

Figure 3-31D. Two small accessory windscreens.
(Sennheiser MZW-22 and MZW-411) [Sennheiser photos]

121

SHOCK MOUNTED MICROPHONES
*In the first two examples, the shock mount system
provides for some slack in the cable, to prevent
transmission of vibration along the
cable to the microphone.*

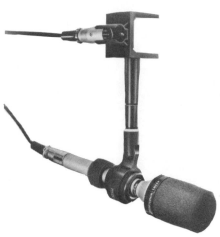

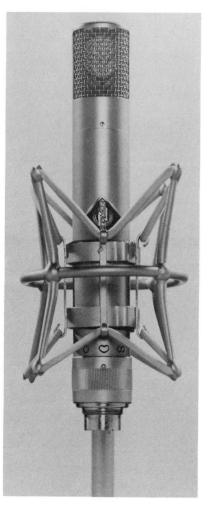

*Figure 3-32A. Shure SM-53 with
A-55M shock mount.
[Shure Bros. photo]*

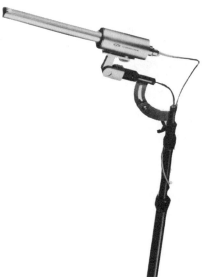

*Figure 3-32C. Neumann KM-56
with EA-21 shock mount.
[Gotham Audio photo]*

*Figure 3-32B. Sennheiser
MKH-415T with MZB-415 shock
mount. [Sennheiser photo]*

122

of close-up microphone placement, there is probably little or no problem, but when the microphones are placed at some distance from the instruments, the rumble may be audible during quiet passages.

Even in a rumble-free studio, certain impact noises are accompanied by considerable vibration. For example, an over-enthusiastic bass drum kick may set all the microphone stands in the vicinity vibrating.

Shock Mounts

Most manufacturers produce shock mounts designed to mechanically isolate the microphone from its stand, thus cutting down on vibration-induced noises. Representative examples of shock mounts are seen in Figure 3-32.

Figure 3-33. Cutaway view of a microphone in a double casing to minimize transmitted vibration. (Electro-Voice RE-50) [Electro-Voice photo]

123

In general, cardioid microphones are more prone to mechanical shock and vibration, and in hand-held applications the noises may be quite distracting, especially if the artist is moving the microphone around to any extent. For maximum protection, an omni-directional microphone such as the one seen in Figure 3-33 may be used. Here, the inner shell is suspended within the outer casing, keeping transmitted vibrations at an absolute minimum.

CHAPTER 4

Microphone Technique

Although the successful utilization of microphones is largely a subjective matter, there are certain "ground rules" that should be followed, or at least understood, before preparing for any important recording session. And, the recording engineer should be aware of the different philosophies of microphone placement technique, so that he may intelligently choose the basic approach that will best meet his needs.

The first law of correct microphone usage has been successfully ignored almost from the day of its discovery. It is:

NEVER use more than two microphones.

Although most recording sessions would be impossible (and a great deal of this book unnecessary) if anyone took this law seriously, the engineer should understand its significance before setting up a third, fourth, or twentieth microphone.

It is perhaps no accident that the listener has but two ears. Their positioning, and the interaction between themselves and the brain, allows us to form an incredibly accurate impression of the relative intensity and location of any noise within our hearing range.

With the exception of those few sounds that originate quite close to one ear only (whispers, telephone conversations, and such) we hear almost everything else with both ears, and our impression of direction is apt to be more dependent on phase shifts and time of arrival differences than on intensity. In fact, for most sounds the intensity difference between one ear and the other is probably negligible.

As an example, consider the listener at a concert in a large theatre. The orchestra or band is spread out across the width and depth of the stage. Strings are usually up front, and percussion instruments are to the rear, with brasses in between. If there is a chorus, it may be standing behind the orchestra on risers. The larger the production, the more distance there is between the first row of the violins and the last row of the chorus.

125

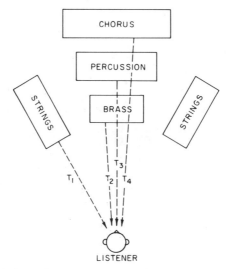

Figure 4-1. Sounds from the more distant orchestral sections take a little longer to reach the listener.

Obviously, the sound of the chorus reaches the listener a little later than the first row of violins, as seen in Figure 4-1. Presumably, the time lag is so slight that it escapes conscious notice, yet the ear/ brain combination processes the information received and correctly concludes that the chorus is behind the orchestra. Even when the chorus is louder than the strings, the listener is not fooled into thinking they have moved forward of the orchestra.

Despite the listener's excellent perception of width and depth, he has no control over what he hears. But in the recording studio, a microphone may often be placed in front of each section of the orchestra and chorus, allowing the engineer considerable control over what he hears. The working distance between the performers and the microphones will be arranged so that each microphone favors a particular section, as in Figure 4-2. To accomplish this, a microphone must be placed reasonably close to each section, to better distinguish it from the rest of the ensemble.

But in arranging microphones in this manner, much valuable directional and spacial information is lost for the sake of greater intensity control over the various sections of the orchestra. Unfortunately, the missing information is all but irretrievable in even the most sophisti-

126

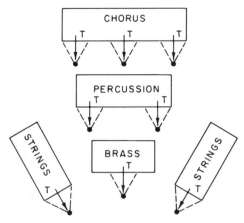

Figure 4-2. With a multiple microphone setup, time of arrival differences are minimized, depriving the listener of much of the spatial information for the sake of improved control over balance.

cated recording systems. The engineer should clearly understand this characteristic of multi-miking before concluding that it is the only way to record.

In a simple two microphone setup, the entire ensemble is heard by both microphones. Presumably, all the subtle differences in performer-to-microphone spacings, angle of arrival, etc. are retained, ideally as if the listener himself were seated at the location of the microphone pair.

In a multi-microphone setup, these subtleties are lost, since each performer or group of performers is recorded close up to a separate microphone. As an obvious consequence, time of arrival differences are minimized or eliminated completely, since each microphone transmits its information simultaneously.

In the control room, the various microphone outputs may be satisfactorily arranged in a left-to-right plane, but there is no completely successful way of creating an illusion of one instrument located behind another one. In other words, a good impression of depth has been sacrificed. It is rarely satisfactory to place the rear instrument microphone outputs at a lower level than the more forward-located instruments, especially if in the actual performance the rear instruments (the chorus, for example) are frequently supposed to be louder.

BINAURAL RECORDING

Figure 4-3A. *A binaural recording setup.*

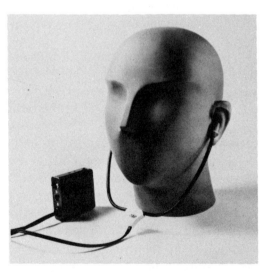

Figure 4-3B. *A dummy head is often used in binaural recording, to closely simulate the actual listening condition. (Sennheiser MKE 2002) [Sennheiser photo]*

Of course, the practical day-to-day realities of the recording studio often take precedence over any theoretically ideal notions of purist technique. Nevertheless, the recording engineer should understand the trade-offs between stereo and multi-miking techniques.

STEREO MICROPHONE PLACEMENT TECHNIQUES

Binaural Recording

There are several methods of selecting and placing a single pair of microphones for a stereophonic pick-up. Perhaps the most obvious technique is to space two omni-directional microphones on either side of an acoustic baffle (Figure 4-3) in an attempt to simulate the condition of actually being seated at the location of the microphones. This technique, known as binaural recording, is most realistic while wearing headphones, since the microphones become an extension of the listener's ears, in effect transporting him to the site of the recording.

A binaural recording played over loudspeakers is often less than convincing. To understand why, consider a sound source off at some distance to the left of the binaural microphone pair, as seen in Figure 4-4A. Both microphones will pick up about the same intensity sound, along with the slight phase shift or time of arrival differences that would give the listener at the site the necessary directional clues. However, over spaced loudspeakers these subtleties will be pretty much lost, and the approximately equal sound intensity at each speaker may give the impression that the sound source is somewhere in the center. On the other hand, a sound close up and say, directly on the left, will be picked up mostly by the left microphone and transmitted primarily to the left speaker, giving the impression that the sound is off to the extreme left, rather than close up as is actually the case. These distortions of directional information rule out the effectiveness of binaural recording in most practical applications.

The Stereo Microphone

For other stereo recording techniques, a so-called stereo microphone may be used. This is actually two separate microphone systems, housed in one case, as shown in Figure 4-5A. The upper microphone capsule may be rotated through 90° or more, and the two outputs are kept electronically separate.

129

THE EFFECT OF LISTENING TO A
BINAURAL RECORDING OVER LOUDSPEAKERS

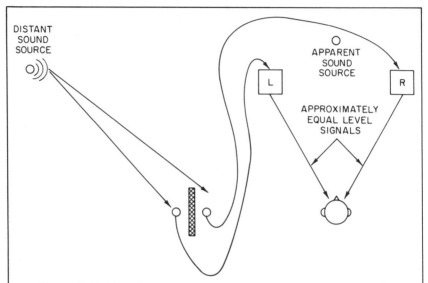

Figure 4-4A. When loudspeakers are used, the listener may think the sound source is somewhere in the center of the room, rather than on the extreme left.

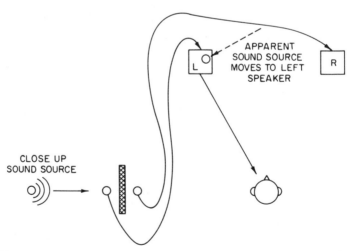

Figure 4-4B. As the sound source moves in closer, the listener hears the apparent source move from center to extreme left.

THE STEREO MICROPHONE

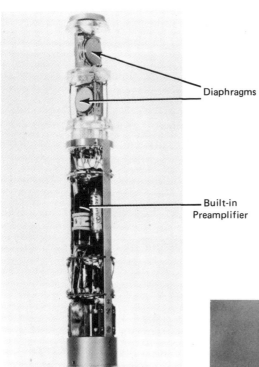

Diaphragms

Built-in
Preamplifier

Figure 4-5A. A condenser stereo microphone. (Neumann SM-2) [Gotham Audio photo]

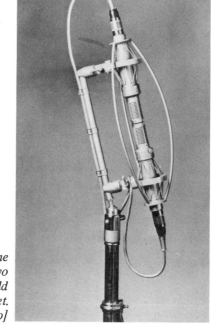

Figure 4-5B. A stereo microphone may also be made from two separate microphones, held together in a special bracket. [Schoeps photo]

Stereosonic Recording

In this technique, the stereo microphone consists of two bi-directional elements. The front of one microphone is pointed towards the left side of the orchestra, while the other is pointed towards the right, as shown in Figure 4-6A. The distance between the microphone and the orchestra is usually equal to about half the width of the ensemble, so that the angle between the microphone axes is 90°. With one microphone routed to the left speaker and the other to the right, the reproduced sound conveys a very accurate impression of both the width and depth of the orchestra. It is quite easy to determine which instruments are in the foreground and which are further back, although the engineer has no control over the internal balance of the ensemble. The ambiguities of the binaural pickup are considerably lessened, since off-center sounds reach the live front of one microphone and the dead side of the other. Centered sounds are picked up equally by both microphones, and the ratio of direct to reverberant sound gives the listener an impression of the distance between microphone and performer.

X-Y Recording

In the X-Y technique, a stereo microphone with cardioid polar patterns is used, as shown in Figure 4-6B. A preference between this, and the stereosonic technique, is largely a function of the room in which the recording is being made. The stereosonic microphone might be well suited to a recording of a pipe organ in a large cathedral, whereas the off-axis attenuation characteristics of a cardioid pair might be better suited to miking a concert performance in front of a large, and perhaps noisy, audience.

As a variation of the X-Y technique, the two cardioid microphones may be spaced some distance apart, as shown in Figure 4-7. Typical distances between the microphones are from 6 to 12 inches; at greater distances, the stereo image may seem to have a "hole in the middle"; that is, sounds are for the most part left or right of center, with little or nothing happening in the middle.

M-S Recording

This technique also uses a centered coincident microphone pair, although here a cardioid microphone is pointed straight at the middle

STEREO MICROPHONE POLAR PATTERNS

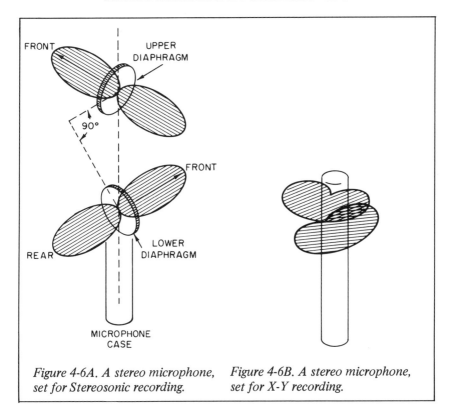

Figure 4-6A. A stereo microphone, set for Stereosonic recording.

Figure 4-6B. A stereo microphone, set for X-Y recording.

Figure 4-7. Stereo miking with two cardioid microphones. (Electro-Voice RE 16 microphones)

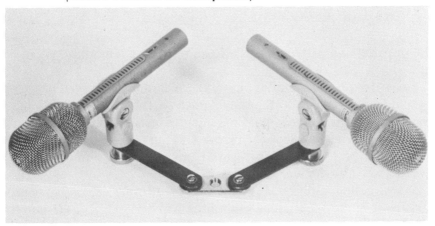

of the orchestra, while a figure-8 microphone is pointed sideways, so that one of its dead sides faces the orchestra. The M-S (Middle-Sides) technique is illustrated in Figure 4-8A, and it should be apparent that the cardioid microphone picks up the entire ensemble, while the figure-8 microphone favors the extreme left and right hand sides. (Center information reaches the dead side of the figure-8 pattern, and is pretty much cancelled out.)

To form a suitable stereo image, the outputs of the two microphones are combined in a matrix system. To understand how the matrix works, assume that the front of the figure-8 microphone is pointed to the left. Therefore, signals originating left of center will be picked up by both the front of the cardioid microphone and the front of the figure-8 microphone. If their outputs are combined, these signals will add together. On the other hand, right-of-center signals will be picked up by the rear of the figure-8 microphone, and the same combination will tend to cancel these signals. Therefore, this cardioid/figure-8 combination will favor left-of-center information.

On the other hand, if the output of the figure-8 microphone is simply reversed in electrical polarity, the effect will be the same as if its left-to-right orientation had been physically reversed. Now, a simple combination with the cardioid output will yield a right-sided signal instead. As shown in Figure 4-8B a matrix system provides both types of signal combinations; one for the left — the other for the right hand signal.

One advantage of the matrix system is that the cardioid microphone output alone may be used for a monaural program. When stereo is required, the output of the figure-8 microphone may be combined with the mono signal, as just described.

Use of Additional Microphones With a Coincident Pair Setup

Since the practical limitations of the recording environment may not allow the engineer to achieve a satisfactory balance with just one stereo microphone, additional microphones may be used to accentuate one or more sections of the orchestra. However, they must be used very carefully, so as not to detract from the stereo perspective produced by the main coincident pair.

If the section with an additional microphone placed nearby is on say, the left, the microphone's output must be mixed with the stereo pair in such a way that the apparent location of the section is not

THE M-S RECORDING TECHNIQUE

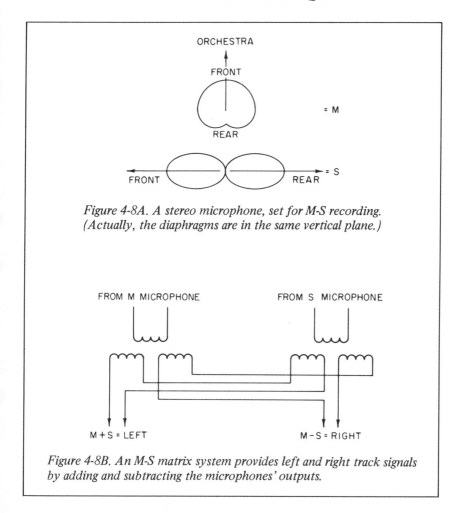

Figure 4-8A. A stereo microphone, set for M-S recording. (Actually, the diaphragms are in the same vertical plane.)

Figure 4-8B. An M-S matrix system provides left and right track signals by adding and subtracting the microphones' outputs.

changed. Otherwise, there is apt to be a considerable "blurring" of the stereo image.

And since the extra microphone is somewhat closer than the main stereo pair, its output will reach the listener's ear some fraction of a second earlier, focussing his attention on it. To keep these extra microphones from thus deteriorating the overall pickup, their output will probably have to be kept quite low in level.

The advantage of the various stereo techniques just described is that the sound of the orchestra as an ensemble is well preserved.

There is a good illusion of depth, as well as left-to-right information. Within reason, low level instruments may be clearly heard and located within the ensemble, despite the presence of louder instruments in the same general vicinity.

The obvious disadvantage of this technique is that the engineer has no control over the instrumental balance, and at a later date may not modify the sound of one instrument without simultaneously affecting the entire ensemble.

MULTI-MICROPHONE PLACEMENT TECHNIQUES

Although the advantages of the various stereo microphone techniques should be clearly understood, the needs of the contemporary recording session may often prevent their successful application.

Due to budget limitations, it may be out of the question to hire an orchestra of sufficient size to be self-balancing, even with the help of a skillful conductor. Or, the musical arrangement may be such that an instrument, or instruments, be heard out of proportion to its natural balance within the ensemble. At times (frequently, on contemporary music sessions) it may be necessary to modify the signal produced by one instrument without similarly affecting the rest of the group. Or, the various instruments may be recorded one (or a few) at a time.

In any of these cases, stereo microphone techniques are perhaps best left alone, and the engineer must be prepared to develop a multi-miking technique more appropriate to the demands of the session.

SOME RULES OF MICROPHONE USAGE

The beginner is always anxious to learn proper multi-microphone techniques, and is often disturbed to find little or nothing published concerning "correct" microphone placement. He often insists that experienced engineers should be able to tell him which microphone is best for each instrument, and where that microphone should be placed. However, beyond a few simple rules, microphone technique is largely a matter of personal taste, and engineers rarely agree on anything that has to do with choice, and placement, of microphones.

Many of the rules have already been covered, and they are paraphrased here.

1. Take off-axis coloration and proximity effect into consideration when selecting microphones.
2. Avoid overload, either with an attenuator in the microphone line, or in the case of a condenser microphone, by inserting a pad between the diaphragm capsule and the microphone's own preamplifier, if this preamplifier is being overloaded.
3. Protect the microphone against wind and vibration noises.
4. Exercise caution when using acoustic baffles. Listen *first*.
5. Make sure all microphone lines are properly shielded.
6. Make sure there are no electrical phase reversals in the signal path.
7. Don't use two microphones when one microphone will do a better job.

Beyond these rather obvious precautions, microphone usage is largely a matter of personal taste, and the remainder of this chapter should in no way be considered as a "rule book" of microphone technique.

Avoiding Phase Cancellations

In Chapter 2, Figure 2-12 showed how the outputs of two electrically in-phase microphones might nevertheless cancel if a musical instrument was located somewhere between them. Unless the instrument was perfectly centered and did not move – an unlikely event – some wavelengths would reach the microphones acoustically out-of-phase. And with each slight movement, a different set of wavelengths – and therefore frequencies – would be affected, as the relative path lengths between the instrument and each microphone fluctuated. Figure 4-9A illustrates the problem. A slightly off-center instrument creates a path length difference of three inches. The frequency with a half-wavelength of 3 inches (that is a wavelength, λ, of 6 inches) is

$$F = \frac{V}{\lambda} = \frac{1100 \text{ ft/sec}}{.5 \text{ ft/cycle}} = 2200 \text{ cycles/sec (Hz)}.$$

Therefore, this frequency would be prone to cancellation whenever the path length difference approached 3 inches.

Although it is certainly impossible to completely eliminate all interaction between microphones, most phase cancellation problems can be minimized by observing a 3:1 rule. That is, if a microphone is 1 foot away from an instrument, no other microphone should be

AVOIDING PHASE CANCELLATIONS

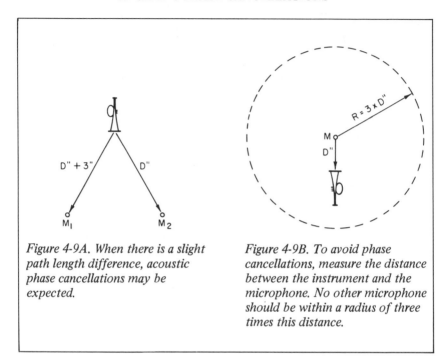

Figure 4-9A. When there is a slight path length difference, acoustic phase cancellations may be expected.

Figure 4-9B. To avoid phase cancellations, measure the distance between the instrument and the microphone. No other microphone should be within a radius of three times this distance.

within 3 feet of this microphone, as shown in Figure 4-9B. Although small path length differences still occur, the distance ratio is sufficiently large to minimize or eliminate any cancellations.

Close Miking Techniques

Any microphone will hear a proportion of direct-to-indirect sound; the direct sound coming from the instrument just in front of the microphone, and the indirect sound comprising reflections plus the sound of other instruments in the immediate vicinity.

Obviously, the closer the microphone to the sound source of interest, the less it will hear other sounds within the same room. As the working distance decreases, the ratio of direct-to-indirect sound increases, until at extremely close working distance, the microphone hears—for all practical purposes—just the direct sound of the instrument in front of it. This was illustrated earlier, in Chapter 3 (Figure 3-9B).

Minimizing Leakage

As mentioned earlier, leakage (that is, unwanted sounds from other instruments in the room) may be minimized by close miking, or by interposing some acoustic barriers between the wanted and the unwanted sounds. However, these techniques must be applied with great care so that in the attempt at greater control, the overall sound quality does not deteriorate unnecessarily. Although the loss of depth may be unavoidable with a close miking technique, some other pitfalls may be avoided through a better understanding of microphone usage.

Microphone Placement For Maximum Separation

In an effort to provide greater electrical separation between instruments, the engineer's first impulse may be to use a cardioid microphone, reasoning that its comparative insensitivity to off-axis sounds will help keep leakage at a minimum. However, the off-axis response of the microphone *must* be taken into account. A cardioid microphone with poor off-axis response may very well attenuate rear-originating high frequencies, yet function pretty much like an omni-directional microphone at lower frequencies. As an obvious disadvantage of this off-axis coloration, consider such a cardioid microphone aimed at say, an acoustic guitar, and pointed away from the drums, as seen in Figure 4-10. The higher frequencies of the cymbals and snare drum may be significantly attenuated at the microphone, yet the lower frequency tom-tom and bass drum will still be heard. The resultant drum sound, as heard by the microphone will consequently

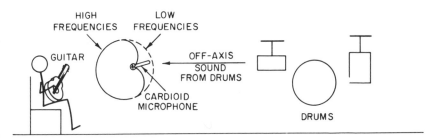

Figure 4-10. A cardioid microphone with poor off-axis response may pick up too much low frequency off-axis sound.

be "bottom-heavy," although the on-axis guitar itself may be entirely satisfactory. If there are several such microphones in use—each contributing some amount of high frequency-lacking leakage—the cumulative effect may very well be an unpleasantly muddy sound with a great sacrifice in overall clarity.

In an effort to further minimize off-axis coloration, the microphone may be moved even closer to the guitar, to keep the leakage at an absolute minimum. However, the poor off-axis response of some cardioid microphones is often accompanied by a pronounced proximity effect. At very small working distances, the bass rise may be excessive. And, the slightest movement of the instrument will produce a noticeable change in the sound frequency characteristic.

In many applications, these various operating restrictions may be effectively by-passed by using an omni-directional microphone. Free of proximity effects and off-axis coloration, the microphone may be used very close to the sound source without excessive bass build-up. Slight changes in working distance will not cause frequency response fluctuations and whatever leakage the microphone hears will at least be free of frequency distortions.

Here it should be remembered that the omni-directional pattern on dual diaphragm microphones may retain the undesirable characteristics of the cardioid microphone since, as mentioned earlier, its omni characteristic is derived from two cardioid patterns.

Using the Figure-8 Microphone For Greater Separation

It should be kept in mind that the sides of a microphone with a figure-8 pattern are generally far less sensitive than the rear of a cardioid pattern. Accordingly, it is often possible to obtain great separation by pointing the dead side of the microphone towards the unwanted sound, as shown in Figure 4-11. The technique is particularly effective when miking several instruments or a small chorus with one microphone. Some members of the group may be placed on either side of the microphone, as shown in the figure, and an internal balance achieved by moving closer or further away as required.

In an attempt at greater control, the temptation to use two cardioid microphones, back-to-back, should probably be avoided. As mentioned earlier in the discussion of dual diaphragm microphones, the combination of two such cardioid microphones produces an omni-directional pattern, thereby defeating the off-axis attenuation characteristic of the figure-8. If the microphones are connected to-

140

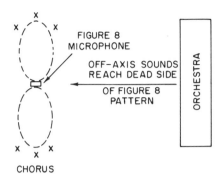

Figure 4-11. Using a Figure-8 microphone on a small chorus.

gether out-of-phase, a figure-8 pattern will indeed result, but any re-balancing in the control room will alter the shape of the figure-8 pattern. Therefore, if the engineer attempts to balance the group by "riding gain," the amount of leakage will rise and fall as the relative level between the two microphones is changed.

Acoustic Separation—Isolation Booths, Baffles & "Goboes"

In a further attempt at minimizing leakage, various acoustic bar-riers are often set up between the microphone and the unwanted sounds. The most obvious—and effective—barrier is the isolation booth; a completely enclosed room (Figure 4-12) in which a musi-cian, or group of musicians, may be placed. Although such a room may provide the required isolation, it may also be somewhat of an artistic compromise, since the musicians thus isolated will often find it difficult to perform in ensemble with the rest of the group, despite whatever sophisticated earphone monitoring system may be at hand.

Movable acoustic barriers, popularly known as "goboes"—a word of uncertain derivation—are frequently seen in use in modern record-ing studios. The idea is to establish greater acoustical isolation be-tween instruments by arranging the goboes as required. The goboes may be easily moved to meet the needs of the particular recording session. However, they too should be used with discretion, since an improperly placed gobo can do more harm than good.

Goboes are often used on the supposition that they will help keep unwanted sounds from reaching a microphone. The goboes are placed somewhere between a loud sound source and a microphone

141

Figure 4-12. An isolation booth at Ultrasonic Recording Studios, Hempstead, N.Y.

that is to be shielded from this sound, so that the microphone may better hear the specific instrument placed in front of it. A typical set-up is shown in Figure 4-13A.

There are several reasons why this gobo may create more problems than it solves. If the microphone is a cardioid, its rear and side entry ports must not be obstructed, if the microphone is to function as intended. Assuming that the gobo is a perfect sound absorber (which it surely isn't), it has effectively absorbed the off-axis sounds which otherwise would have reached these ports, as illustrated in Figure 4-13B. Therefore, all sounds (including the unwanted ones) reach the microphone diaphragm by the front entrance only. The gobo has temporarily created an omni-directional pattern, thus defeating the microphone's built-in attenuation of off-axis sounds.

But of course, the gobo is *not* a total absorber of all frequencies. Since it is often placed quite close to the microphone, its surfaces— though absorptive—will nonetheless reflect some frequencies back

USING ACOUSTIC BARRIERS, OR "GOBOES"

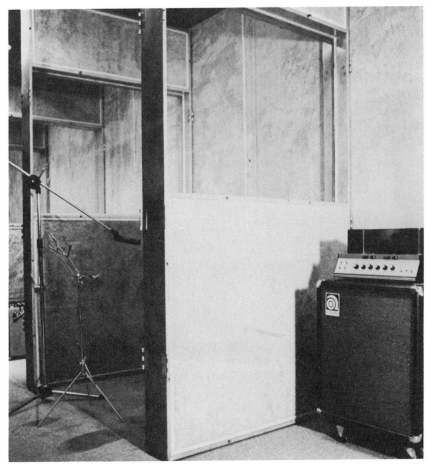

Figure 4-13A. A typical setup using goboes.

towards the microphone, while absorbing others. In so many cases, the net result is a deterioration of the overall sound that far outweighs whatever partial isolation has been accomplished.

As yet another consideration, the diffraction phenomenon discussed in Chapter 2 must be taken into account. As sound energy travels past the gobo, low frequencies are diffracted appreciably, while high frequencies are not. Therefore, the gobo offers incomplete protection against unwanted sounds. The microphone hears the diffracted low frequencies all too well, while the absence of high frequency components results in an unpleasantly muddy sound pickup.

USING ACOUSTIC BARRIERS, OR "GOBOES"

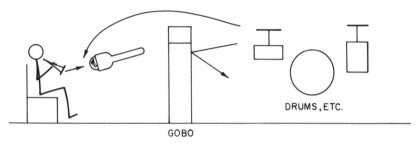

Figure 4-13B. The gobo may prevent off-axis sounds from reaching the cardioid microphone's rear entry ports.

USE OF SOME SPECIAL PURPOSE MICROPHONES

Contact Microphones

The contact microphone responds to the mechanical vibrations of the musical instrument to which it is attached. Therefore, it hears little or nothing of the sounds of other instruments within the studio. Specific operating principles vary from one manufacturer to another; one type may actually contain a very small microphone, while another works like an electric guitar pickup.

Representative examples of contact pickups are shown in Figure 4-14.

The contact microphone is of course the ultimate extreme in close microphone placement, as it hears only the direct sound of one instrument. Although it offers the engineer maximum control, the sound may not be as "musical" as would be desired. We are after all accustomed to at least some indirect sound along with any instrument we hear, and the contact microphone's ultra-close perspective completely eliminates this component of the total sound.

On the other hand, when isolation booths are either unavailable or undesired, the contact microphone may permit the engineer to pick up a relatively quiet instrument in the midst of a loud ensemble. This type of pickup allows the musician to be located wherever he is most comfortable—an important advantage that cannot be ignored. And, when the contact microphone is used to emphasize an instrument that would otherwise be inaudible, its characteristic "dry" sound may actually work to advantage.

CONTACT MICROPHONES

Figure 4-14A. A contact microphone attached to a guitar. (AKG D 401) [AKG photo]

Figure 4-14B. An electrostatic piano pickup. Five pickup transducers sense the string vibrations directly, rather than via the traditional sounding board. (Countryman Piano Pickup) [Countryman photo]

At times, the contact microphone may be used even when acoustic conditions in the studio would permit the engineer to use more conventional methods. It's ultra-close perspective may create the type of sound that suits the particular requirements of the session.

Lavalier Microphones

The lavalier microphone in Figure 4-15A is designed to be worn on a cord around the neck. Specifically intended as an announcer's microphone, its irregular frequency response becomes smoothed out when the microphone is placed close to the user's chest. The rising high end response compensates for the fact that the speaker's clothing will tend to absorb high frequencies.

The lavalier microphone's apparently poor frequency response no doubt makes it unsuitable for most studio work. However, in some unique applications, it may be used to advantage. When the microphone is wrapped in foam rubber, as shown in Figure 4-15B, it may

THE LAVALIER MICROPHONE

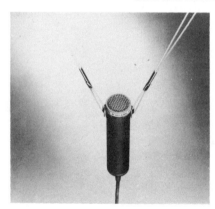

Figure 4-15A. A lavalier microphone, designed to be worn on a cord around the neck. (AKG D 110) [AKG photo]

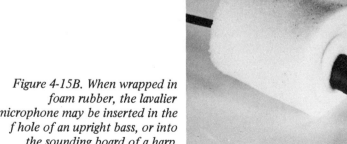

Figure 4-15B. When wrapped in foam rubber, the lavalier microphone may be inserted in the f hole of an upright bass, or into the sounding board of a harp.

146

be placed in the f hole of an upright bass, or into the sounding board of a harp. Conventional microphone placements are often difficult when these instruments are surrounded by other much louder instruments. But a regular microphone placed in either of the locations just mentioned would faithfully reproduce a rather "muddy" sound, since it will hear mostly low frequencies. The lavalier microphone's rising high end response will help bring out the higher frequencies, resulting in a more acceptable sound. Of course, an even more acceptable sound could be realized with a microphone spaced some distance from the instrument, but when this is impossible, the lavalier microphone may become a most practical way to retain some control over the sound of the instrument.

MIKING VARIOUS MUSICAL INSTRUMENTS

The Electric Guitar

The electric guitar is by now such an integral part of the recording scene that its use is taken almost for granted, and the guitar amplifier is a fixture in most, if not all, modern studios.

A sketch of the signal path from guitar to control room monitor (Figure 4-16) reveals the several energy conversions that must take place before the guitar sound reaches the control room listener. Note that the first energy conversion is from mechanical to electrical: although this electrical energy serves primarily as the input to the guitar amplifier, it may also be routed directly to the console, bypassing several intermediate steps in the signal path.

As always, there are advantages and disadvantages to this type of direct pickup. Since guitar amplifier outputs are at times noisy and/or distorted, the direct pickup may give the engineer a much cleaner, "tighter", signal with which to work. On the other hand, the guitar amplifier is usually considered an integral part of the electric guitar sound: when it is bypassed, its controls have no effect on the signal heard in the control room. The direct pickup eliminates any unwanted leakage from other instruments, yet it also eliminates the characteristic sound of the guitar amplifier speaker.

Matching Transformers

The output from the guitar itself is usually high impedance, and so a transformer is required to step down the output to microphone line

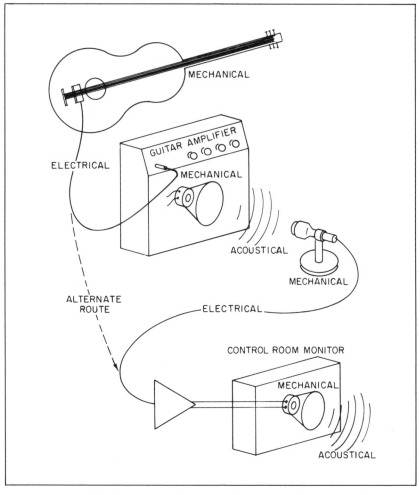

Figure 4-16. The signal path from guitar to control room monitor, showing the energy conversions that occur along the way.

impedance. (For the reasons cited earlier, the guitar's high impedance output cannot be fed directly through a long cable to the console input). And in the studio, the guitarist will want to hear the output from his amplifier, so a split feed, or "Y" connector is used, as shown in Figure 4-17.

If the guitar amplifier has an "external amplifier" output, the transformer may be plugged in to this jack instead. This eliminates the need for the Y connection, and also passes the signal through the

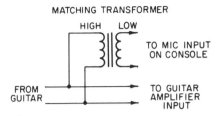

Figure 4-17. A split feed from an electric guitar to console input and guitar amplifier input.

guitar amplifier before it is routed to the recording console. Consequently, the amplifier's controls (tone, tremolo, reverberation, etc.) will have an effect on the recorded signal.

Transformers suitable for these applications are readily available, and a typical style is shown in Figure 4-18A. The use of the transformer is illustrated in Figures 4-18B and C.

Electronic Keyboard Instruments

The transformers just described may be similarly used with most electronic keyboard instruments. It should be noted though, that some keyboard outputs are divided between two output jacks, each feeding a separate section of the instrument's regular amplifier. In the event of a direct pickup, two transformers may therefore be required. These may either be mixed together at the console, or recorded on separate tracks.

The Leslie Organ Cabinet

The Leslie organ cabinet is a speaker enclosure system typically used with a Hammond organ. The cabinet contains two speaker systems, as shown in Figure 4-19. Built-in motors rotate the speakers, creating a tremolo effect. A microphone is usually placed somewhere in front of the speaker cabinet, since a transformer pickup would by-pass the effect of the rotating speakers. However, since the overall sound is distributed between the low frequency speaker at the bottom of the cabinet, and the high frequency speaker at the top, the microphone may have to be placed at some distance to pick up a satisfactory blend.

As an alternative, a figure-8 microphone may be placed close to

THE LINE MATCHING TRANSFORMER

*Figure 4-18A. A typical line matching transformer.
(Shure A95P) [Shure Bros. photo]*

*Figure 4-18B. The line matching transformer plugged into the
external amplifier plug on a bass amplifier.*

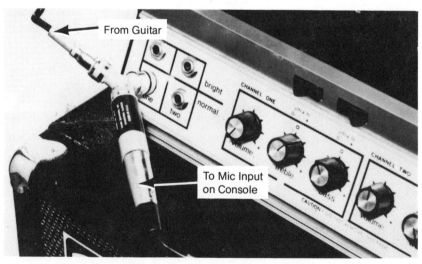

Figure 4-18C. The line matching transformer used for a split feed.

the cabinet, as shown in Figure 4-19. The microphone may be moved up and down to achieve the desired balance, while the dead side points into the room, thus keeping leakage from other instruments at a minimum.

The rotating speakers in the Leslie cabinet may be used as a special effect with many instruments, both electronic and acoustic. For example, the preamplifier within the Hammond organ contains an auxiliary input jack, into which an electric guitar may be plugged. The guitar will then be heard through the Leslie speaker system. Or, a microphone may be used to feed the sound of any non-electric instrument through the system.

The Acoustic Guitar

When an acoustic guitar is used as part of the rhythm section, a single microphone is usually placed fairly close up, to keep leakage at a minimum. Here, proper technique is mostly a matter of choosing the microphone that produces the most pleasing sound. Perhaps the greatest advantage is in a guitar player who understands enough of the nature of multi-track recording to make sure he remains at a reasonably constant distance from the microphone.

However, when the guitarist is also the vocalist, correct microphone placement is not quite so straightforward. If the vocal and guitar are separately miked, as is often done, some question arises as to how to satisfactorily balance the two microphone outputs. If one microphone is routed to the left and the other to the right, we have the unlikely situation of the musician singing and playing from opposite sides of the room. Yet if both microphones are center-placed, the monaural combination conveys little or no stereo perspective.

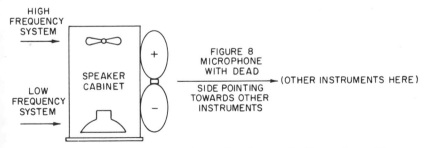

Figure 4-19. A Figure-8 microphone placed near a Leslie speaker cabinet.

151

In many cases, a better recording could be made with a stereo microphone placed somewhere in front of the musician. Assuming the performer is capable of balancing his vocal and guitar performance, the stereo microphone will pick up a blend of the two, and at the same time convey the feeling that the recording is in fact in stereo. Of course, two regular microphones may be used in place of the stereo microphone, providing they are well matched.

Percussion Instruments

In studio practice, the term "percussion" is usually applied to all such instruments, except the drum set. The instrumentation for a session may list "drums and percussion", thus informing the engineer that there will be both a drummer and a percussionist, with the latter playing a variety of percussive instruments; typically, tambourine, shaker, bell tree, marimba and/or vibes, tympani, etc.

In many sessions, the percussionist will move quickly from one instrument to another, and no single microphone placement will provide adequate coverage. It is a common practice to place a variety of microphones in the general area, and as the musician moves from one instrument to another, he will play into the closest microphone. In this case, the microphone-to-instrument spacing will be quite small, and each microphone may be kept at a low output level, keeping leakage from nearby instruments at a minimum.

The Drum Set

The engineer will often use a quantity of microphones for his drum setup. Since each part of the drum set has its own distinctive "sound", the engineer may balance—or re-balance—the overall sound to suit the needs of the session. A typical setup is shown in Figure 4-20. Two overhead microphones are used as an overall pickup, and there are additional microphones on the snare drum, the floor tom-tom, and the bass drum. And it is not at all uncommon to find additional microphones in use, closely placed near the cymbals and small tom-toms.

Although the choice, and specific placement, of individual microphones will depend—as always—on personal taste, the engineer should keep in mind the consequences of the multi-microphone setup.

152

Figure 4-20. A typical multi-microphone drum setup. Note padding in bass drum, to help deaden its sound.

Transient percussive peaks—especially from the snare drum and cymbals—will surely be way above the apparent levels seen on the VU meters. Until the engineer has some practical experience relating the VU levels to the peaks recorded on tape, particular caution should be used to prevent overloading either the recording console input or the tape. It is particularly likely that a condenser microphone placed very close to a snare drum will require an attenuation pad between the capsule diaphragm and the microphone's preamplifier.

To keep the individual drum sounds better isolated for maximum control, cardioid microphones are often used. These cardioid microphones should be chosen carefully though, since the disadvantage of proximity effect and off-axis coloration may outweigh the directional sensitivity advantage of the microphone. For example, a cardioid microphone may be aimed at the snare drum; however it will certainly hear at least some sound from the nearby cymbals. Proximity effect may give the snare drum a tubby sound, while off-axis coloration may distort the frequency response of the cymbals. In many cases, an omnidirectional microphone will be more suitable, for the reasons mentioned earlier (Chapter 3).

When multi-microphone pickups are used, there is often little physical clearance between the microphones and the various parts of the drum set. And of course, the microphones must be carefully placed where they will not accidently be struck as the drummer moves from one part of his set to another. Several condenser microphone systems offer a series of extension tubes and swivels, which enable the microphone pre-amplifier to be placed at a distance from the diaphragm capsule. These accessories allow considerable flexibility in microphone placement when physical clearances are a problem. A representative example of these accessories is shown in Figure 4-21.

The overall pickup is a potential source of phase cancellation, particularly in the case of cymbals, which may move considerably each time they are struck. The movement creates continually varying path lengths to the two microphones, and if their outputs are not being combined at the time of recording, it is a good idea to spend a little time listening to a mono mixture over the monitor system, to make sure there will be no serious cancellation problems later on. Often moving one microphone slightly will clear up a potentially troublesome acoustic phase problem.

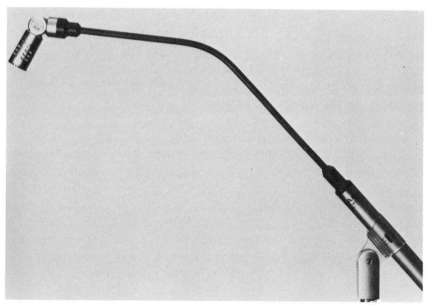

Figure 4-21. The right angle and extension tube accessories shown allow the engineer great flexibility in arranging ultra-close microphone placements. (AKG A 51 and VR 1)

On many sessions, the rear skin of the bass drum is removed, and a blanket is stuffed inside the drum, against the front skin. Although this certainly affects the tonality of the drum, it seems to produce a more percussive attack, emphasizing the all-important "beat" of the song. (A method of restoring the bass drum's tonality is discussed in Chapter 8 [Using the Expander for Special Effects.]).

The bass drum microphone may also be placed inside the drum, and here the proximity effect may be used to advantage, although care must be taken that the bass rise is not so severe as to overload the console preamplifier.

Some engineers have used ribbon microphones in the bass drum, although this is probably about the worst place to put such a microphone. The severe pressure changes inside the drum are enough to tax any microphone, and unless the ribbon is exceptionally sturdy, it may very quickly become damaged.

The Piano

To achieve adequate overall coverage of a grand piano, a single microphone might have to be placed several feet away, due to the instrument's size. Since this may present problems with leakage from other instruments, the engineer will often use two or more closely placed microphones instead, in order to gain good coverage with maximum isolation of other instruments in the surrounding area. In such cases, there is inevitably some acoustic phase interaction between the microphones, and an eventual combination of the microphone outputs may produce some severe frequency cancellations. As before, it is important to monitor the microphone outputs in mono from time to time, to make sure there will be no mixing problems later on.

The open lid of the grand piano acts as a reflector of the piano sound, and of course also reflects the sounds of other instruments in the nearby area. A microphone placed somewhere between the strings and the lid will pick up both wanted and unwanted reflections from the lid, as seen in Figure 4-22.

In the figure, notice that the unwanted reflections shown are all from points on the lid above the microphone height. Sounds reaching the lid below this height are mostly reflected away from the microphone. A microphone placed very close to the lid will not pick up as many reflections, and will favor the direct sound of the piano. The ideal placement will depend on the angle of the lid and the music

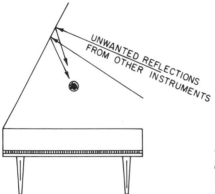

Figure 4-22. A microphone placed as shown may pick up the reflections of other instruments from the piano lid.

being played, but some experimentation should reveal a suitable location in most situations.

The engineer should bear in mind that most of the piano sound comes from its sounding board, and that there is little point in aiming the microphone(s) at the hammers, as is so often seen. In fact, the microphones may be placed under the piano, pointing up, or in the case of an upright piano, behind the piano. Both locations favor the sounding board, and may help keep unwanted reflections at a minimum.

Strings, Brass, and Woodwinds

The close up perspective that so often works well on rhythm instruments (guitars, keyboards, drums, percussion and bass) may be less effective on strings, brass, and woodwinds. In most cases, these instruments should sound as though they are spread over a reasonably large area. Pin-point localization is usually not nearly so musically effective as a diffuse, spacious kind of perspective. The close-up sound of a violin or brass instrument is often apt to be rather unpleasant, and moving the microphones back a little bit will create a better illusion of listening to an ensemble, rather than to a collection of isolated point source sounds.

Of course, if other instruments are playing loudly at the same time, a distant microphone pickup may be impossible due to leakage problems, especially if the string section is quite small, as is so often the case.

CHAPTER 5

Loudspeakers

In evaluating a microphone, the environment in which it is placed may often be ignored, when ultra-close miking reduces the contribution of the room's acoustics to a negligible factor. On the other hand, the effect of the listening room on the loudspeaker must never be ignored, since it has a great influence on what the listener hears. But before describing the room/speaker interface, some background information on loudspeaker theory and application is required.

Schematically, the microphone and the loudspeaker bear a striking resemblance in operating principle if not in outward appearance. In both, the diaphragm is the center of the transducing system. In the microphone, its motion converts acoustic energy into electrical energy. The loudspeaker diaphragm reverses the process; electrical energy is converted back into acoustic energy.

MOVING-COIL LOUDSPEAKERS

A typical moving-coil loudspeaker is shown in Figure 5-1. When an alternating current signal is applied to the voice coil, the diaphragm moves back and forth, displacing the surrounding air molecules and creating a sound wave which eventually reaches the listener. Due to its structural reliability, the moving-coil system is the basis of practically all studio monitor systems.

RIBBON LOUDSPEAKERS

In principle, the operation of the ribbon loudspeaker is analagous to the ribbon microphone, except that the energy conversion process is of course reversed. Although ribbon loudspeakers have been manufactured in the past, their fragility and physical limitations seem to make them impractical as wide range studio quality transducers. Nevertheless, ribbon transducers are occasionally found in the high

157

Figure 5-1. Cutaway view of a moving coil loudspeaker. (JBL LE 8T) [JBL photo]

frequency section of multi-speaker systems, where power handling requirements are not quite so demanding.

CONDENSER, OR ELECTROSTATIC, LOUDSPEAKERS

In loudspeaker terminology, a speaker working on the condenser principle is referred to as an electrostatic transducer. A simplified electrostatic loudspeaker is shown in Figure 5-2. As with the condenser microphone described earlier (Figure 3-6A), it consists of a

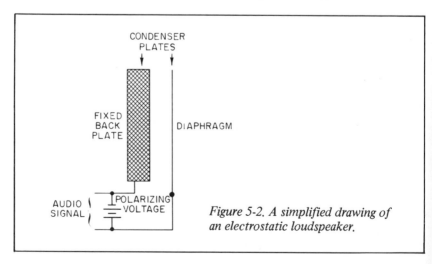

Figure 5-2. A simplified drawing of an electrostatic loudspeaker.

fixed back plate and a moveable diaphragm plate. The audio signal voltage is applied across the plates, and the diaphragm plate moves back and forth, as described earlier. Figure 5-3 shows a representative electrostatic speaker system.

SOME LOUDSPEAKER TERMINOLOGY

Later in the chapter, terms such as compliance, resonance, efficiency, etc. are introduced. These terms—as they apply to the loudspeaker—are briefly described below.

Resonance

The fundamental frequency at which a tuning fork or taut string vibrates may be called its **resonant frequency**. Although the device may actually be vibrating at many frequencies, at the frequency of resonance, the opposition of the surrounding air is at a minimum. This frequency is a function of the device's mass and stiffness.

All vibrating devices have a resonant frequency, and the loudspeaker is no exception. Depending on the mass and stiffness of the

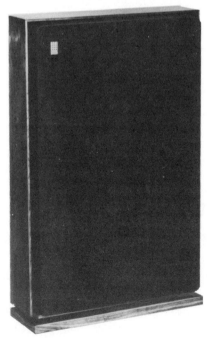

Figure 5-3. An electrostatic speaker system.
Since the capacitor-like diaphragm does not require a massive permanent magnet/voice coil assembly, the system has a relatively slim profile.
(Koss Model One) [Koss photo]

speaker cone and diaphragm/voice coil assembly, this frequency will vary. Generally, the larger the speaker diameter, the lower will be the resonant frequency.

Transient Response and Damping

Just as a tuning fork continues to vibrate long after it is struck, a speaker diaphragm does not instantly cease its motion the moment the applied signal is withdrawn. Accordingly, its **transient response** — the ability to follow precisely the more percussive waveforms — may suffer, especially at or near the speaker's resonant frequency.

To improve transient response, some form of acoustical, mechanical, or electrical resistance may be applied to the moving system. This opposition, or **damping**, helps to keep the speaker movement directly related to the applied signal, and in the absence of that signal, the speaker diaphragm is brought to an almost instantaneous halt.

Compliance

Compliance — expressed in Newtons per meter (abbreviated N/m) — is the ease with which a speaker diaphragm moves, and is measured by dividing the diaphragm displacement by the applied magnetic force. A highly damped speaker will have little compliance, since the diaphragm movement per unit of applied force will be quite small. Without damping, compliance will reach a maximum at the speaker's resonant frequency. As damping is increased, compliance is reduced, and as a result, the resonant frequency of the speaker is likewise increased.

Efficiency

As in other physical systems, speaker **efficiency** is a ratio of power output-to-power input. In this case, the input power is electrical, while the output power is acoustical.

THE IDEAL SOUND SOURCE

In the study of acoustics, reference is often made to an **ideal sound source.** This is usually considered to be a point source of sound, suspended in free space. It is described as a pulsating sphere of infinitely small dimension. As the sphere releases energy, sound

THE EFFECT OF ROOM
SURFACES ON THE IDEAL
SOUND SOURCE

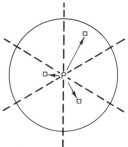

THE MEASURED SOUND LEVEL AT ANY
POINT ON THE SPHERE IS THE SAME

Figure 5-4A. An ideal sound source, radiating into full space (4π steradians).

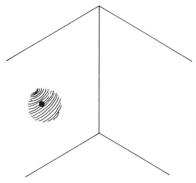

Figure 5-4B. When the point source is placed against a wall, the total energy radiates into half space (2π steradians).

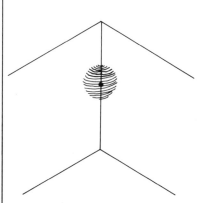

Figure 5-4C. When the point source is at the intersection of two surfaces, the total energy radiates into 1/4 space (π steradians).

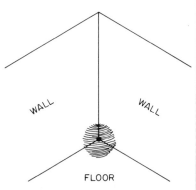

WALL   WALL

FLOOR

Figure 5-4D. When the point source is placed at the intersection of three surfaces, the total energy radiates into 1/8 space π/2 steradians).

161

waves radiate away from it in all directions. This is often referred to as **radiation into full space** (or **free space**), described in mathematical terms as a radiation angle of 4π steradians.

If the point source is considered to be at the center of a larger sphere, the measured sound level will be the same at any point on this sphere's circumference, as illustrated in Figure 5-4A.

The Effect of Room Surfaces on the Ideal Sound Source

If our ideal sound source is now moved against a wall, as shown in Figure 5-4B, the radiation sphere will be bisected by the wall. Assuming this to be a solid, the total sound energy from the point source will now be forced to radiate into half-space only, or 2π steradians. Therefore, at any point on the hemisphere, the measured sound level will be 6 dB greater than if the measurement was made in full space. (Intensity is analogous to voltage, and therefore its decibel value increases by 6 dB when it is doubled.)

If the point source is now moved into a corner, the intersection of the two walls will cut the radiation angle in half again, and the intensity rises another 6 dB, as shown in Figure 5-4C.

Finally, if the point source is placed at floor—or ceiling—level, the intersection of the three surfaces will again halve the radiation angle, and the intensity will rise once more by 6 dB, as in Figure 5-4D.

Loudspeaker Radiation, or Polar, Patterns

Polar patterns may be drawn for each of the theoretically ideal conditions just described. Although similar in principle to the microphone polar pattern, the loudspeaker pattern is an indication of the intensity radiated from the sound source into the surrounding space. The patterns are shown in Figure 5-5, and the room surfaces that have influenced the radiation are indicated in the illustration. Since both vertical (walls) and horizontal (ceiling or floor) surfaces may affect the radiation angle, patterns are often given in both the horizontal and vertical planes, as seen in the figure.

PRACTICAL LOUDSPEAKERS

As with other theoretically ideal systems, the point source of sound does not exist in reality. Practical loudspeakers may, by no stretch of the imagination, be considered to be spherical radiators.

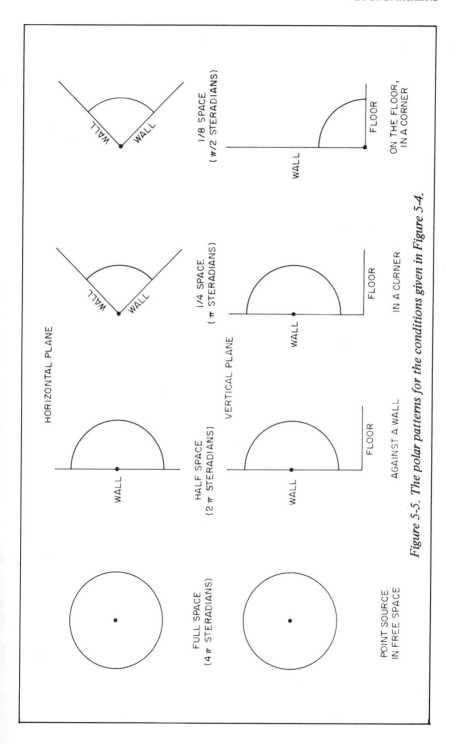

Figure 5-5. The polar patterns for the conditions given in Figure 5-4.

163

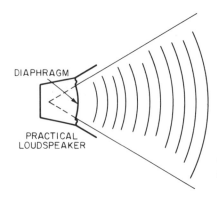

Figure 5-6. The radiation angle of a practical loudspeaker.

For example, if we draw a speaker diaphragm schematically, as in Figure 5-6, we can anticipate that it may radiate into the angle shown, rather than into full space. For one thing, the speaker housing gets in its own way, just as the body of a flashlight prevents its light from radiating backwards.

Diffraction

It will be found that a speaker's radiation angle varies considerably with frequency, for once again the diffraction phenomenon described in Chapter 2 must be considered. The size of the speaker itself becomes an obstacle to small wavelengths (high frequencies), tending to focus them into a narrow radiation angle. On the other hand, long wavelengths (low frequencies) are readily diffracted around the speaker assembly. Therefore, the radiation pattern of a practical loudspeaker suspended in free space may be as shown in Figure 5-7. Note that low frequencies are radiated over a wide angle, while higher frequencies are focused into a progressively narrower beam of sound.

Provided the listener is directly in front of the speaker, the frequency response is flat, as seen in the illustration. But, as with some microphones, off-axis response may be quite distorted, or colored.

The Effect of Room Surfaces on the Practical Loudspeaker

From our brief study of the ideal sound source, it will be realized that speaker placement within the room will severely affect performance. For example, if the loudspeaker represented in Figure 5-7 is

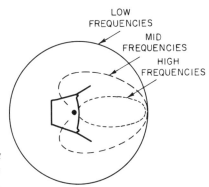

Figure 5-7. Radiation patterns of a practical loudspeaker, showing the effects of diffraction.

placed against a wall, this surface will reflect whatever rear energy there is back towards the front. Since this rear energy is predominantly longer wavelengths (due to diffraction) the apparent on-axis low frequency response will rise, while the high frequency response remains unaffected. And if the speaker is moved into a corner, or to the floor or ceiling, the low frequency response will rise even more. When the speaker is placed at the intersection of three room surfaces, the low frequency response will be boosted to a maximum. Figure 5-8 illustrates the effect that the room exerts on the speaker for each of these conditions.

THE DIRECT RADIATOR
Speaker Enclosure Systems

Just as the walls, ceiling and floor influence the loudspeaker's performance, so does the cabinet in which it may be enclosed. Speaker enclosures may be classified as direct or indirect radiators, and examples of both types are described here.

As its name implies, the **direct radiator** system is designed so that the speaker radiates directly into the listening room.

The Infinite Baffle

As shown in Figure 5-9, the **infinite baffle** is the simplest form of direct radiator, consisting simply of a hole cut in a wall. Assuming that the other room surfaces are sufficiently distant, the speaker's full space radiation pattern is minimally affected, since the speaker is free to radiate pretty much as it would in free space. Of course, the

THE EFFECT OF ROOM SURFACES ON THE PRACTICAL LOUDSPEAKER

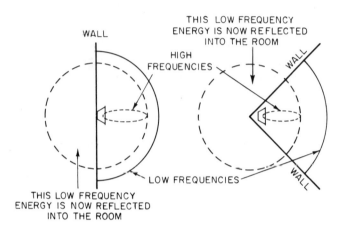

THIS LOW FREQUENCY ENERGY IS NOW REFLECTED INTO THE ROOM

WALL

HIGH FREQUENCIES

WALL

LOW FREQUENCIES

THIS LOW FREQUENCY ENERGY IS NOW REFLECTED INTO THE ROOM

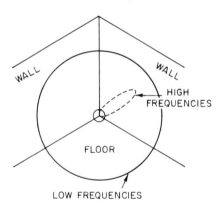

WALL

WALL

HIGH FREQUENCIES

FLOOR

LOW FREQUENCIES

Figure 5-8. Each additional room surface reflects more of the refracted low frequency energy into the room. The more directional high frequencies may not be affected by the room surfaces.

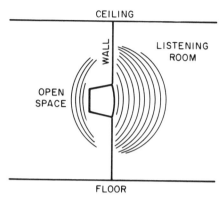

Figure 5-9. The Infinite Baffle. The speaker's full space radiation pattern is minimally affected by the wall.

energy that is dissipated in the rear is wasted, from the point of view of the listening room, and the infinite baffle also makes the impractical assumption that a large space behind the speaker wall is readily available.

The Open Baffle

The **open baffle** system is likewise impractical, but should be discussed at some length since it forms the beginning of the practical speaker enclosure. To understand its purpose, consider an unmounted loudspeaker, as shown in Figure 5-10. As the diaphragm moves forward, the air molecules directly in front of it are compressed, while at the same time there is a rarefaction immediately behind the dia-

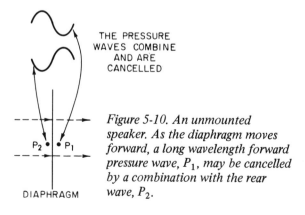

THE PRESSURE WAVES COMBINE AND ARE CANCELLED

Figure 5-10. An unmounted speaker. As the diaphragm moves forward, a long wavelength forward pressure wave, P_1, may be cancelled by a combination with the rear wave, P_2.

phragm. As the diaphragm moves back and forth, sound waves should be radiated away from the speaker, as indeed is the case with high frequency sounds. However, when the diaphragm is moving relatively slowly (low frequencies), the sound pressure wave on one side of the diaphragm may simply cancel with that on the other, as seen in the figure.

To prevent this type of low frequency cancellation, the speaker may be mounted in an open baffle, as shown in Figure 5-11. Now, sound waves from the rear must travel around the baffle before they

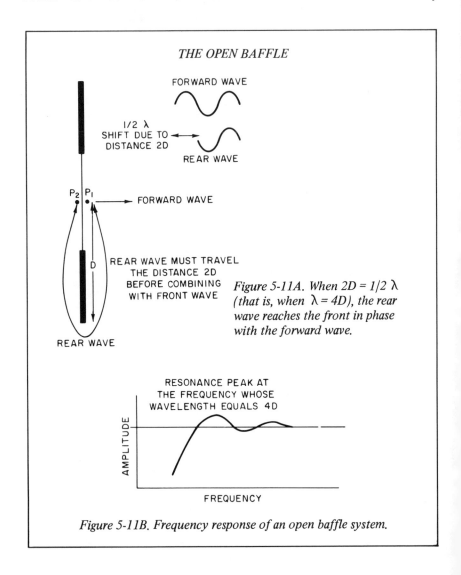

Figure 5-11A. When 2D = 1/2 λ (that is, when λ = 4D), the rear wave reaches the front in phase with the forward wave.

Figure 5-11B. Frequency response of an open baffle system.

are combined with those from the front. It has been found that the longer the baffle length, the lower will be the frequency at which cancellations begin. The baffle length should equal one quarter the wavelength of the lowest frequency that it is desired to reproduce without cancellation. As seen in Figure 5-11, a frequency whose wavelength equals four times the baffle length (λ = 4D) will now arrive at the front of the speaker in phase with the forward wave, producing a maximum reinforcement.

Longer wavelength signals will be progressively attenuated, due to both phase cancellations and the speaker's own inherent low frequency limit. Frequencies whose wavelengths are somewhat shorter than 4D will also tend to be attenuated somewhat, although as the wavelength decreases, the rear wave has less and less of an effect, due to the diminishing radiation angle described earlier.

Open Baffle Resonance Frequency

The frequency response (or rather, wavelength response) of the open baffle system will appear as shown in Figure 5-11B. Note that there is a peak at the frequency where λ = 4D, for it is at this point that the rear and front waves add to produce a maximum sound pressure level, or resonance peak.

Another disadvantage of the open baffle is the dimension required for good low frequency response. A little arithmetic will reveal that the quarter wavelength of 50 Hz is about 5.5 feet. Therefore, an open baffle tuned to this resonant frequency must be 11 feet in diameter; that is, 5.5 feet in radius from the speaker cut-out; hardly a practical dimension!

The Folded Baffle

The **folded baffle** seen in Figure 5-12 offers some relief in size over the open baffle system. By folding the baffle as shown, it is possible to achieve a smaller enclosure without raising the resonant frequency described earlier. However, when the sides take on any appreciable dimension, the speaker cabinet acquires the acoustic properties of an open column of air. That is, it produces a resonance at the frequency whose wavelength equals four times the length of the column created by the baffle sides. Therefore, if the baffle sides are 1 foot long, the enclosed air column will resonate at 275 Hz, while the baffle itself will continue to resonate at λ = 4D, as described earlier.

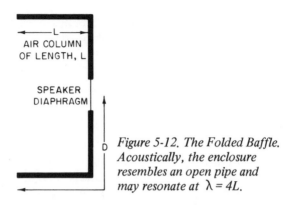

Figure 5-12. The Folded Baffle. Acoustically, the enclosure resembles an open pipe and may resonate at $\lambda = 4L$.

The Sealed Enclosure, or Acoustic Suspension System

The **sealed enclosure** – shown in Figure 5-13 – eliminates the acoustic resonance peaks of the open and folded baffle systems, since it is impossible for rear waves to reach the front of the speaker. In addition, the enclosed volume of air acts as an acoustic resistance (damping) against the rear of the speaker cone, thus lowering the system's compliance. As the compliance is reduced, the speaker's resonant frequency is raised, as was noted earlier, in the description of compliance.

Depending on the design parameters, the resonant frequency of the speaker/enclosure system may be an octave or more above the resonant frequency of the speaker itself in free space.

Since in the sealed enclosure the speaker is, in effect, resting on the enclosed air column, it is often referred to as an **acoustic suspension system**. A representative example is shown in Figure 5-14.

Figure 5-13. The Sealed Enclosure, or Acoustic Suspension System.

Figure 5-14. An Acoustic Suspension System. The woofer's free space resonance frequency is 18 Hz, while the system resonance frequency is 42 Hz. (Acoustic Research AR-11) [Acoustic Research photo]

The sealed enclosure is often called an infinite baffle, since, like the true infinite baffle described earlier, the system prevents rear waves from reaching the front of the speaker. However, the true infinite baffle has an unlimited air space behind it, while the sealed enclosure does not.

The Vented, or Bass Reflex, Enclosure

One limitation of the acoustic suspension system is that rear waves are trapped within the enclosure; consequently the speaker's efficiency rating is reduced, since this portion of the total output power is lost. The vented enclosure, shown in Figure 5-15, allows the rear waves to reach the front, thus improving the system's efficiency.

171

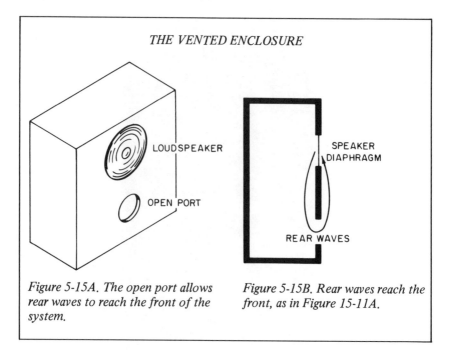

Figure 5-15A. The open port allows rear waves to reach the front of the system.

Figure 5-15B. Rear waves reach the front, as in Figure 15-11A.

The Tuned Port

The volume of air within an enclosure has a certain compliance; that is, it acts as an acoustic capacitance, affecting the system's resonant frequency, as was discussed earlier. If a port is cut into the enclosure, the opening allows sound waves to escape. However, the port has a certain acoustic inertance, analogous to inductance in an electrical circuit. The system becomes, in effect, a capacitance (the enclosure) in parallel with an inductance (the port). The dimensions of both may be designed to create an acoustic resonance at a specified frequency. It has been found that if this frequency is the same as the speaker's own resonant frequency, the system resonance will drop in amplitude. In fact, it will exhibit two resonance points—one above and the other below the original speaker resonant frequency. As a result, the usable low frequency response of the system is extended downwards. However, due to open baffle-type cancellation effects, the low frequency attenuation below resonance will probably fall off at a sharper rate than in the sealed enclosure system.

In the open baffle systems described earlier, baffle dimensions had to be quite large to keep phase cancellations at as low a frequency as possible. In the vented system, the acoustic phase shift of the enclo-

Figure 5-16. A Vented Enclosure System. In this speaker system, several small ports are used to prevent structural weakening of the front baffle. (JBL 4350 [prototype]) [JBL photo]

sure and port accomplishes the same thing, and low frequencies (above resonance) emerge from the port in phase with the front of the speaker, as is illustrated in Figure 5-15B. An example of a vented enclosure system is seen in Figure 5-16.

Vented Enclosure with Passive Radiator

As sound waves travel through the open port just described, a certain amount of acoustic friction acts against the air particles. The friction is greatest at the edge of the opening, diminishing toward the center.

To make the movement of the air particles more uniform across the entire opening, a passive radiator may be placed in the port. Sometimes called a slave or drone cone, the passive radiator may be nothing more than an unpowered speaker assembly. The air pressure against the back of the passive radiator forces it to move in and out. In the front, a sound wave is radiated that is more uniform than one from a simple open port. Figure 5-17 shows a vented enclosure system using a passive radiator.

SUMMARY OF DIRECT RADIATORS

A direct radiator is a speaker that is coupled directly to the air in front of it. Although at each stage in the development from infinite baffle to vented enclosure with passive radiator the efficiency of the acoustic coupling of diaphragm-to-air increased, the direct radiator remains a relatively inefficient system. The poor efficiency is a function of the high mechanical impedance of the speaker diaphragm attempting to transfer energy to the low acoustic impedance of the surrounding air.

173

Speakers

Passive Radiator

Figure 5-17. A Vented Enclosure with a passive radiator.
(Electro-Voice Interface:A) [Electro-Voice photo]

In an electrical circuit, when maximum power transfer is required, an impedance-matching transformer may be used between any two stages where there is a significant impedance mismatch. For example, without such a transformer, a high impedance microphone will function with minimum efficiency when connected to a low impedance microphone preamplifier.

In a direct radiator speaker system, the diaphragm-to-air coupling is pretty much a "brute force" method; a high electrical input power applied to the speaker terminals produces a low acoustical output power in front of the diaphragm. Even a so-called high efficiency direct radiator system may have an efficiency of not much more than 5 percent.

174

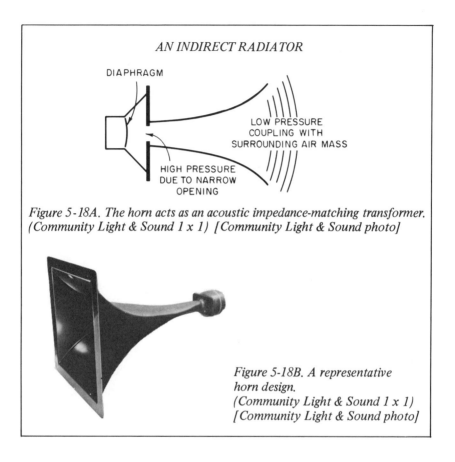

AN INDIRECT RADIATOR

DIAPHRAGM

LOW PRESSURE
COUPLING WITH
SURROUNDING AIR MASS

HIGH PRESSURE
DUE TO NARROW
OPENING

Figure 5-18A. The horn acts as an acoustic impedance-matching transformer. (Community Light & Sound 1 x 1) [Community Light & Sound photo]

Figure 5-18B. A representative horn design. (Community Light & Sound 1 x 1) [Community Light & Sound photo]

HORN LOADED SYSTEMS
The Indirect Radiator

In an **indirect radiator**, the speaker diaphragm is coupled to the surrounding air by a device that functions as an acoustic transformer. The horn system shown in Figure 5-18 is a well known example of this type of indirect radiator.

Note that the speaker diaphragm with a horn in front of it is no longer able to radiate into a large air mass. The throat of the horn is considerably smaller than the diaphragm diameter, and like the action of water being forced into a narrower diameter pipe, there is a resultant high pressure area developed at the beginning of the throat. This high acoustic impedance is closer to the mechanical impedance of the speaker, resulting in a more efficient transfer of power.

As the sound wave travels the length of the horn, its gradually

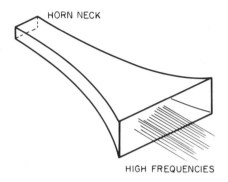

HIGH FREQUENCIES

Figure 5-19. The tapered horn tends to narrow the radiation angle of high frequencies.

flaring shape disperses the sound pressure over a progressively larger cross sectional area. Eventually, the sound wave reaches the open air, by which time its pressure has been reduced substantially. The original high pressure/high impedance sound wave has become a low pressure/low impedance wave front. The transformer action of the horn results in a more efficient coupling with the surrounding air. As a result, the sound level will be considerably higher than with a direct radiator system. This type of indirect radiator is often referred to as a **horn loaded system.**

Radiation Characteristics of Horn Loaded Systems.

Although the horn loaded indirect radiator system has a higher efficiency than a direct radiator, its radiation pattern tends to narrow appreciably at higher frequencies, as the neck and inner surfaces of the horn focus the high frequencies into a narrow beam, as shown in Figure 5-19.

Multi-Cellular Horns

In an effort to widen the radiation pattern, **multi-cellular horns** of the type seen in Figure 5-20 have been developed. The multi-cell construction distributes the sound wave among two or more horn sections, resulting in a wider radiation pattern in both the horizontal and vertical planes. The horizontal radiation angle is usually wider than the vertical angle, but this is usually not a significant drawback since a wide vertical angle is probably not required in the majority of applications.

Figure 5-20. A Multi-Cellular Horn.
(Community Light & Sound 2 x 5) [Community Light & Sound photo]

The Acoustic Lens

The **acoustic lens** is designed to provide a wider radiation angle for high frequencies, especially in the horizontal plane. Based on optical principles, the lens bends the sound "rays" passing through it, dispersing them over a greater area. Figure 5-21 shows examples of the acoustic lens.

Folded Horns

A straight horn designed for low frequency operation would be quite long, and physically impractical. However, the horn may be folded as shown in Figure 5-22 to fit within a physically manageable area. The long wavelength efficiency of such a design is excellent, since the diffraction phenomenon allows low frequencies to readily pass through this acoustic labyrinth. However, high frequency output will be very inefficient, and a separate high frequency system will be required.

The speaker system shown in Figure 5-23 is a combination of a low frequency folded horn and straight horns for mid-and high frequencies.

177

THE ACOUSTIC LENS

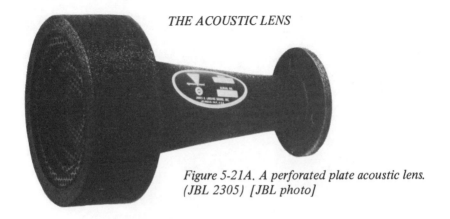

Figure 5-21A. A perforated plate acoustic lens. (JBL 2305) [JBL photo]

Figure 5-21B. A slanted plate acoustic lens. (JBL HL 91) [JBL photo]

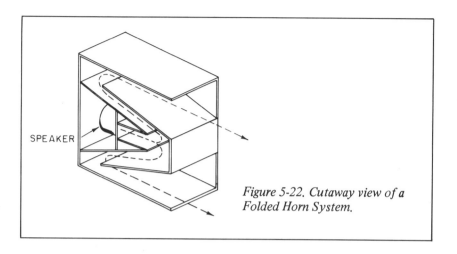

SPEAKER

Figure 5-22. Cutaway view of a Folded Horn System.

Middle and high
frequency
straight horns

Low frequency
folded horn system
(As in Figure 5-22)

Figure 5-23. A speaker system using the folded horn principle. (Electro-Voice Sentry IV) [Electro-Voice photo]

179

The Compression Driver

The **compression driver** is a special-purpose transducer designed to be used in mid- and high-frequency horn systems. The unit shown in Figure 5-24 has a 4 inch diameter aluminum voice coil/diaphragm and a 2 inch diameter throat. The relatively small diaphragm has a high resonant frequency and is generally more efficient in horn loaded applications than a massive speaker cone assembly. The comparatively narrow throat diameter is designed for maximum efficiency coupling with the horn assembly.

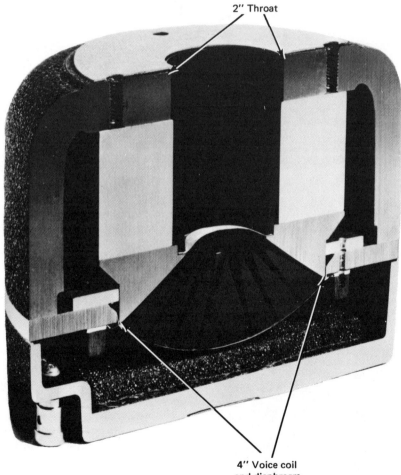

2" Throat

4" Voice coil
and diaphragm

Figure 5-24. Cutaway view of a
Compression Driver.
(JBL 2440) [JBL photo]

MULTI-SPEAKER SYSTEMS

Like most musical instruments, a given loudspeaker may be most efficient over a portion of the audio bandwidth. For example, a family of stringed instruments ranging in size from the treble violin to the oversized double bass is required to cover the entire music spectrum. Likewise, a small high frequency speaker may be incapable of reproducing low frequencies, and *vice versa*. Accordingly, many studio speaker systems employ two or more speakers, each optimized for a specific segment of the audio bandwidth.

In its simplest form, a wide range system may comprise a high frequency tweeter and a low frequency woofer. (The terms describing accurately, if irreverently, the sound output of the two speakers.)

Crossover Networks

In most cases, a **crossover network** is used with a multi-speaker system, as shown in Figure 5-25. The network passes the appropriate frequency band to each speaker, while suppressing frequencies outside the band. Thus, neither speaker receives unusable power from a signal outside its own pass-band. In addition, the tweeter is protected against overload from high level, low frequency signal components.

Crossover Phase Distortion

In Figure 5-25, note that there is some overlap in the frequency pass-bands, and that the output from both speakers is down 3 dB at the crossover frequency. Therefore, both speakers deliver the same amount of power at the crossover frequency, flattening out the response over the crossover range. This assumes, however, that the speakers are in phase at the crossover frequency, when in fact this is most often not the case. Each filter introduces a phase shift as it attenuates frequencies outside its bandwidth. In one typical situation, each filter shifts the output signal by 90° at the crossover frequency. However, the phase shifts are in opposite directions, giving a net phase shift of 180° between speakers at the crossover frequency. Therefore, there will be a severe acoustic phase cancellation in this region unless one of the speakers is electrically reversed in phase. This reversal puts the speakers back in phase at the crossover frequency, and out-of-phase within their pass bands. However, since the speakers are only reproducing the same signal in the vicinity of cross-

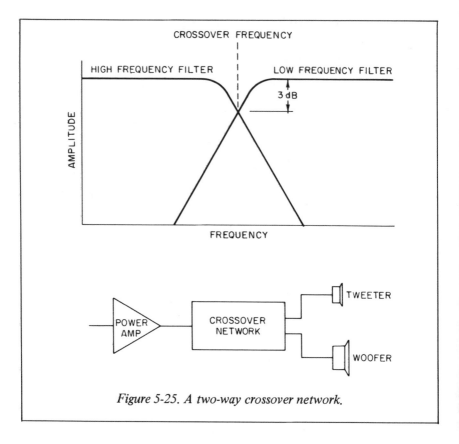

Figure 5-25. A two-way crossover network.

over, there will be little cancellation over the rest of the audio band-width. Of course, if the phase shift at the crossover frequency is not exactly ±90°, the wiring reversal will be ineffective.

Acoustic Phase Shift in Multi-Speaker Systems

The **acoustic center** of a loudspeaker is the point at which sound waves appear to originate. Especially in horn loaded systems, the acoustic center may be somewhat removed from the actual center line of the diaphragm at rest. When more than one speaker is to be used in an enclosure, it is important that their acoustic centers all lie in the same vertical plane, to prevent acoustic phase cancellations in the vicinity of the crossover frequency.

However, if the electrical phase shift at the crossover frequency cannot be corrected by the wiring reversal described above, one of the speakers may be moved slightly so that its acoustical center is

182

shifted by the distance required to cancel out the crossover network's electrical phase shift.

Bi-Amplification

In a **bi-amplification** system, the tweeter and the woofer are driven by separate amplifiers, with the crossover network placed before the amplification, as shown in Figure 5-26.

When a single amplifier drives a passive crossover network, the network itself must be capable of sustaining the full power output of the amplifier. In addition, harmonic distortion components of the low frequency output may be delivered to, and reproduced in, the high frequency output section.

On the other hand, an active crossover network placed ahead of the amplification completely isolates low and high frequency components. Distortion in one side will not be transmitted to the other. And, since woofers characteristically require more power than tweeters, a lower power amplifier may be used in the high frequency leg of the system. In fact, a well designed bi-amplified system may require less total power than the same speaker driven by a single amplifier.

THE ROOM/SPEAKER INTERFACE

As we have already seen, room surfaces are a considerable influence on loudspeaker performance. However, this influence extends far beyond the effects on bass response that have already been discussed.

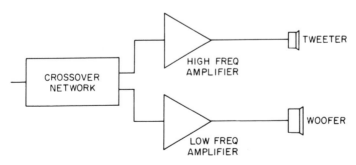

Figure 5-26. A bi-amplification system. The crossover network is placed ahead of the amplification.

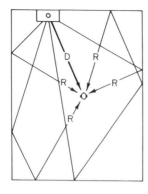

Figure 5-27. The listener hears mostly reflected signals, although the direct sound does arrive first. D = direct signal R = reflected signals

Earlier, it was seen (Figure 5-8) that nearby surfaces reflect low frequency energy back into the room. And, as the sound energy radiates away from the speaker, it eventually reaches the more distant room surfaces. These in turn reflect some portion of the sound wave back into the room. The listener hears not only the direct sound coming from the speaker, but also the multiplicity of reflections from all the room surfaces. In fact, in most cases the amplitude of the reflections near the listener's ear is greater than that of the direct sound, as may be seen in Figure 5-27. Therefore, the character of these reflections will play a very important part in the listener's impression of what he hears.

Room surfaces are neither perfect reflectors nor perfect absorbers. The frequencies that are efficiently reflected — or absorbed — depend on surface textures and density, air space behind the surfaces, rigidity, and so on. In fact, a change in any one of these parameters may very well exert an influence on the overall sound that is greater than would be heard if the speaker system itself was replaced with a different type.

Depending on the complex interaction between the speaker and the room, the overall sound quality may be described as bright, dull, live, dead, boomy, shrill, or by any of a seemingly endless number of similar adjectives. In other words, the room becomes part of the monitor system, and its effect must be taken into consideration when evaluating any speaker.

Standing Waves

When a sound wave strikes a wall and reflects back into the room, there may be areas in the room where the direct and reflected waves interact to form a **standing wave** — an apparently stationary waveform. The phenomenon may be quite apparent when listening to a single frequency tone from an audio signal generator.

To explain the standing wave, consider a sound wave reflected back on itself, as seen in Figure 5-28. The sound source, **S**, eventually strikes the wall, **W**. The listener, **L**, standing somewhere on the line, **S-W**, may hear either a strong signal or none at all, depending on the wavelength of the signal and the listener's distance from the wall.

When the round trip distance from **L** to **W** is a whole number multiple of the wavelength, the reflected sound wave reinforces the direct wave, and the listener hears a strong signal. But when the distance brings the wave back shifted by a half wavelength, the waves cancel and the listener hears nothing.

The first dead spot will be ¼ wavelength from the wall, and there will be others at half wavelength intervals (¾λ, 1¼λ, 1¾λ, etc.) as

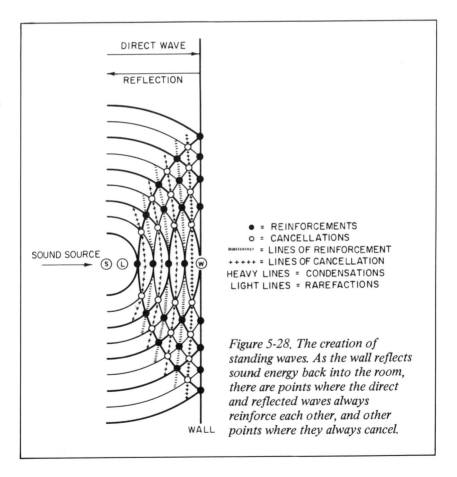

● = REINFORCEMENTS
○ = CANCELLATIONS
⫶⫶⫶⫶ = LINES OF REINFORCEMENT
+++++ = LINES OF CANCELLATION
HEAVY LINES = CONDENSATIONS
LIGHT LINES = RAREFACTIONS

Figure 5-28. The creation of standing waves. As the wall reflects sound energy back into the room, there are points where the direct and reflected waves always reinforce each other, and other points where they always cancel.

the listener moves away from the wall. In between these dead spots will be points at which the waves always reinforce each other. Since these live and dead areas remain stationary, the condition is known as a stationary, or standing, wave.

Standing waves make it difficult-to-impossible to evaluate intelligently what one hears over the monitor system. For example, the producer—although sitting next to the engineer—may hear an entirely different balance due to the different cancellation/reinforcement patterns at each location.

Minimizing Standing Waves

An effective means of minimizing standing waves is to construct non-parallel wall surfaces in the listening room, as shown in Figure 5-29. In the illustration, sound waves striking the walls are reflected back into the room at an angle, thus helping to minimize the build-up of standing waves.

Wall Treatment

As noted earlier, the major portion of the sound energy within the room is made up of reflected signals. If there is an excessive amount of reflections, clarity will be sacrificed, and it may be difficult to pinpoint the actual location of each sound source. On the other hand, when wall treatment reduces the reflections to a minimum, the room becomes acoustically lifeless.

Many well designed control rooms have adjacent wall surfaces that are alternately reflective and absorptive. The reflective walls give the room a reasonable amount of liveness, while the absorptive surfaces prevent multiple reflections from interfering with clarity.

Room Resonance Modes.

Just as each speaker system enclosure has its characteristic resonance point, the listening room itself will have certain resonances, or **room modes**. These occur at frequencies whose wavelengths are twice one of the room's dimensions. Thus, a room that is 15 feet in length will have a main resonance frequency of $F = V/\lambda = V/2L = 1100/30 = 36.67$ Hz.

If the room is 10 feet wide, it will have a secondary resonance at $1100/20 = 55$ Hz.

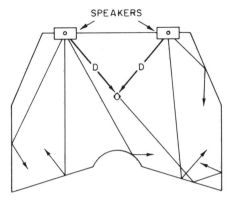

SPEAKERS

D   D

O

Figure 5-29. Non-parallel surfaces help to minimize standing waves.

Not unlike the other speaker enclosures discussed earlier, the room enclosure will attenuate frequencies whose wavelengths exceed 2L. In other words, an extended low frequency response is a function of both the design of the loudspeaker and the dimensions of the room. Regardless of the speaker system in use, it is unlikely that a small room will have a satisfactory bass response.

Room Dimension Ratios

The length, width, and height of a listening room should be unequal, so that the same resonance frequency is not created in two dimensions, thereby accentuating it even more. In addition to the fundamental resonance frequencies of the room's dimensions, there may also be resonances at the harmonics of these frequencies. Therefore, ratios of length-to-width-to-height should be chosen so as to avoid common harmonic resonances in two or more dimensions. Over the years, several "ideal" ratios have been proposed by acousticians. An often-quoted formula is the **golden section**, (1:1.62:2.62) first recommended by the ancient Greeks, but still much favored today. Needless to say, there is very much more to room acoustics than choosing the right ratio. But the point is to try to avoid those dimension ratios that will obviously cause room mode problems.

Room Equalization

Room equalization is the practice of tailoring the frequency response of the signal delivered to the speaker to correct for certain frequency anomalies created by the room. For example, if the room modes create a substantial resonance peak at 100 Hz, a filter in the speaker line may be tuned to attenuate the power output at this frequency, thus flattening out the system response. Peaks throughout the audio spectrum may likewise be attenuated, and to a lesser extent, slight dips in response may sometimes be brought up.

As may be expected, the room equalization process is ineffective against standing wave cancellations, and in general should not be used in an attempt to cover up serious deficiencies in room design.

SUMMARY

Loudspeaker performance is a complex function of speaker design, enclosure style, and the room in which the system is placed. In effect, the room becomes part of the speaker system, and has a profound effect on what the listener hears.

While microphones may be (and are) moved or replaced with ease, the speaker and its location tends to become somewhat of a permanent fixture in the control room. The engineer who insists that only his favorite speaker tells what's "*really* on the tape" is no doubt blissfully unaware of all the variables at work in his control room, helping him to form his impression of the perfect system. One need only hear the same program over the same speaker in another room to realize that the speaker itself is but a small part of the total monitoring system.

Section III
SIGNAL PROCESSING
DEVICES

Introduction

The path between the microphone and the loudspeaker is rarely an electronically straight line. Along the way, the signal may pass through one or more processing devices, designed to make it more (or perhaps less) realistic.

Artificial echo and reverberation may be applied, to simulate the concert hall, or to create an otherwise unattainable effect. Equalization may subtly correct, or deliberately distort, the frequency response of an instrument or group of instruments. Compression and expansion are used to modify the dynamic range of the program, while phasing and flanging create unique sonic effects not found outside the recording studio control room.

In the four chapters of Section III, each of these important signal processing devices is discussed in some detail.

CHAPTER 6

Echo
and Reverberation

With the exception of the anechoic chamber, all monitoring environments have some effect on what the listener hears. The perceived sound of a musical instrument will vary from one room to another, and an acoustically dead studio will never be confused for a concert hall with superb natural acoustics.

When the listener is at a reasonable distance from a musical instrument, he hears something quite different than the direct output of the instrument. Although some sound certainly reaches the ear via a direct path from the instrument, other signals are also present, as the sound radiates from its source to the various room surfaces: walls, ceiling, floor. Each of these surfaces absorbs some portion of the signal and reflects other portions back into the room. Consequently, the listener hears an incredibly complex mixture of direct and reflected information; the proportion varies according to where he is seated. If very close to the sound source, he will hear mostly the direct signal. On the other hand, the listener at the rear of a large concert hall may hear a signal that is almost totally reflected sounds.

The character of the reflected sound is influenced by the construction of the room surfaces and the room's volume. Some materials are more reflective than others, and all have some influence on the frequency response of the reflected signal. Carpeting, for example, tends to absorb higher frequencies, while glass may efficiently reflect these same frequencies.

In the older concert halls, one often finds mirrored walls, paneling, thick plaster surfaces and perhaps parqueted wood floors—all of which reflect sound and contribute to that illusive concert hall realism.

On the other hand, the surfaces of a well-designed rock studio may reflect very little sound back into the room. And, since so much recording is done with close microphone placement, the microphone "hears" a signal that is, for all practical purposes, only the direct

Figure 6-1A. The Mormon Tabernacle–Salt Lake City, Utah. The hard plaster ceiling, wood surfaces and large volume make the room quite reverberant. Dimensions: 250 ft. long, 150 ft. wide, 80 ft. high. [LDS photo]

sound of the instrument.

Whether the primarily direct pickup is due to close miking, a dead studio, or a combination of both, the resultant sound is usually described as "dry", or "tight", or by some other subjective term that suggests the absence of reflected information.

As a corrective measure, some sort of signal processing is often required to simulate a more natural sound. Or, for a special effect, an apparently greater than normal amount of reflected information may be sought. The engineer has several tools at his disposal to either simulate the ambience of the concert hall, or, create a unique effect that would otherwise be unattainable.

Before describing these methods, a few definitions, and a brief discussion of room acoustics, are required.

*Figure 6-1B. RCA Studio A –
New York City. A large studio,
designed for "concert hall"
acoustics. 95 ft. long, 56 ft.
wide, 19-29 ft. high (variable).*

*Figure 6-1C. RCA Studio E –
New York City. A small rock
studio, designed for a minimum
amount of reverberation.
[RCA photos]*

TERM	GENERAL DEFINITION	SPECIFIC DEFINITION
Echo	A repetition of a sound.	One (or a few at most) repetitions of an audio signal.
Reverberation	A re-echoed sound.	Many repetitions, becoming more closely spaced (denser) with time.
Delay	To postpone to a later date.	The time interval between a direct signal and its echo(es).
Decay	Progressive decline.	The time it takes for the echo(es) and reverberation to die away.

193

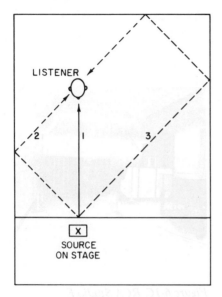

Figure 6-2. Echo and reverberation within a room. The listener hears a combination of:
1. Direct sound.
2. Early reflections (echoes).
3. Later reflections (reverberation).

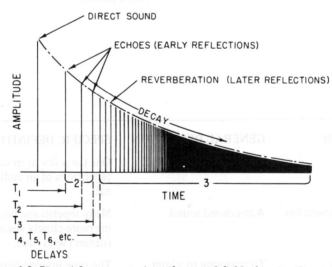

Figure 6-3. Pictorial representation of a sound field, showing direct sound, echoes, and reverberation.

Room Acoustics

The total energy present within any listening environment is a mixture of three components: 1) the original, or direct sound, 2) the early reflections, and 3) the later, more diffuse reflections, or "reverberation". These three components are illustrated in Figure 6-2. Although there is of course only one direct path from sound source to listener, there will probably be a few paths for early reflections and many more for later reflections within the typical music listening room. In fact, a pictorial representation of an actual sound field might appear as shown in Figure 6-3.

At first, the direct sound (1), is heard. After a very short interval (T_1), a repetition is heard as the direct sound, reflected from a nearby surface, reaches the listener's ear. Still later (T_2), another repetition is heard, and then (T_3), perhaps another, as the sound reflects from other nearby surfaces. As time passes, more and more repetitions occur, as the sound waves spread through the listening environment, striking and being reflected from the myriad surfaces within the room. By now $(T_4, T_5, T_6, \ldots)$, the reflections have become so closely spaced that they fall almost on top of one another and the listener is no longer aware of their individual identities.

As a matter of fact, even the very earliest reflections (T_1, T_2, T_3) are seldom conciously noted as such. Instead, their presence is sensed rather than distinctly heard. However, in some cases, an early reflection may become audibly noticeable, and perhaps distracting. In certain concert halls, for example, the space under a balcony may produce an undesirable echo that is heard as an acoustic slapback a moment after the direct sound. However, in the well-designed room, echo and reverberation will not distract from the direct sound, yet their presence will add a richeness that is conspicuously lacking in a deadened rock studio.

Referring again to Figure 6-2, we may label four variables within the listening environment; after some **delay**, there is an **echo**, (or echoes), then after further delay, there are many closely spaced echoes, or **reverberation**. In time, the reverberation will die away, or **decay**.

In order to simulate this natural condition, the engineer may be called upon to artificially produce one or more of these variables.

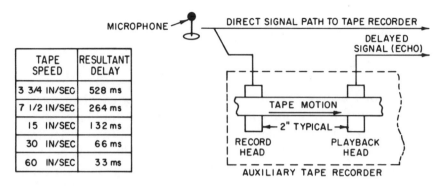

TAPE SPEED	RESULTANT DELAY
3 3/4 IN/SEC	528 ms
7 1/2 IN/SEC	264 ms
15 IN/SEC	132 ms
30 IN/SEC	66 ms
60 IN/SEC	33 ms

ms = MILLISECONDS (THOUSANDTHS OF A SECOND)

Figure 6-4. Artificial echo, produced by a tape delay system.

ECHO AND DELAY

The Tape Delay System

To produce an echo, some sort of signal delaying process is required. Until recently, this delay was accomplished with an auxiliary
tape recorder. In addition to the normal recording process, the signal
to be treated would also be fed to this extra machine. Depending on
tape speed and the distance between the record and playback heads,
the output would be delayed by some fraction of a second. Figure
6-4 illustrates the tape delay process, and lists the delays available
when the heads are about 2 inches apart, which is typical of many
professional tape recorders.

If it is possible to continuously vary the speed of the machine over
a wide range, additional delays become available. But although the
tape delay system is certainly usable, it may be inconvenient, since
the "echo tape" must be rewound frequently, and at the slower
speeds, the record/playback responses may not be equal to the demands of the session.

The Digital Delay Line

With the introduction of digital technology to audio, the so-called
digital delay line may take over the task of the tape delay system.
The advantage of the digital delay line is that the delay is provided
electronically, with no moving parts in the system. And, the delays

may be continuously variable over a very wide range (0-200 milliseconds, typical), with no effect on the frequency response. A modern digital delay line (Figure 6-5) may also have two or more outputs, so that the input signal may produce two or more echoes, each of which is delayed by a different amount. To create more than one echo using tape delay, each output would have to feed an additional input on the auxiliary tape recorder. Consequently, each additional delay would add one more generation of tape noise.

Acoustic Delay Line

Another recent development in delay lines is the so-called Cooper Time Cube, developed by Dr. Duane H. Cooper of the University of Illinois. The device uses acoustical delay lines in the form of coiled tubes, through which the signal to be delayed travels. A pickup hears the sound after it has travelled the length of the tube. Two tubes are provided, giving delays of 14 and 16 milliseconds. The two may be combined in series to produce a delay of 30 milliseconds; however no other delays are available without physically altering the lengths of tubing. Of course, some care must be taken to protect the units from mechanical vibration, which would be transmitted to, and then through, the tubes. The electronic circuitry is less complex than the digital delay line, and it is consequently less expensive — though admittedly not quite so flexible as devices using digital technology.

Figure 6-5. A versatile digital delay line. The unit shown has two outputs, which are here set at 198 and 113 milliseconds. The delays are continuously variable in 1 millisecond increments. (Eventide DDL 1745A) [Eventide Clockworks photo]

197

Doubling

It is of course possible to produce a delay so short that the ear cannot recognize it as such, even if its level equals that of the direct sound. Generally, as the delay is increased between 20 and 40 milliseconds, there comes a point within that range at which the echo separates from the direct signal and becomes clearly audible. The actual time value at which this happens depends on the nature of the signal in question. The echo of a drum figure might be clearly heard at 20 milliseconds, while a legato string line may require twice that delay or more before the echo is heard.

These very short delays may often be used to simulate the effect of, say, a larger string section. In a large string section, the ensemble is never precisely synchronized. In fact, the very slight imprecision of attack within the ensemble gives the listener an aural clue that the group is large. (Of course, once the imprecision becomes overdone, the listener will object to the sloppy playing.)

Now, by selecting a delay that is too short to create an audible echo, the engineer can apparently double the size of the string section. The almost instantaneous repetition of the signal simulates that very slight imprecision which is characteristic of a large group. The result may be particularly effective if the delayed signal is placed somewhat away from the direct signal, to create the illusion that the ensemble is spread out over a wider area.

Once sufficiently delayed signals have been produced, they may be mixed with the direct signal to simulate the early reflections (echoes) of a concert hall. Or, for a special effect, these echoes may be combined out of proportion to the direct sound. However, the natural reverberation content of the concert hall cannot be satisfactorily created with a time delay system.

REVERBERATION AND DECAY

Reverberation was described earlier as a series of closely spaced reflections—so closely spaced that they are not perceived as discrete echoes. Rather, their cumulative effect creates an impression of room liveness.

The time intervals between the multiple reflections are entirely random, and to create such an irregular pattern with a series of delay lines would require a rather involved—and expensive—system. At this time, it is more practical to use an artificial reverberation device,

REVERBERATION PLATES

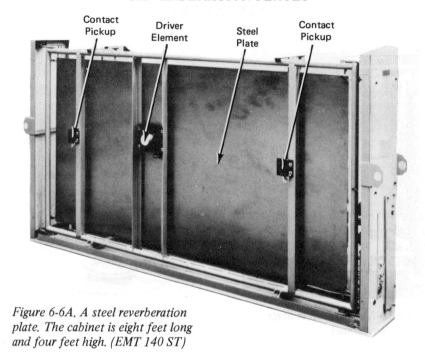

Contact Pickup   Driver Element   Steel Plate   Contact Pickup

Figure 6-6A. A steel reverberation plate. The cabinet is eight feet long and four feet high. (EMT 140 ST)

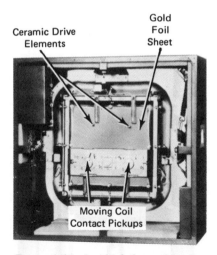

Ceramic Drive Elements   Gold Foil Sheet

Moving Coil Contact Pickups

Figure 6-6B. A gold foil reverberation plate – front view. A thin gold foil sheet replaces the original steel plate. (EMT 240)

Figure 6-6C. A gold foil reverberation plate – rear view. The vertical "venetian blinds" are a mechanical damper used to vary the reverberation time. (EMT 240) [Gotham Audio photos]

A SOPHISTICATED SPRING REVERBERATION SYSTEM
(AKG BX 20E)

Figure 6-7A. The system in its protective cabinet.

Figure 6-7B. The complete spring system.

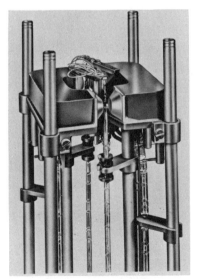

Figure 6-7C. Detail of spring suspension.

Figure 6-7D. Detail of mechanical damping system. [AKG photos]

200

which simulates the random multiple echo pattern of natural reverberation, without actually producing discrete echoes. Basically, an elastic medium is set into motion by an applied audio signal, and the to-and-fro vibration is sensed by a special type of microphone attached to the vibrating medium. When the applied signal is removed, the vibration gradually diminishes, simulating the natural decay of room reverberation.

The Reverberation Plate

In professional studios, perhaps the most widely used device is the artificial reverberation plate. This unit consists of a steel plate, protectively suspended within a wooden cabinet, as seen in Figure 6-6. Attached to the plate is a driver element, not unlike a very small loudspeaker. The element is driven by an audio signal, and sets the plate in motion. As the plate flexes back and forth, the motion is sensed by two contact pickups also attached to the plate. The audio signal produced by these pickups simulates the reverberant field of a large concert hall. When the applied signal ceases, inertia keeps the plate in motion for several seconds, although via a mechanical damping system, this decay time may be reduced as desired.

Spring Reverberation Systems

Although the steel plate produces a remarkably good simulation of reverberant sound, it is rather large and quite expensive. Later generation plates, although considerably smaller, are no less costly and may be somewhat beyond the reach of studios with a modest equipment budget.

Reverberation devices using coiled springs are available over a wide price range and although the least expensive ones certainly are not the equal of the steel plate, they are easily within the financial reach of the smallest studio operation.

Although specific construction details vary from one manufacturer to another, this type of system uses a long coiled spring, suspended

THE ACOUSTIC REVERBERATION CHAMBER

Figure 6-8A. Although the room is not
large, its highly reflective surfaces
simulate the natural reverberation
characteristics of a concert hall.

Figure 6-8B. The convex surfaces help
create a more diffuse sound.

between a driver and a pickup element. The applied signal sets the spring in motion, and this motion is sensed by the pickup element. The simplest spring units are easily recognized by a characteristic metallic sound quality which is unconvincing as a simulation of natural reverberation. However, as a special effect on, say, an electric guitar, the "springy" sound may create a unique sound texture not otherwise attainable. Inexpensive spring units have been built into a wide variety of guitar amplifiers and electric keyboard instruments with considerable success, and the well-equipped studio may have a few available for use as the occasion demands.

The more sophisticated spring systems have decay time adjustments and a sound quality that many find comparable in quality to the steel plate. In addition, the decay time may be varied while the unit is in use, since this adjustment does not produce any mechanical vibration which might be sensed by the pickup element. Representative spring type reverberation systems are shown in Figure 6-7.

Acoustic Reverberation Chambers

The most elegant reverberation device is the acoustic reverberation chamber, actually a highly reverberant room in which all surfaces have been treated for maximum reflectivity. A loudspeaker placed within the room transmits the signal to be processed, and a microphone placed some distance away picks up the multiplicity of echoes produced as the signal is reflected again and again within the room. Such a room is shown in Figure 6-8.

Although the room is unsatisfactory for normal listening, the overly reverberant sound, combined with the direct unprocessed signal, creates the illusion that the recording was made in a very large room with normal reverberant characteristics.

The acoustic reverberation chamber is a luxury many studios cannot afford. In order to function adequately, the room must be reasonably large, and of course carefully isolated from extraneous noise sources. Especially in high rent districts, it may be difficult to justify setting aside an appreciable area solely for the creation of reverberation. And, decay time may not be varied with ease, as on the steel plate or high quality spring system. To significantly alter the room's characteristics, some acoustic padding, perhaps in the form of drapes, may be added or removed. Although this is certainly effective, it can be a time-consuming process to tailor the reverberant sound to fit the immediate needs of the session. However, the well-designed chamber does produce a most pleasant reverberant field, and is perhaps the closest approximation of natural concert hall reverberation that is available at this time.

Stereo Reverberation

By its nature, natural reverberation is diffuse, and the listener is scarcely conscious of a recognizable location from which the reverberation is coming. Rather, the reverberation envelops the listener from all sides.

But, regardless of construction details — steel plate, spring, or room — a reverberation device with only one output is limited in its effectiveness to simulate the natural condition. A single output, panned to some specific point, will be just that; a point source of sound, reverberant in quality but not diffuse.

Consequently, the definitive stereo reverberation system should have two outputs, both derived from the same input. For example, the steel plate mentioned earlier has two pickup devices, located at different distances from the driver element. As the plate flexes, the instantaneous deflection is randomly dissimilar at the two pickup locations. However, if the two outputs were compared, one at a time, they would sound practically identical since they are of course reacting to the same input. But if one output is routed to the left and the other to the right, the subtle variations in phase will create an overall ambient sound field that more closely resembles natural reverberation.

In the acoustic reverberation chamber, two microphones may be set up within the room to create the same effect.

Using Stereo Reverberation

If a direct signal is routed to, say, the right, and also fed to a stereo output reverb system, as described above, the reverberation will appear to be coming pretty much from the left side. Although it is of course actually coming from both left and right speakers, on the right side the reverberation is masked somewhat by the actual direct signal. The effect approximates natural reverberation, where the direct signal path tends to mask any reverberation coming from the same general direction. A center-placed signal will seem to be surrounded by reverberation if a stereo return is used. A single (mono) return panned to the center along with the direct signal will not be nearly so effective.

At this point it should be clearly understood that any single source of sound panned to the center is **not** the same as a stereo signal, in which left and right may be practically identical, yet different because of random phase shifts. Although the center-panned mono signal comes out of both speakers it still lacks the stereo "dimension."

On the other hand, if the reverberation is to come only from the same side as the direct signal, a separate single output device should be used. (Or, of course, one side of a stereo unit may be used.)

An advantage of artificial reverberation is that different reverberation characteristics may be applied to various instruments. For example, a long decay may be added to the string section, while a shorter decay is applied to a percussion track. Of course, for each variation, a separate reverberation system is required.

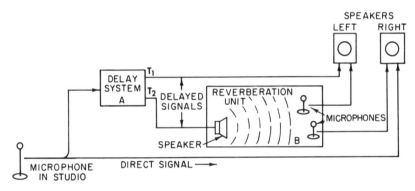

Figure 6-9. The complete Echo/Reverberation System.

The Complete Echo – Reverberation System

A totally flexible echo-reverberation system will provide separate control of delay time, echo, reverberation, and decay. Figure 6-9 illustrates the basic signal routing paths of a well-designed system.

As described earlier in the chapter, the delay system may be either a tape recorder or a digital delay line. In the illustration, a delay line with two outputs is shown. One output (T_1) feeds the left track directly to create an echo effect. Another output (T_2) feeds the stereo reverberation system, whose outputs are fed to the left and right speakers to create the illusion of a diffuse reverberant field. The

205

figure is a simplified drawing of a fairly involved system. In practice, the various signal paths feeding the speakers would first be combined so that there would be one feed only to each speaker. And once the desired mixture of direct sound, echo, and reverberation was established, this complex program would of course be fed to a two track tape recorder to produce the master tape.

CHAPTER 7

Equalizers

The term **equalization** may be somewhat misleading, since–like **alignment**–it seems to imply some sort of necessary adjustment process to bring an audio signal within published specifications. Some equalization is of course done for this reason. For example, frequency adjustments are made to overcome the limitations of the recording medium; however these adjustments–when correctly made–should have no apparent effect on the program as heard by the listener. On the other hand, equalization may be a form of signal processing, when the adjustments are made to modify noticeably the frequency response of the signal being treated. Here, there is no intention to conform to a standard; changes are made according to the taste of the listening engineer or producer. The signal is equalized to suit the standards of the moment, and these may change at the very next moment, according to the taste of the listener.

The well equipped studio will have a variety of equalizers on hand. Some are built into the recording console and permanently assigned to specific signal paths. Others may be installed in an auxiliary equipment rack, to be used when and where required. Both types are shown in Figure 7-1.

The equalizer may provide one or more variable controls with which the engineer can modify various portions of the audio bandwidth. Typically, these controls are distributed among low, middle, and high frequencies.

Low Frequency Equalization

Figure 7-2 shows the effect of two types of low frequency equalization. The solid lines sloping downward illustrate typical high pass filter curves, while the solid lines sloping upward are shelving curves showing low frequency boost. The dashed line also illustrates a shelving curve, but with low frequency attenuation.

STUDIO EQUALIZERS

Figure 7-1A. An equalizer designed for in-console installation. The dual concentric knobs save console space. The upper knob selects the frequency, and the lower knob controls the amount of equalization.
(API 550A) [API photo]

Figure 7-1B. An equalizer designed for mounting in an auxiliary equipment rack. On this model, frequency selection is continuously variable. (Orban Parasound 622B) [Orban/Parasound photo]

The High Pass Filter (or Low Frequency Cut-off Filter)

The **high pass filter** is usually identified by its cut-off frequency; that is, the frequency at which the output level has fallen by 3 dB. Beyond this point, the level falls off at a steady rate, or slope, expressed in decibels per octave (dB/8va). Generally, an equalizer offers a choice of several cut-off frequencies. The dB/8va slope is usually given in the published specifications, and is not adjustable by the user.

Low Frequency Shelving Equalization

Note that the shelving curves in Figure 7-2 show a response that rises (or falls), and that the slope eventually flattens out, or shelves, at some low frequency. This equalizer is identified by its turnover frequency, that is, the frequency at which the slope begins to turn over or flatten out to a shelf. This frequency is generally 3 dB below the maximum amount of boost (or attenuation). Thus, if the shelving equalizer has been set for a maximum boost of +18 dB, and the turnover frequency selected is 100 Hz, then the level at 100 Hz will be +15 dB (3 dB below +18 dB).

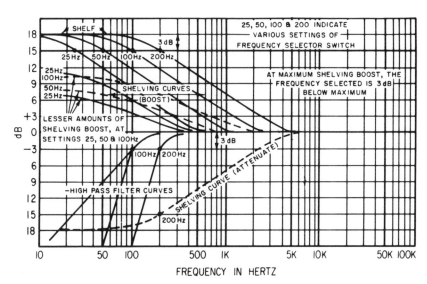

Figure 7-2. Typical low frequency equalization curves.

209

*MID FREQUENCY
EQUALIZATION*

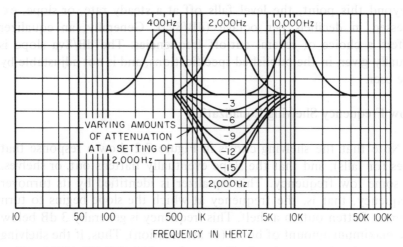

Figure 7-3A. Typical mid frequency equalization curves.

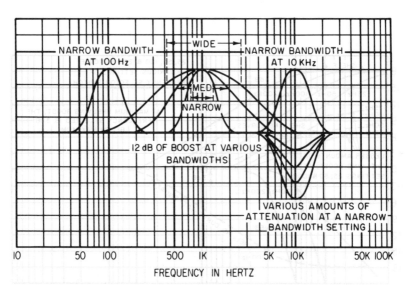

Figure 7-3B. Typical mid frequency equalization bandwidth curves.

Mid Frequency Equalization

Figure 7-3A shows some typical mid frequency equalization settings. Note that the response reaches a maximum boost or attenuation at the frequency selected, and then returns to zero as the frequency is raised or lowered beyond this point. This type of equalization is often referred to as a "haystack" due to the characteristic shape of the response curve.

Mid Frequency Bandwidth, or "Q"

In Figure 7-3B the three boost settings at a 1,000 Hz center frequency illustrate narrow, medium, and wide bandwidths. Note that when the same narrow bandwidth curve is drawn at 10,000 Hz, the bandwidth is arithmetically much greater. At 100 Hz, it is, of course, much smaller. Therefore, a bandwidth expressed in hertz is only meaningful when the center frequency is also known. To eliminate this ambiguity, the bandwidth is often expressed in terms of Q, a ratio that is equal to the center frequency, f_c, (in hertz) divided by the bandwidth, (in hertz), or $Q = f_c/B.W.$ From the graph, it should be seen that the Q of all three narrow bandwidths remains the same, regardless of the center frequency chosen.

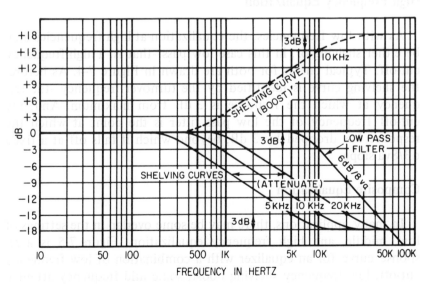

Figure 7-4. Typical high frequency equalization curves.

211

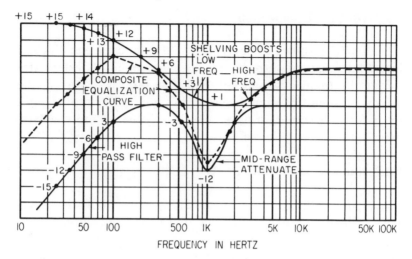

Figure 7-5. A composite equalization curve. The dashed line illustrates the overall equalization that results from the addition of the low, mid, and high frequency curves shown on the graph.

Some equalizers have a variable Q control, allowing the engineer to vary the bandwidth as required.

High Frequency Equalization

As with low frequencies, the equalization at high frequencies may be either shelving or, in this case low pass—that is, a high frequency cut-off. Typical curves for both are drawn in Figure 7-4. As before, the shelving curve is identified by the turnover frequency—the frequency at which the response is 3 dB from maximum. And, the cut-off frequency of the low pass filter is the point at which the response has dropped by 3 dB, beyond which it falls off at a fixed dB/8va slope.

Composite Equalization

In many applications, there may be some overlap in the settings of low, middle, and high frequency equalization. Figure 7-5 is a response curve for an equalizer with a combination of low frequency cut-off, low frequency shelving boost, some mid frequency attenuation, and a high frequency shelving boost. The individual effect of

212

each equalizer section is shown, together with a dashed line curve representing the resultant composite response of the four sections.

Parametric Equalizers

The frequency selector control on most recording console equalizers is in the form of a rotary stepped position switch. Each position selects a different turnover or cut-off frequency, and, depending on the equalizer's versatility, there may be between two and six or more frequencies selectable.

On a **parametric equalizer**, this frequency selection control is continuously variable over a wide band of frequencies. This allows the

GRAPHIC EQUALIZERS

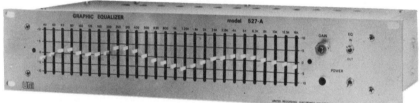

Figure 7-6A. A Graphic equalizer with controls at 1/3 octave intervals. (UREI 527-A) [UREI photo]

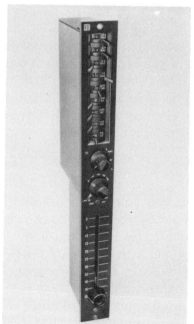

Figure 7-6B. A small graphic equalizer, built into a console input module. The unit shown has nine cut/boost controls, spaced at octave intervals. (Cetec) [Cetec photo]

213

engineer to tune the equalizer to any frequency within the equalizer's range. Or, while recording, the frequency selector may be swept back and forth as a special effect.

Graphic Equalizers

The **graphic equalizer** is so-called because the physical positioning of the controls gives a graphic display of the resulting frequency response, as shown in Figure 7-6A. Here, each slide switch boosts or attenuates the response around the frequency assigned to it. The shape of the response for each switch is like the mid frequency boost/attenuate settings shown in Figure 7-3A. Individual bandwidths are not adjustable, but should be sufficiently small to limit the effect of each switch to a narrow bandwidth centered around the frequency selected.

A full range graphic equalizer is usually found as an auxiliary piece of equipment, since its size and cost preclude it from being included in each separate signal path. However, smaller graphic equalizers are now available in a format that makes them physically compatible with other equalizers built into the recording console (Figure 7-6B).

Notch Filters

The **notch filter** is a specialized form of frequency attenuator, generally used to tune out a very narrow band of frequencies. A typical application is shown in Figure 7-7A, where a notch filter has been set at 60 Hz, to remove a.c. hum from a program. The very narrow bandwidth prevents the severe attenuation at 60 Hz from unduly affecting the rest of the audio bandwidth.

Band Pass Filters

A **band pass filter** is an equalizer with both low and high frequency attenuation. The band of frequencies between the two cutoff points is "passed"; that is, it is not affected by the equalizer. Although any such arrangement of low and high frequency filtering constitutes a band pass filter, the term is usually reserved for applications where the "pass band" is fairly narrow. Figure 7-7B shows the face plate of an equalizer that combines the functions of notch and band pass filtering.

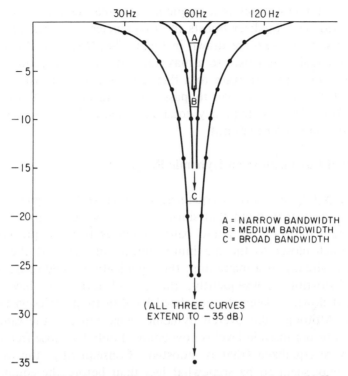

Figure 7-7A. A notch filter, set for 35 dB attenuation at 60 Hz.
A = narrow bandwidth.
B = medium bandwidth.
C = broad bandwidth.

Figure 7-7B. A combination notch and band pass filter.
(UREI 565) [UREI photo]

215

The band pass filter is a frequency attenuating device, while the mid frequency equalizer boosts the frequencies in its pass band. For comparison, the two are drawn in Figure 7-8. Note that the mid frequency equalization rises to a maximum at its center frequency and then quickly falls off again to a flat response. By contrast, the band pass filter remains flat over its pass band, and falls off at either end. Therefore, the mid frequency equalizer passes all frequencies, while the band pass filter does not.

Effect of Equalization on Dynamic Range

In applying any sort of equalization to a high level signal, it is important to bear in mind that since a frequency boost raises the level of certain parts of the audio band, it places these frequencies just that much closer to the maximum permissible level. If the overall signal is already at a maximum, the equalization could cause noticeable distortion. Consequently, the overall level may have to be brought down to keep the equalized band of frequencies within safe limits. Although the overall dynamic range remains the same, the maximum permissible level is now enjoyed only by those frequencies that were equalized (that is, boosted). Consequently, the dynamic range may seem to be somewhat less than before the equalization was applied.

On the other hand, some attenuation of a troublesome band of frequencies may permit the overall level to be brought up, resulting in an apparently (and actually) louder program.

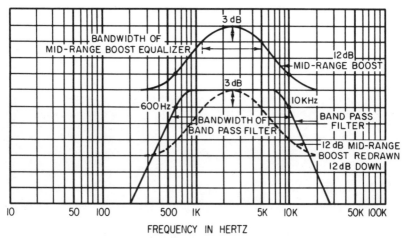

Figure 7-8. Comparison of a band pass filter and a mid range boost equalizer.

EQUALIZER PHASE SHIFTS

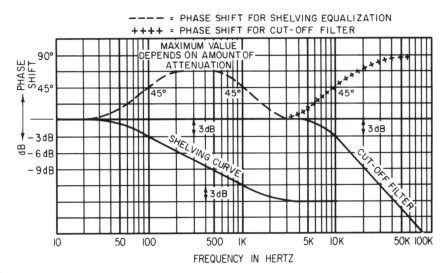

Figure 7-9A. Typical phase shift characteristics for shelving equalization and cut-off filters.

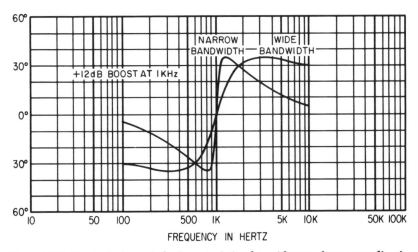

Figure 7-9B. Typical phase shift characteristics for mid range boost equalization.

Equalizer Phase Shift

Since the equalizer achieves its frequency boost or attenuation through the use of reactive components (inductors and capacitors), a certain amount of phase shift accompanies any equalization added to a signal path.

Figure 7-9A shows typical phase shift characteristics for shelving and cut-off filters. Figure 7-9B illustrates the effect of a mid frequency boost equalizer.

Active and Passive Equalizers

An **active equalizer** is actually an amplifier, so designed that certain frequencies are amplified while others are not, according to the equalizer settings chosen. The basic active equalizer may be a unity gain amplifier, with additional gain supplied only to those frequencies that are to be boosted.

On the other hand, a **passive equalizer** does not amplify any frequencies, since it contains no active elements (transistors or tubes). In a passive equalizer, a boost at, say, 1,000 Hz is actually accomplished by attenuating the rest of the audio band, using passive elements only, that is — resistors, capacitors and inductors.

CHAPTER 8

Compressors, Limiters and Expanders

At the present state-of-the-art, there are still some practical restrictions on the dynamic range of magnetic tape, as compared to the live performance. The sound level of a symphony orchestra may reach 100+ dB, and the enthusiastic rock groups may be even louder. By comparison, the dynamic range available on the recorded medium may be about 70 dB, or even less if a safety margin for peaks is allowed.

There are two reasons for the restricted dynamic range. One is the cumulative noise level of the tape recorder electronics and the tape itself. Even in the absence of an audio signal, a tape that has passed over the record head will contain a measurable, low level, noise signal. Audio signals must be recorded above this residual noise level if they are to be heard. On the other hand, the tape is also limited in the amount of high level program it will accept. As discussed in greater detail later on (Chapter 11), the recorded program becomes distorted once the capacity of the tape is exceeded.

Therefore, the dynamic range of the recorded program must be compressed so that it does not exceed these limitations of the recording system. There are several ways in which this may be done.

Gain Riding

While recording, the engineer may raise the recorded level of low level program, and decrease the level during louder passages. This **gain riding** plays an important part of many successful recordings, yet it will not solve all dynamic range problems. In many cases, the engineer cannot anticipate and control every high level peak that comes his way. Also, occasional high level signals from a few instruments may not be troublesome in themselves, but when from time to time they occur simultaneously, the cumulative signal will exceed the maximum permissible level. In many cases, it is unlikely that the engineer could anticipate these conditions in time to take corrective steps before they occur.

Dynamics Restricted in Performance

As an alternative to mechanical gain riding, the orchestra or group may attempt to restrict its own dynamic range while playing. Although this is widely done, an undue restriction on the performers' own dynamics invariably takes its toll on musical expression too.

COMPRESSORS AND LIMITERS

As a complement to these methods of narrowing the dynamic range, the engineer may use signal processing devices known as compressors and limiters to meet the restrictions of the recording medium. The terms compression and limiting have been in the audio vocabulary for years, yet there is often some confusion over their definitions. The confusion arises from the fact that both the compressor and the limiter are devices that restrict the dynamic range of a signal, and the difference between them is one of degree, with the limiter having the most effect. To simply define:

> **Compressor:** *An amplifier, whose gain decreases as its input level is increased.*
> **Limiter:** *A compressor, whose output level remains constant, regardless of its input level.*

Both definitions are valid only after the signal being processed reaches a certain level. Therefore, we have one more definition:

> **Threshold:** *The level above which the compressor or limiter begins functioning.*

These terms are further defined in Figure 8-1, which is a graph of input *versus* output for an idealized combination compressor/limiter. Notice that as the input level increases from -10 dB to 0 dB, the output level likewise increases from -10 dB to 0 dB. Here, the device is functioning as a simple unity gain amplifier, with no effect on the signal level.

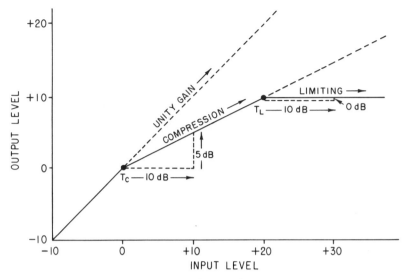

Figure 8-1. A graph of compressor and limiter functions.
T_c = *compression threshold.* T_l = *limiting threshold.*

Compression

However, once the signal level exceeds the compression threshold of 0 dB, the output level is found by following the compression curve, and it may be seen that a further increase of 10 dB in input will yield only 5 dB more output level. In other words, the device now has a compression ratio of 10/5, or 2:1. Since this 2:1 ratio took effect only after the signal level exceeded 0 dB, we call 0 dB the compression threshold; that is, the point at which the compressor begins functioning.

Limiting

Once the input level reaches +20 dB, there is no further increase in output level. Hence, the device is now operating as a limiter, with a limiting threshold of +20 dB. As drawn in Figure 8-1, the limiter's compression ratio is ∞ :1, or simply ∞ . In actual practice, compression ratios of 10:1 or greater are usually considered as limiting.

Notice that once the +20 dB limiting threshold has been reached, the output level remains at +10 dB, despite further increases in input level. Therefore, it should be understood that the limiter threshold

221

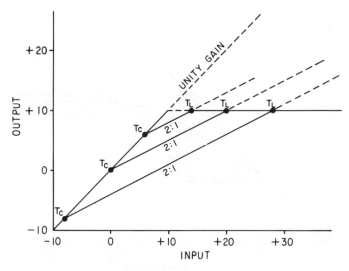

Figure 8-2. To prevent output levels in excess of +10 dB, the limiter threshold setting will vary, depending on where the compression threshold was set.

Figure 8-3. A compressor/limiter with variable compression threshold. (Neve 2254A) [Rupert Neve photo]

does not necessarily indicate the maximum allowable output level of the device. Rather, it indicates the input level at which the limiter begins working.

Variable Thresholds

In Figure 8-2, note that the same compression ratio of 2:1 will have different effects on the overall dynamic range depending on the point at which the compression begins. Also, the position of the compression threshold will influence the point at which limiting must begin, if a certain maximum output level is not to be exceeded. For example, note that when output levels are to be kept below +10 dB, then the lower the compression threshold, the higher the limiting threshold may be.

In Figure 8-3, the faceplate of a combination compressor/limiter is shown. Note that the compression threshold may be varied from -20 dB to +10 dB, allowing considerable control over the point at which compression begins. However, in the case of a compressor that does not have such a control, the same effect may be realized by inserting an amplifier/attenuator combination before the compressor,

Figure 8-4. In a compressor with a fixed threshold, the output dynamic range may be varied by boosting (or attenuating) the input signal level before compression.

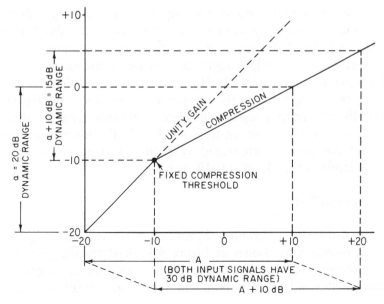

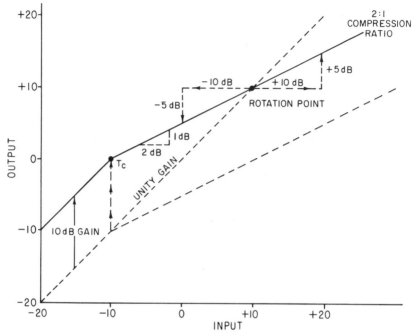

Figure 8-5. Graph of a compressor, with gain before threshold.
Input levels below the rotation point are raised.
Input levels above the rotation point are lowered.

and a complementary attenuator/amplifier—if necessary—after it. For example, consider a compressor with a fixed threshold of say, -10 dB. In Figure 8-4, input signal **A**, with a dynamic range of 30 dB is compressed to an output signal, **a**, with a dynamic range of 20 dB, and a maximum level of 0 dB. However, if the input signal is amplified 10 dB before reaching the compressor, as shown in the figure by **A +10 dB**, the output signal will have a dynamic range of only 15 dB, and its maximum output level will be +5 dB. This increased output level may now be attenuated by 5 dB, if it is necessary to keep the maximum output level at 0 dB, as before.

The Rotation Point

When there is some amount of gain before compression, Figure 8-4 may be re-drawn as shown in Figure 8-5. Here, the dB gain before threshold raises the transfer characteristic above the unity gain line, as shown. Beyond the threshold, the system gain steadily decreases as the compression curve approaches the unity gain line. The point at which they intersect is known as the rotation point. At this point only, the gain of the compressor is 1, or unity. Beyond the rotation point, the gain continues to decrease.

It should be noted that, as a consequence of the gain before threshold, the compressor raises low level (below rotation point) signals, and lowers high level (above rotation point) signals. Thus, low level signals may be brought up above the residual noise level while at

THE EFFECTS OF VARIOUS COMPRESSION RATIOS

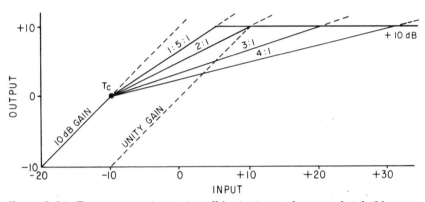

Figure 8-6A. Four compression ratios, all beginning at the same threshold.

Figure 8-6B. Four compression ratios, each passing through the same rotation point. Note that each ratio begins at a different threshold.

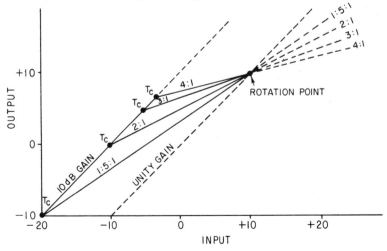

the same time high level signals are prevented from driving the tape into distortion.

Variable Compression Ratios

Many compressors offer the engineer a variety of compression ratios from which to choose. Figure 8-6A illustrates four different compression ratios, all beginning at the same threshold point. Assuming that the output level must be kept below +10dB, it will be seen that the greater the compression ratio, the wider may be the dynamic range of the input signal.

On the other hand, the four ratios of Figure 8-6A might each begin at a different threshold, as seen in Figure 8-6B. In this illustration, each threshold/ratio combination passes through the same rotation point, and each has a different effect on the total program. The relatively gradual 1.5:1 ratio affects the program from -20 dB, while the more severe 4:1 ratio does not begin until the input signal level reaches -3 dB.

Pumping or Breathing

It is an easy matter to graphically determine the compression ratio and threshold required to prevent a wide dynamic range program from exceeding a specified output dynamic range. However, it should be realized that—especially at high compression ratios—the action of the compressor may become audibly obtrusive. To understand why, remember that the compressor is a variable gain device. As defined earlier, the compressor is an amplifier whose gain decreases as the input level increases, and *vice versa*. And the higher the compression ratio, the greater is this gain change.

The gain (or attenuation) of an amplifier may be expressed either as a positive number (0.25, 1, 3.5, etc.) or as a dB value (-10 dB, 0 dB, +10 dB, etc.). The positive number value is a ratio of output to input voltage. Thus, if the input voltage is 0.5 volts, and the output is 0.2 volts, the gain is 0.2/0.5, or simply, 0.4. If the input and output are equal, the gain is, of course, 1, or unity. However, it is usually more convenient to express the output in terms of dB above or below the input level. Thus, a unity gain amplifier has a gain of 1, which would be expressed as a decibel gain of 0 dB. A compressor will have a negative dB gain, usually called a gain reduction.

Figure 8-7 graphs the gain reduction for several compression ra-

THE GAIN REDUCTION OF A COMPRESSOR

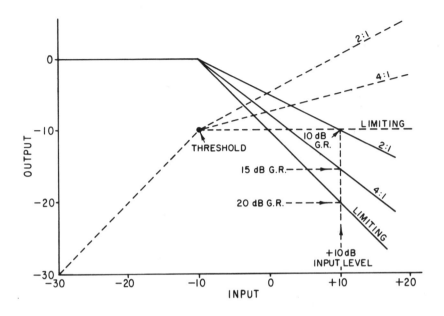

	2:1 RATIO		4:1 RATIO		LIMITING	
INPUT	OUTPUT	GAIN REDUCTION	OUTPUT	GAIN REDUCTION	OUTPUT	GAIN REDUCTION
-30	-30	0	-30	0	-30	0
-25	-25	0	-25	0	-25	0
-20	-20	0	-20	0	-20	0
-15	-15	0	-15	0	-15	0
-10	-10	0	-10	0	-10	0
-5	-7.5	2.5	-8.75	3.75	-10	5
0	-5	5	-7.5	7.5	-10	10
+5	-2.5	7.5	-6.25	11.75	-10	15
+10	0	10	-5	15	-10	20
+15	+2.5	12.5	-3.75	18.75	-10	25
+20	+5	15	-2.5	22.5	-10	30

Figure 8-7. The solid lines show the amount of gain reduction at various compression ratios. The corresponding compression ratios are drawn as dashed lines.

tios. It will be seen that as the compression ratio is increased, a constant high level signal, say +10 dB, will cause more gain reduction. When the high level input is removed, the amount of gain reduction decreases, as the compressor returns to unity gain. If the gain reduction fluctuates rapidly, it may be quite audible as the background noise goes up and down in time with the compressor action, causing a breathing-like sound. On the other hand, if the compressor takes a relatively long time to restore itself after a high level signal has caused gain reduction, then other low level signals following the high level signal will also be reduced in gain.

THE EFFECTS OF VARIOUS RELEASE TIMES

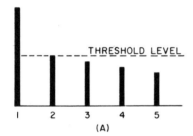

Figure 8-8A. A series of beats, only the first of which is above the compressor's threshold.

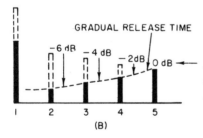

Figure 8-8B. Progressively less gain reduction, as compressor recovers from the initial beat.

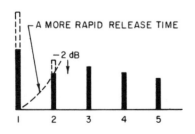

Figure 8-8C. A relatively fast release time prevents the initial gain reduction from having a long-time effect.

228

Compressor Release, or Recovery Time

The amount of time it takes for a compressor to return to its normal gain-before-threshold is known as its release, or recovery time. Some compressors have an operator-adjustable release time. Figure 8-8 shows the effect of various release times on a series of beats. In the illustration, the first beat is above the compressor's threshold. The next four beats are all below threshold, and will not cause the compressor to react. However, if the release time is relatively long, these beats may be affected by the initial gain reduction caused by the first beat, as shown in Figure 8-8B. Here, the compressor gradually returns to unity gain. At the time of the second beat, there is still 6 dB of gain reduction; at the third beat there is 4 dB, and so on. As a result of this gradual release time, the dynamic range of the series is considerably changed.

In Figure 8-8C, the release time has been considerably shortened, and only the second beat is affected by the gain reduction. In this case, the rapid return to unity gain may cause an audible breathing sound, as the system gain rapidly increases.

There is no inherently correct release time setting. More often than not, the release time is varied by the engineer to produce the least objectionable effect. A reasonable amount of breathing or pumping on an individual signal may very well be masked when the compressed signal is combined with other signals that are not compressed.

Variable Attack Time

The attack time of a compressor is the time it takes for it to react to a signal above threshold level. On some compressors, it too may be adjustable. In many cases, a long attack time will allow the first part of a sustained note to pass through the compressor unaffected. If the note persists in duration, the compressor will attenuate it after a fraction of a second. Subjectively, the note may sound more percussive, due to this type of compression. For example, a longer attack time may help to accentuate a compressed bass line that is otherwise difficult to distinguish, especially in a busy instrumental arrangement.

Using the Compressor for Special Effects

The use of a long attack time to help bring out a bass line is one of the ways a compressor may be put to creative use beyond its function of acting as a dynamic range restrictor.

Very often, it may be desirable to compress the dynamic range of an instrument even when there are no problems due to noise level or high level distortion. An instrument with a fluctuating sound level may be difficult to balance against other instruments. Some compression may help create a more manageable signal, although in many cases it would of course be more desirable if the musician himself could control his dynamic range somewhat.

The use of an extremely short attack time and a longer release time may create a backward-like sound, especially on some percussive instruments. The fast attack immediately drops the level of the signal, and then as the signal naturally decays, the release time setting brings up the gain, working against the normal decay. The effect is particularly noticeable on a drum set, and especially on cymbals.

Program Limiting

Often compression may be applied to the overall program rather than to an individual instrument. Known as program limiting, (or compression) this practice will prevent the cumulative levels of the various instruments from getting too high or too low. This type of gain reduction must be approached with care though, since the adverse effects of the compression action are heard on the entire program, and excessive compression will probably be audibly distracting.

Program limiting is often used to raise the apparent loudness of a record. As mentioned earlier in the discussion on VU meters, (Chapter 1), the ear averages the sound level over a period of time. Thus a

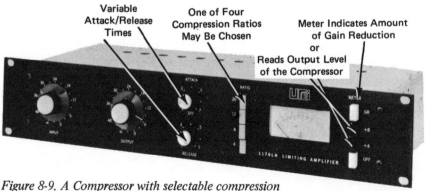

Figure 8-9. A Compressor with selectable compression ratios and variable attack and release times. (UREI 1176 LN) [UREI photo]

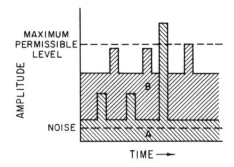

Figure 8-10. Program B will sound a lot louder than program A despite the latter's peaks, since its average level is higher.

low level program with occasional high level peaks will not seem to be as loud as an average level program with no high level peaks. Figure 8-10 illustrates this. Program **B** will sound much louder than **A**, despite **A**'s higher peaks, since its average level is obviously much higher. If program **A** was compressed about a suitable rotation point, (as in Figure 8-5) the high level peaks would be attenuated and the low level portion would be raised, resulting in a louder sounding program. In the race for louder sounding records and broadcasts, this type of loudness boosting is often overdone, much to the detriment of the finished product.

Stereo Program Limiting

When a stereo tape or broadcast is program limited, the gain regulating sections of the left and right track compressors must be electronically interlocked, so that compression in one track causes an equal amount of compression in the other track. This keeps the overall left-to-right stereo program in balance.

Consider a stereo program in which the right track occasionally needs some compression. During compression, a center placed soloist would apparently drift to the left whenever the gain of the right track is reduced by the compressor. To prevent this center channel drift, the stereo interlock function reduces the gain of both channels whenever either one goes into compression. This keeps the center placed information from moving from side to side with each action of one or the other compressor.

The De-esser

As mentioned earlier (Chapter 2), the energy distribution of the human voice is such that sibilants are apt to be significantly louder than other voice sounds. The high frequency/high energy content of many 's' sounds may overload an amplifier even when the apparent listening level does not appear to be unduly loud.

Some compressors feature a de-esser function that helps to keep these sibilants under control. A high frequency equalization boost is inserted in the compressor's gain reduction control circuit, so that frequencies in the sibilant range will cause more compressing action than do other frequencies. Therefore, during those fractions of a second when a distortion-prone sibilant passes through the compressor, the gain is reduced by a more than usual amount.

On most compressors, the gain reduction lowers the level of the entire signal. However, on more sophisticated devices, the audio bandwidth may be split into several sections, each of which is separately treated and then re-combined. In this way, the sibilant band may be isolated, and compressed more than the rest of the audio program. When the signal is re-combined, the sibilant sounds are reduced in level without affecting the rest of the program.

The Voice-Over Compressor

The voice-over compressor permits an announcer's voice to take precedence over a musical background. The musical program is first routed through a compressor and then combined with the voice sig-

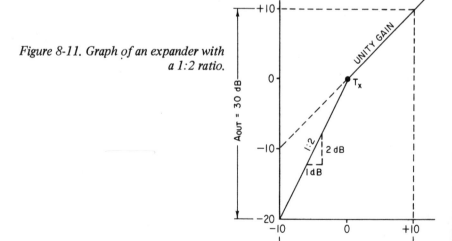

Figure 8-11. Graph of an expander with a 1:2 ratio.

232

nal. However, the voice signal also actuates the compressor, causing gain reduction in the musical background, but not in the voice path itself. Now, as the announcer speaks, the background level of the music is automatically lowered.

As a further refinement, some voice-over compressors provide voice-actuated gain reduction only when the musical program is above a certain level. Therefore, if the music is already sufficiently low in level so as not to obscure the announcer's voice, no further gain reduction is provided.

EXPANDERS

Like the compressor, the expander affects the dynamic range of a program. But, as its name suggests, the expander widens — or expands — the dynamic range, rather than restricting it. Two definitions describe its operation:

> **Expander**: *An amplifier whose gain decreases as its input level is decreased.*
> **Threshold**: *The level below which the expanding action takes place.* (Note that the expander functions *below* threshold — just the opposite of a compressor.

Figure 8-11 is a graph of input *versus* output for an expander with a 1:2 expansion ratio. Note that when the input level lies below the expander threshold, the output level changes 2 dB for every 1 dB change in input level. As drawn, an input signal with a 20 dB dynamic range produces an output with a 30 dB range. Although the maximum output level equals the maximum input level, the dynamic range has been expanded, since the minimum output level is now 10 dB below the minimum input level. In other words, the dynamic range has been expanded downward.

Expansion, when used before recording to increase the dynamic range of a program, must be approached with caution, since the low level components of the signal are now even closer to the residual noise level of the tape. On the other hand, if the overall level is raised after expansion, the high level components are brought closer to the tape's maximum permissible level. Since it is so often necessary to compress the dynamic range to meet the restrictions of the medium, this application of expansion is rarely used. .

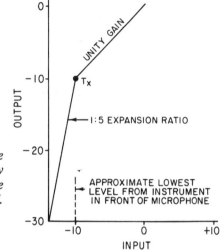

Figure 8-12. The expander as a noise gate. Noise signals at a level below the expander threshold are significantly attenuated.

The Noise Gate

In many typical recording situations, there is often a certain amount of undesirable low level sound present in the studio. Air conditioner rumble, chair squeaks, outside traffic noise, and the sounds of nearby instruments are some of the many noises that a microphone may hear. These sounds may be adequately masked when the sound level from the instrument in front of the microphone is sufficiently high. However, when the instrument is not playing, this background noise becomes audible.

An expander may be used to reduce this noise by selecting a large expansion ratio, with a threshold level at a point above the noise level, but just below the lowest output level of the instrument in front of the microphone. As seen in Figure 8-12, the low level noise signals are practically eliminated. This function of the expander is often called a **noise gate** since the effect is to cut off the noise without affecting the musical program. Of course, the line between the noise and the music is not often clearly defined, and it is all too easy to cut off the very quietest musical passages along with the noise. As before, this type of expansion must be approached with care.

"Tightening" Sounds with an Expander

As just mentioned, an expansion threshold that is set too high will cut off the low level end of a program along with the noise. Although this is certainly not desirable in most cases, it may be very effective on some percussive sounds (drums, hand claps, etc.). As an example, a snare drum produces a series of high level transients, each of which should quickly fade away. If each drum attack sustains too long, the overall sound may lack the subjective tightness that is usually sought. An expander threshold set at a relatively high level—well into the drum sound itself—will bring the level down quickly after each attack, as shown in Figure 8-13.

The same technique may be applied to most percussive instruments to attenuate or remove any low level extraneous noises or instrument ringing in between each attack. During the attack itself, the expander cannot remove the background noise, since it reacts of course to the overall program level and has no way of distinguishing wanted from unwanted sounds. For this reason, the noise gate function of the expander may be marginally effective on sustained instruments, such as organ, or strings. When either instrument is not playing, the expander may attenuate the noise, but as before, the noise will reappear whenever the instrument begins playing. And, due to the sustained nature of the instrument, the noise may be heard through the music. Consequently, its sudden disappearance and re-

THE EFFECT OF AN EXPANDER ON PERCUSSIVE TRANSIENTS

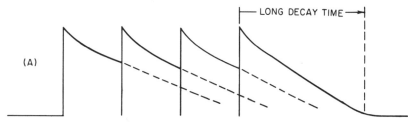

Figure 8-13A. A series of transient attacks, with long decay times.

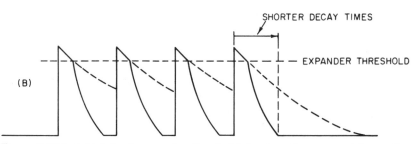

Figure 8-13B. A high level expansion threshold shortens the apparent decay time of each transient.

235

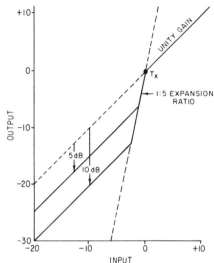

*Figure 8-14. Graph of an expander,
showing 5 and 10 dB attenuation
ranges.*

appearance in time with the music may be more of a distraction than a help.

In any case, despite the effectiveness of the noise gate on some occasions, it is not a substitute for good musicianship, and should not be expected to transform mediocre players into skilled artists.

Expander Release Time

The release time of an expander is the time it takes for the gain to fall to a minimum, once the input signal is removed. If the input signal is not entirely removed, the release time will simply govern the speed at which the gain falls along the expansion ratio curve. As with the compressor, very short release times are more noticeable than longer values.

Expander Range

Since it may be desirable to restrict the amount of low level attenuation provided by the expander, a variable range control may be provided. Its effect is shown in Figure 8-14, where it will be observed that low level signals are attenuated by only 5 or 10 dB. The range control may be continuously variable from 0 to about 60 dB.

236

BLOCK DIAGRAM OF AN EXTERNALLY KEYABLE
PROGRAM EXPANDER

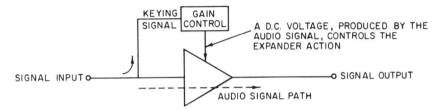

Figure 8-15A. Normal expander operation.

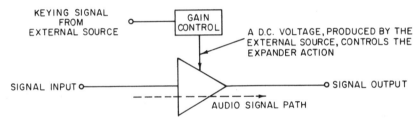

Figure 8-15B. Externally keyed operation.

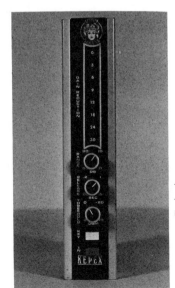

Figure 8-15C. The "KEPEX", a popular KEyable Program EXpander. (Allison 501)

237

Using the Expander for Special Effects

So far, the expander has been described as a self-keying device; that is, the expanding action is controlled by the program passing through the expander, as shown in Figure 8-15A. However, some expanders may instead be controlled, or keyed, by an external signal, as in Figure 8-15B. Here, it is the level of the external keying signal, rather than the signal being expanded, that regulates the amount of expansion. If the keying signal is a constant sine wave voltage at a level above the threshold, the expander will simply stay on, functioning as a unity gain amplifier, regardless of the dynamic range of the audio program passing through it.

It should be clearly understood that the keying signal is *not* heard at the expander's output. It simply provides a control voltage to regulate the gain of the expander and thus of the level of whatever signal is passing through it. If the keying voltage is gradually reduced below threshold, the signal level will likewise gradually fall off, and if the voltage is removed entirely, the audio signal will completely fade out. The length of the fade will depend on the release time of the expander. An automatic fade-out may be made by setting the expander range to maximum attenuation, and the release time to about 3 to 6 seconds. Now when the keying voltage is suddenly removed, the program through the expander will gradually fade out over 3 to 6 seconds.

Figure 8-16. An expander used to modify the sound of one instrument with the envelope of another.

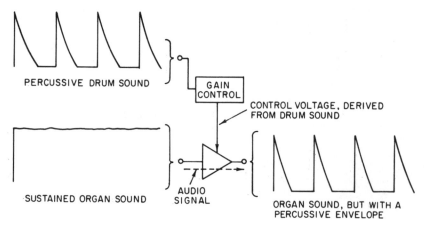

PERCUSSIVE DRUM SOUND

GAIN CONTROL

CONTROL VOLTAGE, DERIVED FROM DRUM SOUND

SUSTAINED ORGAN SOUND

AUDIO SIGNAL

ORGAN SOUND, BUT WITH A PERCUSSIVE ENVELOPE

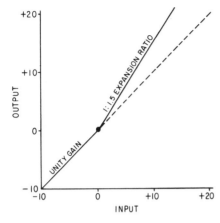

Figure 8-17. A graph of peak expansion. Higher level inputs are boosted during playback to create a wider dynamic range program.

Unique effects may be created with an expander by keying a sustained musical instrument with a control voltage derived from a percussive instrument. With a maximum range setting and a relatively short release time, the sustained instrument, say a Hammond organ, is routed through the expander. The expander is then keyed on and off, perhaps by a drum track. The expander switches on and off with every drum transient attack, and imposes this percussive envelope on the sound of the organ, as shown in Figure 8-16.

In another application, a sub-sonic sine wave (under 10 Hz.) may be applied to the keying input. As the sine wave amplitude slowly increases and decreases, a tremolo effect is imposed on the audio signal passing through the expander.

Since few signal generators produce the very low frequencies required for this effect, the outputs from two signal generators tuned to any convenient low frequency may be used. The generators are slightly de-tuned to produce a beat frequency of several cycles per second. The rising and falling amplitude produced by the beat frequency is fed to the keying input to produce the tremolo effect.

As yet another interesting application of the keyable expander, a bass drum or tom-tom (and some other percussion instruments) may be "tuned" by feeding a low frequency audio signal through the expander. This time, the intention is to hear the low frequency every time the expander is keyed on. The expander is keyed by the signal from say, the bass drum, thus passing the low frequency tone every time the drum is struck. The signal generator may be tuned as desired, and the expander output is mixed with the regular drum sound to impart a definite tonality to the sound.

239

Peak Expansion

Peak expansion, or "unlimiting" is another form of expansion, used during playback of a program that was compressed while being recorded. This expansion-after-compression system forms the basic foundation of several noise reduction systems, and will be discussed in greater detail in the chapters on Noise and Noise Reduction. (Section V.).

As a result of improvements in expander technology that came about as a result of the interest in noise reduction techniques, expanders are now available to enhance the dynamic range of conventionally recorded programs. Here, the expansion takes place above the unity gain curve, as seen in Figure 8-17, so that higher levels — perhaps representing peaks that were compressed earlier — are raised to restore the original program dynamic range. This type of expansion may also be used as a program enhancer to expand the range of music that was not necessarily compressed in the first place. As before, the amount of expansion should not be excessive, lest it become noticeably distracting.

CHAPTER 9

Phasing and Flanging Systems

Many attempts have been made to describe in print the unique effect known as **flanging**, or **phasing**. The effect is created by canceling some frequencies within the audio bandwidth while others are reinforced. Moreover, the frequencies at which cancellation and reinforcement take place are continuously shifting up and down the audio range.

For the person who has not heard the effect at first hand, descriptive phrases may not contribute much to an understanding of just what flanging or phasing really sounds like. However, as an attempt at description, a somewhat similar type of sound may be heard when two aircraft engines are rotating at slightly different speeds. A throbbing sound is superimposed on the roar, and there seems to be a shifting of frequency as this "beat" fades in and out. In the studio, the effect was first produced when a signal was fed to two tape recorders whose outputs were combined. The speed of one of the recorders was varied just a little bit by applying a slight pressure to the flange of the supply reel (hence the term "flanging"). As the machine speed varied, so did the tape's transit time between the record and playback heads. Compared to the other tape recorder, the very slight time delay differential produced a series of phase shift cancellations, as the outputs of the two machines were mixed together. As the time delay varied, the cancellations moved up and down the audio bandwidth, producing the effect that is now known as flanging.

Electronic Phasing System

In an effort to produce a suitable flanging effect without the use of auxiliary tape recorders, electronic phasing systems were developed. In these, the cancellations were produced by combining the outputs of a series of phase shift networks with the direct signal. Although the cancellations, or nulls, could be moved up and down

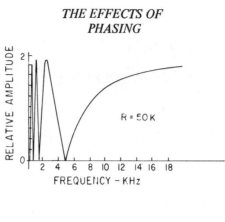

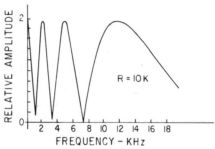

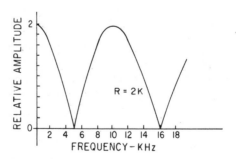

Figure 9-1A. Phasing.
The output of an 8 section phase shift network
is combined with the direct signal.
Varying a resistance produces the phasing effect,
as the cancellations move up and down the audio bandwidth.

THE EFFECTS OF
FLANGING

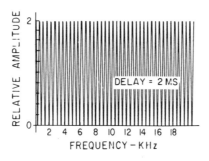

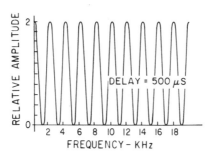

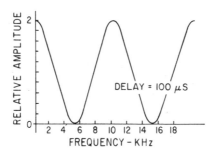

Figure 9-1B. Flanging.
The output of a delay line is combined with the direct signal.
Varying the delay time produces the flanging effect.
(graphs courtesy of Eventide Clock Works).

the audio bandwidth by varying a resistance value in each phase shift network, the number of cancellations was dependent on the number of phase shift networks built into the circuit. The frequency ratio between nulls was a function of the circuit values chosen and did not bear any sort of constant harmonic relationship as the nulls were shifted up and down.

Although the electronic phasing unit produces an interesting effect, it does not have the depth of sound of the flanging effect produced by the auxiliary tape recorder system.

Electronic Flanging System

Digital technology has made possible a variable delay line that more closely resembles tape recorder flanging. Here, the tape recorder's time delay differential is simulated by a delay system that is variable between about 200 microseconds and 15 milliseconds. The delayed signal, when combined with the direct signal, produces a series of nulls that are spaced at regular odd harmonic intervals over the entire audio bandwidth. As the delay time is increased, the spacing between adjacent nulls decreases. The flanging sound is created by continually varying the system's time delay. Figure 9-1 is a series of frequency response curves, showing the effects of flanging and phasing, while Figure 9-2 shows the face plate of a typical flanging system.

Figure 9-2. The faceplate of an Electronic Flanger.
(Eventide FL 201) [Eventide Clock Works photo]

Section IV
MAGNETIC RECORDING

Introduction

The tape recorder is rarely thought of as a signal processing device, for at all times its output is expected to be a faithful replica of its input. And yet it does indeed process the signal – first from electrical to magnetic energy, and later back to electrical energy again.

Chapter 10 is a brief introduction to the basic principles of magnetic recording, in which the tape and the tape recorder are viewed as component parts of a total system. Together with some explanation of elementary magnetic principles, the basic "building blocks" of the system are briefly described. In the next two chapters, the tape and the tape recorder are discussed separately, and in some detail. Finally, Chapter 13 describes the alignment of the system, in which the performance of the tape recorder is optimized to suit the parameters of the particular type of magnetic recording tape which will be used during the recording session.

CHAPTER 10

Magnetic Tape and Tape Recorder Fundamentals

An Overview of the Tape Recorder as a "System"

Regardless of the amount of technical sophistication built into the modern tape recorder, it consists basically of the few essential parts listed below. Since the recorder is of no use without something to record upon, we may begin with;

1. The magnetic recording tape.
2. a) The record head.
   b) The record amplifier.
3. a) The playback head.
   b) The playback amplifier.
4. The transport system.

Theory of Operation

The theory of operation may be simply stated; as illustrated in Figure 10-1 the transport system moves the magnetic tape past the recording head, where the program to be recorded is magnetically stored on the tape. When the stored program passes the playback head, the playback amplifier produces a signal that corresponds to the input signal, as originally applied to the record amplifier. In practice, the record/playback process is of course considerably more involved, and to better understand it we need to review some basic

Figure 10-1. The basic tape recorder system.

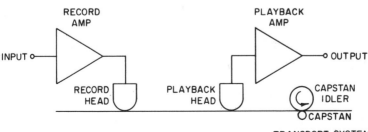

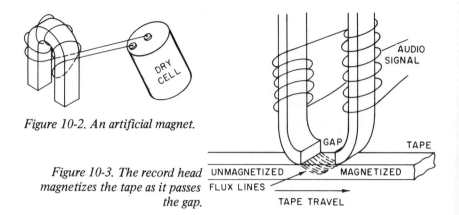

Figure 10-2. An artificial magnet.

Figure 10-3. The record head magnetizes the tape as it passes the gap.

principles of magnetism.

Basic Magnetism

The ancient philosophers knew that a certain kind of rock, now known as lodestone, would mysteriously draw to it particles of iron. This power came to be known as magnetic attraction, and in time it was recognized to be a physical, not spiritual quality. Materials possessing this power are now called magnets.

An artificial magnet may be created by winding a coil of wire around a bar of metal—as shown in Figure 10-2. When a direct current is applied to the coil, a magnetic field is set up, and the bar becomes a magnet. Depending on the particular material, the bar may or may not remain magnetized after the current is withdrawn. Hardened steel will retain its magnetic properties long after the applied current ceases, whereas soft iron is considered a temporary magnet. Although readily magnetized, it does not retain the magnetization in the absence of an applied current.

If a hard ferrous material—that is, a material with the capacity to acquire permanent magnetic characteristics—is temporarily subjected to a magnetic field and then removed from the vicinity of the field, the residual magnetism now stored in the magnet can be measured later on. The measurement will enable us to determine the strength of the force that magnetized the material. This measurement may be made whenever it is convenient to do so, since the material was permanently magnetized at the instant it was withdrawn from the applied magnetic field.

It follows then that a series of ferrous particles may be magnetized, each by a different magnetic field strength, and later, measurements of each particle will tell us, as before, of the strength of the applied magnetic field at the instant the particle was magnetized. Basically, this is the principle of magnetic tape recording.

Magnetic Tape

Magnetic tape consists of an acetate or polyester base material coated with a binder in which ferric oxide (magnetic) particles are suspended. The particles become magnetized when they pass through the magnetic field that has been created around the record head. Later, the magnetic tape may be played back and the stored magnetization retrieved, via the playback head and the playback amplifier.

The Record Amplifier

The record amplifier converts the signal voltage from microphone or console into the current that flows through the record head.

The Record Head

The record head is, in effect, a temporary magnet. An alternating current, proportional to the audio signal to be recorded, is fed through the coil in the head. The coil is wrapped around an iron ring core, in which the applied current creates an intense magnetic field (Figure 10-3).

A gap has been cut in the core, and this gap is bridged by magnetic lines of force, known as **flux**. Flux is the magnetic equivalent of current flow. As the magnetic tape passes by the gap, some of the flux passes through the tape, magnetizing it. The flux lines readily penetrate the tape, since this path offers less reluctance to the flux than the air gap itself. **Reluctance** is the term for opposition to a magnetic force, and is analogous to resistance in a purely electrical circuit.

The Playback Head

The playback head is similar to the record head in construction. A coil of wire is wrapped around a soft iron core. The tape, previously magnetized by the record head, passes by the gap in the play-

249

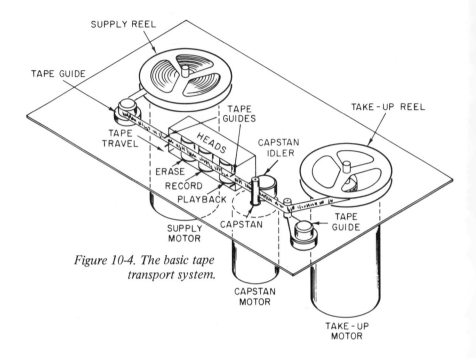

Figure 10-4. The basic tape transport system.

back head. The tape flux penetrates this gap, inducing a current, proportional to the flux, within the coil winding.

The Playback Amplifier

The playback amplifier converts the current induced within the playback head into a voltage which then appears at the output terminals of the tape recorder.

Tape Transport System

Figure 10-4 shows the essential components of the tape transport system. The tape to be recorded (or played back) is placed on the supply reel side of the transport. The tape is threaded past the tape guides and head assembly to the empty take-up reel. The capstan idler presses the tape against the capstan, pulling it past the heads at the required speed, while the take-up motor winds the tape onto the empty reel.

In the fast forward, or rewind mode, the reel motors quickly wind the tape onto the supply or take-up reel, as required.

CHAPTER 11

Magnetic Recording Tape

In the previous chapter, it was noted that magnetic tape consists of a base material upon which has been placed a magnetic coating.

The coating consists of a binder solution, in which gamma ferric oxide particles are suspended. Depending on the particular application for which the tape is intended, each particle may be from 7 to 20 μin in length. The particles are generally one third to one sixth as wide as they are long.

Before the binder has set, the tape is passed through a strong d.c. magnetic field which physically arranges the particles in a lengthwise orientation with respect to the tape. (For some video applications, the particles would be oriented in a cross-wise direction.)

Each particle consists of one or more **domains**. A domain is defined as 10^{18} molecules of gamma ferric oxide, and is the smallest physical unit that can be considered a magnet. The domains are thought to be totally magnetized at all times, but since their magnetic orientation within the oxide particles is random, the net total magnetization of the tape is zero.

When an applied magnetic force, as in a record head, supplies a weak magnetic field, only those domains whose existing magnetic orientation approximates the direction of the applied field will be forced from their natural "unstressed" state into magnetic alignment with the field. When the field is withdrawn, most—if not all—the domains will return to their original unstressed random orientation. In other words, the tape remains unmagnetized.

If a stronger magnetic force field is applied, many more domains will be forced into alignment with it. When the field is withdrawn, some domains will return to their original random, or unstressed, orientation, while many other domains will remain in the orientation forced upon them by the application of the magnetic field. Consequently, the tape will remain magnetized. This residual magnetism is not quite as strong as the applied magnetic force (since some of the domains returned to the unstressed orientation when the force was

251

withdrawn) yet the tape definitely remains in a measurable state of magnetization.

Tape Saturation

If an even stronger magnetic force is applied, *all* the domains will be forced into alignment with it. When this happens, the tape is said to be saturated, that is, no further magnetic action can take place. Now, when the applied force is withdrawn, very few domains will return to their original unstressed orientation. The tape is now in its maximum possible magnetized state.

Once the applied magnetic field forces the tape into saturation, any further increase in the field strength will have no further effect on the tape. When all the domains have been forced into alignment with the applied magnetic field, the tape is incapable of further responding to even greater field strengths.

SUMMARY OF THE EFFECT ON MAGNETIC TAPE OF VARYING FIELD STRENGTHS

A very weak magnetic field will have little or no lasting effect on the magnetization of a tape. Moderate field strengths will magnetize the tape, more or less in proportion to the strength of the applied magnetic field. A strong magnetic field will totally magnetize the tape and it will be considered saturated. Even stronger magnetic fields may be applied, but they will cause no further influence on the tape, once the saturation point has been reached.

In order to be of practical use as a program storage medium, a magnetic tape must possess a linear transfer characteristic. That is, its playback output must be a non-distorted (or linear) replica of the original recorded input signal. Low and high level signals must maintain their proper relative amplitudes if a usable recording is to be made. But, when we apply the basic properties of magnetism to recording tape, we may find that very weak audio signals do not get recorded at all. While moderate level signals are recorded satisfactorily, very high level signals are distorted if the signal strength is sufficient to drive the tape into saturation. In other words, magnetic tape recording seems at the moment to be a non-linear process, as in fact it is, if corrective steps are not taken.

Before describing these corrective measures, we may illustrate the magnetic properties of recording tape by drawing the so-called hys-

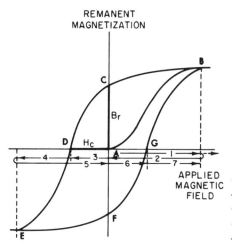

REMANENT
MAGNETIZATION

APPLIED MAGNETIC FIELD

Figure 11-1. The Hysteresis Loop. A graph of the magnetism left on a recording tape by an applied magnetic field. B_r = retentivity, H_c = coercivity.

teresis loop, as shown in Figure 11-1. The loop may be explained as follows:

The Hysteresis Loop

Magnetic force, measured in units called *oersteds,* is symbolized by the letter H. When a tape passes through a magnetic field, the magnetization that remains on the tape is called **remanent magnetization**; that is, the magnetization remaining after the applied magnetic force, H, has been removed. This remanent magnetization is measured in *gauss,* and is symbolized by the letter B. A tape's ability to store magnetization is referred to as its **retentivity, B_r.** To illustrate the magnetic tape's storage capabilities, we shall apply a direct current to the record head. Starting at zero, the current will be gradually increased in the positive direction. In Figure 11-1, the applied current creates a gradually increasing positive magnetic force (arrow 1) and the positive magnetization of the tape increases, non-linearly, from zero (**A**) to positive saturation (**B**). Once the saturation point has been reached, any additional increase in magnetic force (the dashed-line extension of arrow 1) has no further effect on the tape.

When the applied force is gradually decreased to zero by decreasing the applied d.c. (arrow 2), the magnetization left on the tape decreases, not to the zero value at (**A**), but to (**C**). The heavy vertical line, B_r, represents the retentivity of the tape, that is, the residual magnetism left on the tape after the applied magnetic force has been reduced to zero. If we ceased our experiment at this point the tape

253

would remain magnetized. But if a gradually increasing negative force is now applied (arrow 3), the tape's magnetization will be reduced to zero (D), when that force reaches the magnitude represented by the solid horizontal line, H_c. H_c is the **coercivity** of the tape; the force required to completely demagnetize it.

As the negative force continues to increase (arrow 4), the tape will be negatively magnetized. The magnetization will increase from zero (D), to negative saturation (E). In either condition of saturation, all the domains are magnetically aligned with the applied magnetic field. The terms, positive and negative, simply refer to the opposite directions that the lines of force, and consequently the orientation of the domains, may take.

Now, when the negative force is diminished to zero (arrow 5), the residual magnetism falls off to (F). Once more, the tape is left in a magnetized state, but the polarity is opposite to that shown earlier as B_r.

Now, to restore the tape to an unmagnetized state (G), a gradually increasing positive force must be re-applied (arrow 6), and a further increase in the positive direction (arrow 7) will once again drive the tape to positive saturation (B).

In this rather tedious step-by-step explanation of the properties of the magnetic tape medium, direct current was used so that we could observe the effect of a force of gradually changing magnitude and polarity. In practice, of course, we shall apply an alternating current, such as a sine wave, to the record head and thence to the tape. However, in terms of the properties of magnetic tape, frequencies within the audio range may be considered as fluctuating d.c. voltages.

The Transfer Characteristic

To study the effect of recording an alternating current signal onto tape, we may draw a transfer characteristic, such as the one shown in Figure 11-2. This transfer characteristic is simply a graph of retentivity versus applied magnetic force.

Although the curve superficially resembles the line between (A) and (B) in Figure 11-1, it is actually derived mathematically from a series of hysteresis loops. The hysteresis loop shown in Figure 11-1 illustrates the retentivity of a tape that was driven to the saturation point. However, if the applied force had been somewhat less, the hysteresis loop would have been smaller and somewhat differently shaped, thereby giving a different value of retentivity. And of course,

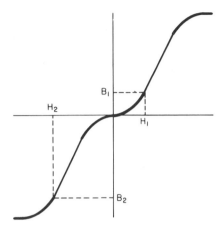

Figure 11-2. A typical transfer characteristic for magnetic tape. An applied magnetic force of H_1 will store a magnetic field of B_1 on the tape.

for any value of applied force, there is a corresponding value of retentivity, once that force is withdrawn. For example, if a positive force of H_1 is applied, as shown in Figure 11-2, the tape will be left with a retentivity of B_1; if a negative force, H_2, is applied, the retentivity will be B_2, and so on. Therefore, the curve of Figure 11-2 should be understood to be a plot of retentivity for any value of magnetic force applied, between negative and positive saturation.

In Figure 11-3, the transfer characteristic is redrawn in exaggerated form, for clarity of explanation. Five waveforms, A - E, are shown, representing various magnitudes of alternating current supplied to the record head. In waveform A, the progressively longer arrows indicate an increasing magnetic force, first positive, and then negative. The smallest arrows indicate forces that do not permanently affect the tape. The next two sets of arrows indicate forces that do affect the tape slightly. The largest arrows indicate an applied force operating for the moment within the linear segment of the transfer characteristic.

The resulting magnetism left on the tape as a result of waveform A may be plotted as shown on the output side of the transfer characteristic. Obviously, the output is quite distorted, both in waveshape and amplitude.

The output is redrawn at A', and the outputs from the other waveforms, B - E, are shown as B' - E'. Note that waveform C does not reproduce at all, and that output waveform E' is flat-topped, since the magnitude of the input signal has driven the tape into saturation.

255

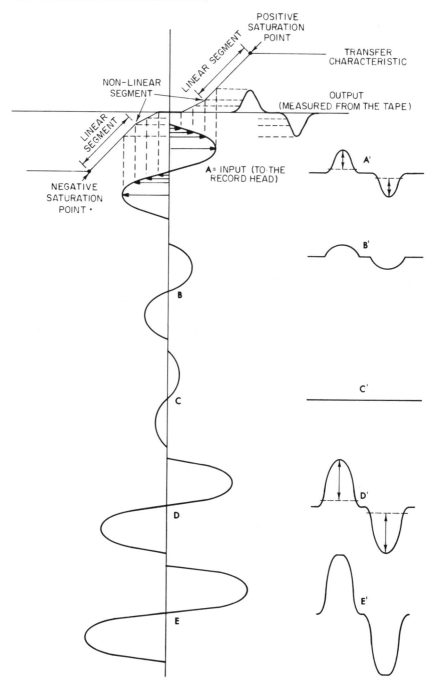

Figure 11-3. The effects of a non-linear transfer characteristic. Various levels of input signals (A through E) produce distorted (non-linear) output waveshapes (A' through E').

These output waveforms illustrate the non-linear properties of tape as a storage medium. However, it should be noted that there are two segments of the transfer characteristic which *are* linear. (These segments have been identified in Figure 11-3.) Any portion of an input waveform that falls within these segments will be linearly reproduced. This may be noted in output waveforms **A'** and **D'**, where the sections measured by the vertical arrows are seen to be non-distorted reproductions of the equivalent section of the input.

AN INTRODUCTION TO BIAS

In Figure 11-3, the applied signal is an alternating current, varying between zero and some positive – and then negative – maximum amplitude. And, as noted, only when the amplitude forces the tape's magnetization into the linear segment of the transfer characteristic will the output be a faithful reproduction of the input.

However, if an additional direct current were also applied, the audio signal would now alternate above and below that d.c. value instead of about the zero point as before.

D.C. Bias

In Figure 11-4, a positive direct current, called a **bias current**, is applied to the record head. The magnitude of this bias current places it, as shown, midway in the positive linear segment of the transfer

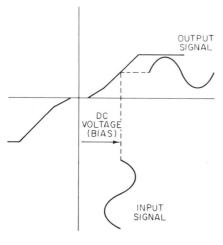

Figure 11-4. Achieving a linear transfer characteristic by using D.C. bias. The D.C. bias shifts the applied signal into one of the linear portions of the transfer characteristic.

OUTPUT
SIGNAL

DC
VOLTAGE
(BIAS)

INPUT
SIGNAL

257

characteristic. Now, when the audio signal is also applied, the resulting magnetization will vary about this bias level, and the output, (that is, the magnetization left on the tape) will fall within this linear segment.

Despite the obvious improvement in linearity, d.c. biasing does not allow the tape to be used to its full potential. By observation, it may be seen that now only a small portion of the transfer characteristic is being used. Consequently, the full magnetic storage capacity of the tape is not being utilized. Furthermore, input levels must be considerably restricted so that peak levels do not fall outside the positive linear segment of the transfer characteristic.

As a further disadvantage, d.c. biasing tends to magnetize the record head permanently, introducing noise onto the tape, and perhaps erasing it partially.

Yet despite these practical limitations, d.c. biasing is a marked improvement over recording without any bias. Due to the relative simplicity of d.c. bias circuitry, it was sometimes found in early non-professional tape recorders.

A.C. Bias

Using a very high frequency alternating current as a source of bias provides a more satisfactory method of overcoming the non-linear properties of magnetic tape.

Typically, a frequency on the order of 150,000 to 180,000 Hz is selected for biasing. The frequency is well beyond our hearing limits, and indeed may be too high to be reproduced by some playback heads. However, the bias *is* actually recorded on the tape, and may be heard as a very high pitched squeal if a segment of recorded tape is very slowly rocked back and forth—as in editing—across the playback head.

From the shape of the transfer characteristic, it might be expected that the bias frequency would be recorded in distorted form, much like any of the other frequencies illustrated in Figure 11-3. However, it has been found that at very high frequencies, the transfer characteristic apparently becomes quite linear over most of the range between positive and negative saturation. The degree of apparent linearity seems to increase with the amplitude of the bias, as shown by the curves in Figure 11-5.

There have been many explanations of a.c. bias, most of which seem to add more confusion than enlightenment to the subject. A.c.

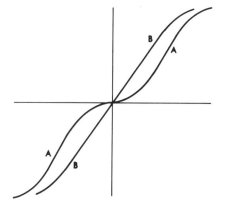

Figure 11-5. The apparent linearizing properties of high frequency A.C. bias.
A = typical non-linear transfer characteristic of magnetic tape (no bias signal applied).
B = apparent transfer characteristic in the presence of an applied high frequency bias voltage.

bias seems at times to be in a class with the aerodynamically-impossible bumble bee; everyone knows that it works, but no one is quite sure why!

Reduced to its simplest terms, it would seem that the rapid alternations of the bias frequency overcome the magnetic medium's inertia to change in applied force. Remember that the non-linear transfer characteristic, first seen in Figure 11-2, was mathematically derived from a series of hysteresis loops. As such, it represents the effects of gradually changing values of applied magnetic force. In magnetic terms, any audio frequency may be considered to be a gradually changing force. By comparison, the bias frequency is a rapidly changing force. The tape is in a state of continuous magnetic agitation, and its resistance to change has been overcome.

Of course, the transfer to tape of a bias frequency, while no doubt academically intriguing, is of questionable artistic interest. We are, after all, concerned with recording music and speech, and not with the behavior of some frequency many times beyond the range of human hearing.

However, a.c. bias allows us to store on tape a faithful reproduction of the applied audio signal, at an amplitude that takes advantage of the full storage capability of the tape.

The Application of A.C. Bias

Rather than simply applying the audio signal directly to the record head, it is first combined with the bias frequency, which is supplied by a bias oscillator built into the electronics. The bias frequency may

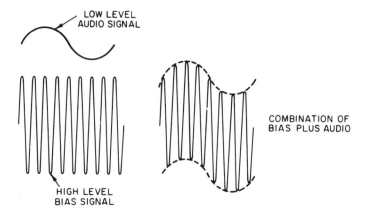

Figure 11-6. Combining bias and audio signals at the record head.

be about ten times the amplitude of the audio signal. Consequently, the mixture of the two will appear as shown in Figure 11-6. The figure shows that the audio signal has become an envelope on the larger amplitude bias signal. This simple addition of bias-plus-audio is fed to the record head. The bias frequency is linearly recorded (apparently) on the tape, along with the relatively slight amplitude changes caused by the audio envelope.

The Effect of Bias Level on the Audio Signal

When an audio signal is recorded without bias, the output shows a large segment of third harmonic distortion. That is, the output wave-form shows a component that is three times the frequency of the applied audio signal. As bias is added, the distortion is reduced, as the bias apparently linearizes the transfer characteristic.

But the linearizing effect of the bias signal is a function not only of its frequency, but of its amplitude as well. As the bias amplitude is increased from zero, the transfer characteristic becomes more and more linear, resulting in less and less third harmonic distortion. Or, conversely, as bias level is decreased below optimum, distortion increases. This may lead us to think that optimum bias level is that amount which is required to reduce third harmonic distortion to an absolute minimum.

Unfortunately, it may not be that simple. In a typical situation, it may be found that at some point before minimum distortion is reached, the high frequency response of the audio signal begins to fall off significantly, while at the same time, low frequency response increases. This is because the bias level affects the sensitivity of the tape.

Remember again that, without bias, the tape is relatively insensitive to low *levels* of applied audio. With bias, the tape responds (is sensitive) to these low levels, but the sensitivity varies over the audio frequency band, depending on the level of the bias.

For example, if the bias level is gradually increased from zero, while recording a high frequency — say 15,000 Hz — that frequency will be recorded on the tape at a gradually increasing amplitude, until the optimum bias level for 15,000 Hz is reached. Further increase in bias level will result in a decrease in the amplitude of the recorded frequency. As a matter of fact, the level will fall off rather sharply at high frequencies, due to the self-erasing tendencies of high frequencies.

If we now record a low frequency, we will discover that the bias level must be increased several dB in order to achieve the maximum possible output. But, this increased bias level will tend to erase the higher frequencies, as explained above.

A compromise setting must be sought, keeping in mind that distortion increases as bias decreases, in addition to the effects on frequency response described here.

Bias Traps

A bias trap is a very high-frequency cut-off filter, designed to prevent the bias signal from overloading the record and playback electronics. Even though the bias frequency is far beyond audio limits, its high amplitude could overload any audio amplifier to which it was applied, thereby distorting the amplifier's audio output severely. As shown in Figure 11-7, bias traps may be located just after the record amplifier and before the playback amplifier. The first one prevents the bias signal from backing up and overloading the record amplifier output, while the second one filters out any bias that may be in the playback line.

Bias Beats

When two frequencies, f_1 and f_2, are combined, beat frequencies are produced which correspond to the sum and difference of f_1 and

261

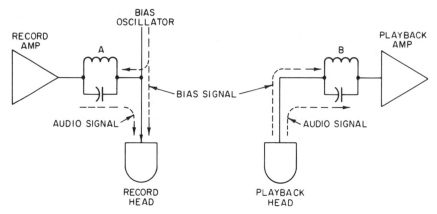

Figure 11-7. Bias traps.
A prevents bias from overloading the record amp output.
B prevents bias from overloading the playback amp input.

f_2. If two bias oscillators are slightly detuned, at frequencies of, say 180,500 Hz and 179,500 Hz, a difference frequency of 1,000 Hz will be produced. Although neither bias frequency is audible, the difference frequency certainly is, and if the corresponding tracks on the tape recorder are mixed together, this audible bias beat will be definitely objectionable.

To prevent this audible bias beat frequency, the individual bias oscillators for each tape recorder track may be linked together electronically to keep them all at precisely the same frequency. On later model multi-track tape recorders, a single master bias oscillator is often used in place of individual bias oscillators. Within each set of record/playback electronics, the bias adjustment controls regulate an amplifier that is connected to the master bias oscillator. Therefore, the engineer has control over the bias level for each track, while the single master oscillator assures that there will be no discrepancies in frequency from one track to another.

SUMMARY OF BIAS

Without bias, magnetic recording is a non-linear process. That is, the audio program stored on the tape is a distorted replica of the applied signal.

Bias is a high frequency (typically 150,000 to 180,000 Hz) high amplitude signal, applied to the tape to overcome its non-linear transfer characteristic.

As bias level is increased, third harmonic distortion decreases.

Optimum bias level varies with the frequency of the applied audio signal. As frequency increases, optimum bias level decreases.

OPERATING PARAMETERS OF MAGNETIC RECORDING TAPE

The engineer should be aware that the operating parameters of magnetic recording tape may differ appreciably from one manufacturer to another, as well as between different types of tape from the same manufacturer. Although tape recorder alignment will be covered later, (Chapter 13) here it should be understood that if a tape recorder is aligned using a certain type of tape, it will not necessarily give optimum performance when a different tape type is substituted. There should certainly be consistency between one reel and another of the same type of tape, but in all other cases, the engineer should be prepared to realign his tape recorders when changing tape.

Manufacturers may specify the magnetic, physical, and electroacoustical characterisitics of their product, each of which is discussed below.

MAGNETIC PROPERTIES

Coercivity

The coercivity (abbr. H_c) of a tape — measured in oersteds — is an indication of its sensitivity to an applied magnetic field. The published specifications usually list the strength of the magnetic field required to bring a saturated tape to complete erasure. The coercivity of representative studio tapes generally ranges between 280 and 380 oersteds.

Retentivity

As discussed earlier, retentivity is a measure of a magnetic tape's flux density after a saturation-producing magnetic field has been withdrawn. Retentivity is expressed in gauss (i.e., magnetic flux lines per cross-sectional square centimeter of tape.)

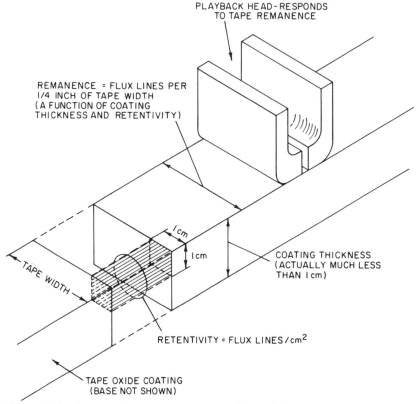

Figure 11-8. A comparison of remanence and retentivity.

Remanence

Remanence also describes the same condition, but is expressed in lines of flux per linear quarter inch of tape width. This specification is particularly significant, since the playback head's output level is a direct function of the tape's remanence.

Figure 11-8 illustrates the measurement of both retentivity and remanence.

Sensitivity

Sensitivity is an indication of tape's relative output level, as compared to some specified reference tape. Thus (given the same input level) a tape with a sensitivity of +2 will produce an output level 2 dB higher than the standard reference tape.

High Output Tapes

As a result of advances in oxide formulation techniques, tapes with relatively high sensitivities have now become available. The sensitivity improvement is a function of the greater retentivity of these so-called high output tapes. For a given oxide coating thickness, this greater flux density results in a higher remanence value, and therefore, a higher output level.

Harmonic Distortion and Headroom

Recorded third harmonic distortion, in addition to being a function of bias level, will also be found to increase as the recorded level of the tape approaches saturation. Maximum allowable recorded level is usually defined as that level at which the third harmonic distortion reaches 3%.

A tape's headroom is defined as the difference between standard operating level (+4 dB) and the 3% distortion point. Thus, if a tape reaches 3% third harmonic distortion when the applied input level is +10 dB, it is said to have a 6 dB headroom (10 dB - 4 dB = 6 dB).

Some of the newer tapes have greater headroom than standard tapes, and this may be used in two ways: the signal may be applied to the tape at a higher level, taking advantage of the headroom improvement and raising the program above the residual noise level by the amount of the increase. Or, the tape may be recorded at standard operating level, with the increased headroom allowing occasional high peaks to be recorded with less distortion.

PHYSICAL PROPERTIES

In addition to the oxide coating described earlier, magnetic tape consists of a base material upon which the oxide is coated, and a back coating, both of which are described here.

Base Material

Both cellulose acetate and polyester have been widely used as a base material for magnetic recording tape, with the thickness of the base ranging from 0.6 mils to 1.42 mils. So-called "extended play" tapes use a thin base, so that more tape may be wound on a given reel size.

Some years ago, cellulose acetate was generally preferred for professional applications, since under tension the tape would break rather than stretch. On the other hand, polyester based tape would usually become severely stretch-deformed before it would break under tension.

Although a simple break is easily fixed with a piece of splicing tape, a stretched tape cannot be salvaged. But the acetate-base tapes had a disadvantage, in that they would eventually dry out, becoming quite brittle after being stored for a while. Polyester tapes remain stable, even when stored for a long time, and as manufacturing techniques have greatly increased their stretch resistance, acetate is being used less and less.

Back Coating

As with the oxide coating described earlier, the back coating of a tape is a thin layer of carbon pigment (rather than oxide particles) suspended in a binder. The resultant surface texture generally reduces the slippage between the tape and the capstan/capstan idler, and provides a more even tape wind, especially at high speeds. The back coating is generally more abrasion-resistant than uncoated polyester and in addition, its low resistivity minimizes the build-up of static charges. Typical back coating thicknesses range between 0.05 and 0.12 mils.

Figure 11-9 summarizes some of the magnetic and physical parameters of various commercially available recording tapes.

ELECTRO-ACOUSTICAL PROPERTIES

Under this heading appear some of the other characteristics of magnetic tape which must be taken into account in its evaluation.

Modulation and Asperity Noise

A completely de-magnetized tape will nevertheless contain a very low level background noise. It has been found that this background noise level rises considerably during the recording process, and may be particularly noticeable when a single frequency is recorded. For example, Figure 11-10 shows the effect of recording a single frequency on tape. As may be seen, the noise level rises across the entire audio bandwidth, with the increase greatest in the vicinity of the frequency being recorded. The wide band noise is known as **modulation noise**, and a narrow band segment on either side of the recorded signal itself is known as **asperity** (i.e., roughness) **noise**. It is so-called because of the resultant harshness of sound. Although modulation noise may not be objectionable on many recorded programs, asperity noise is often quite noticeable when recording single frequency test tones.

Drop Outs

Drop outs are momentary signal losses which may be caused by imperfections in the magnetic tape coating, or by dust particles lifting the tape away from the record head. In some cases, over biasing may help minimize drop outs, for as the dust particles come between the tape and the head, the bias reaching the tape is slightly lessened, with a resultant increase in recorded sensitivity.

Print-Through

Since magnetic tape is stored on reels, each segment is wound between two other segments. The tape's magnetic field may be sufficient to partially magnetize these segments, resulting in **print-through**; an audible pre- and post-echo of the signal on the two tape layers that come in contact with it. On many recordings, the program itself will mask the print-through, especially the post-echoes. However, print-through may be noticeable at the beginning and end of a recording, and during sudden changes in dynamic level, where a quiet passage is not loud enough to mask the echo of a loud passage immediately before or after it.

Since print-through is usually greatest on the outer tape layer, it is advisable to store tapes tails out; that is, without rewinding after playing. This way, the worst print-through comes as a post-echo and stands the greatest likelihood of being masked by the program itself.

Print-through is particularly noticeable during narration recordings, since there are so many open pauses between, and within, sentences. In some cases, one or two rewindings of the recorded tape—just prior to playback—will remove a slight amount of print-through. Tapes should never be stored in high temperature areas, since this usually increases the amount of print-through.

MANUFACTURER TAPE NUMBER	AGFA	AMPEX			AUDIOTAPE		BASF	
	468	406	407	GRAND MASTER	2506	2507	26LH	50LH
MAGNETIC PROPERTIES								
COERCIVITY [OERSTEDS]	380	285	285	295	315	315	325	330
RETENTIVITY [GAUSS]	1060	1050	1050	1300	1050	1050	1200	1100
PHYSICAL PROPERTIES								
BASE MATERIAL*	P	P	P	P	P	P	P	P
BASE THICKNESS [mils]	1.2	1.42	.88	1.42	1.50	.95	.6	1.5
OXIDE THICKNESS [mils]	.6	.5	.5	.50	.53	.53	.39	.55
BACK COATING THICKNESS [mils]	.1	.05	.05	.05	INCLUDED IN BASE DIMENSION		NONE	
TOTAL [mils]	1.9	1.97	1.43	1.97	2.03	1.48	.99	2.05

*P = Polyester
C = Cellulose Acetate

Figure 11-9. Recording Tape Characteristics.

MANUFACTURER TAPE NUMBER	CAPITOL		MAXELL		111	201	3M			
	678	968	UD-50	UD-35			206	207	209	250
MAGNETIC PROPERTIES										
COERCIVITY [OERSTEDS]	315	315	315	315	270	315	320	320	320	380
RETENTIVITY [GAUSS]	1200	1200	1180	1180	920	790	1050	1050	950	1200
PHYSICAL PROPERTIES										
BASE MATERIAL*	P	P	P	P	C	C	P	P	P	P
BASE THICKNESS [mils]	1.48	.94	1.43	.95	1.42	1.42	1.52	.95	1.52	1.30
OXIDE THICKNESS [mils]	.53	.53	.45	.45	.44	.51	.56	.56	.40	.65
BACK COATING [mils]	INCLUDED IN BASE DIMENSION		INCLUDED IN BASE DIMENSION		NONE		INCLUDED IN BASE DIMENSION			.08
TOTAL [mils]	2.01	1.47	1.88	1.40	1.86	1.93	2.08	1.51	1.92	2.03

*P = Polyester
C = Celluslose Acetate

Figure 11-9. Recording Tape Characteristics.

269

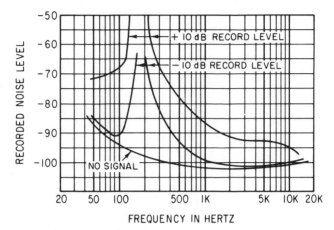

Figure 11-10. Noise in tape recording. When a single frequency is recorded on tape, the noise level across the entire audio bandwidth rises.

CHAPTER 12

The Tape Recorder

THE RECORD PROCESS

The Record Head

The **record head** is the transducer that converts the applied audio signal (the record current) into magnetic lines of force (flux) which in turn pentrate and magnetize the tape.

In an effort to achieve a flat frequency response, it might seem that the record current should be kept constant regardless of the frequency of the applied audio signal. However, as we shall see, there are several good reasons why this is not the case.

If we were to analyze any piece of music from an acoustical power point of view, we might find that much of the energy lies within the middle frequency range. For example, if a series of sound level meters were tuned to respond to various segments of the audio bandwidth, we might find the situation illustrated in Figure 12-1. The

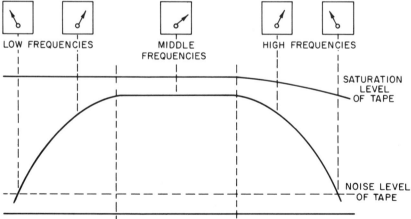

Figure 12-1. Energy distribution curve of a musical program. The exact shape of the curve will vary, according to the nature of the program.

meters tuned to the frequency limits—the extreme lows and highs—would show readings considerably less than the meters tuned to the mid-range frequencies.

This is because there is often less going on at very low or very high frequencies. Accordingly, if we were to record the music as is, the mid-range frequencies would be the first to near the saturation level of the tape. (Note that the saturation line slopes downward at the high frequency end of the spectrum, to represent the tape's tendency towards earlier saturation at higher frequencies.)

From the illustration, we can see that if the level is kept down so that the mid range is just below saturation, the low and high frequencies are well below saturation. And of course, they are just that much closer to the residual noise level of the tape.

Tape Recorder Equalization

If these low and high frequencies were boosted somewhat, just before the record head, they would be recorded at a higher than normal amplitude, well above the residual noise level. The resultant recording would now have an unnatural amount of bass and treble, but complementary circuitry just after the playback head could restore the signal to its normal balance, and in so doing, lower the apparent noise level. For, as the playback circuit restored the frequencies to normal balance by lowering the lows and highs, the recorded noise would likewise be lowered.

It should be clearly understood that tape recorder equalization has nothing to do with changing the apparent frequency balance of the program as heard by the listener. All equalization described within this chapter is intended solely as a compensation for various limitations of the recording medium and to improve the faithfulness of the recording to the original program. When a properly adjusted tape recorder is in use, the listener should be unaware of the tape recorder equalization. This is in marked contrast to "program equalization" done at the recording console to audibly change the frequency balance according to the tastes of the engineer or producer.

Record Equalization (Pre-Emphasis)

The boosting of low and high frequencies, just before the applied audio signal reaches the record head, is known as **pre-emphasis.**

Due to the properties of magnetic recording tape, high frequencies will cause saturation sooner (that is, at a lower level), than mid range or low frequencies. Accordingly, high frequencies may not be boosted quite as much as low frequencies. There is also some tendency toward self erasure at high frequencies; therefore, beyond a slight high end boost, further increases may become self-defeating.

THE PLAYBACK PROCESS

The playback circuit must compensate for the record pre-emphasis, to restore the signal to normal balance. And, additional compensation must be included, to compensate for the output characteristics of the playback head itself.

The Playback Head

The **playback head** is the transducer that responds to the magnetic flux stored on the tape, producing an output voltage directly proportional to the rate of change of this magnetic flux. Since this rate of change doubles every time the frequency doubles, we find that as the frequency increases, the output voltage rises according to the formula:

$e = N (d\phi/dT)$ e = output voltage
N = number of coil turns of wire in the playback head
$d\phi/dT$ = rate of change of flux (analagous to frequency)

Now, since a doubling of voltage equals a 6 dB increase, we may say that, for a constant-level recorded signal, the playback output will increase at the rate of 6 dB per octave. This rise will continue until the wavelength of the recorded signal is equal to twice the length of the playback head's gap. It is at this point that the rate of change of flux within the gap is the greatest, and so the output voltage is at its maximum. It is the gap itself which measures the flux level. As the word implies, the gap is a physical air space, across which the tape passes. The distance across the gap has been called gap width by some and gap length by others, resulting in some mild confusion. For our purposes, the dimension will be called simply, **gap space**, and labelled, **G**.

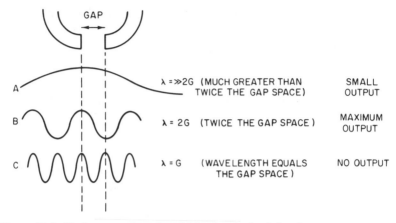

Figure 12-2. Various wavelengths within the playback head gap space.

To understand the effect of the gap on output level, wavelengths for several frequencies are shown in Figure 12-2. It should be understood that these wavelengths are passing across the gap at a constant velocity. (For example, 15 in/sec.) Although it is convenient to think of these wavelengths in terms of some frequency, it should be kept in mind that each wavelength represents a certain length of tape, and depending on the tape speed, the frequency produced by this wavelength will vary. For example, at 15 in/sec., a 1 mil wavelength will produce a 15,000 Hz tone. If we play the same tape at half speed, (7½ in/sec.) the same 1 mil wavelength now produces a tone of 7,500 Hz.

In Figure 12-2, wavelength A corresponds to a relatively low frequency. The flux level is changing slowly; that is, the rate of change within the gap is relatively slow, and the output voltage is therefore small. As the frequency increases, so does the rate of change within the gap, until the frequency corresponding to wavelength B is reached. At this wavelength, (λ = 2G) the rate of change is at its greatest since, as a positive peak crosses one side of the gap, a negative peak crosses the other, and *vice versa*.

Gap Losses

Beyond this wavelength, the output level falls off sharply, and at half this wavelength (λ = G) the output is zero, because as one positive peak crosses one side of the gap, another crosses the other, for a net change of zero. Across the gap there is no rate of change, and therefore no output voltage. This is illustrated by wavelength C in Figure 12-2. At each successive halving of the wavelength, the output will again be zero, while in between these points the output will sharply rise and fall, as shown in Figure 12-3.

On a professional quality playback head, the gap space is typically 0.2 mils. Therefore, a frequency whose wavelength is 0.2 mils (λ = G), would give zero output, as just described.

Remember that, on tape, the wavelength is the physical distance taken up by one cycle of the frequency in question. Every time the tape speed is doubled, (7½ to 15 in/sec. for example) twice as much tape is used, and the wavelength for any frequency is therefore twice as long. Consequently, the frequency at which maximum output occurs is likewise doubled. This is why high frequency response is extended with each doubling of tape speed.

At 15 in/sec., 0.2 mils corresponds to a frequency of 75,000 Hz, certainly well past the audio range, so zero output at this frequency would be of no concern. Maximum output would occur at a frequency with an 0.1 mil wavelength; that is, 37,500 Hz. At 7½ in/sec., this same wavelength would yield 18,750 Hz, which is still sufficiently high for audio purposes.

If this gap loss was the only limitation on upper frequency response, we might safely ignore it when operating at speeds of 7½ in/sec. or greater. At 7½ in/sec. the rapid fall-off in output level – from maximum to zero – occuring within the octave which beings at λ = 2G (18,750 Hz at 7½ in/sec.), poses no practical problem.

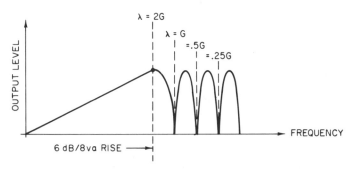

Figure 12-3. Output characteristic of a playback head when reproducing a constant flux tape.
The output level rises at 6 dB/8va until the wavelength equals twice the gap space. Then the output falls off rapidly to zero at λ = G.

275

Other Head Losses (Record and Playback)

However, there are other limitations within the playback head, and in the tape itself, which will account for losses that affect the upper audio frequencies even at 15 in/sec.

The cumulative effect of these losses, added to the gap loss effect, may noticeably restrict the upper audio frequency response, even at 15 in/sec.

These losses are due to a variety of causes. On the tape, higher frequencies have a tendency towards self erasure, and bias current may also reduce high frequency response somewhat.

Within the heads, eddy currents are a further contribution to high frequency roll-off. And the slightest separation between tape and heads is also most noticeable at high frequencies.

Further losses will occur if the record and playback heads are not in correct mechanical alignment with respect to each other, and to the tape path. These losses will be described in detail in the chapter on machine alignment.

Playback Equalization (Post-Emphasis)

To compensate for the 6 dB/8va rise in output voltage which occurs over most of the audio range, a playback equalization circuit with a 6 dB/8va cut is employed. But at the highest audio frequencies, this 6 dB/8va cut must be replaced with a high frequency boost to help overcome the losses described above. Of course, once $\lambda = G$, there is zero output from the playback head and no amount of equalization will help. However, proper playback equalization should keep the frequency response flat within the entire practical audio range.

The NAB Standard Reproducing Characteristic

The NAB (National Association of Broadcasters) Standard Reproducing Characteristic is shown in Figure 12-4. It should be understood that this post-emphasis equalization is in addition to the 6 dB/8va cut described above. The combination of the NAB characteristic and the 6 dB/8va cut is shown in Figure 12-5.

The low end roll-off within the NAB standard is to compensate for the low end boost in the record circuit, and it restores these frequencies to their normal balance.

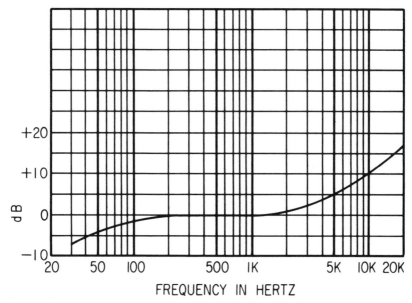

Figure 12-4. The NAB Standard Reproducing Characteristic. (7½, 15 in/sec.)

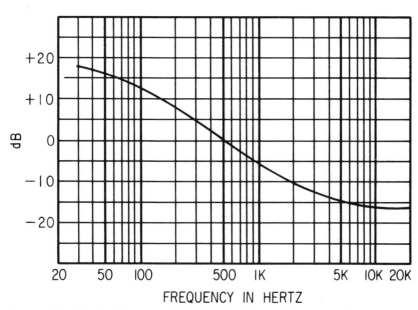

Figure 12-5. The NAB Standard Reproducing Characteristic, combined with a 6 dB/8va roll-off. (7½, 15 in/sec.)

Since the high end was also boosted in the record circuit, it might seem that a complementary roll-off would be required in the play-back circuit, as indeed would be the case if the record and playback losses described earlier were not a factor. However, the high end pre-emphasis (in the record circuit) only partially overcomes these losses, and so, additional boost, rather than a roll-off, is required in the playback circuit.

As a consequence of the record/playback losses, there is no pub-lished record equalization standard. At the lower frequencies, the boost is merely the opposite of the NAB Reproducing Characteris-tic. However, the cumulative effect of the various high frequency losses occurring within the record/playback chain cannot be predict-ed, since they are so dependent on the bias level setting, the recorded level, the type of tape used, etc. Therefore, the proper record equali-zation is simply that which will yield a flat frequency response when the playback circuit has been aligned according to the NAB stand-ard.

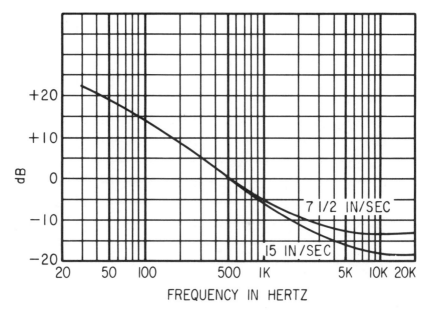

Figure 12-6. The CCIR Standard Reproducing Characteristic, combined with a 6 dB/8va roll-off.

CCIR Reproducing Characteristic

Tapes, and recording equipment, produced in Europe will often conform to the CCIR Standard (International Radio Consultative Committee), which is illustrated in Figure 12-6. High frequency post-emphasis is somewhat greater than that prescribed by the N.A.B. characteristic.

SUMMARY OF NAB PRE- AND POST-EMPHASIS

Figure 12-7 summarizes the frequency characteristics and corrective equalization found within the modern tape recorder.

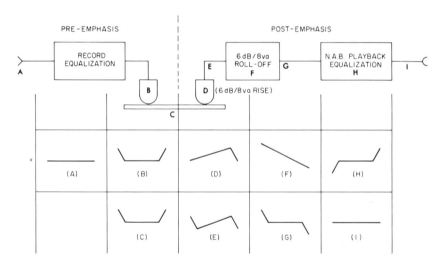

Figure 12-7. Summary of the frequency characteristics and corrective equalization within a tape recorder.
A. *A flat frequency response is applied to the input.*
B. *Record equalization boosts low and high frequencies.*
C. *Tape is recorded with boosted low and high frequencies.*
D. *Playback head exhibits 6 dB/8va rise in output level, with rapid fall-off beyond λ = 2G.*
E. *Recorded response, c, as reproduced by playback head with 6 dB/8va rise. High end boost of response c may partially counteract rapid fall-off beyond λ = 2G.*
F. *6 dB/8va. roll-off to compensate for playback head characteristic.*
G. *Resultant response after 6 dB/8va roll-off.*
H. *N.A.B. equalization to restore flat response.*
I. *Resultant flat frequency response corresponds to input response a.*

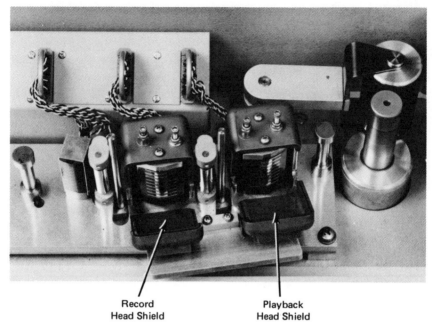

Record   Playback
Head Shield   Head Shield

Figure 12-8. Tape recorder head shields.
The shield protects the head against stray magnetic fields. A similar shield
protects the record head.
(Ampex MM-1000) [Ampex photo]

Playback Head Shielding

Since the playback head responds to the magnetic field surrounding the recording tape, it follows that it will also respond to stray
magnetic fields in the immediate vicinity. Accordingly, magnetic
shielding is used to protect the head, particularly against 60 Hz hum
picked up from the transport motors. A representative example of a
playback head shield is shown in Figure 12-8.

The Erase Head

The function of the **erase head** is to remove any remanent magnetization from previous use of the tape. The need for an efficient erase
mechanism is not unique to magnetic recording. Notebook pages,
blackboards, and magnetic tape are alike in that they must be erased
after each use if they are to be re-used. To simply record over an al-

ready recorded tape would be just as confusing, aurally, as the visual confusion that would result from writing over a previously used page of notes.

In the tape path, the erase head immediately precedes the record head. Generally, the tape recorder's high frequency bias oscillator also supplies a very strong alternating current to the erase head. This "erase current" completely saturates the tape, and of course, there is no audio signal mixed with it, as in the record head circuit.

The heavy erase current forces the tape's magnetic particles out of their previous magnetic orientation, and into saturation. The high frequency of the erase current alternately drives the tape from positive to negative saturation, and as each segment of tape moves out of the magnetic field around the erase head, the effect of the field on that segment becomes less and less. The hysteresis loop for the segment grows smaller and smaller—consequently the remanent flux diminishes eventually to zero, and the tape segment leaves the vicinity of the erase head completely demagnetized.

Of course this all happens very quickly, as the tape travels past the erase head on its way to the record head. By the time the tape arrives at the record head, all traces of previously recorded information have been removed, and the tape is ready for re-use.

Bulk Erasers

A **bulk eraser**, or **degausser**, is a device for erasing entire rolls of tape at once. The bulk eraser usually takes the form of a non-magnetic turntable, or perhaps just a simple table-top, (as shown in Figure 12-9) upon which the tape to be erased is placed. Underneath the tape is a very powerful electro-magnet, to which current is gradually applied, while slowly rotating the tape. After maximum current is reached, the current is gradually decreased again to zero, at which time the tape is completely demagnetized.

If the bulk eraser does not allow the gradual application and withdrawl of the erase current, then it must be turned on *before* the tape is placed on it. Now, the tape is slowly brought near the eraser, rotated several times, and then slowly withdrawn from the field.

Since bulk erasers invariably operate at line frequency (50 or 60 Hz), the alternate positive-negative saturation takes place at a much slower rate than when the tape is being demagnetized by an erase head operating at bias frequency. Therefore, the tape must be moved in and out of the magnetic field very slowly, so that a high ratio of

281

Figure 12-9. A commercially available bulk eraser.
(Taberaser) [Taber photo]

frequency-to-tape speed is maintained.

Although bulk erasers certainly lack the operational flexibility of a multi-track erase head, their intense magnetic field is usually more efficient than that created by the erase head. A well functioning erase head should certainly handle most erasing needs with ease, yet an occasional loud passage may require several erasures before the tape can be re-used.

Consequently, it is good engineering practice to use a bulk eraser whenever circumstances permit the complete erasure of a previously used tape. It is also a good idea to routinely bulk erase fresh tape prior to first use.

Bulk erased tapes are generally lower in noise level than tapes erased on a tape recorder; however this advantage is for the most part academic, since erase head-less tape recorders would impose severe operational limitations on any modern recording session. And, for making simple tape copies, where stop-and-start operation is not required, the practical nuisance of disabling the erase head without affecting bias level to the record head probably outweighs the slight advantage in noise reduction.

282

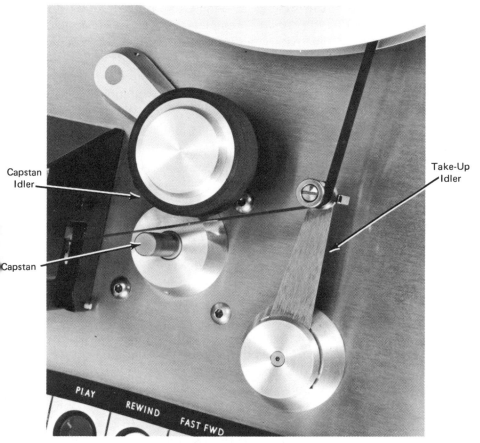

Figure 12-10. The capstan/capstan idler system.
(The capstan idler is often called a pinch roller)
(Ampex AG-440C) [Ampex photo]

THE TAPE TRANSPORT SYSTEM

For optimum performance of the recorder's electronics system, it is essential that the magnetic tape maintain constant contact with the heads over which it passes. The slightest up-and-down movement, or variation in tape-to-head pressure will seriously degrade the tape recorder's performance. Even a slight speed error will become a serious problem if the tape thus recorded is played back on a different machine later on.

283

In addition to the supply, take-up, and capstan motors briefly mentioned in Chapter 10, the complete tape transport system includes a series of tape path guides, located on either side – as well as within – the head assembly.

What follows is a description of the various components within the complete tape transport system. Although construction details vary from one tape recorder model to another, most of the components mentioned below may be found on every studio grade tape recorder.

Capstan/Capstan Idler

Figure 12-10 is a close up of the capstan/capstan idler assembly. As shown, the machine is stopped, and the capstan idler has swung away from the spinning capstan. When the play button is depressed, the idler swings down against the capstan, pinching the tape between them, and pulling it past the heads at a constant speed.

Supply and Take-up Motors

In Figure 12-11A, the tops of the supply and take up reel motors are seen. When the machine is in the play or record mode, both motors attempt to wind the tape onto their respective reels. But, since the capstan motor is pulling the tape in the direction of the take-up motor, the tape winds off the supply reel and onto the take-up reel, as intended. However, the reverse torque applied to the supply reel prevents the tape from spilling off this reel too quickly. If this torque were excessive, the tape might become stretched as the capstan and supply motors attempted to pull the tape in opposite directions. In normal operation, the supply motor will keep the supply reel of tape under moderate tension, keeping the tape in good contact with the heads, but not stretching it.

Reel Size (Tension) Switches

Both reels are kept under tension by a current applied to both the supply and the take-up reel motors; the greater that current, the greater the tape tension. With a constant applied current, the actual mechanical tension on the tape varies with the amount of tape left on the reel. As less and less tape remains on the supply reel, the hold-back tension on the tape becomes greater and greater. Similarly, the

THE TAPE
TRANSPORT SYSTEM

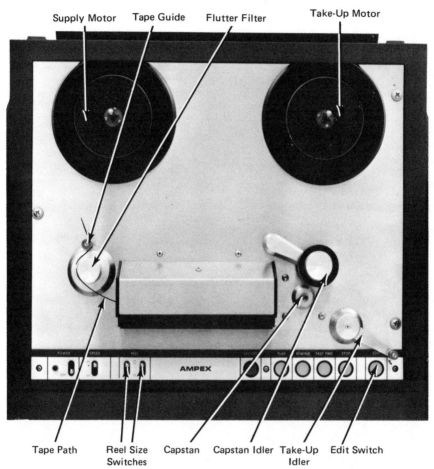

Supply Motor   Tape Guide   Flutter Filter   Take-Up Motor

Tape Path   Reel Size   Capstan   Capstan Idler   Take-Up   Edit Switch
           Switches   Idler

Figure 12-11A. Top view.
(Ampex AG-440C) [Ampex photo]

THE TAPE
TRANSPORT SYSTEM

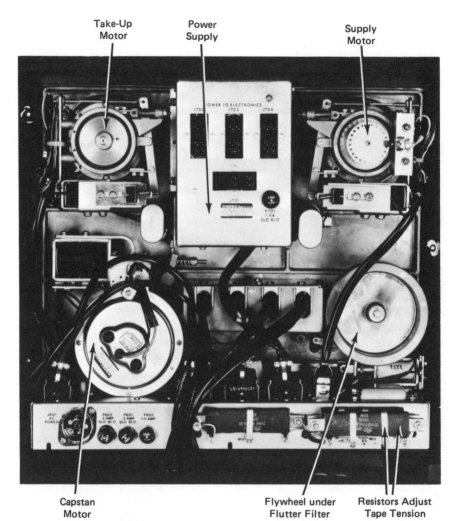

Figure 12-11B. Underside view.
(Ampex AG-440C) [Ampex photo]

286

take-up tension on the take-up reel decreases as it fills up with tape. Overall, the tension must be sufficient to maintain good tape-to-head contact, yet not so great as to cause tape stretching or to affect the speed of the tape past the heads. Although a full roll of tape on either reel requires more tension than an almost empty reel, the tension is usually adjusted for some mid-point value between the optimum tension for full and empty reels.

Most studio recording is done with reels of tape wound on NAB hubs, similar to the ones shown in Figure 12-12. The inner diameter of these hubs is 4½ inches. Nevertheless, it is often necessary to use small plastic reels, also shown in Figure 12-12.

These have an inner diameter of only 2¼ inches, and the normal tension adjustment–made with an NAB hub–would place an undue amount of tension on tape being wound on such a reel. Many tape recorders therefore have a reel size switch (or switches) which changes the tension to a lesser amount when small hub diameter reels are to be used. These switches may be seen in Figure 12-11A.

Figure 12-12. Tape reels of various sizes.
Note the relatively large inner diameter on the metal reels. The plastic reels have much smaller inner diameters, with the exception of the test tape reel (upper right). Its extra large inner diameter protects the tape against excessive reel tension.

Take-Up Idler

Located just beyond the capstan/capstan idler assembly, the take-up idler serves as a guide for proper tape height and as a mechanical on/off switch. In Figure 12-10, the tape is correctly threaded around the guide on the idler, and the machine is ready to play or record. In Figure 12-11A, the idler has dropped (due to a spring) to the off position, since there is no tape holding it up. In this position, the machine will not go into the play or record modes. In the event of tape breakage, the idler will fall to the off position, thus stopping the transport. Similarly, when either reel runs out of tape, the idler stops both reels from spinning.

Braking Systems

Some tape recorders employ a mechanical braking system on both reel motors, as seen in Figure 12-13. In the stop mode, a clutch system may allow the reels to spin freely in one direction only, allowing tape to be wound up on either reel, yet preventing it from accidentally spilling off.

In the play, fast forward, and rewind modes, the brakes may be applied only to the reel motor from which the tape is being unwound, as a precaution against tape spillage. Once the machine stops, the brakes are applied to both reel motors.

Figure 12-13. The under side of the tape transport, showing the braking system on the take-up motor. (Ampex AG-440C) [Ampex photo]

In some recorders, mechanical brakes have been completely eliminated, with all braking being done electronically. In the stop mode,
the reels are kept under tension by a current applied to both motors.
Since both reels are attempting to take up tape, the tape may slowly
creep across the heads while the machine is stopped, if the braking
currents are not properly balanced.

On this type of machine, there is usually a photocell in the tape
path, which senses the presence of tape. When the tape runs out,
the photocell circuit stops the reel motors from rotating. Without
this function, the machine's electronic braking system would keep
the reels spinning slowly when tape was not threaded from one reel
to another.

Edit Switch

When the edit switch is depressed, the capstan/capstan idler pulls
tape across the heads in the usual manner; however, the take-up motor is disabled, so that the tape spills off the machine, rather than
winding onto the take-up reel. This function allows the engineer to
discard sections of tape while listening to the segment being removed. The edit switch may be seen in Figure 12-11A, just below the
take-up idler.

Fast Forward and Rewind Switches

When either the fast forward or the rewind switch is depressed, the
capstan idler releases the tape, and the appropriate reel motor begins
spinning very quickly, winding or rewinding the tape at high speed.
In either mode, tape lifters hold the tape away from the heads. These
tape lifters may be seen in Figure 12-14.

Motion Sensing

A motion sensing system will prevent the tape from being damaged when the machine is switched from rewind or fast forward into
play. On machines without motion sensing, the transport should
come to a complete stop before the play switch is depressed; otherwise the tape may be stretched as the capstan idler forces the tape
against the capstan, and into the play mode.

On some machines, the motion-sensing mechanism is a micro-
switch in the tape path which senses the tape's direction. When the

Tape Lifter   Tape Path Guide   Scrape Flutter Filter   Tape Lifter

Tape Path Guide

Tape Path Guide

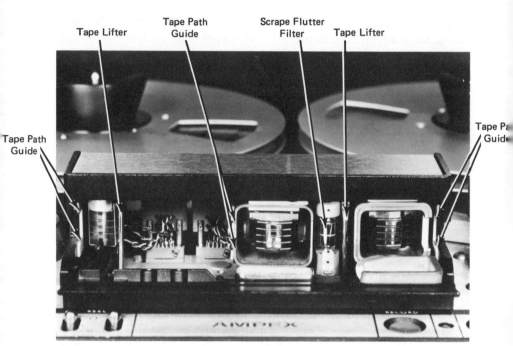

Figure 12-14. Detail view of the head assembly, showing tape lifters, tape path guides, and scrape flutter filter.
(Ampex AG-440C) [Ampex photo]

play switch is depressed, the machine will come to a complete stop before going into the play mode, thereby protecting the tape from damage. On later model machines, the motion sensing system may be an integral part of the overall tape transport control system.

Wow and Flutter

Proper, uniform tape speed is a function of the capstan motor, capstan idler pressure, and the torque applied to the reel motors. Two common irregularities in tape speed are termed wow and flutter. The terms closely describe the type of sound that may be heard if the irregularity becomes excessive.

Wow is a slowly varying speed change, which may be caused by a variety of factors: a mis-alignment in the transport system may cause a once-around slowing of one of the motors; there may be an out-of-round capstan or flywheel; or a worn bearing may cause a low frequency fluctuation in tape speed that results in an audible wow especially noticeable on sustained tones.

290

Flutter, as the word implies, is a very rapid speed fluctuation, producing a fluttering kind of sound. It is usually traced to some sort of tape vibration, not unlike that of a string on a guitar. For example, as the tape moves across the transport system, at various locations it passes over, and is supported by, tape guides. The unsupported tape between these guides may be forced into mechanical vibration, and if a record or playback head detects this vibration, or flutter, the listener hears a high-frequency modulation of the musical program.

Scrape Flutter Filters

To keep the flutter frequency as high as possible — well beyond the audio range — so-called **scrape flutter filters** may be installed between the heads as seen in Figure 12-14. The scrape flutter filter reduces the length of unsupported tape, thus raising the resultant vibration, or flutter, frequency. A larger flutter filter, seen in Figure 12-11A, mechanically isolates the supply reel from the head assembly and also reduces the length of unsupported tape on this side of the transport.

The Closed Loop Tape Path

An interesting variation in the tape path is seen in Figure 12-15A. Note that here the capstan pulls tape into, as well as out of, the head assembly. When both capstan idlers are against the capstan, the tape segment within the head assembly is part of a **closed loop** and is mechanically isolated from the rest of the transport system. Thus it is unaffected by supply and take up reel tensions, and excellent speed stability is achieved.

In the profile view of the capstan/capstan idler assembly, note that the roller on the supply side is indented into the capstan, while the take-up roller is not. This small discrepancy in diameters imposes a slight tension on the tape within the closed loop, assuring firm and constant tape-to-head contact.

VARIABLE SPEED OPERATION

Variable Frequency Oscillators for Speed Control

Many capstan motors are designed to run at their rated standard speed when operated from a standard 60 Hz power line. Although

291

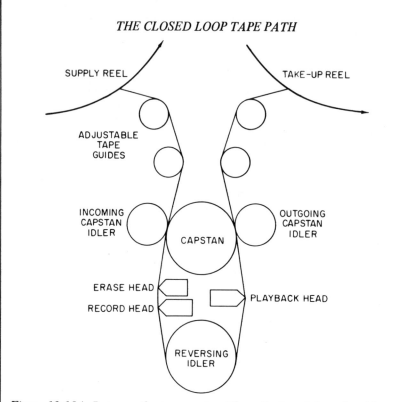

THE CLOSED LOOP TAPE PATH

SUPPLY REEL

TAKE-UP REEL

ADJUSTABLE TAPE GUIDES

INCOMING CAPSTAN IDLER

CAPSTAN

OUTGOING CAPSTAN IDLER

ERASE HEAD

RECORD HEAD

PLAYBACK HEAD

REVERSING IDLER

Figure 12-15A. Between the two capstan idlers, the tape is in a closed loop, mechanically isolating it from the rest of the transport system.

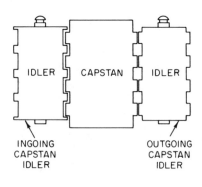

IDLER   CAPSTAN   IDLER

INGOING CAPSTAN IDLER

OUTGOING CAPSTAN IDLER

Figure 12-15B. Profile view of the capstan idler in the closed loop system. (3M Co. M-56)

the motor speed is a function of the line frequency, this frequency is quite stable, and so the machine may be depended upon to run on-speed at all times. However, it is sometimes desired to run a machine off-speed. For example, the musical key of a song may be changed by varying the speed – and therefore the pitch – of the recorded tape. To do this, an audio frequency signal generator may be fed into a power amplifier capable of delivering the required power to the cap-stan motor. As the signal generator frequency is varied above or be-low 60 Hz, the tape speed changes accordingly. Providing the signal generator frequency is reasonably drift-free, this method of speed control works very well, within the frequency limits of the capstan motor.

D.C. Servo Motors

The capstan on some more recent tape recorders is driven by a d.c. servo motor. Here, a tachometer registers the motor speed (and hence the tape speed) and compares it to a reference signal supplied by a built-in oscillator. An error signal equivalent to any difference between the signals from the tachometer and the reference oscillator continuously corrects the capstan motor, keeping it precisely on speed.

However, for variable speed operation, the built-in oscillator may be replaced by an external oscillator, such as the one shown in Figure 12-16. This device provides a reference signal which can be varied by the operator. As the reference signal is changed, the tape speed varies, either in quarter-tone increments, or continuously, over a wide range, as the error signal brings the capstan motor into syn-chronization with the applied reference signal.

*Figure 12-16. A commercially available variable speed oscillator.
(Ampex VS-10) [Ampex photo]*

293

Tape Transport Remote Control

Most multi-track tape recorders are equipped for remote control operation, so that the engineer may control the transport from his position at the console. Figure 12-17 shows such a remote control panel. The unit shown has the capability of automatically returning the tape to the same position over and over again, or of moving the tape to some other pre-determined location if desired. In either case, the desired location is entered on the keyboard seen in the illustration, and this location is displayed on one of the readouts, B, while the other one, A, indicates the actual location of the tape. On command, the transport system rewinds or advances the tape until the A readout corresponds to the B readout, at which point the transport stops. When the engineer wishes to move the tape to another known location, he merely enters the new location on the keyboard, thus changing the B readout.

The remote control panel may also control the record/playback mode of each track. This feature will be discussed in Chapter 17.

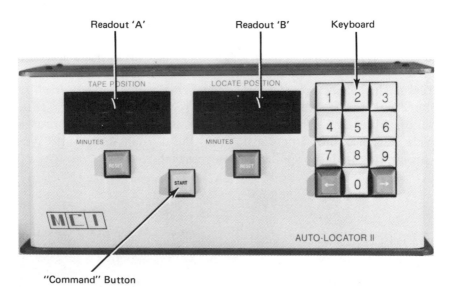

Figure 12-17. A remote tape transport control.
When the start button is depressed, the transport winds the tape to the location indicated on readout B. Other controls, mounted separately, allow remote control of fast forward, rewind, start and stop.
(MCI Auto-Locator II) [MCI photo]

CHAPTER 13

Tape Recorder Alignment Procedures

In order to evaluate completely a tape recorder's level and frequency response performance, a test recording must be made and then played back. Since the recording is evaluated by observing the machine's own playback meter, the playback circuit must be properly aligned first, after which adjustments may be made to the record circuit.

Cleaning

Before beginning the alignment procedure, all tape guides and heads should be thoroughly cleaned. Head cleaning fluid is readily available, and should be applied with a cotton swab to all surfaces with which the tape comes in contact, except the capstan. Other types of solvent cleaners should be avoided, since these may damage the laminations of the heads.

Since some head cleaners may damage the rubber capstan idler, the capstan and the idler should be cleaned with denatured alcohol.

Demagnetization

Heads and tape guides should be routinely demagnetized at regular intervals, since after a few hours of use it is possible for these surfaces to become slightly magnetized. In severe cases, a tape passing over a magnetized head or tape guide will be partially erased.

With the tape recorder turned off, a head demagnetizer should be brought slowly towards the heads and slowly moved away again. The demagnetizer must be well clear of the heads when it is turned on and off.

Test Tapes

To properly align the tape recorder's playback electronics, precision test tapes must be used. These tapes—made under controlled laboratory conditions—contain a series of test tones at a standard reference fluxivity, measured in nano-webers/meter (abbreviated nWb/m). The specification refers to the number of flux lines per unit of tape width. It is these flux lines that will be detected by the playback head and converted into an output signal voltage. Fluxivity should not be confused with remanance, which was described earlier as the magnetism left on a tape after a saturation-producing force has been withdrawn. **Fluxivity**, on the other hand, is an indication of the magnetic field strength of the test signal recorded on the tape. Consequently, for a given playback head, a greater fluxivity on the tape will produce a higher playback output level.

There is still some discrepancy in reference fluxivities between test tape manufacturers. Values range between 150 and 200 nWb/m, which is equivalent to an almost 3 dB range in output levels. Recently, even higher fluxivity test tapes have been introduced, for use with so-called high output tapes, both of which will be discussed later in this chapter.

For purposes of explanation, adjustments to the electronic and mechanical systems are discussed separately. However, there is a certain amount of interaction between these systems; as each is adjusted, the performance of the other should be verified.

THE ELECTRONICS SYSTEM

On most tape recorders, the electronics system parameters are screwdriver-adjustable, as may be seen in Figure 13-1.

Playback Level Adjustment

Generally, the first tone on the test tape is 700 or 1,000 Hz, and is used for setting the proper playback output level. When this tone passes the playback head, the tape recorder's output level is adjusted so that the machine's meters read 0 VU (= +4 dBm). Thus, a reference fluxivity of say, 200 nWb/m, will produce an output level of 0 VU.

High Frequency Playback Equalization

Just after the level-set tone, the test tape usually contains a series of high frequency tones, which are monitored while adjusting the

THE ELECTRONICS SYSTEM ADJUSTMENTS ON A MULTI-TRACK
TAPE RECORDER

Figure 13-1A. On many studio tape recorders, the electronic system parameters are screwdriver-adjustable, from the front of the machine. The photo shows four tracks of record/playback electronics from a multi-track recorder. [Ampex photo]

Figure 13-1B. The bias/erase, record, and playback electronics are on separate plug-in cards for easy servicing or replacement. (Ampex MM-1100)

machine's high frequency playback equalization control. The tones have been recorded in accordance with the NAB standard reproduce characteristic (see Figures 12-4, -5) so that when the machine is properly aligned, the tones will all read 0 VU on the playback meters.

Low Frequency Playback Equalization

Some tape recorders contain an additional equalization control to adjust the low frequency response of the playback circuit. However, the **fringing phenomenon** – an apparent low frequency boost – must

297

be taken into account when evaluating the machine's low frequency performance. To explain, most test tapes are made in a full track format; that is, the reference tones are recorded across the entire width of the tape. In this way, the tape can be used with any head format available for that particular tape width.

However, at long wavelengths (low frequencies), a playback head tends to respond to flux recorded over an area greater than its normal track width. Accordingly, the machine's low frequency response appears to be higher than normal. If the test tape had been recorded over just the width of the track being measured, this fringing effect would not occur. The amount of fringing varies from one playback head to another, and so no attempt has been made to compensate for it in the preparation of the test tape. Hopefully, in time, manufacturers will indicate how much fringing is to be expected with various head configurations. However, when the actual amount of fringing is unknown, low frequency playback adjustments may be deferred until after the record circuit adjustments are completed. Low frequency tones at standard reference level are then recorded and the low frequency playback equalization is adjusted for flat response. Since the tones are being recorded at the proper width for the playback head in use, there will be no fringing, and the low frequency response may be adjusted to read 0 VU. (This procedure makes the assumption that the low frequency record equalization is correct).

Playback Alignment for CCIR Tapes

Since the NAB playback characteristic is standard in American studios, few are likely to have a CCIR test tape available. Never-

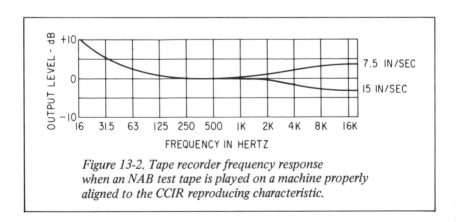

Figure 13-2. Tape recorder frequency response when an NAB test tape is played on a machine properly aligned to the CCIR reproducing characteristic.

theless, many U.S. studios regularly receive tapes from abroad that may have been recorded using the CCIR characteristic. Assuming a tape recorder's playback response has been properly aligned for CCIR playback, an NAB test tape played on such a machine should display the response shown in Figure 13-2. Therefore, when it is necessary to adjust a machine for CCIR playback, an NAB test tape may be used, and the playback adjusted to match the response shown in the figure.

Erase Level Adjustments

In most multi-track tape recorders, a single oscillator provides both the erase and bias signal. A high level, high frequency signal erases the tape, as was described in Chapter 12. The same signal – at a much lower level – is also mixed with the audio program and routed to the record head. In principle, the circuit is as shown in Figure 13-3. From the illustration, it may be seen that the erase control affects both the erase and bias levels, and so it must be adjusted first. On most tape recorders, a bias position on the meter selector switch (Figure 13-4) allows the meter to measure the bias oscillator output, as also shown in the simplified circuit sketch. With the meter switch in the bias position, and the transport in the record mode, the erase control is adjusted for maximum meter deflection. Once maximum deflection has been reached, turning the control further will reduce

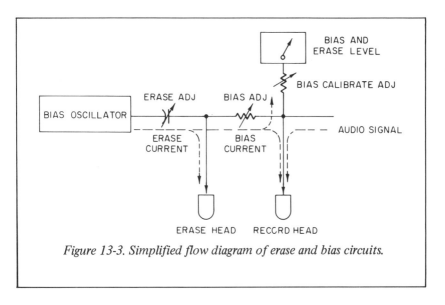

Figure 13-3. Simplified flow diagram of erase and bias circuits.

299

Figure 13-4. A selector switch allows the meter to measure the tape recorder's output, input, or bias level.

the erase current, and the meter reading. During this adjustment, the position of the bias potentiometer is unimportant, so long as it is high enough to allow a readable meter deflection.

Bias Level

Once the erase adjustment has been completed, the meter switch is returned to the playback (or repro) position. A single frequency tone is recorded on the tape, and the bias potentiometer is adjusted for a maximum output reading on the meter. At its minimum position, the tape is underbiased, and as the potentiometer is advanced, the bias level increases towards maximum. Once the output level begins falling off, the tape is overbiased, and the bias current begins to erase the tape as it is being recorded, thus accounting for the level drop.

As discussed in Chapter 11, optimum bias level varies, depending on the frequency of the audio signal. And, from the point of view of minimum distortion, the optimum level may again be different. In setting the bias level, the tape manufacturer's instructions should be consulted. For example, the performance characteristics of two types of magnetic recording tape are shown in Figure 13-5. The manufacturer recommends that bias be adjusted for maximum while recording a 10,000 Hz tone at about 0 dB. Then the bias level should be further increased until the recorded output level drops about 3 dB. At this point, the tape's sensitivity is fairly uniform across the audio bandwidth, and the third harmonic distortion is quite low. In Figure

13-5B, it will be noted that a further increase in bias level will lower the distortion even more; however, the tape's sensitivity also falls off and modulation noise begins to increase again. Accordingly, the 3 dB overbias point is considered as the best compromise setting for these tapes.

Record Level Adjustment

With the tape recorder's playback circuit properly aligned and erase and bias adjustments completed, the record circuit may now be aligned.

Generally, an audio frequency signal generator, set at 700 or 1,000 Hz is used to apply a +4 dBm signal to the tape recorder, where it is recorded on a fresh piece of tape. The machine's record level is adjusted until the playback meter reads 0 VU. In other words, with a +4 dBm input level applied to the tape recorder input, the tape's

Figure 13-5. Electrical performance characteristics of two types of magnetic recording tape.

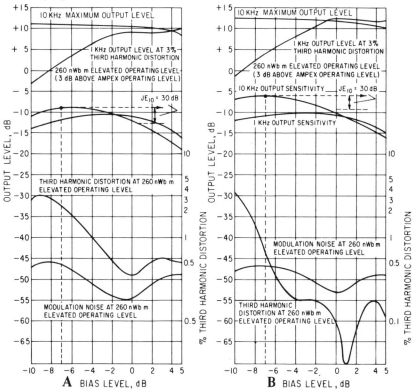

recorded fluxivity will produce a 0 VU output level when the tape is played back.

Record Equalization

The record equalization potentiometer is used to adjust the record circuit response at high frequencies. The setting will vary depending on the characteristics of the tape being used, the bias level, and the design of the record head itself.

A high frequency tone (typically 10-15,000 Hz) is recorded, and the equalization adjusted, as before, until the machine's output level matches the input level. Once the high frequency response has been adjusted, the signal generator output frequency should be varied over the entire audio bandwidth to verify that the system response is within the required specifications. It is important to have available a signal generator with a continuously variable frequency adjustment rather than one with just a few fixed frequencies. Although the latter is adequate for routine signal tracing and spot checks of performance, it may not reveal response errors lying between the switch-selected frequencies.

Elevated Level Test Tapes

With improvements in the manufacture of magnetic recording tapes, the available headroom on some new tapes has been increased by several dB. Therefore, higher levels may be recorded without distortion. However, the meters on both the console and the tape recorder continue to read 0 VU = +4 dBm. So, if a higher operating level is used, the meters may read off-scale much of the time. To prevent this, an elevated level test tape may be used to align the tape recorder. This tape may have a reference fluxivity of, say, 250 nWb/m. Therefore, if it is simply played back on a machine originally calibrated with a standard level test tape, the meters will read about 3 dBm too high. If the tape recorder output level controls are accordingly reduced to read 0 VU, a standard level (+4 dBm) signal applied to the tape recorder input will appear (on the playback meters) to be 3 dBm lower than before, despite the fact that the record level has not yet been touched. But now, the tape recorder's record level controls may be raised 3 dBm to restore the original +4 dBm output level.

As a result of this realignment, there is no apparent change in the system's input/output relationship. A +4 dBm test tone is applied to the tape recorder input and the output meter reads +4 dBm (0 VU) as before. However, the signal is recorded on the tape at a higher flux level.

In the event that an elevated level test tape is not available, a standard test tape may be used, and the playback level set 3 dBm down. The record level is then raised by the same amount, as before.

If, on the other hand, it is desired to take advantage of the greater headroom capability of the newer tapes, the recorder's input and output controls may remain calibrated to a standard fluxivity test tape. This provides increased capability for handling sudden program peaks without distortion, as was mentioned earlier, in Chapter 11.

Calibrate Controls

Some tape recorders contain record and bias calibrate adjustments. These controls do not affect the performance of the tape recorder; they are merely an operating convenience for making quick checks on the machine's performance during a session. For example, once the bias level has been set, the meter selector switch may be placed in the bias position. This places the meter across the bias signal path, as was shown earlier, in Figure 13-3. The bias calibrate control is then adjusted until the meter reads zero, after which the switch is returned to its normal output position. Later, bias level may be checked simply by verifying that the meter continues to read zero when the meter selector is switched to the bias position. Or, if it becomes necessary to change the bias temporarily to accommodate a non-standard type of tape, the original bias may be re-set later simply by adjusting the bias adjust control until the meter reads zero – again with the meter switch in the bias position.

In a similar manner, the record calibrate control is adjusted until the meter reads 0 VU, with the meter switch in the input position and a 0 VU tone applied to the tape recorder input. Later, the record level may be verified by making sure the meter continues to read 0 VU under the conditions just described. If it does not, the record level control may be quickly adjusted for a 0 VU reading. The record calibrate control also makes it unnecessary to play the test tape to make spot checks on the playback output level. With the record and record calibrate controls properly adjusted, a 0 VU tone may be re-

303

THE TAPE-TO-HEAD INTERFACE

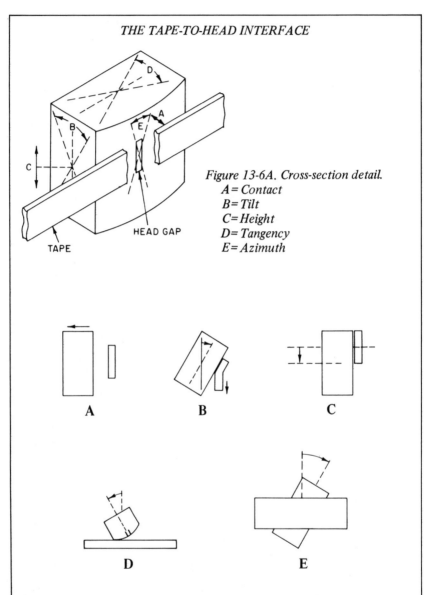

Figure 13-6A. Cross-section detail.
A = Contact
B = Tilt
C = Height
D = Tangency
E = Azimuth

TAPE

HEAD GAP

Figure 13-6B. Exaggerated misalignment of the tape head.
A. Contact — Tape does not make good contact with the head.
B. Tilt — Tape makes uneven contact with head, and may skew away from centerline.
C. Height — Head height is misadjusted.
D. Tangency — Tape does not make good contact with head gap.
E. Azimuth — Tape head is not perpendicular to tape path.

corded. With the meter switch in the playback (or repro) position, the meter should read 0 VU. If it does not, the playback output level control may be quickly adjusted until it does.

THE MECHANICAL SYSTEM

In order for the tape recorder system to function properly, the tape must remain in good physical contact with all three heads. The slightest misalignment may cause errors in level and response that may be incorrectly attributed to the electronics system.

Figure 13-6 illustrates five mechanical adjustments that may be required in the alignment of a head. They are:

A. **Tape-to-head contact.** The tape must, of course, remain in firm contact with the head at all times. Since the head is convex, a slight wrap around this surface will help maintain good contact.

B. **Tilt.** The pressure of the head against the tape must be distributed evenly across the entire tape width. If the head (or the tape) is not truly vertical, the contact pressure may be greater at one edge than at the other, resulting in a skewing of the tape away from the center line of the head.

C. **Height.** Head height must be properly adjusted so that each track is properly aligned with its corresponding head gap. A slight discrepancy between head heights may result in loss of output, inter-channel crosstalk, increased noise level and/or improper erasure.

D. **Tangency.** As part of the tape-to-head criteria, the tape must remain tangent to the head gap for optimum performance. An error in tangent adjustment may cause the tape to enter or leave the gap area prematurely.

E. **Azimuth.** Azimuth adjustments are particularly critical, especially in the case of short wavelength signals. If the head gap is not exactly perpendicular to the direction of tape travel, segments of the same recorded wavelength will enter and leave the gap at different increments of time, as shown in Figure 13-7. In the drawing, lines A and B represent an identical signal recorded on two tracks (or for that matter, A and B may be the edges of any one track). The sine waves represent the instantaneous amplitude of the signal(s). As shown, the head azimuth is misaligned and as a positive maximum passes over a line in the gap, a negative maximum passes over the same line.

305

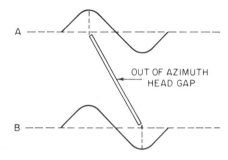

OUT OF AZIMUTH
HEAD GAP

Figure 13-7. An out-of-azimuth head gap. Different segments of the recorded wavelength cross the gap at the same time. A and B represent an identical signal recorded on two tracks.

Azimuth Alignment

Whether the illustration mentioned above represents a single track width, or two tracks that may eventually be combined, the total output will be zero. (In practice, a single track will rarely, if ever, cancel out completely, although two adjacent tracks that are out of azimuth will be severely attenuated when they are combined.)

In the case of some multi-track tape recorders, all head alignment adjustments have been made by the manufacturer and are permanently fixed. However, the heads on most machines with four or less tracks are user-adjustable. Generally, the head is held in place, and adjusted, with a series of screws, which may be seen in Figure 13-8. A properly installed head should not require repeated mechanical adjustments, with the exception of azimuth, which should be checked periodically as a matter of routine.

Use of the cathode ray oscilloscope—described in Chapter 2—is the preferred method of verifying azimuth alignment. In Figure 2-14, various 'scope displays were shown, to illustrate the phase and coherency relationships between two signals. Here, Figure 13-9 shows the 'scope display when a test tape is monitored on the oscilloscope. If the head azimuth is correctly aligned, an in-phase display will be seen, since there is zero phase shift between the two 'scope inputs. However, if the head is slightly off-azimuth, there will be a phase shift displayed on the 'scope.

Figure 13-9A (same as Figure 2-14C) indicates a properly aligned head, while the other 'scope displays indicate various amounts of phase shift, and therefore azimuth error. (The error in degrees refers to the phase shift, and not the angle of the head!)

When checking the alignment of an adjustable multi-track head, the azimuth of two adjacent tracks may be checked first, and then, successively, more distant tracks may be checked, one at a time.

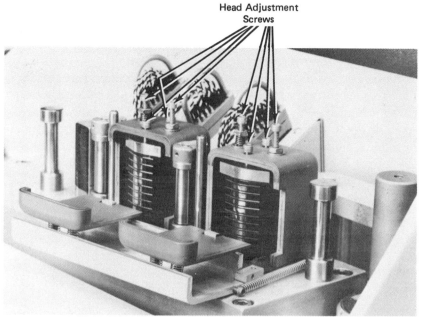

Figure 13-8. On many tape recorders, the heads are held in place with a series of screws, allowing the user to make head alignment adjustments.

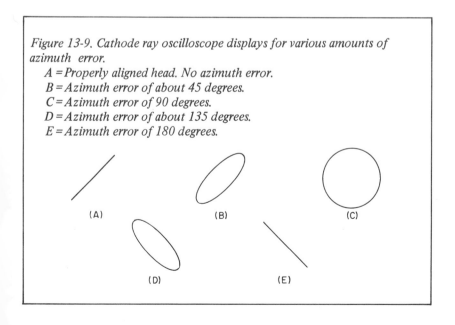

Figure 13-9. Cathode ray oscilloscope displays for various amounts of azimuth error.
A = Properly aligned head. No azimuth error.
B = Azimuth error of about 45 degrees.
C = Azimuth error of 90 degrees.
D = Azimuth error of about 135 degrees.
E = Azimuth error of 180 degrees.

307

Ideally, a single setting will bring all tracks into perfect alignment, but in practice this is often not the case. Within the head itself, the gaps may be slightly misaligned, making complete azimuth alignment of all tracks impossible.

As mentioned above, azimuth alignment becomes more critical as the frequency increases. Therefore, it is often a good idea to make coarse azimuth adjustments at 1,000 to 5,000 Hz, and then play the successively higher tones on the test tape while making finer adjustments. With this in mind, some test tapes are now prepared with the lowest tones first, so that progressively finer adjustments can be made as the machine's playback frequency response is being checked.

When the azimuth alignment procedure is completed, the azimuth should remain aligned over the entire audio bandwidth. If the scope display goes in and out of phase as the frequency is varied, the azimuth is improperly set.

Once the playback head azimuth is aligned, the record head may be aligned by observing the playback head output on the 'scope while recording a tone and adjusting the azimuth screw on the record head.

On machines with sync (record head) output capability, the test tape may be played while direct readings are made from the record head output.

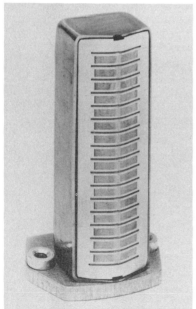

Figure 13-10. A representative example of a multi-track head stack. [Nortronics photo]

Section V
NOISE AND
NOISE REDUCTION

Introduction

Although noise was discussed briefly in Section IV, here the subject is covered in greater detail. Chapter 14 begins with a description of noise in its various forms, and then covers the basic principles upon which the well known studio noise reduction systems are based.

The several noise reduction systems now in popular studio use are incompatible. That is, a recording produced using one system will not play back properly through another. (Fortunately, this state of affairs does not exist in other types of studio hardware, such as tape recorders or recording consoles!)

Since the noise reduction system has become such an important part of the modern well equipped studio, Chapter 15 describes each of the popular commercially available systems separately.

The application of noise reduction is often referred to as **encoding** and **decoding**. For example, a tape that has been recorded using the Dolby Noise Reduction System is said to be "Dolby encoded." Later, when the tape is played back through a Dolby playback system, it is "decoded."

Frequently, the encoded tape is said to be "stretched", which in this case fortunately does not imply any physical abuse. As might be expected, the decoded tape is then "unstretched."

310

CHAPTER 14

Noise and Noise Reduction Principles

Noise, like music, is sound. However, unlike music, it is unwanted sound. For our purposes, we will ignore the fact that one man's music may be another man's noise, and concentrate on those noises that all may agree do not belong in the recording studio.

With care, some of these noises may be minimized or eliminated completely. Coughs, chair squeaks or the sounds of traffic outside the studio may be removed by editing, doing a re-take, or sound proofing the studio. However, there are not yet available any devices that will remove the sound of a chair squeak from a violin solo, or a falling music stand in front of a trombone. And, if a percussionist strikes the microphone instead of the instrument in front of him, the noise will be painfully obvious.

Other noises are a function of the recording medium itself. For example, it is all too well known that every component in the signal path, from microphone to amplifier, introduces a little noise into the system. This noise may be in the form of a hum resulting from faulty shielding, or a hiss from an amplifier output.

In a well functioning studio, the cumulative effect of all these noise makers should remain negligible, and the greatest noise source will probably be the magnetic tape itself. For even if a totally noise-less program could be recorded, on playback the tape will be found to contain modulation and asperity noises that weren't there before.

These noises are a by-product of the magnetic recording process, as was discussed earlier, in Chapter 11. Although some of the more recent advances in tape manufacture have impressively lowered them, they are not yet gone completely, and perhaps will never be totally removed.

But just as a loud thunderclap will momentarily block out the sound of falling rain, loud programs will effectively mask low level noise, and the listener will be entirely unaware of its presence. However, at lower levels, the program may not be loud enough to mask the noise and the listener will hear it along with the music.

Although asperity noise is often masked by the signal causing it, the increase in modulation noise may be apparent over the rest of the audio bandwidth. In fact, even during a rather loud passage of low frequency music, the program may not completely mask the noise present in the higher frequencies.

The Nature of Noise

Now since noise is sound, perhaps it might seem that it should have some particular frequency, or frequencies, associated with it. And indeed certain kinds of noise are identified by frequency. For example, the hum induced in poorly shielded cables is readily recognized as a 60 Hz tone. Rumble, either in a studio building or on a turntable, may also have a measurable center frequency.

But what of the ever present tape hiss? The term "hiss" suggests that this particular noise is a high pitched, or hissy, sound. And there are other quite similar sounds, or rather, noises. Amplifier noise and the noise between stations on an FM radio are not at all unlike the sound of tape hiss.

White Noise

All three are a form of **white noise**. The term is analagous to white light—light containing energy at all wavelengths, such as sunlight. When passed through a prism, white light is dispersed into hundreds of equal intensity hues, each representing the light energy at a particular wave length. Likewise, white noise contains equal sound energy at each frequency within the audio bandwidth.

But despite the equal energy present at each and every audio frequency, white noise is thought of as being a hissy, or high pitched sound. This is because each successively higher octave contains twice as many discrete frequencies as the octave just below it. For example, the octave that begins at 1,000 Hz (1,000 to 2,000 Hz), contains 1,000 discrete frequencies; that is, twice the number as in the octave that ends at 1,000 Hz (500 to 1,000 Hz). (By definition, the octave is the interval between *any* two frequencies, f_1 and f_2, when $f_2 = 2f_1$)

Therefore, any octave contains twice the energy of the octave immediately below it, and so seems louder. The higher (louder) octaves mask the sound energy of the lower ones, and the ear hears a

sound aptly described as hiss. However, there is definitely low frequency energy, or noise, present with tape hiss.

Pink Noise

With white noise, the doubling of energy per octave signifies a
power gain of 3 dB/8va. Although generated white noise is often
used in acoustic measurements, it is often more meaningful to make
use of a wide band noise source that maintains a constant energy
level per octave. This may be realized by inserting a 3 dB/8va filter
after the white noise generator, thus cancelling its inherent 3 dB/8va
rise. This filtered white noise is known as **pink noise**. White and pink
noise energy spectra are illustrated in Figure 14-1.

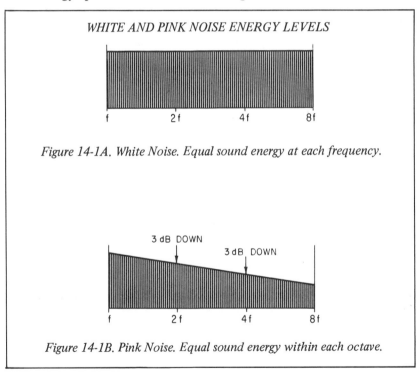

WHITE AND PINK NOISE ENERGY LEVELS

Figure 14-1A. White Noise. Equal sound energy at each frequency.

Figure 14-1B. Pink Noise. Equal sound energy within each octave.

Residual (or Quiescent) Noise Level

The residual **noise level** of a device is its output level in the
absence of an applied signal at the input. With a sensitive meter, a
very small voltage may be read, which represents the amount of
white noise present in the system.

Recording consoles, amplifiers, and tape recorders will usually include within their specifications some reference to a residual noise level. For example, a tape recorder may have a noise level of -65 dB. Obviously, this means that the noise voltage is 65 dB below some reference level. Sometimes, in the race for better and better specifications, the reference level is not clearly stated; therefore the same noise level may be quoted as -65 dB (65 dB below zero reference level) or perhaps as -73 dB (73 dB below the peak record level of a particular type of magnetic tape). Uncommonly low noise level specifications should be regarded with suspicion until the actual reference level can be determined with certainty.

It should be understood that the noise level of a tape recorder represents the output voltage level when the machine is on, but not running. If a roll of bulk erased tape is now played, the measured noise level will be somewhat higher, and when the machine is placed in the record mode — still with no input signal applied — the noise level will again increase.

Signal-to-Noise Ratios

Noise measurements are often discussed in terms of a signal-to-noise ratio (abbr. s/n). Since a ratio is either a fraction (2/5, 1/4, etc.) or a comparison of two quantities (4 to 3, 10 to 1, etc.), it might seem that a signal-to-noise ratio should include two values, one for the signal — another for the noise.

For example, if the level of our reference signal is +4 dB, and the noise level is measured at -65 dB, we might expect to find the signal-to-noise ratio written as +4 dB/-65 dB. This fractional format suggests that some sort of division is possible, but, since decibel values cannot be divided directly, they must first be converted into voltages (or powers, if more convenient). The equivalent voltages are: +4 dB = 1.226 volts; -65 dB = 0.435 millivolts. Therefore:

$$s/n = \frac{+4 \text{ dB}}{-65 \text{ dB}} = \frac{1.226 \text{ v.}}{.435 \times 10^{-3} \text{ v.}} = 2.818 \times 10^3$$

Now although 2.818×10^3 is a mathematically correct signal-to-noise ratio, it is not of much practical use to the recording engineer who is concerned with the decibel difference between signal and noise. The decibel quantity equal to $20 \log 2.818 \times 10^3$ is a more useful figure.

$$N_{dB} = 20 \log s/n = 20 \log (2.818 \times 10^3) = 69 \text{ dB}$$

Because of the nature of the log, it will be noted that 69 dB is the simple arithmetic difference between +4 dB and -65 dB and it tells us exactly what we wish to know: how much below the reference signal level is the noise level?

So, although this decibel value is really twenty times the log of the signal-to-noise ratio, in practice it has come to be popularly known simply as the signal-to-noise ratio. As in other popular mis-uses of terminology, little harm is done, provided the engineer is not confused by the practice.

INTRODUCTION TO NOISE REDUCTION

Good engineering practice demands that noise levels be kept as low as possible. Particularly in multi-track recording, the engineer must be concerned with the gradual increase in noise level as many tracks are mixed together to create a stereo master tape.

It is a common procedure to record each individual track at a high level, regardless of the eventual track-to-track balance. For example, a background vocal track may be recorded at maximum level, so that it is as far above the noise level as possible. During mixdown, the track will be mixed in at a lower level, to create the balance required. Of course as the track is lowered in level, the noise level is also reduced, helping to keep the total noise level within reason.

The practice is not without its hazards, since it is very easy to exceed safe levels while recording. Particularly while observing percussive instruments on volume indicators, an apparently safe recording level may actually be causing severe distortion as high level peaks drive the tape into saturation. Yet, if the track is recorded at a more conservative level, the noise may be quite noticeable.

NOISE REDUCTION DEVICES

Although signal processing devices are usually thought of as a means of altering the signal to produce a desired effect, there are now available several such devices whose sole purpose is to reduce the noise level without audibly affecting the quality of the signal itself. Basically, these noise reduction devices may be classified as static or dynamic, and as complementary or non-complementary devices.

Static and Dynamic Signal Processors

The terms, **static** and **dynamic**, refer to the way in which a noise reduction device (or any other device, for that matter) reacts to the signal passing through it. An equalizer is a static device; that is, its settings do not change once they have been set by the engineer. On the other hand, a limiter reacts to the program and is therefore considered to be a dynamic device.

Complementary and Non-Complementary Signal Processors

In a complementary system, some processing is done before recording, with equal and opposite (complementary) processing done on playback. In a tape recorder, pre- and post-emphasis might be considered as a complementary equalization process.

In a non-complementary system, processing is done only once, either before or after recording. The signal processing devices discussed in Section III are all non-complementary devices.

A brief discussion of noise reduction devices falling into the categories listed above follows.

Static, Non-Complementary Noise Reduction

In its simplest form, noise reduction may consist of a filter, adjusted to attenuate the frequency band in which the noise is found. Such filters may be marginally effective, for with the exception of a few noise sources (60 Hz hum, for example), most noise is wide band, that is, it exists over all, or most of, the audio spectrum.

Filtering also affects the signal frequencies as well as the noise. In the case of a very low frequency cut-off filter—to minimize rumble (building or turntable)—the effect on the program may be negligible. But in most other cases, the filter becomes musically objectionable long before the noise is removed.

Static, Complementary Noise Reduction

In another form of noise reduction, high frequency boost is applied before recording in an effort to keep these frequencies well above the noise level. Then during playback, a complementary roll-off restores the high end to normal, while lowering the tape noise level.

316

This form of noise reduction may also be minimally effective. The high end pre-emphasis puts these frequencies just that much closer to the saturation point of the tape. Therefore, if the program has a significant amount of high frequency energy already, the overall record level will probably have to be lowered, negating any noise reduction advantage. For many typical musical programs, the pre- and post-emphasis in the tape recorder itself furnishes about as much of this type of noise reduction as is practical.

Both of the above examples of noise reduction are called static, since their noise reduction properties are fixed; that is, the nature of the program in no way affects the action of the filter or of the pre/post-emphasis.

Dynamic, Non-Complementary Noise Reduction

The expander may be considered as a dynamic non-complementary noise reduction device. The expansion threshold may be set just above the residual noise level. Therefore, as the signal falls below threshold, the system gain is reduced, sharply attenuating both signal and noise. As another way of looking at the same action, a gradually increasing low level input signal is quickly boosted above the noise level. Higher level inputs (above threshold) follow the unity gain slope.

Expanders are frequently used as noise gates, to attenuate a microphone line, or tape recorder output, in the absence of a program signal. However, since the device is reacting to overall program level, there is always the risk that very low level signals will be lost if they fall much below the expander's threshold point. Therefore, as a noise reduction device, the expander must be used with caution. Its effectiveness varies greatly, according to the nature of the program being treated. For a more detailed discussion of the expander's operating characteristics, see Chapter 8.

A compressor, too, might be considered in the same category of noise reduction. By compressing the dynamic range of the program, the overall gain may be brought up, thereby raising the lower level segments above the noise, while preventing peaks from saturating the tape.

However, both expansion and compression generally leave something to be desired in the area of noise reduction. The signal processing effects of either device become noticeably audible long before any significant noise reduction has been accomplished. Therefore, while compressors and expanders are valuable studio tools, they are—with the exception of the noise gate—rarely considered for noise reduction.

Dynamic Complimentary Noise Reduction—Companders

As just described, neither the compressor nor the expander is an effective noise reducer. However, a complementary combination of the two devices may achieve a degree of noise reduction not anticipated by observing the characteristics of either unit used alone.

The compressor/expander combination is termed a **compander**, and it is the basic principle behind the operation of several commercially available noise reduction systems. Noise reduction technique has not become standardized, and the various systems currently in existence are not compatible. That is, a tape that has been recorded using one system will not be played back properly on another system. Due to the impact of noise reduction systems within the recording system, the various systems will be described in the next chapter in some detail.

CHAPTER 15

Studio Noise Reduction Systems

Introduction to The dbx Noise Reduction System

In theory, the compressor/expander (compander) noise reduction system is reasonably straightforward, though in practice some highly sophisticated circuitry is required. To help understand the basic principles, consider a musical program with a dynamic range of 100 dB, and a recording medium whose maximum dynamic range is 75 dB. A simple compressor with a 100:75 (that is, 4:3) compression ratio will keep the high level program peaks at or below 75 dB. However, as pointed out in Chapter 8, such compression will also attenuate low level signals, placing them even further below the residual noise level. As a noise reducer, the system doesn't look promising. After recording, we may recover our 100 dB dynamic range with a complementary expander (3:4 ratio), but the expansion will bring up the noise level along with the program. A more likely approach would be to select a convenient compressor rotation point so that input levels above this point would be reduced in level, while levels below the rotation point would be raised, thereby bringing them up somewhat above the noise level.

dbx Noise Reduction System

The dbx Noise Reduction System uses a compander similar to the one just described. However, certain refinements have been made in order to minimize the audible effects of compression and expansion. In the basic compander system, the noise level continually varies according to the degree of expansion in the playback circuit. Now, although the ear eventually may disregard a steady level of noise, a fluctuating one—even at low level—becomes a distraction. And, as mentioned earlier in the chapter, hiss may be quite audible when the program is primarily in the lower frequency range. Therefore, al-

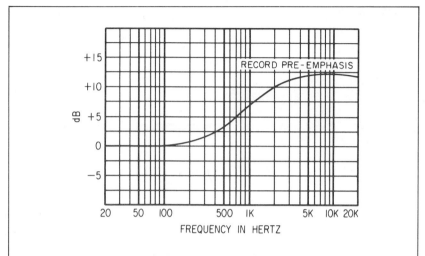

Figure 15-1. The 12 dB high frequency pre-emphasis in the dbx system's record circuit.

though the basic compander may allow us a greater dynamic range, its noise reduction capabilities require improvement.

In the dbx system, that improvement is realized by a 12 dB high frequency pre- and post-emphasis network. High frequencies are boosted before recording (Figure 15-1) and then attenuated on playback. Since tape noise occurs after the pre-emphasis, the post-emphasis reduces the noise, while restoring the normal frequency balance.

If the tape's saturation and self-erasing characteristics could be ignored, this high frequency pre- and post-emphasis might be the extent of the noise reduction system. High frequencies would be boosted above the hiss before recording, and then returned to normal on playback, with the resultant post-emphasis dropping the hiss level below audibility. However, in the presence of any sort of high frequency program material, the dbx's considerable high end boost will certainly drive the tape into saturation. To prevent this, the level-sensing circuit in its compressor (record mode) contains an additional high frequency boost. Consequently, when the program contains high frequency components, the compressor over-reacts and in effect works against the program pre-emphasis by bringing the entire level down, thereby keeping the boosted high frequencies from overloading the tape.

Actually, when the program contains a substantial amount of high level/high frequency information, protection against hiss is unnecessary, since it will be masked by the music itself. Only when the high frequency content of the program is slight will the hiss be noticeable, and here the pre/post emphasis effectively reduces it.

Figure 15-2 is a block diagram of the dbx record/playback system, and Figure 15-3 is a graph of the compressor/expander functions. On the graph, a program with a 100 dB dynamic range is applied to the dbx system's input. In the record mode, the system functions as a compressor with a 2:1 compression ratio. The program's -80 dB to +20 dB range is compressed to -40 dB to +10 dB. As a result, low level program is raised above the noise level of the tape, while high level peaks are kept below the saturation point.

When the compressed program is played back, the dbx functions as an expander, as shown in Figure 15-3B. The dynamic range is restored to 100 dB, and the -60 dB noise level is reproduced at -120 dB.

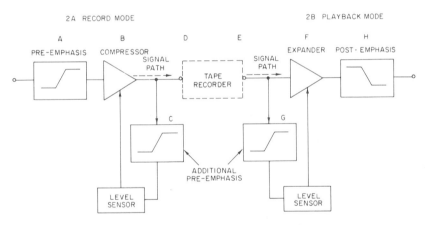

Figure 15-2. Block Diagram of the dbx Noise Reduction System.
A. High frequency equalization boost is applied to input signals.
B. Input signal is compressed.
C. Significant high frequency components cause greater amounts of compression due to additional pre-emphasis in the level sensing circuit.
D. Input signal is recorded.
E. Output signal is reproduced.
F. Output signal is expanded.
G. Significant high frequency components cause greater amount of expansion.
H. High frequency equalization attenuation restores original flat frequency response of program.

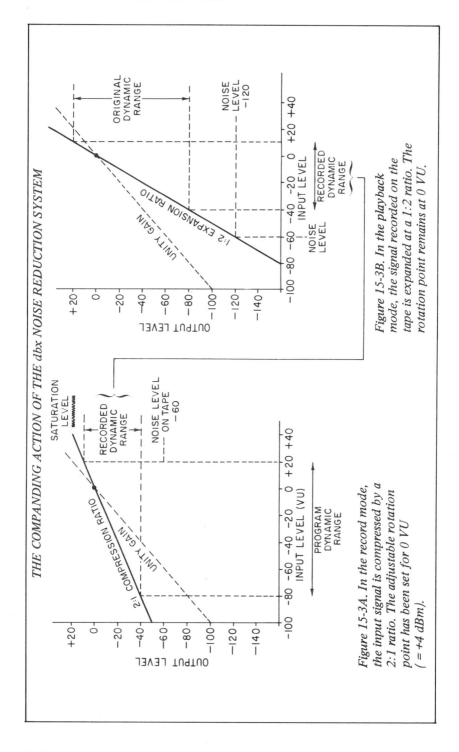

THE COMPANDING ACTION OF THE dbx NOISE REDUCTION SYSTEM

Figure 15-3A. In the record mode, the input signal is compressed by a 2:1 ratio. The adjustable rotation point has been set for 0 VU (= +4 dBm).

Figure 15-3B. In the playback mode, the signal recorded on the tape is expanded at a 1:2 ratio. The rotation point remains at 0 VU.

Headroom Improvement

Note that the compressor reduces input levels that lie above the rotation point. Therefore, higher level output signals from the console may be handled by the tape recorder. Although the magnetic capacity of the tape has not improved, the dbx expander restores the compressed high level signals to their original value, thus improving the tape's apparent headroom capabilities.

Figure 15-4 is a partial listing of the dbx Noise Reduction System's specifications. Note that the specifications claim 10 dB noise reduction *on signals with dominant energy below 500 Hz.* This type of signal takes full advantage of the system's pre- and post-emphasis circuit, since most of its musical energy lies below the high frequency equalization boost that was shown in Figure 15-1.

The specifications also claim varying amounts of additional noise reduction, depending on the level of the input signal. This may be seen from Figure 15-5, which shows that the dbx's compressor raises the input levels cited in the specifications by 10, 20, and 30 dB, respectively. Therefore, the complimentary playback expander will lower these levels the same amount, simultaneously reducing the noise level by 10, 20, or 30 dB.

Reduction of noise added to the signal by the tape recorder	At +4 dBm signal level, hiss and high frequency modulation noise are reduced by 10 dB on signals with dominant energy below 500 Hz.
	At -16 dBm signal level there is an additional 10 dBm of noise reduction.
	At -36 dBm signal level there is an addition 20 dB of noise reduction.
	At -56 dBm input level there is an additional 30 dB of noise reduction.
	At -76 dBm input level there is a total of about 40 dB noise reduction.

Figure 15-4. dbx Noise Reduction System specifications.

The Burwen Noise Eliminator

The Burwen Noise Eliminator System is similar to the dbx system in that pre-emphasis and compression in the record mode are followed by expansion and post-emphasis in the playback mode. In the

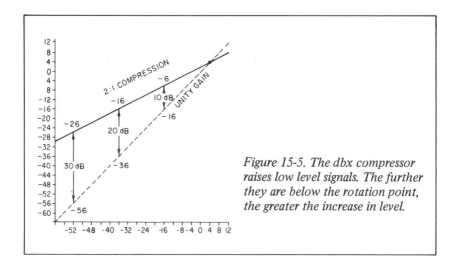

Figure 15-5. The dbx compressor raises low level signals. The further they are below the rotation point, the greater the increase in level.

Burwen system however, there is a pre-emphasis equalization boost of both low and high frequencies, as shown in Figure 15-6. Unlike the dbx system, there is no additional pre-emphasis in the level sensing circuit. And the Burwen system compression ratio (record mode) is 3:1, as shown in Figure 15-7. For comparison, the dbx compression ratio is also shown in the figure.

Note that the dbx and Burwen compression ratios intersect at an input level of about -85 dB. Therefore, input levels above this point

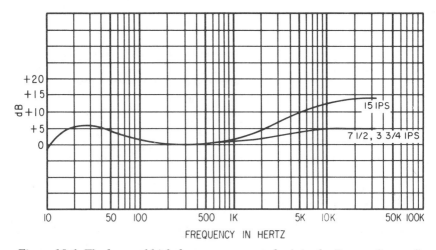

Figure 15-6. The low and high frequency pre-emphasis in the Burwen System's record circuit. (compare with the dbx System shown in Figure 15-1)

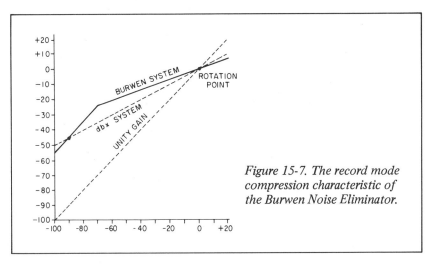

Figure 15-7. The record mode compression characteristic of the Burwen Noise Eliminator.

are boosted somewhat more by the Burwen system. For example, a -60 dB input level will supply a -30 dB output from the dbx compressor, and a -20 dB output from the Burwen system. When these signals are later restored by their complementary playback mode expanders, the Burwen system reduces the gain, and therefore the noise, by 10 dB more than the dbx system. As can be seen in Figure 15-7, this difference varies with input level, and at levels below the intersection, the dbx system supplies more gain reduction. [Production of this noise reduction system has recently been discontinued by the manufacturer.]

The Burwen Noise Filter

Unlike the other noise reduction systems described in this chapter, the Burwen Noise Filter is a dynamic non-complementary device. It functions as a combination high- and low-frequency roll-off filter. At normal program levels, the frequency response of the noise filter is flat; however, as the program level decreases, the filters gradually attenuate the high and low ends of the audio spectrum. The filters are controlled by the level and frequency content of the program, and take advantage of the fact that in many cases instruments playing softly do not produce as many overtones as the same instruments played somewhat louder. Therefore, quieter musical passages may not require a wide bandwidth audio system for satisfactory reproduction.

As noted earlier, tape hiss is particularly noticeable when high fre-

325

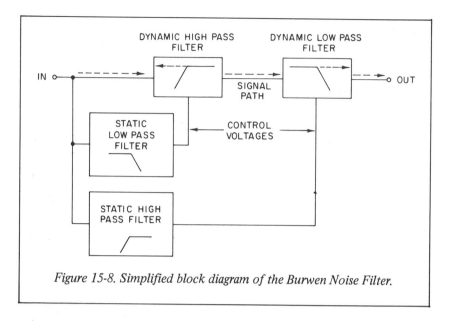

Figure 15-8. Simplified block diagram of the Burwen Noise Filter.

quency program is lacking; therefore as program level diminishes, more and more high frequency attenuation is applied to the signal path. A similar filtering action also takes place at low frequencies.

Figure 15-8 illustrates the basic operation of the noise filter. The applied audio signal is passed through a high- and low-pass filter. Unlike the filters described in Chapter 7, the actual cut-off frequency of these dynamic filters varies according to the program content. Each filter is controlled by a voltage derived from a static filter, as shown in the figure.

The static low-pass filter produces a control voltage proportional to the low frequency content of the program. As the low frequency content increases, the control voltage shifts the dynamic high-pass filter's cut-off point progressively lower.

The static high-pass filter performs a similar function. A high level/high frequency program will shift the cut-off frequency of the dynamic low-pass filter progressively higher.

In the presence of a wide range/high level program, the cut-off frequencies are at 12 Hz, and 37,000 Hz. In effect, the filters are out of the circuit, since these cut-off frequencies are well beyond the audio bandwidth. As the frequency/level content at either end of the audio bandwidth diminishes, the filter cut-off frequencies move inwards until at no signal, the low and high frequency cut-offs are at 400 Hz and 1,200 Hz respectively. Figure 15-9 illustrates the resultant vari-

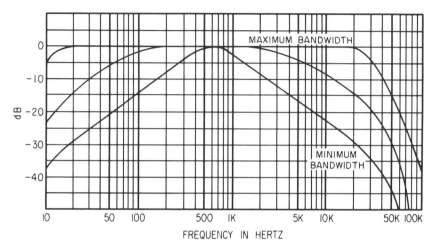

Figure 15-9. The variable bandwidth characteristics of the Burwen Noise Filter.

able bandwidth of the system. From Figures 15-8 and 15-9, it should be seen that the bandwidth of the Burwen Noise Filter varies according to program content. When the program lacks significant energy at either frequency extreme, the system bandwidth is accordingly reduced, thereby filtering out the residual noise level of the recording medium. As the bandwidth of the program increases — thereby masking the noise level — the frequency response of the system likewise increases.

The Dolby Type 'A' Noise Reduction System

Unlike the dbx and Burwen Noise Reduction Systems, the Dolby system does not react to high level program. In the former systems, high as well as low levels are compressed before recording and expanded later on, during playback.

The Dolby system takes into account the fact that compression and expansion actions are most likely to be audible at high levels and that noise reduction is unnecessary once the program level is sufficient to mask the background noise. Accordingly, the noise reduction is restricted to low level signals only.

Figure 15-10A is a simplified description of the basic principle of the Dolby system in the record mode. To explain how the system works, consider a very low level input signal, with a value of, say, 2.5 millivolts (about -50 dB). This input signal is routed, a) via a com-

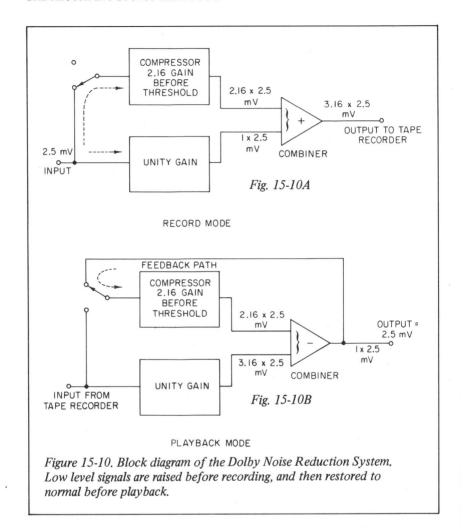

Figure 15-10. Block diagram of the Dolby Noise Reduction System. Low level signals are raised before recording, and then restored to normal before playback.

pressor in the side chain, and b), directly, to a combining amplifier. The compressor's gain-before-threshold is 2.16. Therefore, low level signal voltages through the compressor are multiplied by 2.16. Via the direct path, the signal is multiplied by 1 (unity gain). At the summing amplifier, the two signals add to produce an output voltage that is 3.16 (= 2.16 + 1) times the input voltage. Therefore, the dB gain of the system is:

$$N_{dB} = 20 \log \frac{\text{Output}}{\text{Input}} = 20 \log \frac{3.16 \times 2.5 \text{ millivolts}}{2.5 \text{ millivolts}} = 20 \log 3.16 =$$

$$20 \times 0.49968 = 10 \text{ dB}$$

In other words, the low level signal has been amplified by 10 dB.

As the input level is increased beyond threshold, its gain through the compressor is reduced, and the compressor's output contributes less and less to the summing amplifier. By the time the input signal has increased to -10 dB, the system has become a simple unity gain device, since the compressor's contribution to the summing amplifier is now negligible compared to the direct path.

In the playback mode, the compressor is placed in a feedback path, as seen in Figure 15-10B, and its output is combined subtractively with the direct signal; that is, with the boosted low level signal that was recorded on the tape. If the feedback path were not there, the system's output would equal the input, since the combining amplifier itself is a unity gain device. However, the feedback loop reduces the overall system gain, in this case by the amount of gain through the compressor.

The principles of feedback require a textbook of their own, but we may get a fair idea of the nature of this type of circuit if we can assume, for the moment, that the output of the combining amplifier is 2.5 millivolts. Therefore, the input to the compressor is also 2.5 millivolts. The compressor's gain-before-threshold remains at 2.16; consequently, its output is 2.16 x 2.5 millivolts. This output, combined subtractively with the direct input signal that was boosted earlier to 3.16 x 2.5 millivolts, gives us a system output of (3.16 - 2.16) x 2.5 millivolts = 1 x 2.5 = 2.5 millivolts. The playback mode system has thus attenuated the recorded signal back to 1 x 2.5 millivolts, that is, to its original value.

This brief analysis leaves many questions about feedback unanswered. For example, we have assumed that the playback mode output is what we want it to be (2.5 mV), and then used this value in the feedback path to the compressor, after which it is subtracted from the unity gain signal. Despite this superficial explanation of the feedback system, it should show that in the playback mode the Dolby Noise Reduction System restores low level signals to their original value by lowering the system gain, and therefore the accompanying noise level, by 10 dB.

As in the record mode, higher level signals routed through the side chain are compressed; as the signal level increases, the compressor's gain decreases, and it contributes less and less to the total output. Once more, by the time the program input level has reached -10 dB, the compressor's output is negligible, with respect to the direct path signal.

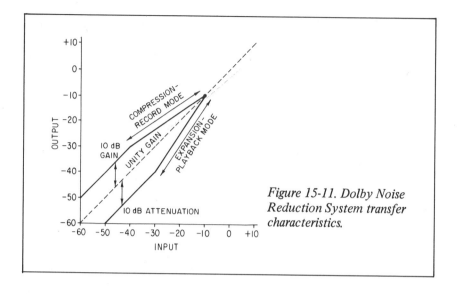

Figure 15-11. Dolby Noise Reduction System transfer characteristics.

Figure 15-11 is a graph of the Dolby system transfer characteristics in both the record and playback modes. The graphs summarize the noise reduction action; in the record mode, low level signals are boosted by 10 dB, while higher level signals are passed at unity gain. In the playback mode, the boosted low level signals are attenuated to the original level, while once again the higher level signals are passed at unity gain.

Note that even though the side chain remains a compressor, its subtractive combination with the direct signal produces an expansion characteristic in the playback mode.

From a study of the graph, it will be seen that the compression/expansion action takes place over a relatively small segment of the total dynamic range. Therefore, much of the signal is unaffected by the companding action.

To further reduce the audible effects of companding, the audio bandwidth is split into four sections, each of which is separately compressed and expanded. Above 5,000 Hz, the companding characteristic increases gradually, until at 15,000 Hz and above, there is 15 dB of noise reduction.

The four frequency bands are:
1. 80 Hz—low pass.
2. 80 Hz—3,000 Hz—band pass.
3. 3,000 Hz—high pass.
4. 9,000 Hz—high pass.

The selection of these bands takes into account the fact that at low-to-moderate program levels, most of the music may lie within the 80 Hz to 3,000 Hz band, with much less energy found at higher (and lower) frequencies. Therefore, the full noise reduction capability may continue in operation in the high frequency (above 3,000 Hz) ranges, keeping tape hiss at a minimum. This is somewhat like the action of the Burwen Noise Filter, which restricts the bandwidth when program signal conditions permit.

The Dolby type 'B' Noise Reduction System

A simplified version of the Dolby Noise Reduction System is available in many consumer tape recorders. Known as the 'B' system, it is a single band device, affecting only the high frequency portion of the audio spectrum. Its function is to reduce the most audible (high frequency) portion of tape noise.

Recently, the 'B' system has been put into use by several FM radio stations, which use the system in the record mode, thereby transmitting a Dolby B-encoded signal. The listener uses his Dolby decoder to restore the signal to normal, while at the same time lowering the level of the broadcast's transmission noise.

TRACKING ERRORS

When a dynamic complementary noise reduction system is used, it is particularly important that the tape recorder's electronics are properly aligned. In the playback mode, the noise reduction system's expander restores the recorded signal to its proper level and frequency response, while the noise level is brought down. For optimum operation, the tape recorder itself must be well aligned so that the expander does not react to errors of gain or frequency response within the tape recorder. If the noise reduction system's output does not match the original input, the deviation is known as a **tracking error**.

The dbx System

Figure 15-12, Table 1, shows the effect of a 5 dB gain error within the tape recorder. The input levels in Column A are compressed and recorded at the levels shown in Column B. However, due to an alignment error, the machine's output level is 5 dB down, as shown in

A System Input	B Recorded	C Played Back	D System Output	A System Input	B Recorded	C Played Back	D System Output
- 50	- 25	- 30	- 60	- 50	- 40	- 45	- 55
- 45	- 22.5	- 27.5	- 55	- 45	- 35	- 40	- 50
- 40	- 20	- 25	- 50	- 40	- 30	- 35	- 45
- 35	- 17.5	- 22.5	- 45	- 35	- 27	- 32	- 42
- 30	- 15	- 20	- 40	- 30	- 23	- 28	- 37.5
- 25	- 12.5	- 17.5	- 35	- 25	- 20	- 25	- 32.5
- 20	- 10	- 15	- 30	- 20	- 17	- 22	- 28
- 15	- 7.5	- 12.5	- 25	- 15	- 13	- 18	- 22.5
- 10	- 5	- 10	- 20	- 10	- 10	- 15	- 17.5
- 5	- 2.5	- 7.5	- 15	- 5	- 5	- 10	- 10
0	0	- 5	- 10	0	0	- 5	- 5
+ 5	+ 2.5	- 2.5	- 5	+ 5	+ 5	0	0
+10	+ 5	0	0	+10	+10	+ 5	+ 5
+15	+ 7.5	+ 2.5	+ 5	+15	+15	+10	+10
+20	+10	+ 5	+10	+20	+20	+15	+15

(Table 2 rows -35 through -10 bracketed as TRACKING ERROR)

Table 1
dbx System

Table 2
Dolby System

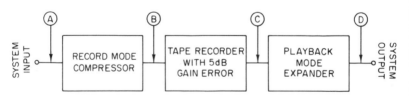

Figure 15-12. The results of a gain error at the tape recorder.
A = input levels, applied to the compressor.
B = resultant levels applied to the tape recorder.
C = tape output levels: all are 5dB down, due to a misalignment
of the tape recorder electronics.
D = resultant output levels from the expander.
(dbx levels are taken from Figure 15-3.
Dolby levels are taken from Figure 15-11)

Column C. Consequently the expander outputs are as listed in Column D. Notice that the system output is consistently down 10 dB, as compared to the input levels.

This gain error is double the gain error of the tape recorder, but is constant over the entire dynamic range. Therefore, there is no tracking error, since later on a simple gain adjustment could be made at any time to bring the level up 10 dB. Of course, the noise level would also come up by 10 dB, but the tape would not otherwise be affected.

However, if the error was one of equalization rather than of overall level, the equalization error would be doubled while the rest of the bandwidth would be properly reproduced. This type of tracking error would be quite noticeable, and extremely difficult to correct later on.

The Burwen Noise Eliminator

As in the dbx system, the Burwen system is tolerant of overall gain errors within the tape recorder, but extremely sensitive to equalization errors. With either system, it is extremely important that tape recorder equalization be as flat as possible.

The Dolby Noise Reduction System

Since the Dolby system's companding action affects only a small portion of the program's dynamic range, tracking errors will be confined, as seen in Figure 15-12, Table 2. Although the tracking error is less than the tape recorder's gain error, it cannot be corrected later on since it is not consistent over the entire program dynamic range.

The Dolby system is more tolerant of equalization errors since the tracking error is confined—as just noted—to a small portion of the dynamic range of the program.

Dolby Level

Since the Dolby system is sensitive to gain errors within the tape recorder, any such errors must be eliminated before playing back the tape through the Dolby expander. Since there are several "standard reference levels" in popular usage at this time, it is important that all Dolby-encoded tapes contain a Dolby level tone at the beginning for Dolby alignment purposes. This tone may be at any convenient reference level, so long as it matches the level at which the recording was made. When the tape is played back later, the tone is used to verify the input level to the Dolby expander. If the tone does not line up with the Dolby level marker on the Dolby meter panel, the tape recorder output level control (or the Dolby input level control) must be adjusted before playing the tape.

A Dolby level tone is particularly important on tapes that may be sent to other studios, where a different standard reference level is used. By aligning the system to the Dolby level tone recorded on the tape, tracking errors may be eliminated.

SUMMARY OF NOISE REDUCTION SYSTEMS

With the exception of the Burwen Noise Filter, the noise reduction systems described in this chapter are all based on the compander principle; compression before recording, followed by expansion on playback. The gain of low level signals is raised so that they are recorded above the noise level of the recording medium. On playback, the low level signals are restored to their normal level, while the gain reduction reduces the noise level by the same amount.

In the record mode, the dbx Noise Reduction System and Burwen Noise Eliminator compressors reduce high level signals, thus increasing the apparent headroom of the recording medium.

The Dolby system affects only a small section of the total dynamic range, and takes into account that high level program adequately masks the residual noise level of the recording medium.

The Burwen Noise Filter is a dynamic non-complimentary device, which varies the playback bandwidth according to the frequency/level content of the program.

In the majority of cases, the recording medium is magnetic tape, although both the dbx and Burwen systems are available in disc versions and the Dolby system has recently been adapted for use in the motion picture industry. Representative production models of each of the noise reduction systems described in this chapter are shown in Figures 15-13, -14, -15.

Due to the significant differences between the various noise reduction systems, a tape encoded in one system may not be decoded with another system's playback unit. Thus, a dbx-encoded recording will play back improperly through either a Burwen or Dolby playback system, and *vice versa.*

If an encoded tape is played back with no complementary noise

THE dbx NOISE REDUCTION SYSTEM

Figure 15-13A. Four channels of the dbx Noise Reduction System. (dbx 187) [dbx photo]

Figure 15-13B. The dbx System in a 16 track format. (dbx 216) [dbx photo]

335

THE BURWEN NOISE REDUCTION SYSTEM

Figure 15-14A. The Burwen Noise Eliminator.
(Burwen 2000) [Burwen photo]

Figure 15-14B. The Burwen Noise Filter; a dynamic, non-complementary
noise reduction system.
(Burwen DNF-1100) [Burwen photo]

THE DOLBY NOISE REDUCTION SYSTEM

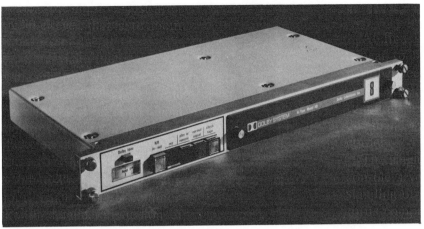

Figure 15-15A. A single channel of the Dolby System.
(Dolby 361) [Dolby photo]

Figure 15-15B. The Dolby System
in a 16 channel format.
(Dolby M16H) [Dolby photo]

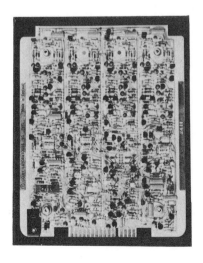

Figure 15-15C. a plug-in card with
one channel of noise reduction
electronics.
(Dolby cat.-22) [Dolby photo]

reduction system, or with the wrong system, its dynamic range and frequency response will be distorted; the degree of distortion depending on the original dynamic range of the program.

Noise reduction systems are often designed with an automatic switching function that inserts the system in the line to the tape recorder during recording and in the playback line at all other times. Thus, the same noise reduction device performs dual functions, though not at the same time. Although obviously an economic advantage, the arrangement prevents the engineer from properly monitoring the tape while recording. However, this slight operating limitation is usually more than offset by the economy of the dual function system.

Section VI
RECORDING CONSOLES

Introduction

At first glance, the up-to-date multi-track recording console may appear to be a hopeless maze of knobs and switches cluttering the path between microphone and tape recorder. Yet despite its apparent complexity, the console is essentially a collection of similar control functions, repeated over and over again, to give the engineer a greater command over each input from the studio, and output to the tape recorder.

The single chapter of this section actually discusses the recording console several times; at first briefly, to give the reader an understanding of its basic functions. Then, each section is broken down into its component parts, which are described in greater detail. Finally, various secondary signal paths are introduced, and our examination of the complete console is at last concluded.

CHAPTER 16

The Modern Recording Studio Console

Under some circumstances, a completely satisfactory recording may be made by simply plugging a microphone directly into a mic level input on a tape recorder. Particularly in the case of a single stereo microphone and a two-track tape recorder, there may be little point in inserting any type of intermediate control device in the signal path. The stereo microphone "hears" what the concert hall listener would hear and this information is directly transferred to tape. Given a well balanced musical ensemble, playing in an acoustically satisfactory environment, an excellent recording may be made in this manner. (For a longer discussion of microphone techniques, see Chapter 4.)

However, for the majority of contemporary recording situations, somewhat more flexibility may be required, and a recording console becomes a necessity. The console may be nothing more than a combining network, where several microphone inputs are mixed together to provide one, or perhaps two, outputs to a tape recorder. At the other extreme, the console may be capable of mixing, in a seemingly endless number of combinations, the outputs of dozens of microphones, and may have perhaps 24 channels of outputs.

In either case, the console becomes an intermediate control point between microphone(s) and tape recorder. Regardless of the apparent complexity of a modern multi-track recording console, it may be analyzed as a combination of three major control sections, each of which is—for ease of operation—further divided into smaller sub-sections.

The three sections, shown in Figure 16-1, are:

1. **Input Section** (inputs to the console, from microphone and tape recorder lines)

2. **Output Section** (outputs from the console, to the tape recorder)

3. **Monitor Section** (observation and measurement of all signals, via meters, loudspeakers, and headphones)

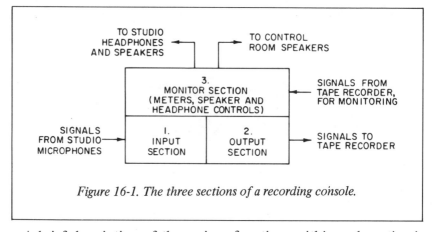

Figure 16-1. The three sections of a recording console.

A brief description of the various functions within each section is given here. This will be followed by more detailed explanations of each component part within the total signal path from microphone to tape recorder.

THE BASIC RECORDING CONSOLE
1. INPUT SECTION

Input Signal Processing

Each signal arriving at the console from a microphone in the studio may be processed individually before being combined with other input signals. Most consoles provide some form of built-in equalization facility within each input signal path, since this form of signal processing is so frequently required. Usually, other types of signal processing devices may be inserted in the input signal path, via patch cords, as required.

Input Signal Level Control

The level of each input signal may be adjusted as required. In the case of several signals that are to be mixed together within the console, the individual input gain controls must be adjusted to produce the desired musical balance.

Input Signal Routing

After signal processing and gain control, each input signal must be

342

routed to the desired output. Several inputs may be combined to form a composite signal that will be recorded on one track of a multi-track tape recorder.

In addition, the input signals may be routed to one or more other points, such as an external delay line or reverberation chamber.

2. OUTPUT SECTION

The Output Bus

In electrical work, a **bus** is a length of copper or aluminum bar stock that is used as a central feeder line, as in a circuit breaker panel. In a recording console, a bus is a common signal line, to which the outputs of many input modules have been routed. On many consoles, the output groups are labelled output buses, and in the monitor section, selecting the bus mode will allow the engineer to monitor these output groups, or buses.

Output Bus Level Control

After all the input signals have been combined and routed as desired, these composite signals, or output groups, may be individually controlled within the console output section. Generally, this control is restricted to a simple gain adjustment, since each individual input signal has presumably been processed within the input section of the console. However, if some form of group signal processing is required, the console should provide patch points within the output signal path so that the appropriate signal processing device may be quickly inserted when and where needed.

Auxiliary Signal Return Control

Output signals from auxiliary devices, such as delay lines and reverberation chambers, may be combined with the direct signals, or routed to a different output group, as required.

3. MONITOR SECTION

Loudspeaker Monitoring

The recording engineer will frequently listen to various signals

THE RECORDING STUDIO HANDBOOK

out-of-context with the level at which they are to be recorded. For example, he may want to listen to the input or output signals one at a time to verify his signal routing arrangement. Or, perhaps a signal that is being recorded at a relatively high level should be heard at a somewhat lower level.

In the case of a tape containing some previously recorded tracks, the producer may wish to concentrate on the recording of the new material. However, during playback he will want to hear the entire program in proper balance.

The monitor section of the console will provide the engineer with the necessary controls to adjust the relative listening levels without affecting the recording level. Of course, if the engineer adjusts his recording levels, these adjustments must be heard on the monitor system. However, adjustments intended for monitoring purposes only must not find their way to the tape. Accordingly, the monitor section of most consoles is physically removed from the area where record level changes are made. The monitoring system must be easily switchable, to points just before and after the tape recorder, so that the engineer may compare (a) the recorded tape with (b) the console output. This comparison, or a similar comparison of one program with another, is popularly known as an **a/b test**, and reference may be made to "a/b-ing" the tape (or other program).

The monitor system will also permit the engineer to select the speaker or speakers over which each output group is heard. In addition, the program may be routed to the studio loudspeakers for monitoring by the musicians during playback.

Headphone Monitoring

As noted above, the engineer or producer may wish to lower the listening level of previously recorded tracks, while concentrating on whatever is being recorded at the moment. On the other hand, the studio musicians must easily hear what was recorded before, if they are to play along in accompaniment. Accordingly, the monitor section will provide a separate set of controls for headphone monitoring in the studio. These controls are independent of both the recording level and the listening level within the control room. On most consoles, the studio headphone monitoring facility is labelled **cue** or **foldback**. On a large console, there may be several separate cue systems, to provide as many different balances to the studio.

Meter Monitoring

The console will also allow the engineer to observe the level of various signal paths via VU or peak-indicating meters. Often, the meters are switched independently of the speaker monitoring system. While the engineer is listening to the console output, for example, the meters may be indicating the tape recorder outputs. Thus the engineer may have his eyes and ears on different parts of the total system.

Basic Console Layout and Signal Flow Diagram

Figure 16-2 identifies the console sections just described. The subsections within the input section are not physically arranged in the

Figure 16-2. A typical recording console, consisting of input, output, and monitor sections, plus patch boy. (Neve 8014) [Neve photo]

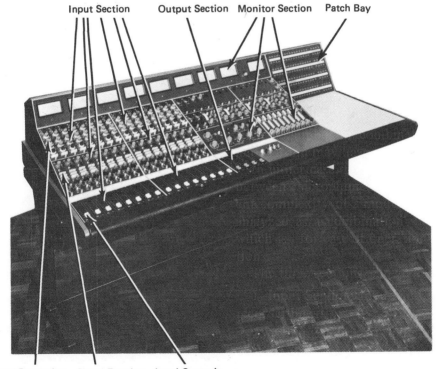

Input Section   Output Section   Monitor Section   Patch Bay

Signal Processing   Signal Routing   Level Controls

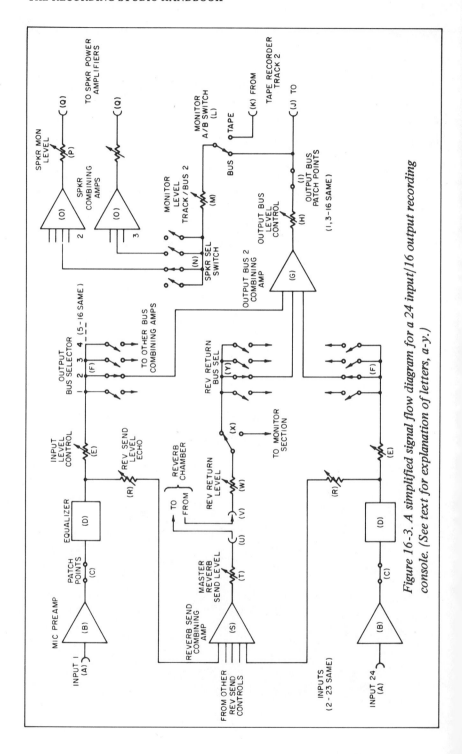

Figure 16-3. A simplified signal flow diagram for a 24 input/16 output recording console. (See text for explanation of letters, a-y.)

order that they will be found in the signal flow diagram shown in Figure 16-3. The physical layout is arranged for the convenience of the operator, who is mostly concerned with gain adjustments while recording. Accordingly, these controls are placed in the most accessible location, while signal routing and built-in equalization controls are located somewhat further away, with their exact orientation varying from one console to another.

In Figure 16-2, note that all input and output patch points are located in one area for operational convenience.

THE COMPONENT PARTS OF A MULTI-TRACK RECORDING CONSOLE

The console to be described and illustrated has 24 inputs and 16 outputs, with provision for 4 monitor speaker systems. Although these specifications are by no means an industry standard, they fairly well describe most consoles, in general outline if not in specific detail. The actual signal paths within a typical console are certainly more complex than those shown in Figure 16-3, yet much of the complexity is a manifold repetition of the basic routing paths shown here. In the figure, each important point in the signal path has been assigned a letter (A through Y) and a detailed description of these points follows. For clarity of explanation, the description simplifies several signal paths, omitting some details which will be added and described later in the chapter.

INPUT SECTION

A) Microphone Input Plugs (1-24)

At the console, each arriving input signal line is generally assigned to a specific input, more or less permanently. In the studio, each microphone input is numbered (Figure 16-4), with each number referring to one of the console's inputs. When the console is installed, the microphone lines may be soldered in place, making later changes difficult, though certainly not impossible. On other consoles, the connections may be made through plugs, allowing for a more easily changeable signal routing (Figure 16-5).

B) Microphone Preamplifier

Microphone output levels are quite low, compared to tape re-

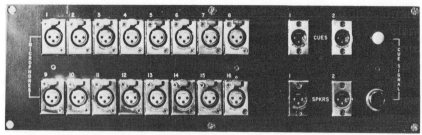

Figure 16-4. A typical microphone input panel in the studio.

Figure 16-5. Microphone input plugs, located on the rear of the console.

corder or line levels, and require amplification before any signal processing takes place. Therefore, a microphone preamplifier just after the input connection boosts the signal to line level; that is, to about +4 dBm.

C) Patch Points

On many consoles, the microphone preamplifier is immediately followed by a set of patch points, physically located in the console jack bay. These points allow the engineer to insert external signal processing devices into the signal path, or to re-route signals in special applications.

D) Console Equalizers

The equalizer shown in Figures 16-2 and 16-3 represents the typical unit built into each individual input signal path—a common practice in most recording consoles. For a detailed discussion of equalizers, see Chapter 7.

E) Input Level Control

This control invariably takes the form of a slide potentiometer, physically arranged so that the engineer may adjust a maximum number of input levels at once, as shown in Figure 16-6. It is at this point that level changes are made to suit the artistic needs of the recording session.

F) Output Bus Selector Switch

After each input signal has been suitably processed, it may be

Figure 16-6. Typical slide potentiometers, or input faders.

routed to one or more outputs by depressing the appropriate bus selector switches. Or, several input signals may be combined and sent to one output. For example, the engineer may wish to use a few microphones on a brass section, mixing their outputs together to form one composite signal which will be routed to, say, track No. 2 on the tape recorder. In Figure 16-3, the bus selector switch routes the input signal to output bus No. 2. By depressing the same switch in other input modules, one or more other input signals may be likewise routed to the same bus.

G) Output Bus Combining Amplifier

At this amplifier, all the input signals that have been routed to output bus No. 2 are combined into one composite output signal. There is a similar combining amplifier for each output.

OUTPUT SECTION

The combining amplifier, (G), marks the boundary between the input and output sections of the console, since it is at this point that the various input signals are combined as desired, for routing to one or more tracks on the multi-track tape recorder.

H) Output Bus Level Control

After the signals assigned to an output bus are combined, the overall level of the composite signal may be regulated by another slide fader, similar to the ones shown in Figure 16-6.

I) Output Bus Patch Points

The fader may be followed by a pair of patch points, similar to those described at (C). An external signal processing device inserted here will therefore affect all the individual signals that were combined at (G).

J) Bus Output Plugs (1-16)

At this point, the signal path leaves the console and goes to a specific track on the tape recorder.

MONITOR SECTION

K) Line Input Plug

Here, the tape recorder output is returned to the console. Although this signal will actually be routed to several points within the console, at this time only the monitoring signal path is shown in Figure 16-3.

L) Bus/Tape Monitor Switch

Depending on the position of this switch, the engineer may monitor either the console output (the buses, or output groups), or the output of the tape recorder.

M) Bus/Tape Monitor Level

This control, usually a rotary potentiometer, regulates the listening level without affecting the recording level. This enables the engineer to set a convenient monitoring balance, while at the same time recording on each track at maximum level if he so desires.

N) Speaker Selector Switch

In addition to setting a convenient listening level (M), the engineer may route each signal to one or more of the four control room monitor speakers. As with the monitor level control, the speaker selector switch in no way affects the recording. It merely permits the engineer to select a convenient speaker, or speakers, for monitoring.

O) Speaker Combining Amplifier

As with the output bus combining amplifier, the speaker combining amplifier is the point at which all signals to be routed to one speaker are combined.

P) Speaker Level Control

This potentiometer functions as a master gain control for the combined signal fed to each speaker. Depending on the particular console, there may be a separate control for each speaker, a master control for all speakers, or both.

Q) Monitor Output Plugs (1-4)

At this point, the monitor signal leaves the console and goes to the power amplifier, and then to the monitor speaker.

ECHO SEND AND RETURN SIGNAL PATHS

R) Echo Send Control

This control, usually a rotary potentiometer, is found in the input section near the input level control (E). It allows the engineer to feed some portion of any input signal to an external echo or reverberation device.

S) Echo Send Combining Amplifier

This amplifier combines all the signals that are routed to the echo or reverberation device.

T) Master Echo Send Level

At this point, also a rotary potentiometer, the level of the combined echo send signal may be regulated.

U) Echo Send Plug

Here, the echo send signal leaves the console, going to the input of the external echo/reverberation system.

V) Echo Return Plug

After the echo send signal has passed through the external echo/reverberation system, the system's output is routed back to the console via this plug.

W) Echo Return Level

Since the external echo/reverberation system is not necessarily a unity gain device, this additional potentiometer gives the engineer control over the output level returned to the console.

X) Reverberation on Monitor

During recording, it is often desirable not to record any echo or reverberation along with the direct signal. This control routes the reverberation signal to the monitor system only, so that although the artificial reverberation is heard, it is not recorded on the tape.

Y) Echo Return to Output Bus Selector

As with the regular input signals, the echo return signal may be routed to any output bus combining amplifier (G), where it is combined with the other signals to form a composite bus output signal.

SUMMARY OF THE SIMPLIFIED SIGNAL FLOW PATH THROUGH A MULTI-TRACK CONSOLE

The microphone input signal is boosted to line level, after which a pair of patch points permit the insertion of external signal processing devices. The signal then passes through the console's built-in equalizer (if any) and its level is adjusted by the input fader. After this, the signal is routed to the desired output bus, from which it goes to the tape recorder. Either the bus or the tape recorder output may be monitored in the control room over any of the available loudspeakers.

Input signals may also be routed through external echo/reverberation systems and then returned to the console.

Once this simplified signal flow path is understood, we may return to the console input section to add further details.

SIGNAL FLOW PATHS IN THE CONSOLE – ADDITIONAL DETAILS

(The letters in parenthesis refer to Figure 16-3.)

A) Microphone Inputs
K) Line Inputs, Mic/Line Selector Switch

So far, the recording console has been discussed as a routing and processing point between microphones and tape recorder. A secondary — yet no less important — function is as a control point between one tape recorder and another. For example, after a multi-track tape has been completely recorded, it must be mixed down to, say, two tracks if a stereo master tape is needed — as is usually the case.

So, the multi-track tape recorder outputs are routed to the console input section in addition to going to the monitor section described earlier at points (K) and (L) in Figure 16-3. In fact, the physical location of the line input plugs (K) is usually in the vicinity of the microphone input plugs (A).

Figure 16-7 is a detail drawing of an actual console input section. Note that the line input (K) goes directly to the monitor selector switch (L) as described earlier. When the switch (L) is in the tape position, the multi-track tape is played back directly through the monitor system. However, for mixdown purposes, the multi-track tape recorder's outputs are returned to the input section of the console via a selector switch in each module. This mic/line selector switch allows the engineer to replace any microphone output with the equivalent track from the tape recorder. Thus, console input No. 1 may control the output from either microphone No. 1 or tape recorder track No. 1, and so on.

Since the tape output, or line levels, are of considerably higher level than the microphone levels, they bypass the microphone pre-

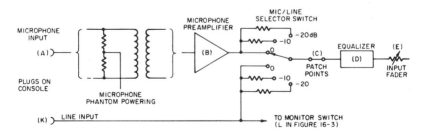

Figure 16-7. Detail of input section of recording console. The mic/line switch graphically demonstrates the selectable sensitivity function. Various amounts of attenuation may be inserted to prevent overload due to high level signals from the microphone or tape recorder playback. (In practice, the sensitivity switch is often an integral part of the preamplifier circuit.)

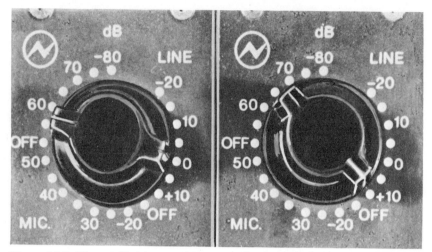

Figure 16-8. The mic/line input selector switch on a console input section module.

amplifier stage, as shown in the illustration. Note that there are several sensitivity positions for line as well as microphone inputs, so that, if either are consistently too high (or low), they may be attenuated (or boosted) as required. The attenuation facility prevents very high level inputs from overloading the following stages, while the boost positions provide extra gain in the case of very low level signals. In actual practice, the sensitivity range may be an integral part of the preamplifier circuit. Figure 16-8 illustrates two microphone/line selector switches, with several sensitivity settings in either mode. The knob points to the input level that will produce a 0 dB output, which in the illustration is a microphone level of -55 dB on the first module, and a line level of +10 dB on the second.

C) Patch Points

A detail drawing of the signal path through some of the patch points in the console jack bay is shown in Figure 16-9. Note that the act of inserting a patch cord into patch point No. 1 allows this signal to be metered, or routed elsewhere, without interrupting the normal signal flow. However, an insertion at patch point No. 2 *does* interrupt the circuit, allowing the path through some external device to take the place of the normal signal flow. This wiring convention, although by no means standard practice, allows the engineer consider-

*DETAIL OF SIGNAL PATHS THROUGH THE
CONSOLE PATCH POINTS*

Figure 16-9A. Patch points not in use – no interruption of regular signal path.

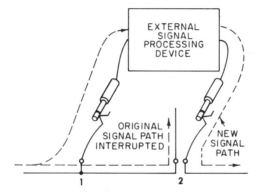

Figure 16-9B. Patch points in use – the regular signal path is interrupted, at patch point 2. Note that a meter could be inserted at patch point 1 without affecting the normal signal path.

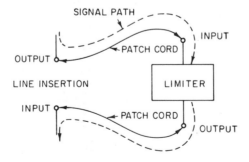

Figure 16-9C. Detail of the flow path through the patch bay when an external device is inserted in a signal path.

able flexibility in changing signal routing paths to meet the needs of the recording session.

A possible point of confusion arises when the jacks within a signal path are labelled **input** and **output**. As at point **(C)** in Figure 16-3, the first jack is the output of the preamp, while the second one is the input to the equalizer. Thus, the usual sequence of input-before-output is inverted. But it should be clearly understood that this in/out pair does not represent patch points at either end of a single device. Rather, the first jack is the output of device No. 1 (the preamp), the second is the input to device No. 2 (the equalizer), and the signal flow is from output No. 1 to input No. 2.

Even if the equalizer also has an output jack immediately following it, the physical layout of the jack bay usually places the former pair together, for patching convenience, with the equalizer output jack placed elsewhere in the jack bay.

On the other hand, when an external device, such as a reverberation chamber or limiter, is wired to the patch bay, its input will of course come before its output, as would be expected. Here the signal path is directly through the device, from input to output. Therefore, the relative orientation of inputs and outputs on the jack bay may vary, depending on whether the patch points are within a signal path or at either end of an unassigned signal processing device. Figure 16-9C illustrates a typical arrangement.

Echo Send Control

In practice, the echo send control may allow more flexibility than is shown in Figure 16-3. A detail drawing of a typical echo send system is shown in Figure 16-10. The echo send signal may be picked up from a point before, or after, the input fader **(E)**, depending on the position of the pre/post-fader selector switch. As shown, the signal to be sent to the echo send line must first pass through the input fader. Consequently, the fader's position influences the echo send signal level. On the other hand, if the selector switch was in the pre-fader position, the signal level to the echo send line becomes independent of the position of the input fader.

There are at least two applications for a pre-fader echo send position. If the input fader is brought way down to attenuate a signal going to the output bus selector switch, there may not be sufficient level after the fader to provide the echo send level that is required. In the pre-fader position, a full level signal is available at the echo send

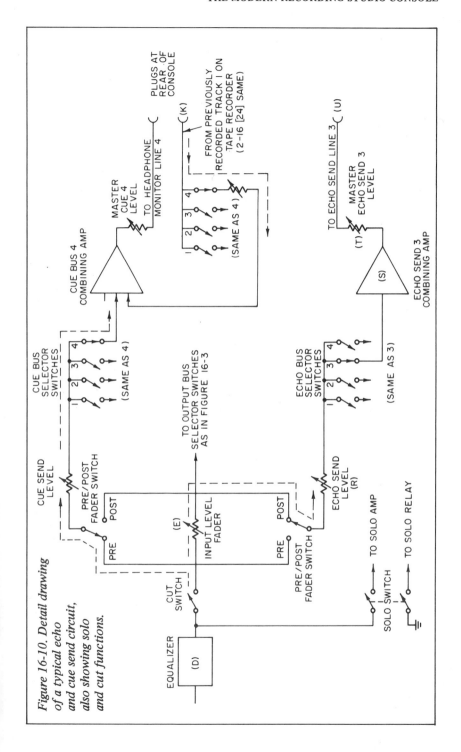

Figure 16-10. Detail drawing of a typical echo and cue send circuit, also showing solo and cut functions.

line, regardless of the position of the input fader.

As a second application, a satisfactory blend of direct and artificially reverberant sound may be established with the input fader at some average level position. Now, as the fader is raised, the direct sound level increases, while the reverberant sound level remains constant. The ratio of direct to reverberant sound changes, and as the direct sound becomes louder, it seems to move closer to the listener. On the other hand, as the fader is brought down, the direct sound fades out, leaving only the reverberation, so the signal seems to recede into the distance.

Cue (Foldback) System

When the studio musicians are acoustically isolated from each other, the engineer must be able to feed a well balanced program into a headphone system so that each musician will be able to hear what the others are doing. The cue system, also shown in Figure 16-10, duplicates the echo send system, except that the cue buses are routed to headphone lines instead of to echo/reverberation devices.

Previously recorded tracks must be sent to the headphone lines so that the musicians may play along in accompaniment. To accomplish this, an additional set of cue bus selector switches are located in the console's monitor section, where each track may be routed to the headphone lines. This additional facility is also seen in Figure 16-10.

Channel Cut Switch

Figure 16-10 also shows a **channel cut switch,** a simple on/off switch that allows the engineer to remove the signal flow entirely without disturbing any of the level, cue, or echo controls. This facility is particularly useful for briefly shutting off a microphone or tape track that must later be turned back on again at the same relative setting.

Solo Function

At times, it may be desirable to listen briefly to the output of one microphone only, in order to check its performance or placement. The **solo** function allows the engineer to do this without affecting the recording in any way.

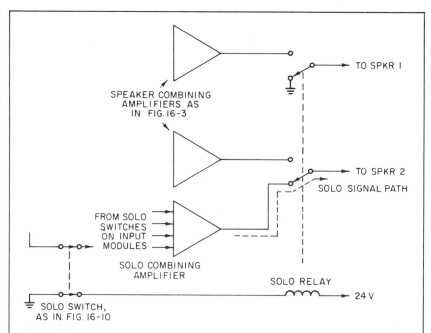

Figure 16-11. The solo function. When any solo button is depressed, a relay interrupts the normal signal path to the monitor switches, and the solo signal only is sent to one of the control room speakers.

From each input module, a solo send line is permanently routed through the solo switch to the solo combining amplifier, also seen in Figure 16-10. When the switch is depressed, the input signal reaches the combining amplifier. Another set of contacts on the same switch energizes a relay which routes the output of the solo combining amplifier to one of the control room amplifiers in place of the signal regularly assigned to it. At the same time, the signal paths to the other control room speakers are interrupted, as shown in Figure 16-11, so that the solo signal alone is heard. Two or more solo buttons may be depressed at once, and the appropriate inputs will be combined and routed to the solo circuit.

Output Bus Selector Switches and Pan Pots

As described earlier, the bus selector switches allow the engineer to route an input signal to one or more output buses. A somewhat more involved switching system will permit the input signal to be routed to two (or more) buses in unequal proportion. A potentiometer, called a **pan pot** (panorama) is used, as shown in Figure 16-12. Note that there are now two sets of bus selector switches, and that bus No. 1 has been selected in one set and bus No. 2 in the other. The pan pot wiper arm is closer to the lower set of switches, so although the signal is routed to both bus No. 1 and No. 2, the power distribution is unequal, with bus No. 2 being favored somewhat. Assuming these buses are monitored on separate speakers, say No. 1 on the left and No. 2 on the right, the position of the pan pot will determine the apparent location of the signal. As shown, the signal would appear somewhat right-of-center. The pan pot is designed so that at its midway position, the signal to both sides is attenuated 3 dB, as compared to the level if the signal is routed to one side only. Since a 3 dB drop represents a halving of power, both buses add up to the same amount of power as when the signal is on one side only, and therefore up 3 dB. Thus, if a signal is gradually panned from one bus to another, there is no change in apparent level as the sound source apparently moves across the room. Without the 3 dB drop feature, a signal would get louder as it moved to the center.

The pan pot on/off switch is shown in the on position, where the only signal path is through the pan pot wiper. When the switch is closed, there is a direct path to both sets of bus selector switches, thus cancelling the effects of the pan pot, regardless of its position.

Direct Outputs

As just described, the bus selector switching system with pan pots offers great flexibility in mixing input signals to one or more outputs. However, when a single microphone is to be routed to one track on a tape recorder, there is little point in going through such a switching system if a more direct route to the tape recorder is available.

On perhaps the majority of recording sessions, very few mixing buses are required at one time. For example, although the drums, string section, and chorus may be recorded using several microphones each, perhaps everything else is done with just one microphone per recorded track. Therefore, a complete mixing bus for each track is not an absolute necessity.

As shown in Figure 16-12, there may be a direct output plug after every input fader. Via these plugs, input No. 1 is routed directly to tape recorder track No. 1, and so on. A single microphone, to be

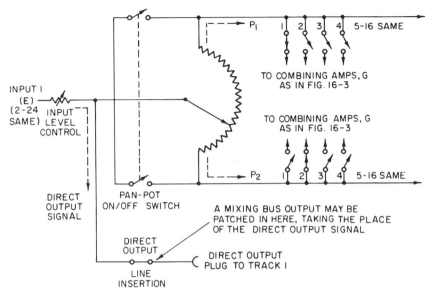

Figure 16-12A. Detail of a flexible bus selector/pan pot switching system, showing additional direct output facility.

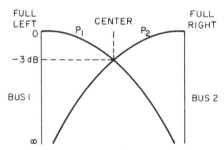

Figure 16-12B. Graph of relative power delivered to buses 1 and 2 by pan pot. At any position, $P_1 + P_2 = 0$ dB.

routed to say, track No. 7, is simply plugged into console input No. 7 at the microphone panel in the studio. In this case, the mixing bus outputs may not be permanently assigned, and are simply routed to the patch bay. A multi-input console with direct outputs may have only four to eight mixing buses. The buses are used only when several microphones are to be combined onto one track. Then, a convenient output bus is selected, and the output of its combining amplifier is routed to the appropriate track at the patch bay.

As an example, four microphones are plugged into inputs 5,6,7,8, and would normally feed tracks 5,6,7,8 on the tape recorder. However, the microphones are all routed to, say, mixing bus No. 2 via the bus selector switches on the input modules. The output of mixing bus No. 2 may be patched directly to any track, and takes the place of the direct output signal normally associated with that track.

Combining Amplifiers

As so far illustrated (Figure 16-3), the combining amplifier must have many inputs, one for each input module in the console. And, additional inputs are required for each echo return line that may have to be combined with the input signals. These multiple inputs are usually in the form of a large number of resistors, as shown in Figure 16-13A. The resistors prevent a group of inputs that are routed to one output from shorting each other out and, in the case of inputs routed to more than one output, keep the outputs isolated from each other.

In many consoles, these resistors are found in the various input modules, as seen in Figure 16-13B. The resistors are wired to the output bus lines as shown, and each bus is routed to a separate combining amplifier, which in this application may be called a line amplifier. Lines from external reverberation devices are also routed to the output buses in the same manner.

Monitor Section

The monitor section of the console may be fairly complex, in order to meet all the requirements of multi-track recording. As seen in Figure 16-14, the signal from output bus No. 1 is being monitored over speaker No. 2. Note that there are separate adjustments for studio and control room listening level. An on/off switch in the studio lines turns these speakers off when required. For convenience, the switch may be linked to the bus/tape monitor selector, so that in the bus mode, the console outputs will not be fed back into the studio speakers, a condition that would cause feedback. As a further safety measure, a record interlock may be provided, so that regardless of the monitor mode, the studio speakers will be turned off while recording.

A cue switch in the studio lines allows the cue signal to be routed

COMBINING AMPLIFIERS

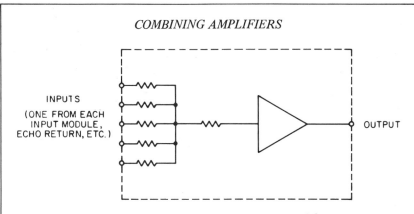

INPUTS

(ONE FROM EACH
INPUT MODULE,
ECHO RETURN, ETC.)

OUTPUT

Figure 16-13A. A typical combining amplifier.

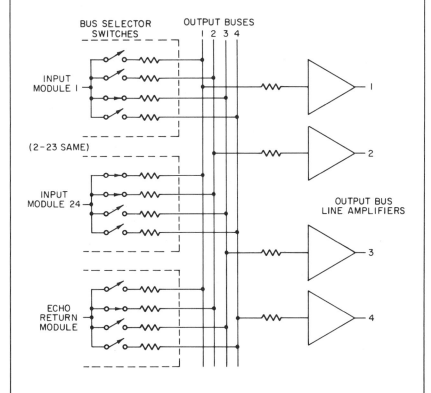

BUS SELECTOR
SWITCHES

OUTPUT BUSES
1 2 3 4

INPUT
MODULE 1

(2–23 SAME)

INPUT
MODULE 24

ECHO
RETURN
MODULE

OUTPUT BUS
LINE AMPLIFIERS

1

2

3

4

*Figure 16-13B. In many consoles, each input module is connected
to each output bus as shown here.*

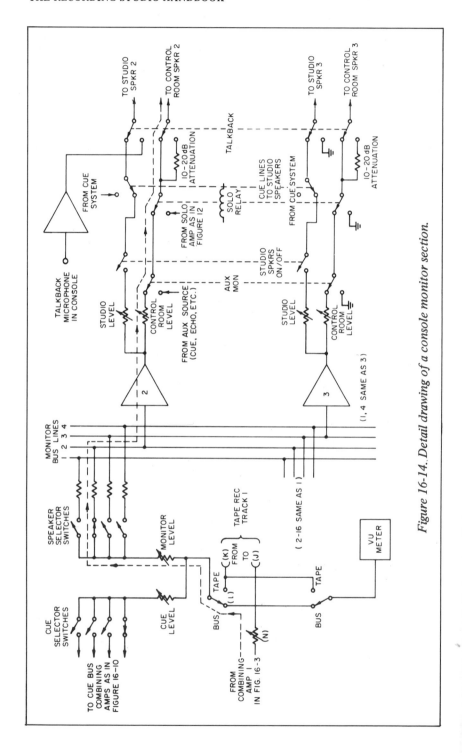

Figure 16-14. Detail drawing of a console monitor section.

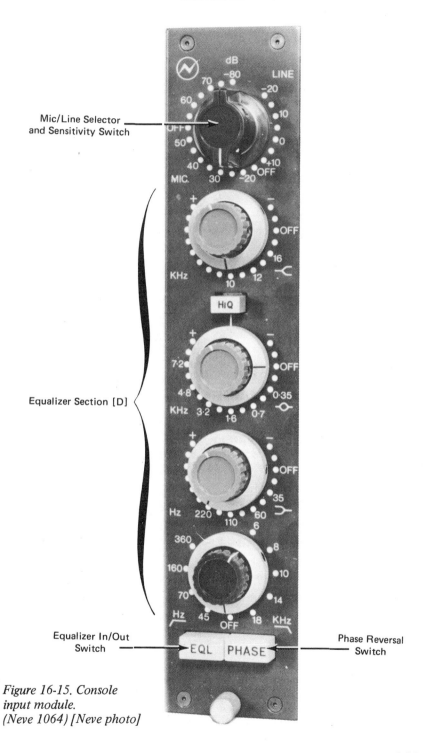

Mic/Line Selector and Sensitivity Switch

Equalizer Section [D]

Equalizer In/Out Switch

Phase Reversal Switch

Figure 16-15. Console input module. (Neve 1064) [Neve photo]

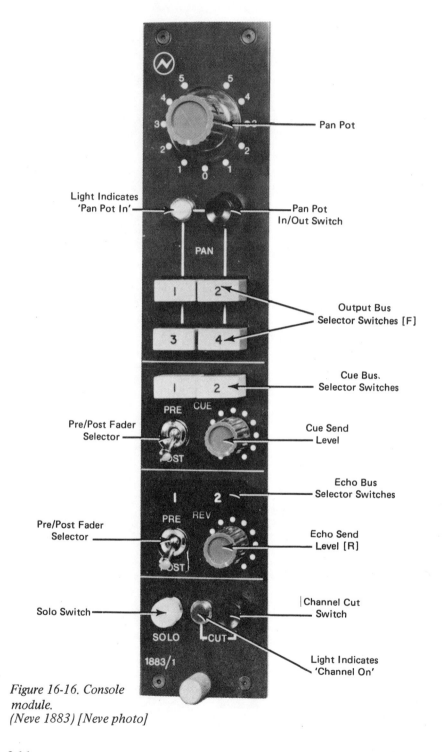

Pan Pot

Light Indicates 'Pan Pot In'

Pan Pot In/Out Switch

PAN

Output Bus Selector Switches [F]

Cue Bus. Selector Switches

Pre/Post Fader Selector

CUE

Cue Send Level

Echo Bus Selector Switches

REV

Pre/Post Fader Selector

Echo Send Level [R]

Solo Switch

Channel Cut Switch

SOLO CUT

1883/1

Light Indicates 'Channel On'

Figure 16-16. Console module. (Neve 1883) [Neve photo]

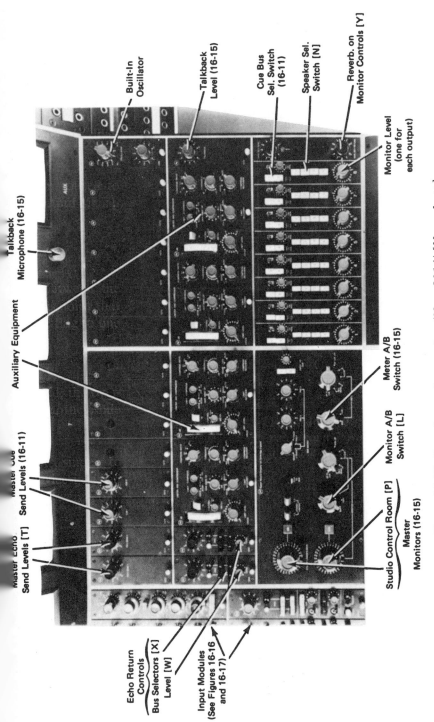

Talkback Microphone (16-15)

Built-In Oscillator

Talkback Level (16-15)

Cue Bus Sel. Switch (16-11)

Speaker Sel. Switch [N]

Reverb. on Monitor Controls [Y]

Monitor Level (one for each output)

Auxiliary Equipment

Master Cue Send Levels (16-11)

Master Echo Send Levels [T]

Meter A/B Switch (16-15)

Monitor A/B Switch [L]

Studio Control Room [P]

Master Monitors (16-15)

Echo Return Controls
Bus Selectors [X]
Level [W]

Input Modules
(See Figures 16-16 and 16-17)

Figure 16-17. Console monitor section. (Neve 8014) [Neve photo]

to the speakers, so that during rehearsal the musicians may hear previously recorded material without wearing headphones.

Independent switches in the control room lines permit the engineer to briefly check various auxiliary functions over one of the speakers while the other speakers are turned off for the duration of the test. And, when any solo button is depressed, the solo amplifier is routed to one control room speaker line, while the other speakers are also turned off.

When the talkback button is depressed, all other signals to the studio are interrupted and the talkback microphone on the console is routed to one of the studio speakers. At the same time, the control room monitor level is attenuated (or turned off completely) to prevent feedback.

Figures 16-15, -16, and -17 are photographs showing most of the controls described in this chapter. The bracketed letters refer to Figure 16-3, the bracketed numbers refer to other figures. It is important to remember that the position and physical appearance of these controls varies considerably from one console to another.

Section VII
RECORDING TECHNIQUES

THE RECORDING STUDIO HANDBOOK

Introduction

In this final section of the book, various aspects of both the recording and mixdown sessions are described.

In Chapter 17, overdub and Sel-Sync sessions are discussed, along with the techniques of "bouncing tracks", "punching in", and the remote control of the tape recorder. Later, pre-session preparation of the studio and the control room is covered, along with a discussion of the use of signal processing devices while recording.

Chapter 18 concludes the book with a discussion of the final step in the recording process; the mixdown session. The mixdown session is actually a form of recording. However, in place of microphones, a previously-recorded multi-track tape is routed through the console, mixed down to a stereo (or perhaps mono or quad) program, and recorded onto another tape recorder.

CHAPTER 17

The Recording Session

Before the introduction of the multi-track tape recorder, recording studio procedures were reasonably standardized; song or symphony would be recorded in its entirety at one sitting. All the musicians would be present, and they would play — and replay — the music to be recorded, until the engineer and producer were satisfied with the balance, the performance, the room acoustics, the soloist's interpretation, and so on.

Longer works might be recorded in sections, which would later on be spliced together to create the complete performance. Chances were the musicians would make several recordings, or **takes**, of each section, and often the best segments from several such takes would be edited together, to form the ideal composite recorded performance. The editing process will be discussed in greater detail in the next chapter.

Beyond the editing process, little could be done to modify the recorded music. Nevertheless, the luxury of tape editing represented a major advance over earlier recordings, made directly to disc. Here, the performance was permanently cut into the groove at the moment of recording, and there was no practical way of making even a simple edit later on.

Overdubbing

Once magnetic tape became the standard studio recording medium, it was only a matter of time before musicians began adding accompaniments to their recordings by playing along with a previously recorded tape. Both the new and the previously-taped performance would be mixed together and recorded onto a second tape recorder. This technique is known as **overdubbing**. At about the time it came into wide use, studio tape recorders with three or four separate tracks were pretty much the industry standard.

During the initial session, all the tracks would be used. Then the tape would be rewound and played, while the musicians added additional parts, by listening over earphones to the first machine, and playing along in accompaniment. The engineer would mix the original recording with the new material, while both were being recorded onto a second machine.

A typical example of the overdub process is illustrated in Figure 17-1A. Earlier, the orchestra was recorded on a four-track tape recorder, and the soloist now listens to the four-track recording and sings along with it. The engineer mixes the four tracks-plus-soloist down to a mono or stereo master tape. If, on playback, the balance is judged unsatisfactory, the soloist will have to be recorded again, while the engineer makes the necessary adjustments.

In many cases, the orchestra might be originally recorded on only two or three tracks, which would be directly transferred to the second recorder while the soloist is recorded on the third and/or fourth tracks during the overdub session. Later, these will be "mixed down" to produce the final mono or stereo master tape, as seen in Figure 17-1B. Although this development allowed more flexibility in arriving at an ideal balance later on, it added an additional generation of tape noise to the final product.

The overdub process brought a measure of efficiency and economy to the recording session. As the orchestral background was being recorded, complete attention could be given to instrumental balance. Later, the solo could be added without the time and expense of having the orchestra make repeated takes while the vocalist searched for the perfect interpretation. Or, the ideal instrumental accompaniment could be assembled, via editing, from several takes, before the solo was added.

In either case, since the accompaniment was recorded first, the soloist became, in effect, the accompaniest, as he or she would be forced to follow the tempi and phrasing of the previously recorded material. However, at the cost of some spontaneity, a technically superior recording could be made, since unsatisfactory balances of soloist-to-accompaniment could be redone at only the cost of the engineer's time.

In the vocabulary of the recording studio, the instrumental background became known as the **basic tracks** or simply, **the tracks**.

Although the overdub process expanded the capabilities of the recording medium, each successive overdub required an additional generation of tape. This presented no real problem on a single overdub, however multiple overdubs could be troublesome, since each would

THE OVERDUB SESSION

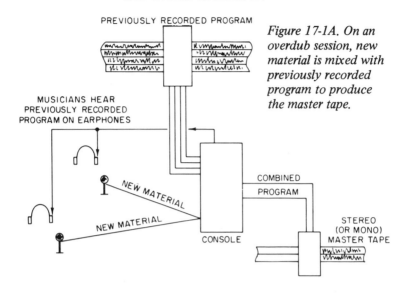

Figure 17-1A. On an overdub session, new material is mixed with previously recorded program to produce the master tape.

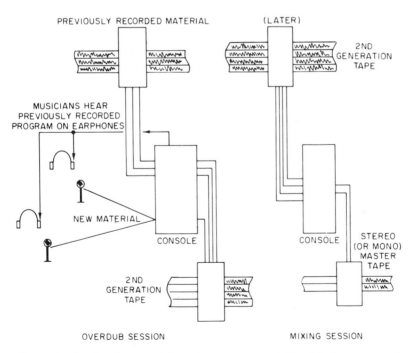

Figure 17-1B. On this overdub session, new material is added on a second generation tape, which is later mixed down to produce the master tape.

373

add another generation of tape noise. And in the case of old material being mixed with new, the only possible balancing that could be done was between the part being recorded at the moment and everything that had gone before. In the case of a recording that consists of many tracks, recorded sequentially, it is difficult or impossible to predict the ideal balance until the recording is totally complete. On a tape that is the product of multiple overdubs, there would be no way to correct the balance of, say, the third overdub, without scrapping everything that was recorded subsequently, and beginning again with a new version of the third overdub.

The Sel-Sync Process (Selective Synchronization)

The Sel-Sync process overcomes this very serious limitation. **Sel-Sync**—a term copyrighted by Ampex—really became popular with the introduction of 8-track tape recorders. The recording begins in the usual manner, using as many tracks as required, but leaving at least one track—and usually more—unused, or open. After recording the basic tracks, the tape is rewound, and new material is recorded on the open tracks, while the musicians listen to what was previously recorded.

In many cases, the rhythm section (drums, bass, guitars, keyboard(s), etc.) is first recorded, and these instruments comprise the basic tracks. Later on, perhaps strings and/or brass or a chorus may be added. These additional sessions are popularly called **sweetening sessions.**

Of course, if the basic tracks are monitored in the usual manner, from the playback head, the new material will be recorded on the tape out-of-sync with the old. This is illustrated in Figure 17-2. Imagine a simple two track tape, with a basic track already recorded on track No. 1. If the musicians listen to the tape, via the playback head of track No. 1, the new material being recorded on track No. 2 will be out-of-sync later, since it is being recorded about two inches behind the original material. The actual distance is that between the record and playback head—and the time delay depends on that distance—and the speed of the tape.

To prevent the out-of-sync effect, the previously recorded track, or tracks, is monitored from the record head while the same record head is adding the new material to the tape. Of course, no individual track within the record head is performing both the record and playback function at the same time. Rather, as in this particular example,

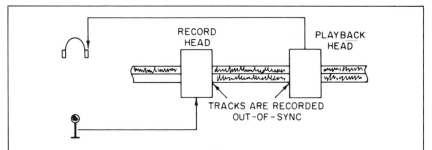

Figure 17-2. When a previously recorded program is monitored from the playback head, new material is recorded out-of-sync.

track No. 1 of the record head is acting as a temporary playback head, while track No. 2 is functioning in the normal record mode.

Since the musicians are now listening to the tape at the precise point at which new material is being recorded, new and old tracks will be in perfect sync. Later on, after all recording is done, the tape may be monitored over the regular playback head in the normal manner. The Sel-Sync process is illustrated in Figure 17-3.

On a machine equipped for Sel-Sync, the finished recording could be monitored in its entirety from the record head. This is, after all, the way an inexpensive home machine functions, with one head performing the dual function of record, and later on, playback. However, since the design parameters for record and playback heads are not identical, the optimum record head leaves something to be desired as a playback head, and *vice versa.*

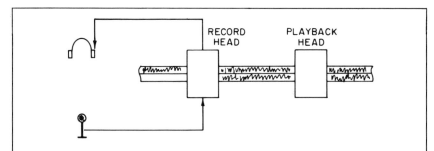

Figure 17-3. The Sel-Sync Process. Previously recorded material is monitored from the record head while new material is being recorded, using the same record head. (The term Sel-Sync is a trademark of the Ampex Corporation. Therefore, other tape recorder manufacturers use a slightly different term to describe the same process, such as sync, self-sync, etc.

Although on recent machines the record head performs quite well as a playback device, such was not always the case. On the earliest machines, playback from the record head was conspicuously inferior, particularly at high frequencies. At the time, this was not considered to be a significant limitation, given the obvious advantages of Sel-Sync over overdubbing. Record head monitoring was merely a production convenience. Critical listening, and mixdown, would come later on, after the recording work was completed. At that time, the regular playback head would be used, and so the poor playback response of the record head was of no consequence.

Transferring, or "Bouncing" Tracks

Of course, there inevitably comes a time when the number of available tracks is not enough, no matter what that number is. In a typical situation, with 15 out of 16 tracks recorded, it may become desirable to have three more tracks available.

Theoretically, this presents no problem. Instead of recording new material on track No. 16, three of the previously recorded tracks (5, 6, and 7, for example) can be monitored from the record head, mixed together, and recorded onto track No. 16, as shown in Figure 17-4. Now, track No. 16 contains a mono mix of tracks 5, 6, and 7, and these three tracks may be reused for new material.

But any imperfections in the record head's behavior as a playback device will show up in the mixdown of tracks 5, 6, and 7. So, when bouncing tracks becomes necessary, the playback response of the record head may no longer be ignored. The frequency response, and level, must be as close to that of the regular playback head as is possible. This requirement becomes even more important if a noise reduction system is being used.

Some state-of-the-art recorders now have separate playback circuitry for use with the record head. Thus, during alignment the sync output may be optimized to give satisfactory output level and frequency response. In Figure 13-1A, the screwdriver adjustment marked "Sel-Sync" allows the engineer to adjust the output level from the record head to match the regular playback head's output level.

Transferring Onto Adjacent Tracks

In planning a session that may require transferring tracks, it is important to remember that material from any track may not be

376

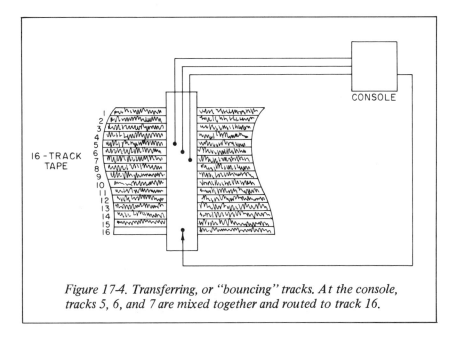

Figure 17-4. Transferring, or "bouncing" tracks. At the console, tracks 5, 6, and 7 are mixed together and routed to track 16.

bounced to an adjacent track. For example, although tracks 5, 6, and 7 may be bounced to track No. 16, as just described, they may not be bounced to either track No. 4 or No. 8, since No. 4 is adjacent to No. 5 and No. 8 is adjacent to No. 7.

The reason for this restriction is that inter-channel separation within the record head is by no means infinite. Consequently, while recording onto track No. 8, track No. 7 section of the record head "hears" some slight portion of what is being recorded (as does track No. 9). This has no significance *unless* track No. 8 is being fed some mixture that includes track No. 7 (or No. 9).

Now, if track No. 7 is being fed to track No. 8, and track No. 7 is also picking up some of track No. 8 internally through the head stack, the feedback squeal thus created will be recorded on track No. 8, preventing the use of the track. The condition is illustrated in Figure 17-5.

"Punching In"

In conventional recording, a series of takes are made until a satisfactory recording is achieved. Or, via editing, the definitive performance may be assembled by splicing together sections from two or more takes. However, when recording tracks on a tape that already

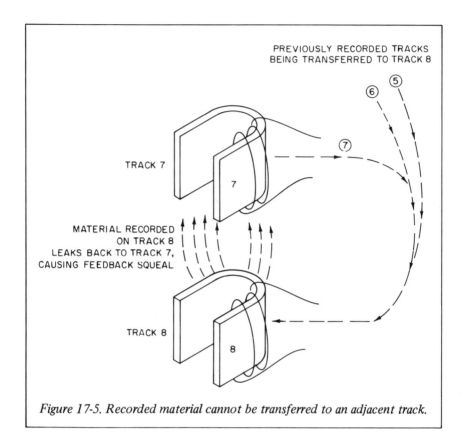

Figure 17-5. Recorded material cannot be transferred to an adjacent track.

contains previously recorded material, the manner of doing re-takes is quite different.

To illustrate, assume that the instrumental background has been recorded and a chorus is now being added to the master tape. The chorus sings the first verse properly, but a mistake is made within the second verse. A new take of the second verse cannot be started on a fresh piece of tape, since the chorus must, of course, fit in with the previously recorded material on the master tape. So, the master tape is rewound to some point before the second verse. The tape is played and just before the point at which the second verse begins, the chorus track is placed in the record mode, while the chorus sings the second verse again. The new performance takes the place of the old, while the previously satisfactory first verse remains as is. The process may be repeated again and again until a complete performance has been recorded, perhaps phrase by phrase.

The practice of putting together a performance in this manner is popularly known as **punching in** since the engineer spends so much of his time punching the record button.

While awaiting the punch-in point, the musicians may wish to listen to the earlier performance, and perhaps play along with it, so that the new portion may closely match the previously recorded parts that are to be saved. If the playback response of the sync output has been properly aligned, there should be no distracting differences in sound quality as the musicians hear first the performance which is being saved, and then the new performance of the sections being redone.

Remote Control of Record/Playback Mode

On any session involving the Sel-Sync process, it is important that the record/Sel-Sync/playback mode of each track be independently controllable. For example, it may be necessary to record on say, tracks Nos. 8 through 12, while the material previously recorded on tracks Nos. 1 through 7 is monitored in the Sel-Sync mode. Tracks Nos. 13 through 16 may be reserved for future use. Obviously, a single record button that puts all tracks into the record mode would be useless, since previously recorded tracks would be erased as new ones were recorded. On the other hand, 16 separate record buttons would be difficult to operate and would make it very easy to accidentally erase the wrong track.

Figure 17-6 shows a typical multi-track remote control unit, providing individual control over the mode of each track. When the single record button is depressed, the machine will record only on those tracks whose safe/ready switches were previously put in the ready position. These switches are, in effect, standby switches, readying the appropriate tracks for recording while protecting the other tracks against erasure. Previously recorded tracks may be monitored from the record or the playback head, depending on the position of the Sel-Sync/repro (i.e., record head/playback head) switch, also seen in Figure 17-6.

The Console in the Sel-Sync Mode

As described earlier, in Chapter 16, the multi-track recording console will contain monitoring facilities which enable the musician in the studio to hear previously recorded tracks. In Figure 16-10, the tape recorder outputs—returned to the console via the line inputs,

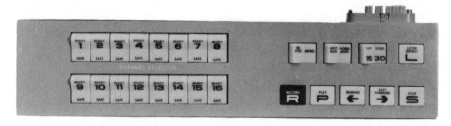

Figure 17-6. A remote control unit, providing individual control over the mode of each track. (AMPEX MM-1100) [AMPEX photo]

K – are routed to the cue system as shown. These previously recorded tracks are also routed to the control room monitor system so the engineer and producer may likewise hear them. In the detail drawing of the console monitor section (Figure 16-14) the bus/tape monitor switch, L, would be in the tape position for each previously recorded track.

Here, Figure 17-7 is a simplified description of the signal routing through the console in the Sel-Sync mode. Note that the engineer must provide the musicians with a balance of previously recorded and new programs, while at the same time the new material is being added to the tape.

The controls for the control room and cue monitor systems are usually independent of each other, so that the engineer may route a suitable headphone balance to the musicians, while in the control room he may listen to, perhaps, just the new material to make sure that it is being recorded properly.

Headphone Monitoring

Depending on the acoustic isolation between instruments in the studio, the engineer will probably have to set up a well balanced headphone cue mix of the program being recorded so the musicians may hear each other in addition to what was previously recorded. In fact, even when no material has been previously recorded, earphones may be required if the isolation between instruments prevents the musicians from adequately hearing each other without them.

Often, several different headphone balances will be required to suit the needs of various musicians. The drummer, for example, may not need to hear himself in the headphones, yet the guitarist in an isolation booth will certainly need to hear the drums in his headphones, if he is to play along in time.

In short, a flexible headphone monitoring system is a very important part of any modern recording console, and the engineer must be prepared to establish quickly one or more headphone balances in addition to the basic recording balance being fed to the tape recorder.

Selection of Headphones

Headphones with open pore ear pieces should be avoided in most studio applications, despite their wearing comfort and frequently excellent reproduction capabilities. Although the headphones allow the musicians to hear each other directly, they also permit a considerable amount of headphone program to be heard in the studio. Consequently, the microphones in the studio pick up a lot of this headphone leakage which then gets recorded on the tape again, along with

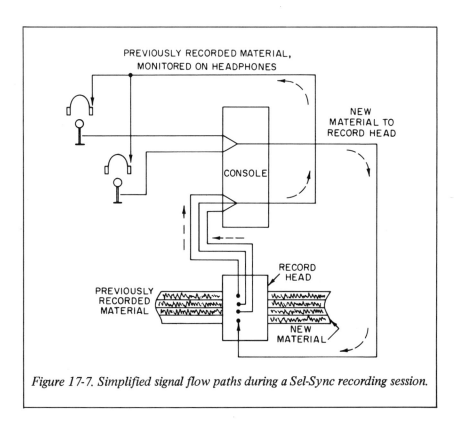

Figure 17-7. Simplified signal flow paths during a Sel-Sync recording session.

the new material. In severe cases, a feedback squeal may be produced if the microphone picks up too much of a headphone feed that already contains a portion of the microphone's output. And, for the same reason, inexperienced musicians should be cautioned against hanging their headphones across an active microphone in-between takes.

When a large number of headphones are in use, the engineer should periodically listen to just the program being recorded at the moment, over the control room monitor system. Very often, some musicians will remove their headphones without unplugging them. The headphone program is thus heard in the studio and picked up by the microphones again. If a musician decides not to wear headphones, they should be unplugged before any recording is done. A periodic check of the material being recorded will verify that headphone leakage is being kept at a minimum. A very quick check may usually be made by depressing one or more solo buttons, and listening for headphone leakage during a pause in the music being recorded.

Loudspeaker Monitoring of Cue System During Rehearsals

When strings and/or brass are to be added to a basic track, the conductor may wish to rehearse without headphones in order to better communicate with the musicians. At this time, the musicians may listen to the basic tracks over a loudspeaker as they rehearse their parts. Although this is certainly no technical problem, the producer should understand that the engineer will probably need some additional rehearsal time, once the loudspeaker is shut off and the musicians are wearing headphones. As long as the loudspeaker is active, all the microphones in the studio hear the cue feed, making it difficult or impossible to establish a meaningful balance of the program about to be recorded. In addition, if the microphones themselves are being routed to the cue system, their output will have to be kept at a minimum so long as the loudspeaker is on, to prevent feedback.

Track Assignment

Beyond operator convenience, there are few precautions to be observed in assigning instruments to the various tracks of the multi-track tape recorder. Whenever possible, it is a good idea to assign the same instrument to the same track on each successive recording session so that later recording and mixdown work may proceed with a minimum of switching changes. For example, if strings and brass are to be added to several songs, a great deal of time may be saved if the same tracks are available on each song. In addition, once a basic cue balance has been worked out, it will probably suffice for much of the session, providing the track assignment has remained constant during earlier sessions.

The mixdown session will be discussed in detail in the next chapter, but here it should be noted that mixdown work will proceed a lot more efficiently if the tracks are arranged in some logical order prior to recording. For example, rhythm instruments may be recorded consecutively from track No. 1, while sweetening tracks begin at track No. 16 (or No. 24) and work backwards towards the center of the tape. This leaves the center tracks open till last, so that additional instruments may be recorded towards the rhythm or sweetening sides, as appropriate. The vocal may be recorded on either outside track, or in the middle, if this is more convenient.

In the early days of the multi-track tape recorder, the outside tracks were often reserved for the least important instruments, since there was apt to be some problem with tape-to-head contact. However, this should no longer be a problem, providing the tape recorder is in proper mechanical alignment.

Bus/Tape Monitoring

While recording, the engineer may listen to either the console bus outputs or the outputs of the tape recorder. Although tape monitoring will immediately show up any distortion occurring at the tape recorder, the slight time delay between record and playback head may be a problem if the engineer is attempting any sort of gain riding or other adjustments during recording.

As a further restriction against tape monitoring, many studio noise reduction systems alternately switch between record and playback modes, depending on whether the tape recorder is recording or simply playing back. As was pointed out in Chapter 15, the noise reduction encoded signal may sound quite distorted, making evaluation without decoding quite difficult.

PREPARING FOR THE
MULTI-TRACK RECORDING SESSION

Seating Plan

In preparing the studio for a recording session, a little pre-planning will go a long way towards improving the efficiency with which the recording work progresses. The first step is to work out a seating arrangement that will be most comfortable for the musicians. Often, they are spaced as far apart as possible, under the mistaken impression that this will keep leakage at a minimum. In a very dead studio this may in fact be true, but in most cases the wide spacing creates more problems than it solves. In the average studio, there is not that much attenuation as the distance between instruments is increased. The further away one musician moves from another, the more reflections each one hears, and the resultant time delay makes it much more difficult to play together in sync. The performance probably suffers far out of proportion to any improvement in the recorded sound.

If leakage is that much of a problem, a far greater improvement might be made by moving the microphone a few inches closer, rather than moving the other musician a few more feet away. For example, if two musicians, A and B, are 1 and 3 feet away from a microphone, this ratio may be doubled by moving musician A 6 inches closer *or* moving musician B back an additional 3 feet. The first alternative will usually be the most satisfactory.

Microphone Setup

Once the seating plan has been worked out and set up, the microphones may be placed in position. When running microphone cables across the studio, a great deal of confusion may be avoided if the cable is plugged into the microphone input panel first and then brought to the microphone, rather than *vice versa*. The cable slack is laid near the base of the microphone stand so that if the microphone has to be moved during the session, it will be possible to do so without too much difficulty. This also prevents the slack from every cable in the studio accumulating in front of the microphone input panel, making it difficult to make quick changes later on.

Console Preparation

It is a good idea to neutralize all console controls before beginning any session. That is, make sure all signal routing switches are off, and that equalizer settings are in their zero position. By following this precaution, signals will not be routed to the wrong place due to a depressed switch that went unnoticed, and unwanted equalization will not be applied to any input.

Monitor System

Many control rooms have four monitor speakers in front of the console, and it is often convenient to distribute the multi-track recording over all of them. However, the engineer should not forget that the eventual recording will be heard over just two speakers, and in very many cases over just one. It's often a good idea to use two speakers only while recording to have a better idea of what the final product will sound like.

The four-speaker setup is convenient during Sel-Sync sessions. Previously recorded programs may be routed to two speakers, while material presently being recorded is routed to the other two. The Sel-Sync program may be monitored at a low level (or turned off) while recording, and then quickly brought up during playback. As mentioned earlier, when drums, piano, or other instruments are recorded on two or more tracks, the tracks should be monitored in mono from time to time to make sure there will be no phase cancellations later on.

Using Artificial Reverberation During Recording

Generally, artificial reverberation is best applied after the recording session, during tape mastering. As noted earlier, stereo reverberation requires two outputs, which are fed left and right. If stereo reverberation were added during the recording session, two tracks would have to be used; one for the left, the other for the right. This of course wastes tracks needlessly, adds tape hiss, and besides, a more suitable reverberant field can probably be created during the mixdown session when the individual tracks are heard, and processed, in context.

Of course, if it is necessary to add reverberation to one or more signals which are being combined during the recording session with other, unprocessed signals, this must be done as the recording is taking place. For example, the drum set may be recorded on one track, using several microphones. A slight amount of reverberation added to the snare drum may enhance the sound, yet no reverberation may be desired on the bass drum. So, during recording, the snare drum microphone feeds the reverberation device, while the bass drum microphone does not. In this case, if reverberation was added later, during the mixdown session, it would affect the total drum sound rather than just the snare drum.

Other Signal Processing Devices

As with echo and reverberation, other types of signal processing should be used with some caution during the recording session. Equalization, phasing, or compression effects that may sound just right during the recording session often turn out to be unsuitable later on, after all the succeeding tracks have been recorded. Most of these effects can be added during the mixdown session, but it is difficult and often impossible to remove the effects of a signal processing device that was applied during the original recording session.

Of course, when several inputs are combined during the recording session, it is necessary to process each one as desired before they are mixed together.

Recorded Levels

In multi-track recording, it's a common practice to record each track at a high level, and achieve the desired balance by adjusting the playback level of each track at the console's monitor section. In this way, each individual signal is recorded as high above the noise level as possible. As mentioned earlier (Chapter 1), the engineer should realize that VU meters are not an accurate indication of the program's peak levels, especially on percussive instruments.

Slating

Prior to each take, the tape is usually **slated**. The term is taken from the film industry, where a slate board with the take number is held in front of the camera before each shooting. In the recording studio, the slate consists of a spoken announcement ("take 3," etc.), usually made from the control room. Some consoles feed a low frequency tone to the tape recorder during the slating announcement. Later on, when the tape is rewound at high speed, the tones are heard as high pitched beeps, which identify the beginning of each take. By counting these beeps, the engineer may quickly locate the beginning of a desired take.

Takes are numbered consecutively. Usually, each new song begins with "take 1." However, it is often a good idea to continue the count for the duration of the session. Thus, if one song ends after take 10, the next one will begin at take 11. This is a great help in recording unfamiliar music, or for tapes that will be sent to other studios for additional recording or mixing. If there is only one "take 17" on the entire collection of master tapes, there can be no question as to the identity of each take.

Count-Offs

When it is known that additional material will be added to the tape, beginning at the first beat, a lot of trial-and-error time may be saved by recording a spoken count-off during the first session. On subsequent Sel-Sync sessions, the musicians will hear the count-off and enter on the first beat, without resorting to guess work or complicated visual cues from the control room.

Where there are to be long pauses during the recording of the basic tracks, during which additional instruments will enter later on, it is a little more difficult to provide a satisfactory entrance cue. If someone in the studio counts time, it will be heard over most of the microphones, especially since there is no music masking it. This will make it very difficult to remove the count later on. In such cases, it is better to have someone in the control room (or in an isolation booth) count time onto just one track. Later on, this track may be erased with little difficulty before the mixing session.

Tuning

If any sort of tuned instruments are to be added later on, it is a good idea to record a reference tone (e.g., A-440) during the recording of the basic tracks. This will enable the musicians on later sessions to tune to the basic track in case there is a slight pitch variation between one session and/or tape recorder and another. Or, in the case of a servo-driven machine with variable speed capability, the tape recorder's speed may be tuned as required.

End of Recording

Many contemporary recordings eventually fade out, rather than coming to a definite musical ending. The fade-out is usually made during the mixdown session, as described in the next chapter. During the recording, the musicians generally play the final phrase over and over again, giving the engineer sufficient material to use during the fade later on. At the recording session, it is often advisable to simulate the eventual fade-out by bringing down the monitor level, thus verifying that the music continues long enough to make a suitable fade during the mixdown session.

For those songs that do not end in a fade-out, it is important to maintain a few seconds of silence at the end of the recording so that reverberation (natural or artificial) will have a chance to die away.

CHAPTER 18

The Mixdown Session

During the mixdown session, the completed multi-track tape is played back through the console. Each track takes the place of a microphone input, and is routed, processed and combined with the other tracks to form a stereo (or quad) program which is then recorded onto another tape recorder.

Editing

After the recording session, the takes that are to be used for the mixdown session may be removed and placed on one or more separate reels. The "out takes" may then be filed or discarded so that the engineer does not have to be encumbered with them while mixing. Often, this type of editing work is done just after the basic tracks are completed, and before the "sweetening sessions". It is important to remember *not* to remove any count-offs at the beginning of each master take and to leave enough extra tape at the end for string and brass parts that may last longer than the basic tracks.

For easy identification, the master takes may be separated from each other by a length of white leader tape. This type of editing is quite simple; the engineer listens for the beginning of the desired take, stops the tape, rewinds it to a point before the beginning of the music and cuts it. A length of white leader tape is wound around an empty reel, and the beginning of the master take is spliced to the end of the leader. The take is wound onto the master reel. At the end of the take, the tape is again cut and leader tape is spliced in. The master reel is put aside and the engineer locates the next desired take and repeats the process, splicing the take onto the master reel. The procedure is illustrated in Figure 18-1.

Musical Editing

When the master take is to be a composite of segments of several

389

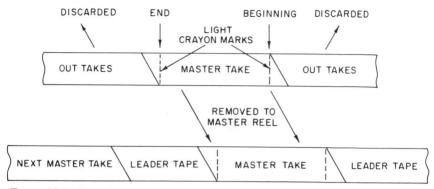

Figure 18-1. The editing process. The takes that are to be used for mixdown work are removed and stored on a separate reel.

takes, the editing process is somewhat more complex, although the basic principle remains as just described. However, great precision of editing may be required, as the beginning of one segment is spliced directly to the end of another. Since the segments come from different takes, the engineer must listen carefully to the proposed splice point *before* cutting the tape. Slight differences in tempo, phrasing, level, pitch, etc., that are not objectionable in themselves may become noticeable if the takes are spliced together. Careful listening will usually reveal whether the splice can be made. However, if an attempted splice turns out to be unacceptable, the segments can be restored to their normal position and a new splice point sought.

Splicing Blocks

Figure 18-2 shows several commercially available splicing blocks. Note that each allows the tape to be cut on an angle. This is done to distribute the cut over a short segment of the tape. A 90° butt joint would probably make an audible "thump" as it passed the playback head, and would be more apt to pull apart as it went over the tape guides, especially at high speed.

Although a 45° angle cut may be made on narrow width tapes, it should be remembered that this angle distributes the cut over a length of tape that is equal to the width of the tape. Thus a 45° angle cut on 2 inch tape takes up 2 inches of tape travel. This means that, at 15 in/sec., the splice will take 2/15 of a second (133 milliseconds) to pass through all the tracks. This length of time could make the splice quite noticeable, and so a narrow angle cut is usually used, as may be seen in Figure 18-2.

Figure 18-2. Splicing blocks for 2-inch, ½-inch, and ¼-inch tapes. (Xedit-2, 2-inch block; Editall S-3.5, ½-inch block; Editall S-3, ¼-inch block)

Track Editing

On a multi-track tape that is the product of many sel-sync sessions, it is very easy to wind up with unwanted material on small segments of various tracks. For example, there may be studio noises on some of the tracks during long pauses. Or a verse or instrumental section may no longer be wanted, once the complete recording has been reviewed.

Some of these segments may be removed simply by switching the appropriate tracks on and off on cue. However, if there are several such segments, it may be difficult to coordinate all the track-on/track-off cues while also concentrating on the mixdown itself. In this case it may be wiser to review each track carefully, and erase those segments before beginning the mixdown work. Before doing any erasing, the engineer should make certain there is sufficient clearance before and after the segment to be erased, so that wanted material is not accidentally lost.

Track Assignment and Panning

During recording, instruments are assigned to various console outputs without regard for their eventual left-to-right orientation. Each track may be heard on the left, center, or right simply by depressing the appropriate switches in the console's monitor section. During the mixdown session, only two console outputs (four for quad) are used. One represents the left track and the other the right track. Tracks that are to be heard in the center are routed to both left and right tracks, or a pan-pot may be used for intermediate positions between left and right. The action of the pan pot was described in Chapter 16, and illustrated in Figure 16-12.

p. 359

THE RECORDING STUDIO HANDBOOK

Preparing for Mixdown

Before beginning the mixdown work, the tracks may be reviewed individually, while equalization, reverberation, and other types of signal processing are tried. Although there is nothing wrong with spending a little time verifying the content of each track, there is little point to spending a lot of time evaluating each track out of context with the total program. By the time of the mixdown session, it really makes no difference what each isolated track sounds like. The signal processing that sounds right when the track is heard by itself will rarely remain effective once the track is mixed with the others. What really matters is the contribution of each track to the total recording.

For example, two guitar tracks heard individually might be processed at great length, only to find out that when they are heard together, they are noticeably out of tune. It makes better sense to spend some time listening to groups of tracks to hear the effect of one instrument against another. The basic tracks may be monitored first, to work out position and balance. Then, rhythm instruments that were added during sel-sync sessions may be mixed in.

Later, the strings and brass – if any – may be reviewed as an ensemble. Once a basic balance is worked out, they are mixed in with the rhythm section. The vocal performance is often added last; however it's a good idea to carefully listen to the vocalist before spending too much time working out the ideal instrumental balance. Depending on the performance, the instrumental balance may have to be substantially modified once the vocalist is added.

Assistance During Mixdown

On a complex mixdown session, there may be more changes to be made than can be handled by one engineer. However, the role of the assistant must be carefully spelled out in advance, to keep confusion at a minimum. One person must remain in complete charge of the mixdown, while the other makes whatever changes have been assigned to him.

If the two engineers attempt to function independently of each other, each will be confused by the action of the other, and little or nothing constructive will be accomplished. Mixing is pretty much like flying: there can only be one pilot at a time.

392

Recording and Monitor Levels

As the mixdown session begins, the engineer establishes a comfortable monitor level in the control room. But as more and more tracks are added, the monitor level rises accordingly, and may have to be turned down to maintain a reasonable sound level. However, the recorded level also rises with each additional track and may become excessive, once all the tracks are being monitored.

The master fader can of course be brought down somewhat; however, this does nothing to protect the stages just before it from high level overload. In most cases, the individual input faders should each be brought down to maintain a safe recording level. But this can be inconvenient, since it means that as each group of tracks is brought into the mix, all the input faders must be readjusted – an awkward procedure at best.

As a practical alternative, the mixdown session may begin with the monitor level control at a higher than normal setting. With the monitor level up, the engineer will not raise the faders quite so high, thus keeping the recording level down. As more and more tracks are added, the monitor level may be brought down, and as the recording level gradually increases, it should still remain within safe limits. A little practice will determine the optimum starting setting for the monitor level control.

As the mixdown wears on, listening levels have a way of creeping gradually upward. (Some engineers swear they can tell how long they have been in the control room by looking at the position of the monitor level control.) But as the listening level increases, the engineer should keep in mind the implication of the equal loudness curves discussed in Chapter 2. Music mixed at a high listening level will sound quite different when played back later on at a lower level. The engineer who disregards this important fact does so at his peril.

Monitor Speakers for the Mixdown Session

Presumably, the well equipped recording studio will have the best monitor system possible within its budget limitations. At this point in the book, the advantages of a well designed, wide range monitor system should require no further discussion.

However, a valid argument may be made for using a reasonably inexpensive monitor speaker during the mixdown session. Despite the impressive technology discussed in the preceding chapters, it is unlikely that the majority of the record buying public will be listening over state-of-the-art professional quality playback equipment. There are more pocket transistor radios in this world than can be counted, and their sound quality is—to put it politely—wretched. Yet this is where much of the final product is heard, and it really doesn't matter what it sounds like on the studio's own super system. The question is: what does it sound like on the beach?—or in the car, over AM radio? One doesn't have to be a degree candidate to realize that mixing subtleties will be forever lost on a two inch speaker in a plastic case.

And so, it is good to have an inexpensive speaker system available in the control room, to get some idea what the ultimate mixdown will sound like in the hands of the consumer. Some ambitious studios even rig up a feed through a small radio receiver so that the engineer and producer may get some impression of what the record buyer may hear when he brings the album home, or hears it in his car.

It is an exercise in futility to attempt a mixdown that will sound ideal on all systems; a review of Chapter 5 should clear up any misconceptions on that point. However, the engineer should have at least some idea of what the master tape may sound like once it leaves the studio.

APPENDICES

APPENDIX 1

Table of Logarithms

Common logarithms

N	0	1	2	3	4	5	6	7	8	9
10	0000	0043	0086	0128	0170	0212	0253	0294	0334	0374
11	0414	0453	0492	0531	0569	0607	0645	0682	0719	0755
12	0792	0828	0864	0899	0934	0969	1004	1038	1072	1106
13	1139	1173	1206	1239	1271	1303	1335	1367	1399	1430
14	1461	1492	1523	1553	1584	1614	1644	1673	1703	1732
15	1761	1790	1818	1847	1875	1903	1931	1959	1987	2014
16	2041	2068	2095	2122	2148	2175	2201	2227	2253	2279
17	2304	2330	2355	2380	2405	2430	2455	2480	2504	2529
18	2553	2577	2601	2625	2648	2672	2695	2718	2742	2765
19	2788	2810	2833	2856	2878	2900	2923	2945	2967	2989
20	3010	3032	3054	3075	3096	3118	3139	3160	3181	3201
21	3222	3243	3263	3284	3304	3324	3345	3365	3385	3404
22	3424	3444	3464	3483	3502	3522	3541	3560	3579	3598
23	3617	3636	3655	3674	3692	3711	3729	3747	3766	3784
24	3802	3820	3838	3856	3874	3892	3909	3927	3945	3962
25	3979	3997	4014	4031	4048	4065	4082	4099	4116	4133
26	4150	4166	4183	4200	4216	4232	4249	4265	4281	4298
27	4314	4330	4346	4362	4378	4393	4409	4425	4440	4456
28	4472	4487	4502	4518	4533	4548	4564	4579	4594	4609
29	4624	4639	4654	4669	4683	4698	4713	4728	4742	4757
30	4771	4786	4800	4814	4829	4843	4857	4871	4886	4900
31	4914	4928	4942	4955	4969	4983	4997	5011	5024	5038
32	5051	5065	5079	5092	5105	5119	5132	5145	5159	5172
33	5185	5198	5211	5224	5237	5250	5263	5276	5289	5302
34	5315	5328	5340	5353	5366	5378	5391	5403	5416	5428

Common logarithms

N	0	1	2	3	4	5	6	7	8	9
35	5441	5453	5465	5478	5490	5502	5514	5527	5539	5551
36	5563	5575	5587	5599	5611	5623	5635	5647	5658	5670
37	5682	5694	5705	5717	5729	5740	5752	5763	5775	5786
38	5798	5809	5821	5832	5843	5855	5866	5877	5888	5899
39	5911	5922	5933	5944	5955	5966	5977	5988	5999	6010
40	6021	6031	6042	6053	6064	6075	6085	6096	6107	6117
41	6128	6138	6149	6160	6170	6180	6191	6201	6212	6222
42	6232	6243	6253	6263	6274	6284	6294	6304	6314	6325
43	6335	6345	6355	6365	6375	6385	6395	6405	6415	6425
44	6435	6444	6454	6464	6474	6484	6493	6503	6513	6522
45	6532	6542	6551	6561	6571	6580	6590	6599	6609	6618
46	6628	6637	6646	6656	6665	6675	6684	6693	6702	6712
47	6721	6730	6739	6749	6758	6767	6776	6785	6794	6803
48	6812	6821	6830	6839	6848	6857	6866	6875	6884	6893
49	6902	6911	6920	6928	6937	6946	6955	6964	6972	6981
50	6990	6998	7007	7016	7024	7033	7042	7050	7059	7067
51	7076	7084	7093	7101	7110	7118	7126	7135	7143	7152
52	7160	7168	7177	7185	7193	7202	7210	7218	7226	7235
53	7243	7251	7259	7267	7275	7284	7292	7300	7308	7316
54	7324	7332	7340	7348	7356	7364	7372	7380	7388	7396
55	7404	7412	7419	7427	7435	7443	7451	7459	7466	7474
56	7482	7490	7497	7505	7513	7520	7528	7536	7543	7551
57	7559	7566	7574	7582	7589	7597	7604	7612	7619	7627
58	7634	7642	7649	7657	7664	7672	7679	7686	7694	7701
59	7709	7716	7723	7731	7738	7745	7752	7760	7767	7774
60	7782	7789	7796	7803	7810	7818	7825	7832	7839	7846
61	7853	7860	7868	7875	7882	7889	7896	7903	7910	7917
62	7924	7931	7938	7945	7952	7959	7966	7973	7980	7987
63	7993	8000	8007	8014	8021	8028	8035	8041	8048	8055
64	8062	8069	8075	8082	8089	8096	8102	8109	8116	8122
65	8129	8136	8142	8149	8156	8162	8169	8176	8182	8189
66	8195	8202	8209	8215	8222	8228	8235	8241	8248	8254
67	8261	8267	8274	8280	8287	8293	8299	8306	8312	8319
68	8325	8331	8338	8344	8351	8357	8363	8370	8376	8382
69	8388	8395	8401	8407	8414	8420	8426	8432	8439	8445

Common logarithms

N	0	1	2	3	4	5	6	7	8	9
70	8451	8457	8463	8470	8476	8482	8488	8494	8500	8506
71	8513	8519	8525	8531	8537	8543	8549	8555	8561	8567
72	8573	8579	8585	8591	8597	8603	8609	8615	8621	8627
73	8633	8639	8645	8651	8657	8663	8669	8675	8681	8686
74	8692	8698	8704	8710	8716	8722	8727	8733	8739	8745
75	8751	8756	8762	8768	8774	8779	8785	8791	8797	8802
76	8808	8814	8820	8825	8831	8837	8842	8848	8854	8859
77	8865	8871	8876	8882	8887	8893	8899	8904	8910	8915
78	8921	8927	8932	8938	8943	8949	8954	8960	8965	8971
79	8976	8982	8987	8993	8998	9004	9009	9015	9020	9025
80	9031	9036	9042	9047	9053	9058	9063	9069	9074	9079
81	9085	9090	9096	9101	9106	9112	9117	9122	9128	9133
82	9138	9143	9149	9154	9159	9165	9170	9175	9180	9186
83	9191	9196	9201	9206	9212	9217	9222	9227	9232	9238
84	9243	9248	9253	9258	9263	9269	9274	9279	9284	9289
85	9294	9299	9304	9309	9315	9320	9325	9330	9335	9340
86	9345	9350	9355	9360	9365	9370	9375	9380	9385	9390
87	9395	9400	9405	9410	9415	9420	9425	9430	9435	9440
88	9445	9450	9455	9460	9465	9469	9474	9479	9484	9489
89	9494	9499	9504	9509	9513	9518	9523	9528	9533	9538
90	9542	9547	9552	9557	9562	9566	9571	9576	9581	9586
91	9590	9595	9600	9605	9609	9614	9619	9624	9628	9633
92	9638	9643	9647	9652	9657	9661	9666	9671	9675	9680
93	9685	9689	9694	9699	9703	9708	9713	9717	9722	9727
94	9731	9736	9741	9745	9750	9754	9759	9763	9768	9773
95	9777	9782	9786	9791	9795	9800	9805	9809	9814	9818
96	9823	9827	9832	9836	9841	9845	9850	9854	9859	9863
97	9868	9872	9877	9881	9886	9890	9894	9899	9903	9908
98	9912	9917	9921	9926	9930	9934	9939	9943	9948	9952
99	9956	9961	9965	9969	9974	9978	9983	9987	9991	9996

Power, Voltage Ratios to Decibels

$$N_{dB} = 10 \log \frac{P_1}{P_2} = 20 \log \frac{E_1}{E_2} + 10 \log \frac{R_2}{R_1} = 20 \log \frac{E_1}{E_2} \text{ if } R_1 = R_2$$

To find the decibel equivalent of any power or voltage ratio (P_1/P_2 or E_1/E_2), locate the ratio in the appropriate column, and read the decibel level in the adjacent column. Note that ratios of less than 1 signify a loss, while ratios greater than 1 indicate a gain, in decibel level.

To find the decibel level for a desired ratio not listed in the table, choose any of the available ratios whose product equals the desired ratio. The sum of the adjacent decibel values is the decibel level of the desired ratio.

Example: What is the level in decibels of a power ratio of 200?

200 = 100 x 2   100 = 20 dB
                            x2 = +3 dB
                        200 = 23 dB

POWER, VOLTAGE RATIOS TO DECIBELS

Power Ratio	Decibel Loss	Voltage Ratio
.00001	-50 dB	.00316
.0001	40	.0100
.0010	30	.0316
.0100	20	.1000
.0125	19	.1122
.0158	18	.1259
.0199	17	.1413
.0251	16	.1585
.0316	15	.1778
.0354	14.5	.1884
.0398	14	.1995
.0446	13.5	.2113
.0501	13	.2239
.0562	12.5	.2371
.0631	12	.2512
.0707	11.5	.2661
.0794	11	.2818
.0891	10.5	.2985
.1000	10	.3162
.1023	9.9	.3199
.1047	9.8	.3236
.1072	9.7	.3273
.1096	9.6	.3311
.1122	9.5	.3350
.1148	9.4	.3388
.1175	9.3	.3248
.1202	9.2	.3467
.1230	9.1	.3508
.1259	9.0	.3548
.1288	8.9	.3589
.1318	8.8	.3631
.1349	8.7	.3673
.1380	8.6	.3715
.1413	8.5	.3758
.1445	8.4	.3802
.1479	- 8.3	.3846

Power Ratio	Decibel Loss	Voltage Ratio
.1514	- 8.2 dB	.3890
.1549	8.1	.3936
.1585	8.0	.3981
.1622	7.9	.4027
.1660	7.8	.4074
.1698	7.7	.4121
.1738	7.6	.4169
.1778	7.5	.4217
.1820	7.4	.4266
.1862	7.3	.4315
.1905	7.2	.4365
.1950	7.1	.4416
.1995	7.0	.4467
.2042	6.9	.4519
.2089	6.8	.4571
.2138	6.7	.4624
.2188	6.6	.4677
.2239	6.5	.4732
.2291	6.4	.4786
.2344	6.3	.4842
.2399	6.2	.4898
.2455	6.1	.4955
.2512	6.0	.5012
.2570	5.9	.5070
.2630	5.8	.5129
.2692	5.7	.5188
.2754	5.6	.5243
.2818	5.5	.5309
.2884	5.4	.5370
.2951	5.3	.5433
.3020	5.2	.5495
.3090	5.1	.5559
.3162	5.0	.5623
.3236	4.9	.5689
.3311	4.8	.5754
.3388	4.7	.5821
.3467	4.6	.5888
.3548	- 4.5	.5957

Power Ratio	Decibel Loss	Voltage Ratio
.3631	- 4.4 dB	.6026
.3715	4.3	.6095
.3802	4.2	.6166
.3890	4.1	.6237
.3981	4.0	.6310
.4074	3.9	.6383
.4169	3.8	.6457
.4266	3.7	.6531
.4365	3.6	.6607
.4467	3.5	.6683
.4571	3.4	.6761
.4677	3.3	.6839
.4786	3.2	.6918
.4898	3.1	.6998
.5012	3.0	.7079
.5129	2.9	.7161
.5248	2.8	.7244
.5370	2.7	.7328
.5495	2.6	.7413
.5623	2.5	.7499
.5754	2.4	.7586
.5888	2.3	.7674
.6026	2.2	.7762
.6166	2.1	.7852
.6310	2.0	.7943
.6457	1.9	.8035
.6607	1.8	.8128
.6761	1.7	.8222
.6918	1.6	.8318
.7079	1.5	.8414
.7244	1.4	.8511
.7413	1.3	.8610
.7586	1.2	.8710
.7762	1.1	.8810
.7943	1.0	.8913
.8128	0.9	.9016
.8318	0.8	.9120
.8511	- 0.7	.9226

Power Ratio	Decibel Loss	Voltage Ratio
.8710	- 0.6 dB	.9333
.8913	0.5	.9441
.9120	0.4	.9550
.9333	0.3	.9661
.9550	0.2	.9772
.9772	0.1	.9886
.9795	0.09	.9897
.9817	0.08	.9908
.9840	0.07	.9920
.9863	0.06	.9931
.9886	0.05	.9943
.9908	0.04	.9954
.9931	0.03	.9966
.9954	0.02	.9977
.9977	- 0.01	.9988

Power Ratio	Decibel Gain	Voltage Ratio
1.000	0.00	1.000
1.002	+ 0.01	1.001
1.004	0.02	1.002
1.006	0.03	1.003
1.009	0.04	1.004
1.011	0.05	1.005
1.013	0.06	1.006
1.016	0.07	1.008
1.018	0.08	1.009
1.020	0.09	1.010
1.023	0.1	1.012
1.047	0.2	1.023
1.072	0.3	1.035
1.096	0.4	1.047
1.122	0.5	1.059
1.148	0.6	1.072
1.175	0.7	1.084
1.202	0.8	1.096
1.230	0.9	1.109
1.259	1.0	1.122
1.288	1.1	1.135
1.318	+ 1.2	1.148

Power Ratio	Decibel Gain	Voltage Ratio
1.349	+ 1.3 dB	1.161
1.380	1.4	1.175
1.413	1.5	1.189
1.445	1.6	1.202
1.479	1.7	1.216
1.514	1.8	1.230
1.549	1.9	1.245
1.585	2.0	1.259
1.622	2.1	1.274
1.660	2.2	1.288
1.698	2.3	1.303
1.738	2.4	1.318
1.778	2.5	1.334
1.820	2.6	1.349
1.862	2.7	1.365
1.905	2.8	1.380
1.950	2.9	1.396
1.995	3.0	1.413
2.042	3.1	1.429
2.089	3.2	1.445
2.138	3.3	1.462
2.188	3.4	1.479
2.239	3.5	1.496
2.291	3.6	1.514
2.344	3.7	1.531
2.399	3.8	1.549
2.455	3.9	1.567
2.512	4.0	1.585
2.570	4.1	1.603
2.630	4.2	1.622
2.692	4.3	1.641
2.754	4.4	1.660
2.818	4.5	1.679
2.884	4.6	1.698
2.951	4.7	1.718
3.020	4.8	1.738
3.090	4.9	1.758
3.162	+ 5.0	1.778

Power Ratio	Decibel Gain	Voltage Ratio
3.236	+ 5.1 dB	1.799
3.311	5.2	1.820
3.388	5.3	1.841
3.467	5.4	1.862
3.548	5.5	1.884
3.631	5.6	1.905
3.715	5.7	1.928
3.802	5.8	1.950
3.890	5.9	1.972
3.981	6.0	1.995
4.074	6.1	2.018
4.169	6.2	2.042
4.266	6.3	2.065
4.365	6.4	2.089
4.467	6.5	2.113
4.571	6.6	2.138
4.677	6.7	2.163
4.786	6.8	2.188
4.898	6.9	2.213
5.012	7.0	2.239
5.129	7.1	2.265
5.248	7.2	2.291
5.370	7.3	2.317
5.495	7.4	2.344
5.623	7.5	2.371
5.754	7.6	2.399
5.888	7.7	2.427
6.026	7.8	2.455
6.166	7.9	2.483
6.310	8.0	2.512
6.457	8.1	2.541
6.607	8.2	2.570
6.761	8.3	2.600
6.918	8.4	2.630
7.079	8.5	2.661
7.244	8.6	2.692
7.413	8.7	2.723
7.586	+ 8.8	2.754

Power Ratio	Decibel Gain	Voltage Ratio
7.762	+ 8.9 dB	2.786
7.943	9.0	2.818
8.128	9.1	2.851
8.318	9.2	2.884
8.511	9.3	2.917
8.710	9.4	2.951
8.913	9.5	2.985
9.120	9.6	3.020
9.333	9.7	3.055
9.550	9.8	3.090
9.772	9.9	3.126
10.000	10.0	3.162
11.22	10.5	3.350
12.59	11.0	3.548
14.13	11.5	3.758
15.85	12.0	3.981
17.78	12.5	4.217
19.95	13.0	4.467
22.39	13.5	4.732
25.12	14.0	5.012
28.18	14.5	5.309
31.62	15.0	5.623
39.81	16.0	6.310
50.12	17.0	7.079
63.10	18.0	7.943
79.43	19.0	8.913
100.00	20.0	10.000
1,000.00	30.0	31.620
10,000.00	40.0	100.00
100,000.00	+50.0	316.20

APPENDIX 3

Frequency, Period and Wavelength of Sound

Frequency F = V/λ	Period T = 1/F	Wavelength λ = V/F				
		In Air, V = 1,100 ft./sec.	On Tape, At a Speed of			
			7½ in./sec.	15 in./sec.	30 in./sec.
10 Hz	100.00 millisec.	110.00 ft.	750.00 mils	1.50 in.	3.00 in.
20	50.00	55.00	375.00	750.00 mils	1.50 in.
31.50	31.74	34.92	238.09	476.19	952.38 mils
63	15.87	17.46	119.04	238.09	476.19
125	8.00	8.80	60.00	120.00	240.00
250	4.00	4.40	30.00	60.00	120.00
440	2.27	2.50	17.04	34.09	68.18
500	2.00	2.20	15.00	30.00	60.00
1,000	1.00 millisec.	1.10 ft.	7.50	15.00	30.00
2,000	500.00 microsec.	6.60 in.	3.75	7.50	15.00
4,000	250.00	3.30	1.87	3.75	7.50
6,000	166.67	2.20	1.25	2.50	5.00
8,000	125.00	1.65	0.93	1.87	3.75
10,000	100.00	1.32	0.75	1.50	3.00
12,000	83.33	1.10 in.	0.62	1.25	2.50
14,000	71.42	942 mils	0.53	1.07	2.14
16,000	62.50	825	0.46	0.93	1.87
18,000	55.55	733	0.41	0.83	1.67
20,000 Hz	50.00 microsec.	660 mils	0.37 mils	0.75 mils	1.50 mils

APPENDIX 4

Conversion Factors

A	B	To convert *A to B, multiply by;* *B to A, divide by*
ampere-hours	coulombs	3.600×10^3
ampere-turns	gilberts	1.257
bars	atmospheres	9.869×10^{-1}
bars	dynes/sq. cm.	$1. \times 10^6$
btu/hr.	watts	2.931×10^{-1}
btu/min.	kilowatts	1.757×10^{-2}
btu/min.	watts	1.757×10^1
centimeters	feet	3.281×10^{-2}
centimeters	inches	3.937×10^{-1}
centimeters	meters	$1. \times 10^{-2}$
centimeters	millimeters	$1. \times 10^1$
coulombs	faradays	1.036×10^{-5}
degrees (angle)	radians	1.745×10^{-2}
degrees/sec.	radians/sec.	1.745×10^{-2}
degrees/sec.	revolutions/min.	1.667×10^{-1}
dynes/sq. cm.	atmospheres	9.869×10^{-7}
dynes	joules/cm.	1.0×10^{-7}
dynes	joules/meter (newtons)	1.0×10^{-5}
dynes/sq. cm.	bars	1.0×10^{-6}
ergs	joules	1.0×10^{-7}
ergs	kilowatt-hrs.	2.773×10^{-14}
ergs	watt-hrs.	2.773×10^{-11}
ergs/sec.	kilowatts	$1. \times 10^{-10}$
farads	microfarads	$1. \times 10^6$

A	B	*To convert* *A to B, multiply by;* *B to A, divide by*
faraday/sec.	ampere (absolute)	9.65×10^4
faradays	ampere-hours	2.68×10^1
faradays	coulombs	9.649×10^4
feet	meters	3.048×10^{-1}
feet/sec.	miles/hr.	6.818×10^{-1}
gausses	lines/sq. in.	6.452
gausses	webers/sq. cm.	1.0×10^{-8}
gausses	webers/sq. in.	6.452×10^{-8}
gausses	webers/sq. meter	1.0×10^{-4}
gausses	amp.-turn/cm.	7.958×10^{-1}
gausses	gilbert/cm.	1.0
gilberts	ampere-turns	7.958×10^{-1}
gilberts/cm.	ampere-turns/cm.	7.958×10^{-1}
gilberts/cm.	ampere-turns/in.	2.021
gilberts/cm.	ampere-turns/meter	7.958×10^1
henries	millihenries	1.0×10^3
horsepower	kilowatts	7.457×10^{-1}
horsepower	watts	7.457×10^2
horsepower-hours	joules	2.684×10^6
inches	centimeters	2.540
internat'l ampere	absolute amp. (u.s.)	9.998×10^{-1}
'internat'l volt	absolute volt (u.s.)	1.00033
internat'l coulomb	absolute coulomb	9.99835×10^{-1}
joules	ergs	1.0×10^7
joules	watt-hrs.	2.778×10^{-4}
joules/cm.	dynes	1.0×10^7
joules/cm.	joules/meter (newtons)	1.0×10^2
kilograms/sq. cm.	dynes/sq. cm.	9.80665×10^5
kilograms/sq. meter	bars	9.807×10^{-5}
kilogram-calories	joules	4.183×10^3
kilowatts	watts	1.0×10^3
kilowatt-hrs.	ergs	3.6×10^{13}
kilowatt-hrs.	joules	3.6×10^6

A	B	To convert A to B, multiply by; B to A, divide by
lines/sq. cm.	gausses	1.0
lines/sq. in.	gausses	1.55×10^{-1}
lines/sq. in.	webers/sq. cm.	1.55×10^{-9}
lines/sq. in.	webers/sq. in.	1.0×10^{-8}
lines/sq. in.	webers/sq. meter	1.55×10^{-5}
maxwells	webers	1.0×10^{-8}
megohms	microhms	1.0×10^{12}
megohms	ohms	1.0×10^{6}
meters	feet	3.281
microfarads	farads	1.0×10^{-6}
millimeters	centimeters	1.0×10^{-1}
millimeters	inches	3.937×10^{-2}
millimeters	mils	3.937×10^{1}
mils	centimeters	2.54×10^{-3}
mils	feet	8.333×10^{-5}
mils	inches	1.0×10^{-3}
minutes (angles)	degrees	1.667×10^{-2}
minutes (angles)	radians	2.909×10^{-4}
newtons	dynes	1.0×10^{5}
ohms	megohms	1.0×10^{-6}
ounces/sq. in.	dynes/sq. cm.	4.309×10^{3}
radians	degrees	5.7296×10^{1}
radians	minutes	3.438×10^{3}
radians	seconds	2.063×10^{5}
radians/sec.	revolutions/min.	9.549
revolutions	radians	6.283
seconds (angle)	degrees	2.778×10^{-4}
seconds (angle)	minutes	1.667×10^{-2}
seconds (angle)	radians	4.848×10^{-6}
square centimeters	sq. inches	1.550×10^{-1}
steradians	spheres	7.958×10^{-2}
watts	btu/hr.	3.4129

A	B	To convert A to B, multiply by; B to A, divide by
watts	kilowatts	1.0×10^{-3}
watts (abs.)	joules/sec.	1.0
webers	maxwells	1.0×10^8
webers	kilolines	1.0×10^5
webers/sq. in.	gausses	1.55×10^7
webers/sq. in.	lines/sq. in.	1.0×10^8
webers/sq. in.	webers/sq. cm.	1.55×10^{-1}
webers/sq. in.	webers/sq. meter	1.55×10^3
webers/sq. meter	gausses	1.0×10^4
webers/sq. meter	lines/sq. in.	6.452×10^4
webers/sq. meter	webers/sq. cm.	1.0×10^{-4}
webers/sq. meter	webers/sq. in.	6.452×10^{-4}

APPENDIX 5

NAB Standard: Magnetic Tape Recording and Reproducing (Reel-to-Reel)

INTRODUCTION

The NAB Recording and Reproducing Standards Committee was originally organized in 1941. Standards proposals issuing from the Committee have been adopted by the Board of Directors in 1942, 1949, 1950, and 1953. The Standards contained herein were adopted by the Board on January 29, 1965. They are presented here in an abridged format.

These standards and recommended good engineering practices are for the guidance of the broadcasting industry and represent the contributions of many of the nation's authorities on the various phases of recording as used by the industry. The NAB Recording and Reproducing Standards Committee has also benefited by contributions made by several international organizations. The Committee was open to participation by any interested individual or organization and consisted of representatives from the manufacturers, broadcasters and producers. Close liaison was maintained with other organizations (as well as foreign countries) to insure the maximum degree of coordinated understanding and recommended standardization, to permit interchangeability, and, at the same time, to embrace the latest technological advances of the art.

Nothing in these standards prohibits or discourages continued progress or advancement of the art. On the contrary, these standards are intended to stimulate continued scientific exploration in the field of recording. It is anticipated that when new techniques and developments are evident, the NAB Recording and Reproducing Standards Committee may request submissions thereon looking toward any needed amendments and additions to keep pace with the art as it affects all forms of AM, FM and TV broadcasting.

Reprinted by permission. Engineering Department, National Association of Broadcasters, 1771 N Street N.W., Washington, D.C. 20036

412

These standards are written to cover full track, two track, and four track magnetic recording systems operating at 7½ inches per second, the speed established as the preferred tape standard speed for program exchange. These standards also contain the supplementary tape speed standards of 15 and 3¾ inches per second in the body of the main high-performance standard.

A second set of standards are contained within the overall framework of these standards. This section is titled "Special Purpose Limited Performance Systems." These specifications are intended to permit interchangeability between recorders where portability and weight are the primary considerations and technical perfection is made secondary to accomplish this greater portability. It is essential that anyone studying these standards appreciate the difference in purpose of these two sets of standards.

Basic to these standards are physical and mechanical properties such as tape speeds, tape specifications, track width, reel specifications, and tape wind and storage conditions.

To simplify compliance with these standards, the specifications called for are referenced to "Standard Test Tapes," which tapes are the primary tools in determining compliance. Three sets of annex cover the details of how such standard test tapes are made and calibrated so that they may be reproduced in the field with the proper equipment.

Recording systems which comply with the "Standard Systems" specifications in the main body of the standard shall be designated as "NAB Standard Recorders". Such recording systems as do not meet these specifications shall be designated as "NAB Special Purpose Recorders," if they meet the Special Purpose Limited Performance System specifications.

1. PHYSICAL AND MECHANICAL SPECIFICATIONS

Magnetic Tape Dimensions

1.01 Width. It shall be standard that magnetic tape width shall be 0.246 inches ± 0.002 inches for nominal one-quarter inch sound recording tape.

1.02 Thickness. It shall be standard that the thickness of magnetic tape shall not exceed 0.0022 inches.

1.03 Length. It shall be standard that magnetic tape be supplied in the following minimum lengths:

Nominal Reel Dia.	Nominal Hub	1.5 mil base	1.0 mil base	0.5 mil base
3 in.	1.75 in.	125 ft.	200 ft.	300 ft.
5 in.	1.75 in.	600 ft.	900 ft.	[1]
7 in.	2.25 in.	1200 ft.	1800 ft.	[1]
10.5 in.	NAB 4.5 in.	2500 ft.	3600 ft.	[1]
14 in.	NAB 4.5 in.	5000 ft.	7200 ft.	[1]

Magnetic Tape Wind

1.04 It shall be standard that tape shall be wound with the oxide coated surface facing toward the hub of the reel.

1.04.01 Recorded tape normally should be wound so that the start of the program material is at the outside of the reel.

1.04.02 It is good engineering practice when storing recorded tapes for long periods of time that the start of the program material be at the inside next to the hub. Tapes so stored or shipped shall be clearly marked to prevent accidental playing in the reverse direction.[2]

Magnetic Tape Level and Uniformity

1.05 It shall be standard that magnetic tape shall have an average output level at 400 Hz at a tape speed of 7½ ips which is uniform within ± 0.5 dB throughout a given reel.

1.05.01 This measurement is to be made at the NAB Standard Reference Level and read on a Standard Volume Indicator (ASA Standard C16.5-1961) with bias adjusted for maximum output for the tape under test.

1.06 It shall be standard that magnetic tapes of any specified type shall have an average output at 400 Hz at a tape speed of 7½ ips which is uniform within ± 1 dB from reel to reel.

1.06.01 This measurement is to be made at the NAB Standard

---

[1] Not recommended.

[2] Tapes stored with the end of the program toward the outside of the reel will have slightly less preprint than postprint. This is generally desirable because postprint tends to be masked by the program material and reverberation effects. Also, rewinding a tape immediately before playing tends to reduce print-through. Another advantage of rewinding before playing is that stresses are relieved and any adhesion of adjacent layers of tape will be eliminated. A further advantage is that tape wound on the take-up reel in the play mode of operation usually is wound more smoothly than when wound at high speed. Therefore, there is less chance of damage during storage or shipment or due to temperature and humidity changes.

Reference Level and read on a Standard Volume Indicator (ASA Standard C16.5-1961) with bias adjusted for maximum output for the tape under test.

Magnetic Track Designations

1.07 It shall be standard that in multitrack recordings, Track One shall be the top track when the tape is moving from left to right with the coated side facing away from the observer and with the leader to the right. The next lower track is designated Track Two, and so on.

Magnetic Track Dimensions

1.08 It shall be standard that the recorded magnetic track for full track recordings be 0.238 inches +0.010 −0.004 inches in width.

1.09 It shall be standard that the recorded tracks for two track monophonic or stereophonic recordings be 0.082 ±0.002 inches in width with a center-to-center spacing of 0.156 ±0.004 inches.

1.10 It shall be standard that the recorded tracks for four track recordings shall be 0.043 +0.000-0.004 inches in width. The center-to-center distances between Tracks 1 and 3, and between Tracks 2 and 4 shall be 0.134 +0.002−0.000 inches. The four tracks shall be equally disposed across the tape with a tape width of 0.244 inches and the outer edges of Tracks 1 and 4 coincident with the edges of the tape.

Two Track Stereophonic Recordings

1.11 It shall be standard that for two track stereophonic recordings, Track 1 shall carry the recording for the left-hand channel as viewed from the audience, and Track 2 shall carry the recording for the right-hand channel.

1.12 It shall be standard that for two track stereophonic recordings, the tracks shall be recorded with head gaps in line and phased for reproduction on equipment so connected that when a full track tape is reproduced, it produces in-phase signals in the two channel outputs.

Four Track Monophonic Recordings

1.13 It shall be standard that for four track monophonic recordings, the track recording sequence shall be 1-4-3-2.

Four Track Stereophonic Recordings

1.14 It shall be standard that Tracks 1 and 3 shall be used simultaneously for one direction of tape travel and Tracks 2 and 4 for the other direction. Tracks 1 and 3 shall be used first as the tape is unwound from the supply reel.

1.15 It shall be standard that Tracks 1 and 4 shall carry the recording for the left-hand channel as viewed from the audience, and Tracks 2 and 3 shall carry the recording for the right-hand channel.

1.16 It shall be standard in four track stereophonic recordings that Tracks 1 and 3 and Tracks 2 and 4 shall be recorded with the head gaps in line and shall be phased for reproduction on equipment so connected that when a full-track tape is reproduced it produces in-phase signals at the two channel outputs.

Magnetic Tape Reel Dimensions (¼ inch tape)

1.17 It shall be standard that NAB magnetic tape reels for ¼ inch tape be identified as Type A or Type B reels.

1.17.01 It shall be standard that NAB Type A reels shall include 10½ or 14 inch metal or filled plastic reels with a nominal 3 inch center hole and shall conform to the dimensions and specifications of Figure 1 and Table 1.

1.17.02 It shall be standard that NAB Type B reels shall include all filled or unfilled plastic reels with a nominal 5/16 inch center hole and shall conform to the dimensions and specifications of Figure 2 and Table 2.

2. SPECIFICATIONS FOR STANDARD SYSTEMS

The following systems specifications apply to all high quality magnetic recording and reproducing equipment used for music and speech programs where superior performance is of primary importance.

Magnetic Tape Speeds

2.01 Preferred Speed. It shall be standard that the preferred tape speed be 7½ inches per second ± 0.2%.

2.01.01 The tolerance on tape speed shall apply to any portion of the reel of tape in use and shall be measured by the method described in Annex A.

2.02 Supplementary Tape Speeds. It shall be standard that 15 and

3¾ inches per second ± 0.2% be supplementary tape speeds.

2.02.01 The tolerance on tape speed shall apply to any portion of the reel of tape in use and shall be measured by the method described in Annex A.

Standard Reference Level

2.03 It shall be standard that the NAB Standard Reference Level shall be that 400 Hz level which is equal to the recorded level on the NAB Primary Reference Tape.[3]

Standard Recorded Program Level[4]

2.04 It shall be standard that recorded program material shall produce the same reference deflection on a Standard Volume Indicator (ASA Standard C16.5-1961) as that produced by a 400 Hz sine wave signal recorded at the NAB Standard Reference Level.

Standard Recorded Response[5,6,7,8]

2.08.01 The recorded response is defined as the difference between the over-all record-reproduce response and the reproduce

---

[3] The NAB Primary Reference Tape is a tape of the normal general purpose type which has been selected for average characteristics of output, sensitivity and distortion. The 400 Hz recording on it was made at 7½ ips with bias adjusted for maximum output, at an output level 8 dB below that which produced 3% third harmonic distortion. This does not imply a failure to meet the 10 dB overload margin of footnote 4. It is rather, a practical convenient method of specification consistent with the magnetic recording and reproducing process. Since neither the tape nor the measurement conditions can be duplicated exactly in the field, all NAB Standard Test Tapes contain a 400 Hz recording at the NAB Standard Reference Level within ±0.25 dB as a means for making this level available.

[4] It is well established that at least a 10 dB margin is required between the sine wave load handling capacity of a system and the level of program material as measured by the Standard Volume Indicator (ASA Standard C16.5-1961). These peak levels are believed to be approximately the maximum flux which can be recorded on presently available tapes without excessive distortion. This is also substantiated by practical experience.

[5] It is recommended that the Standard Reproducing System reponse roll off at the rate of at least 6 dB per octave beyond the frequency limits specified.

[6] Basic Reproducing Characteristics are defined in Annex B, and the values listed in Tables 3 and 4. Precise methods of measuring and calibrating a reproducing system are discussed in Annex C. A reproducer calibrated by these methods and meeting all of the specifications of this Standard is considered suitable for measuring and calibrating Standard Test Tapes.

[7] Since NAB Standard Test Tapes are recorded across the full width of the tape, per section 4.02, a low frequency boost may be expected when the test tape is reproduced on a head of less than full track width. Refer to the instructions supplied with the test tpae for further details.

[8] It should be noted that full track operation at the lower tape speeds may cause some difficulty in consistently meeting the frequency response standards due to possible tape skew and the resultant azimuth errors.

response from an NAB Standard Test Tape of the same speed.[9,10]

2.08.02 The measurement of recorded response shall be made at the same level as that on the NAB Standard Test Tape. Normal operating bias shall be used.

Signal-to-Noise Ratio[11,12]

2.09 It shall be standard that the unweighted signal-to-noise ratio shall be not less than the following:

Tape Speed	Full Track	Two Track	Four Track
15 ips	50 dB	45 dB	not used
7½ ips	50 dB	45 dB	45 dB
3¾ ips	46 dB	46 dB	45 dB

2.09.01 Unweighted noise shall be measured over the frequency range of 20 Hz to 20 kHz. The response of the measuring system shall be uniform ±0.3 dB from 30 to 15,000 Hz. Response at 20,000 Hz shall be 3 dB below the 400 Hz value, falling at the rate of at least 12 dB per octave above 20 kHz. The noise measurement shall be made using a tape previously recorded with bias but with no signal. The reference signal level shall be the 400 Hz NAB Standard Reference Level and the indicating meter shall have the dynamics of the Standard Volume Indicator (ASA Standard C16.5-1961). The measuring system shall have a full-wave rectified average measurement law.

---

[9] The recording equalization of a recorder/reproducer should be adjusted for an over-all response which matches as nearly as possible the response of the reproducer from the NAB Standard Test Tape. This response is standardized, rather than the simple over-all record-reproduce response, in order to assure better interchangeability of recorded tapes.

[10] An alternate definition of a Recorded Characteristic could be in terms of measured surface induction or remanent flux in free space. However, since such measurements are of limited value, particularly when used with ferromagnetic heads at short wave lengths, the definition in 2.08.01 has been accepted as more useful for the purpose of this Standard.

[11] These measurements are intended to give a measure of noise in terms of the NAB Standard Reference Level; they are therefore figures of merit for comparisons of system noise. They do not, however, take into account the program level which may be recorded on a particular tape without excessive distortion. It should be borne in mind that the peak signal-to-noise ratio may be approximately 10 dB better than the figures given when the NAB Standard Recorded Program Level is used on general purpose tape.

[12] The use of 3¾ ips full-track recordings may present practical difficulties in maintaining azimuth.

2.10 It shall be standard that the weighted signal-to-noise ratio shall be not less than the following: [13,14,15]

Tape Speeds	Full Track	Two Track	Four Track
15 ips	58 dB	53 dB	not used
7½ ips	60 dB	55 dB	52 dB
3¾ ips	57 dB	54 dB	52 dB

2.10.01 Weighted noise shall be measured using the ASA "A" curve (ASA Standard S1.4-1961). The noise measurement shall be made using a tape previously recorded with bias but with no signal. Calibration is made (with the weighting network inserted) at 1000 Hz using the 1000 Hz Standard Level which is included for this purpose on the NAB Standard Test Tape. The indicator meter shall have the dynamics of the Standard Volume Indicator (ASA Standard C16.5-1961) and the measuring system shall have a full-wave rectified average measurement law.

Distortion [16]

2.11 It shall be standard that the over-all record reproduce system total harmonic distortion including tape shall be less than 3% rms for a 400 Hz sine wave signal recorded to achieve a reproduce level 6 dB above the NAB Standard Reference Level.

Flutter

2.12 It shall be standard that in the reproduce mode the unweighted flutter content when reproducing an essentially flutter-free recording of 3 kHz at any portion of the reel of tape in use shall not

[13] See footnote 12.

[14] The weighted noise measurement employes a frequency response similar to that of the ear at low volume levels and is intended to give a more useful indication of the subjective signal-to-noise ratio than the unweighted measurement. The noise measurement is approximately comparable to that obtained by the use of a 500 to 15,000 Hz filter in disc noise measurements.

[15] Note that the weighted signal-to-noise ratio is poorer at 15 ips than at 7½ ips. This is due to the fact that the reproduce amplifier equalization remains the same for both speeds while the tape noise increases with tape speed.

[16] The recording amplifier should not overload with high frequency input signals equal in level to the maximum expected low frequency levels. In practice, this means that the recording high frequency pre-emphasis may place an additional demand on the undistorted amplifier output. Distortion of this type is not normally detected by harmonic distortion measurements. Bias leakage into the record or reproduce amplifier circuits may be a source of additional distortion.

exceed the following:

Tape Speed	Flutter (rms)
15 ips	0.15%
7½ ips	0.20%
3¾ ips	0.25%

2.12.01 Unweighted flutter content shall be measured over the frequency range of 0.5 Hz to 200 Hz. The response of the measuring system shall be 3 dB down at 0.5 Hz and 200 Hz, and falling at a rate of at least 6 dB per octave below and above these frequencies, respectively. At low frequencies where the meter pointer follows the wave form, the maximum deflection shall indicate the rms value. The indicating meter shall have the dynamics of the Standard Volume Indicator (ASA C16.5-1961), a full-wave rectified average measurement law, and shall be calibrated to read the rms value of a sinusoidal frequency variation.

2.12.02 It shall be standard that the meter be read for random periods throughout the length of the tape, noting the average of the peak readings, but excluding random peaks which do not recur more than three times in any 10-second period.

2.13 It shall be standard that in the reproduce mode the weighted flutter content when reproducing an essentially flutter-free recording of 3 kHz at any portion of the reel of tape in use shall not exceed the following:[17]

Tape Speed	Flutter (rms)
15 ips	0.05%
7½ ips	0.07%
3¾ ips	0.10%

2.13.01 Weighted flutter shall be measured over the frequency range of 0.5 to 200 Hz. The response of the measuring system shall be as specified in Table 5. At low frequencies where the pointer follows the wave form, the maximum deflection shall indicate the rms value. The indicating meter shall have the dynamics of the Standard Volume Indicator (ASA C16.5-1961), a full-wave rectified average measurement law, and shall be calibrated to read the rms value of a

---

[17] The weighted flutter measurement employs a frequency response similar to the sensitivity of the ear to frequency variations versus the frequency of these variations ("flutter rate") and is intended to give a more useful indication of the subjective effect of flutter than the unweighted measurement.

sinusoidal frequency variation.

2.13.02 It shall be standard that the meter be read for random periods throughout the length of the tape, noting the average of the peak readings, but excluding random peaks which do not recur more than three times in any 10-second period.

Crosstalk[18]

2.14 It shall be standard that for two or four track monophonic systems and for four track stereophonic systems, the adjacent track signal-to-crosstalk ratio shall be not less the 60 dB in the range from 200 Hz to 10 kHz.[19]

2.14.01 For these measurements, bias shall not be applied to the unrecorded tracks.

Stereophonic Channel Separation

2.15 It shall be standard that with stereophonic systems channel separation shall be not less than 40 dB between the frequencies of 100 Hz and 10 kHz.

2.15.01 For measurement of stereophonic systems, bias shall be applied to both tracks.

3. SPECIFICATIONS FOR SPECIAL PURPOSE LIMITED PERFORMANCE SYSTEMS

The use of lightweight portable magnetic recorders is recognized in this section of the Standard. It presents what are considered to be the minimum acceptable performance requirements where adequate voice intelligibility and interchangeability of recorded tapes are of primary importance. Systems meeting these specifications are not suitable for maximum fidelity recording of speech or music.

Tape Speeds

3.01 It shall be standard that tape speeds for Special Purpose Magnetic Recording and Reproducing Systems by 7½, 3¾, or 1⅞ inches

---

18 These measurements shall be made at the recorded level of the frequency response portion of the NAB Standard Test Tape, and must be made with a tuned voltmeter in order to eliminate the effect of noise. The reference level shall be the 400 Hz tone in the frequency response portion of the NAB Test Tape.

19 It should be recognized that two-track monophonic tapes which are duplicated on stereophonic equipment will have the crosstalk characteristics of a stereophonic system and therefore may not meet this crosstalk specification.

per second, ± 2% as measured at any portion of the reel of tape in use, and shall be measured by the method described in Annex A.

Flutter

3.02 It shall be standard that in the reproduce mode, unweighted flutter content, when reproducing an essentially flutter-free recording of 3 kHz, shall not exceed 0.5% rms at any portion of the reel of tape in use.

3.02.01 Unweighted flutter content shall be measured over the frequency range of 0.5 Hz to 200 Hz. The response of the measuring system shall be 3 dB down at 0.5 Hz and 200 Hz, and falling at a rate of at least 6 dB per octave below and above these frequencies, respectively. At low frequencies where the meter pointer follows the wave form, the maximum deflection shall indicate the rms value. The indicating meter shall have the dynamics of the Standard Volume Indicator (ASA C16.5-1961), a full-wave rectified average measurement law, and shall be calibrated to read the rms value of a sinusoidal frequency variation.

3.02.02 It shall be standard that the meter be read for random periods throughout the length of the tape, noting the average of the peak readings, but excluding random peaks which do not recur more than three times in any 10-second period.

Standard Recorded Program Level[20,21]

3.03 It shall be standard that recorded program material shall produce the same reference deflection on a Standard Volume Indicator (ASA Standard C16.5-1961) as that produced by a 400 Hz sine wave signal recorded at the NAB Standard Reference Level.

Reproducing System Response[22]

3.04.01 This specification represents the minimum acceptable limits, and is not intended to restrict the frequency range of voice

---

[20] It is well established that at least 10 dB margin is required between the sine wave load handling capacity of a system and the level of program material as measured by a Standard Volume Indicator (ASA Standard C16.5-1961). These peak levels are believed to be approximately the maximum flux which can be recorded on presently available tapes without excessive distortion. This is also substantiated by practical experience.

[21] At a speed of 1 7/8 ips, it may be advisable to record certain types of program material at a lower level to aviod distortion.

[22] Basic Reproducing Characteristics are defined in Annex B, and the values listed in Tables 3 and 4.

recording systems which have the inherent capability of wide-range recording, without distortion. It is, however, often considered desirable to limit the extreme low frequency response for improved speech intelligibility.

Recorded Response

3.05.01 The recorded response is defined as the difference between the over-all record—reproduce response and the reproduce response from an NAB Standard Test Tape of the same speed.

3.05.02 The measurement of Recorded Response must be made at the same level as that on the Standard Test Tape. Normal operating bias shall be used.

3.05.03 It is recommended that the Recorded Response be attenuated below 100 Hz at the rate of approximately 6 dB per octave in order to improve speech intelligibility. A similar attenuation above 5 kHz is recommended in order to reduce the chance of high frequency tape overload at the lower tape speeds.

Signal-to-Noise Ratio

3.06 It shall be standard that the unweighted signal-to-noise ratio shall be not less than the following:

Full Track	46 dB
Two Track	43 dB
Four Track	40 dB

3.06.01 Unweighted noise shall be measured over the frequency range of 20 Hz to 20 kHz. The response of the measuring system shall be uniform ±0.3 dB from 30 to 15,000 Hz. Response at 20,000 Hz shall be 3 dB below the 400 Hz value, falling at the rate of at least 12 dB per octave above 20 kHz. The noise measurement shall be made using a tape previously recorded with bias but with no signal. The reference signal level shall be the 400 Hz NAB Standard Reference Level and the indicating meter shall have the dynamics of the Standard Volume Indicator (ASA Standard C16.5-1961). The measuring system shall have a full-wave rectified average measurement law.

4. STANDARD TEST TAPES

4.01 The NAB Standard Test Tapes for reel-to-reel equipment

shall be designated as follows:

Speed	Test Tape
15 ips	15 NAB 65
7½ ips	7½ NAB 65
3¾ ips	3¾ NAB 65
1⅞ ips	1⅞ NAB 65

4.02 All test tapes shall be recorded across the full width of the tape.

4.03 Each NAB Standard Test Tape shall contain five parts as defined in the following sections:

4.03.01 An azimuth adjustment tone of 60 seconds duration at the following frequencies:[2][3]

Speed	Frequency
15 ips	15 kHz
7½ ips	15 kHz
3¾ ips	10 kHz
1⅞ ips	5 kHz

4.03.02 A 400 Hz sine wave signal of 20 seconds duration at the following level referred to the NAB Standard Reference Level:

Speed	Level
15 ips	0 dB
7½ ips	-10 dB
3¾ ips	-15 dB
1⅞ ips	-15 dB

4.03.03 A frequency response test containing the following frequencies at the indicated recorded levels. Each tone shall be approximately 12 seconds in duration and preceded by a voice announcement. The signal frequencies are recorded on these tapes in such a manner that they would supply a constant output level when reproduced on an Ideal Reproducing System.[24] The relative levels are

---

[23] The recorded level shall be the same as that of the corresponding frequency in the Frequency Response portion of the tape. The recorded azimuth shall be at 90 degrees ± 1 minute with respect to the edge of the tape.

[24] See Annex B of this Standard for a definition of The Ideal Reproducing System and the equalization to be used. Note that the curves described in Table 3 and 4 are frequency response curves of the Ideal Reproducer with constant flux in the core of the Ideal Head instead of the basic amplifier curve which was used in the 1953 NAB Standard. The concept of expressing a curve in terms of time constants remains unchanged and it is still necessary to modify the amplifier response to compensate for practical reproduce head losses in a Standard Reproducing System.

measured during manufacture of the tape on a reproducing system of known, defined characteristics which are determined by the method described in Annex C.

15 ips	7½ ips	3¾ ips	1⅞ ips
0 dB	−10 dB	−15 dB	−15 dB
15 kHz	15 kHz		
12 kHz	12 kHz		
10 kHz	10 kHz	10 kHz	
7.5 kHz	7.5 kHz	7.5 kHz	
5 kHz	5 kHz	5 kHz	5 kHz
2.5 kHz	2.5 kHz	2.5 kHz	2.5 kHz
1 kHz	1 kHz	1 kHz	1 kHz
750 Hz	750 Hz	750 Hz	750 Hz
500 Hz	500 Hz	500 Hz	500 Hz
250 Hz	250 Hz	250 Hz	250 Hz
100 Hz	100 Hz	100 Hz	100 Hz
75 Hz	75 Hz	75 Hz	75 Hz
50 Hz	50 Hz	50 Hz	50 Hz
30 Hz	30 Hz	30 Hz	30 Hz

4.03.04 A 400 Hz sine wave signal of 20 seconds duration at the NAB Standard Reference Level.[25]

4.03.05 A 1000 Hz sine wave signal of 60 seconds duration at the NAB Standard Recorded Program Level. (See Section 2.04)

---

[25] The level on the NAB Primary Reference Tape is that of a 400 Hz tone at a tape speed of 7½ ips, and thus represents a wavelength of 18.75 mils. Test Tapes for speeds other than 7½ ips are recorded such that they would supply the same ideal head flux at the same wavelength as the Primary Refereance Tape, when measured on an Ideal Reproducing System.

ANNEX A

Methods of Tape Speed Measurement

It shall be standard that tape speed be measured by applying the one-quarter inch wide circumference of a precision pully mounted on precision low friction bearings to the surface of the tape between the capstan and head assembly. The rotational speed of the pulley when driven by the tape may be measured by the use of an ac tachometer generator or by a stroboscope disc mounted on the pulley's flat surface. Tests of tape speed shall be made relative to the power line frequency.

It must be recognized that tape speed depends to some extent on tape thickness and tension, and on room temperature and humidity. Therefore, speed checks should be made under normal operating conditions with the machine adjusted according to manufacturer's recommendations.

Measurements shall be made with a tape the thickness of which is 0.0019 inches ± 0.0002 inches which corresponds to the thickness of nominal 1.5 mil base tape.

A suggested design for a practical stroboscope disc consists of a pulley with a diameter of 1.4305 +0.0002 −0.0000 inches upon which is attached a printed disc having 72 and 36 equally spaced dots or solid lines. A neon lamp operating from the 60 Hz motor supply flashes at a 120 Hz rate. The stroboscope disc, when illuminated by this lamp, will indicate 7½ and 15 ips tape speeds, respectively. For 3¾ ips operation, a diode in series with a neon lamp is required so that the lamp will flash at a 60 Hz rate.

It shall be standard that when using a stroboscope disc as recommended above, no more than 14 dots per minute shall drift past a fixed reference point in either direction for 7½ or 15 ips operation. For 3¾ ips operation the drift per minute shall not exceed 7 dots on the 36 dot disc. These limits of drift correspond to the speed tolerance limits of ± 0.2%.

426

ANNEX B

Ideal Reproducing System

It shall be standard that the NAB Ideal Reproducing System is a theoretical reproducer syster. It consists of an "ideal" reproducing head[1] and an amplifier the output of which shall conform to Table 3 or 4, with constant flux vs frequency in the core of the head.[2]

The curve of voltage vs frequency shall be uniform with frequency except where modified by the following equalizations:

a. The voltage attenuation of a single resistance-capacitance high-pass filter having an RC time constant t_1.

b. The inverse of the voltage attenuation of a single resistance-capacitance low-pass filter having an RC time constant t_2.

The curve expressed in decibels is represented by the following expressions:

$$\text{Where: } N_{dB} = 20 \log_{10} \omega t_1 \sqrt{\frac{1 + (\omega t_2)^2}{1 + (\omega t_1)^2}}$$

$$\omega = 2\pi f$$

$$f = \text{frequency}$$

And, t_1 and t_2 are as follows:

Tape Speed	t_1	t_2
15 ips	$3180\,\mu s$	$50\,\mu s$
7½ ips	$3180\,\mu s$	$50\,\mu s$
3¾ ips	$3180\,\mu s$	$90\,\mu s$
1⅞ ips	$3180\,\mu s$	$90\,\mu s$

---

[1] An "ideal" reproducing head is defined as a ferromagnetic ring head, the losses of which are negligible. This means that the gap is short and straight, the long wave-length flux paths are controlled so that no low-frequency contour effects are present and the losses in the head materials are negligible small.

[2] It is recognized tha the flux in the core of an "ideal" head is not necessarily the same as the surface flux on a tpae in space for various reasons. Since most of these effects are not readily measured, it has been decided to base this standard on "ideal" head core flux rather than surface induction.

ANNEX C

Primary Calibrated Reproducing System[1]

A Primary Calibrated Reproducing System used for the purpose of calibrating Standard Test Tapes shall meet the following specifications:

    A. The system response shall not deviate more than ± 3 dB from the ideal over the frequency range of interest.

    B. Electrical — Apparent core loss at the highest frequency of interest shall not exceed 3 dB, undamped head resonance shall not exceed 3 dB and amplifier deviation from the Ideal Response shall not exceed ±3 dB.

    C. Magnetic — Head gap losses shall not exceed 3 dB at the highest frequency of interest and the head contour effect curve shall not deviate more then ± 2 dB from the average.

Electrical losses shall be determined from measurements of the amplifier frequency response characteristic and the reproduce system output voltage characteristic with constant flux vs frequency in the head core.

Magnetic losses shall be determined from calculations of gap loss and measurements of head contour effects.

The following paragraphs specify the methods by which these characteristics shall be measured and the reproduce system calibrated. The procedure is to determine the various losses independently and consider them as deviations from the theoretical "Ideal Reproducing System."

Electrical Measurements

Three response frequency curves shall be made. First, the amplifier response alone with voltage directly proportional to frequency (voltage doubles for each octave frequency increase) measured by conventional methods; second, the head and amplifier response measured by applying a small voltage proportional to frequency across a low resistance connected in series with the head, and finally, the

---

[1] An NAB Standard Reproducing System need not fulfill the requirements for a Primary Calibrated Reproducing System as described in this Annex.

head and amplifier response measured with a constant flux vs frequency induced into the core of the reproduce head. The third measurement can be made by placing a fine wire over the head gap, securing it firmly in place, and feeding constant current through the wire. Although the resultant flux distribution is not identical to that from a tape, it is considered to be satisfactory for the purposes of this measurement. Ideally, the third curve would follow the Standard Reproducing Characteristic. However, in practice the curve may vary from the ideal because of head resonance effects, and apparent core losses. Resonance effects are determined by comparing curves 1 and 2 while apparent core losses are identified by comparing curves 2 and 3.

Magnetic Measurements

A curve of approximate gap loss vs frequency shall be calculated from the following expression:

$$\text{Gap loss} = -20 \log_{10} \frac{\sin\left[\,(180°)\,(d/\lambda)\,\right]}{\pi d/\lambda}$$

where d = null wavelength
λ = wavelength at which the gap loss is calculated.

The null wavelength is determined by finding the recorded wavelength at which the reproducing head output reaches a distinct minimum of at least 20 dB below maximum output. It is desirable to make this measurement at ½ or ¼ normal speed and with a tuned voltmeter with no greater than a one-third octave band width. In order to reach the 20 dB null the head gap edges must be sharp, straight and parallel.

In order to determine that a gap meets these requirements visual examination of the gap at about 1000x magnification is necessary. This may be accomplished with a toolmaker's microscope or with suitable photomicrographs taken at several locations along the gap. It has been shown that the null wavelength will be 1.14 times the optical gap length for a perfectly constructed head.[2] In practice it is usually greater. However, it is recommended that the null wave-

---

2 W. K. Westmijze, "Studies on Magnetic Recording" Philips Research Reports, Vol. 8, No. 3, pp-161-183, 1953.

length not be greater than 1.25 times the optical gap length for this applications.

A curve of the low frequency reproducing response shall be made using a constant current vs frequency recording made with normal bias and the result compared to the curve of reproduce system response with constant flux vs frequency induced into the head core (Curve 3 above), in order to determine contour effects. This reproducing response curve ideally should follow the Standard Reproducing Characteristic at frequencies below approximately 750 Hz at 7½ inches per second. In practice it is known that all of the flux from a tape at long wavelengths does not enter the head core. The amount that does enter varies with wavelength depending upon the length of tape to head contact, the shields in and around the head and the shape of the pole pieces.

It is important to accurately measure frequency when making the recording so that slight frequency errors are not interpreted as response errors. It is recommended that the slope of the contour effects curve not exceed 10 dB per octave so that a frequency error of ½% will result in a response error of not more than 0.07 dB.

Calibrated System Response

Having determined the various losses or deviations from the Ideal System Response, a calibration of the actual system is obtained as follows: From the system response curve, Curve 3 under Electrical Measurements, subtract the gap loss curve at high frequencies and algebraically add the low frequency portion by the contour effect curve. The resulting curve is the reproducing system response for constant available flux from a tape. The difference between this curve and the Standard Reproducing System Characteristic represents the deviation from the ideal response.

TABLE 1
DIMENSIONS FOR NAB TYPE A REELS
METAL OR FILLED PLASTIC THREE-INCH CENTER HOLE

	Metal	*Plastic*
A	3.002 +0.006 -0.000	3.010 +0.015 -0.000
B	10.500 or 14.000 +0.020 -0.010	10.500 ±0.020
C	4.500 ±0.010	4.500 ±0.015
D	3.250 +0.008 -0.002	3.250 +0.020 -0.000
E	0.219 +0.010 -0.000	0.219 +0.013 -0.000
F	0.109 +0.005 -0.000	0.109 +0.007 -0.000
G	120 degrees ±0.25 degrees	Not applicable
H	0.025 maximum	0.060 maximum
I	0.080 maximum	0.115 maximum
J	0.055 maximum	Not applicable
K	3.031 +0.006 -0.000	Not applicable
M	0.462 ±0.020	0.485 +0.040 -0.000
N	0.350 ±0.005 See Note 4	0.285 ±0.015
Q	3.875 ±0.002	Not applicable
R	60 degrees ±0.25 degrees	Not applicable
S	0.350 ±0.005	Not applicable
T	120 degrees ±0.25 degrees	120 degrees ±0.25 degrees

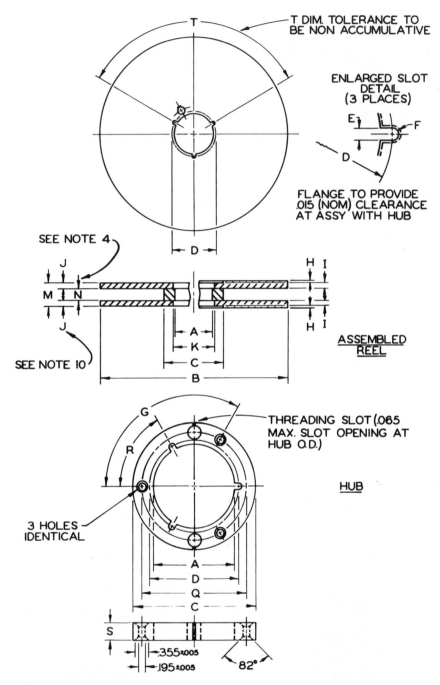

Figure 1. NAB Type A Reels

NOTES FOR FIGURE 1

1. Reels shall bave dimensions in inches as shown in Figure 1 and Table 1.
2. Flanges may have cut outs of random shape. The flange open area shall not exceed 50 percent of the total flange area.
3. Threading slots are shown on the figure but are optional.
4. Dimension N is the distance between flanges at the hub and shall not vary more than ±0.050 inches when measured from the hub to the periphery of the flanges. Flange wobble shall not exceed beyond the hatched areas of Figure 1.
5. The outside cylindrical hub surface (Dimension C) shall be concentric to the center diameter (Dimensions A) within 0.010 inches total indicator reading (TIR), and the flange rim (Dimension B) shall be concentric to the center hole within 0.050 inches TIR.
6. The reel lateral mounting surfaces in the area of Dimension C of both sides of the reel shall be parallel to each other within 0.010 inches at the C diameter when machinist's flats are put in firm contact with each side. The distance between the two machinist's flats is Dimension M.
7. The outside cylindrical hub surface (Dimension C) shall have a taper no greater than 0.002 inches for metal reels and 0.003 inches for plastic reels.
8. Reels shall be symmetrical in that they shall mount and be functional when mounted on either lateral mounting surface.
9. The flanges shall be fastened to the hub with three or more fasteners which shall not protrude above the lateral mounting surface.
10. Dimension J represents flange thickness only for the NAB type A metal reel.

TABLE 2
DIMENSIONS FOR NAB TYPE B REELS
PLASTIC WITH NOMINAL 5/16" CENTER HOLE

Nominal Size 3	5	5	7	7	Tolerance	10½	Tolerance
B 2.938	5.000	5.000	7.000	7.000	+0.031 -0.000	10.500	±0.020
C 1.750	1.750	3.000	2.250	4.000	±0.010	4.500	±0.015
G 120°	120°	120°	120°	120°	±0.5°	120°	±0.5°
H 0.050	0.050	0.050	0.050	0.050	Maximum	0.060	Maximum
I 0.115	0.115	0.115	0.115	0.115	Maximum	0.115	Maximum
M* 0.485	0.485	0.485	0.485	0.485	+.040 -0.000	0.485	+0.040 -0.000
P 1.750	1.750	2.250	2.250	2.250	Minimum	4.500	Minimum
U 0.319	0.319	0.319	0.319	0.319	±0.003	0.319	±0.003
V 0.063	0.063	0.063	0.063	0.063	±0.005	0.063	±0.005
W 0.625	0.625	0.625	0.625	0.625	±0.005	0.625	±0.005
X**							
Y**							
Z**							

* See note 9.
** See note 3.

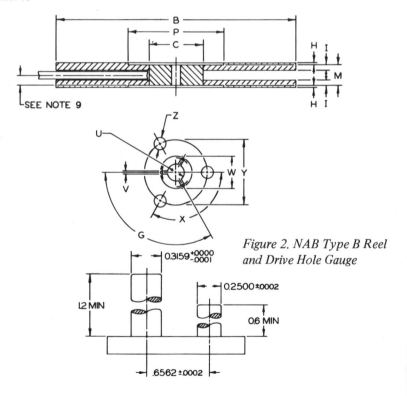

Figure 2. NAB Type B Reel and Drive Hole Gauge

NOTES FOR FIGURE 2

1. Reels shall have dimensions in inches as shown in Figure 2 and Table 2.
2. Flanges may have cut outs of random shape and size, however, flange open area must not exceed 50% of the area between dimensions B and C.
3. Reels may have one, two or three drive holes and must fit on the gauge shown in Figure 2. If more than one drive hole is used, they shall be symmetrically spaced around the center hole.
4. Reels are to be constructed so that any profile section taken through the center axis of the reel will fall within the hatched envelope of Figure 2. This includes warpage and lateral run out of the flanges. Bosses, ribs or other raised designs are permitted on the outside of the flange surfaces but they shall not extend beyond the envelope of Figure 2 when the reel is rotated on its center axis.
5. The reel hub should be provided with a suitable method of tape attachment. Threading slots are optional, but, if used, shall not be wider than 0.065 inches at the hub surface.
6. The outside cylindrical hub surface (Dimension C) shall be concentric to the center diameter (Dimension U) within 0.010 inches total indicator reading (TIR), and flange rim (Dimension B) shall be concentric to the center diameter within 0.020 inches TIR.
7. The outside cylindrical hub surface (Dimension C) shall have a taper in relation to either lateral mounting surface no greater than 0.003 inches.
8. Reels shall be symmetrical in that they shall mount and be functional when mounted on either lateral mounting surface.
9. The intent of this Standard is to accept all plastic reels with an M dimension between 0.485 inches and 0.525 inches. With guides set for a nominal tape path center line of 0.243 inches above the reel mounting surface there will be no flange interference with the tape with the I dimension held at 0.115 inches or less and the M dimension at a minimum. A larger M dimension will merely raise the upper flange further away from the upper edge of the tape.

TABLE 3

NAB STANDARD REPRODUCING CHARACTERISTIC

7½ and 15 ips (3180 and 50 μs)

Reproducing Amplifier Output for Constant Flux
in the Core of an Ideal Reproducing Head

Frequency	Response	Frequency	Response
20 Hz	–8.6 dB	1.5 kHz	+ 0.9 dB
25	7.0	2	1.45
30	5.8	2.5	2.1
40	4.1	3	2.75
50	3.0	4	4.1
60	2.3	5	5.4
70	1.8	6	6.6
75	1.6	7	7.7
80	1.4	7.5	8.2
90	1.2	8	8.6
100	1.0	9	9.5
150	0.45	10	10.35
200	0.2	11	11.1
250	0.1	12	11.8
300	–0.1	13	12.5
400	±0	14	13.1
500	+0.1	15	13.6
600	0.1	16	14.2
700	0.2	17	14.7
750	0.2	18	15.2
800	0.2	19	15.6
900	0.3	20 kHz	+16.1 dB
1 kHz	+0.4 dB		

TABLE 4

NAB STANDARD REPRODUCING CHARACTERISTIC

1⅞ and 3¾ ips (3180 and 90 μs)

Reproducing Amplifier Output for Constant Flux
in the Core of an Ideal Reproducing Head

Frequency	Response	Frequency	Response
20 Hz	−8.8 dB	1.5 kHz	+ 2.2 dB
25	7.2	2	3.4
30	5.9	2.5	4.6
40	4.2	3	5.7
50	3.2	4	7.7
60	2.4	5	9.4
70	1.9	6	10.8
75	1.7	7	12.1
80	1.6	7.5	12.6
90	1.3	8	13.2
100	1.1	9	14.15
150	0.6	10	15.0
200	0.4	11	15.8
250	0.2	12	16.6
300	−0.15	13	17.2
400	±0	14	17.9
500	+0.1	15	18.5
600	0.3	16	19.0
700	0.5	17	19.6
750	0.55	18	20.0
800	0.6	19	20.5
900	0.8	20 kHz	+21.0 dB
1 kHz	+1.0 dB		

TABLE 5

Frequency	dB	Tolerance
0.2 Hz	-30.6	+10, -4 dB
0.315	-19.7	0.315 to 0.5 Hz
0.4	-15.0	±4 dB
0.63	- 8.4	0.5 to
0.8	- 6.0	less than
1.0	- 4.2	4 Hz
1.6	- 1.8	±2 dB
2.0	- 0.9	
4.0	0	±0 dB
6.3	- 0.9	greater than
10	- 2.1	4 Hz to
20	- 5.9	50 Hz
40	-10.4	±2 dB
63	-14.2	50 Hz to
100	-17.3	200 Hz
200	-23.0	±4 dB

APPENDIX 6

Bibliography

The following bibliography may be of service to the reader who seeks additional information. While by no means a complete catalog, it does list the various publications that were consulted during the preparation of *The Recording Studio Handbook*. Titles in quotations indicate papers or articles contained within various journals. Italicized titles represent books. Titles set in regular type identify booklets, pamphlets, instruction manuals, et al.

An abbreviation key follows;

AES Audio Engineering Society, Inc.

BBC British Broadcasting Corporation

CCIR *Comité Consultatif International Radio*

IEC International Electrotechnical Commission

JAES Journal of the Audio Engineering Society

JASA Journal of the Acoustical Society of America

JSMPTE Journal of the Society of Motion Picture and Television Engineers, Inc.

NAB National Association of Broadcasters.

GENERAL REFERENCES

Bernstein, J. *Audio Systems.* Wiley & Sons, 1966.
Crowhurst, N. *Basic Audio Systems.* Tab Books, 1974.
Grob, B. *Basic Electronics.* McGraw-Hill, 1971.
Tremaine, H. *The Audio Cyclopedia.* Howard Sams, 1974.
Villchur, E. *Reproduction of Sound.* Dover Publications, 1965.
Stephens, R. *International Dictionaries of Science and Technology: Sound.* Wiley & Sons, 1974.

Chapter 1
Broch, J.T. Acoustic Noise Measurements. Bruel & Kjaer, 1969.
Davis, D. & C. *Sound System Engineering.* Howard Sams, 1975.

Katz, B. Primer on Sound Level Meters and Acoustical Calibration.
Bruel & Kjaer, undated paper.

Taylor, R. *Noise.* Penguin Books, 1970.

Wilms, H.A.O. Stop Using the Ambiguous 'dBm'! AES Preprint,
unnumbered 1972.

Zellner, F.L. "Audio Testing in a Broadcast Studio." *Audio* Magazine,
November 1968.

– Measurement of Programme Level in Sound Broadcasting. CCIR
Report 292-1, undated.

Chapter 2

Feather, N. *Vibrations and Waves.* Penguin Books, 1964.

Harris and Hemmerling. *Introductory Applied Physics.*
McGraw-Hill, 1963.

Helmholtz, H. *On The Sensations of Tone.* Dover Publications, 1954.

Lamb, H. *The Dynamical Theory of Sound.*
Dover Publications, 1960.

Olson, H. *Music, Physics and Engineering.* Dover Publications, 1967.

Peterson & Gross. *Handbook of Noise Measurement.*
General Radio Co., 1967.

Ribbeck & Schwarze. "The Correlation of Stereo Signals and Its
Indication." *International Elektronische Rundschau,*
Vol. 19, No. 6, 1965.

Stevens & Warshofsky. *Sound and Hearing.* Time-Life Books, 1970.

– Acoustics Handbook. Hewlett Packard Application Note 100,
1968.

Chapter 3

Bore, G. "Powering Condenser Microphones" *db* Magazine,
June 1970.

Burroughs, L. *Microphones: Design and Application.*
Sagamore Publishing Co., 1974.

Davis, A. & D. Microphones for Sound Reinforcement Systems.
Altec Lansing booklet, undated.

Fisher, J. "Microphones." *Studio Sound* Magazine, December 1971.

Nisbett, A. *The Use of Microphones.* Hastings House, 1974.

Pontzen, G.R. Microphones. United Trade Press, Ltd.,
undated booklet.

Robertson, A.E. *Microphones.* Hayden Book Co., 1963.

Weingartner, B. Concepts and Technology Behind the Modern

Dynamic Microphone. AKG booklet, undated.

Weingartner, B. Field Effect Transistor Condenser Studio
Microphone in CMS. AKG booklet, undated.

Weingartner, B. Two-Way Dynamic Cardioid Microphone.
AES Preprint No. 417, 1965.

Chapter 4

Blumlein, A.D. Improvements in and Relating to Sound-Transmission,
Sound-Recording and Sound-Reproducing Systems.
British Patent Specification 394, 325 1931.
(reprinted in *JAES*, April 1958.)

Bore, G. & Temmer, S. "M-S Stereophony and Compatibility."
Audio Magazine, April 1958.

Ceoen, C. "Comparative Stereophonic Listening Tests."
JAES, January/February 1972.

Ceoen, C. Correlation and Virtual Sound Sources.
AES Preprint, unnumbered 1974.

Fouque, M. & Redlich, H. Concerning Spacial Information in
Stereophony. Gotham Audio Corp. application note, undated.

Gardner, M. "Proximity Image Effect in Sound Localization."
JASA, January 1968.

Gardner, M. "Historical Background of the Hass and/or Precedence
Effect." *JASA*, June 1968.

Gerzon, M. "Why Coincident Microphones?"
Studio Sound Magazine, March 1971.

Gerzon, M. "Stabilising Stereo Images."
Studio Sound Magazine, December 1974.

Gerzon, M. "Dummy Head Recording."
Studio Sound Magazine, May 1975.

Madsen, E. "A Ribbon Microphone for Stereo."
Audio Magazine, April 1964.

Snow, W.B. "Basic Principles of Stereophonic Sound."
JSMPTE, November 1953.

Temmer, S. (transl.) Recording Techniques – Compatible
Stereophony. Gotham Audio Corp. application note, 1960.

Weingartner, B. M-S Stereo Recording Techniques.
AKG booklet, undated.

Chapter 5

Allison, R. "The Sound Field in Home Listening Rooms."
JAES, July/August 1972.

Allison, R. "The Influence of Room Boundaries on
Loudspeaker Power Output." *JAES*, June 1974.
Augspurger, G. "The Acoustical Lens."
Electronics World Magazine, December 1962.
Briggs, G.A. *Loudspeakers.* Rank Wharfedale, 1972.
Cohen, A. *Hi-Fi Loudspeakers and Enclosures.*
Hayden Book Co., 1968.
Davis, D.& C. *Sound System Engineering.* Howard Sams, 1975.
Rettinger, M. *Acoustic Design and Noise Control.*
Chemical Publishing Co., 1973.

Chapter 6
Blesser, B. & Lee, F. "An Audio Delay System Using Digital
Technology." *JAES*, May 1971.
Davis, J. "Practical Stereo Reverberation for Studio Recording."
JAES, April 1962.
Factor, R. & Katz, S. "The Digital Audio Delay Line."
db Magazine, May 1972.
Fidi, W. AKG Reverberation Unit BX 20E. AKG Instruction
Manual, undated.
Gerzon, M. "Synthetic Stereo Reverberation."
Studio Sound Magazine, December 1971 & January 1972 (2 parts).
Klepper, D. Application of Digital Delay Units to Sound
Reinforcement Systems. Lexicon application note, 1975.
Steinke, G. A Special Echo-Mixer for a Sound Recording Control
Console. AES Preprint No. 357, 1964.
— Reverberation Unit EMT 140 TS. Gotham Audio Corp. application
note, April 1971.

Chapter 8
Shorter, Manson & Stebbings. The Dynamic Characteristics of
Limiters for Sound Programme Circuits.
BBC Engineering Monograph No. 70, 1970.
— EMT 156 Stereo Compressor + Limiter.
Gotham Audio Corp. booklet, 1970.
— Kepex Keyable Program Expander,
Allison Research, Inc. Operations Manual, undated.

Chapter 9
Bartlett, B. "A Scientific Explanation of Phasing (Flanging)."
JAES, December 1970.

Factor, R. Instant Flanger.
Eventide Clockworks Instruction Manual, 1974.

Chapters 10 through 13
Denham, D. "The Many Faces of Magnetic Tape."
Broadcast Engineering Magazine, June 1960.
Jorgensen, F. *Handbook of Magnetic Recording.* Tab Books, 1970.
Lowman, C. *Magnetic Recording.* McGraw-Hill, 1972.
McKnight, J. "Tape Reproducer Response Measurements With a
Reproducer Test Tape." *JAES*, April 1967.
McKnight, J. "Biasing in Magnetic Tape Recording."
Electronics World Magazine, August 1967.
McKnight, J. "Measuring a Tape Reproducer with IEC Response,
Using an NAB-Response Test Tape." *JAES*, October 1969.
McKnight, J. "The Fringing Response of Magnetic Reproducers at
Long Wavelengths." *JAES,* March 1972.
McKnight, J. Comments on Choice of Frequencies and Reference
Fluxivity on MRL Open-Reel Test Tapes.
Magnetic Recording Laboratories applications note, 1972.
Tanamachi, S. A New Generation of Music Mastering Tapes for
Studio Application. 3M Company applications note, undated.
— Sound Talk. 3M Company applications notes, 1950-1970.
— Magnetic Tape Recording and Reproducing (Reel-to-Reel).
NAB Standard, April 1965.
— Magnetic Tape Recording and Reproducing Systems:
Dimensions and Characteristics. IEC Publication 94, 1968.

Chapters 14 and 15
Blackmer, D. "A Wide Dynamic Range Noise Reduction System."
db Magazine, August/September 1972.
Burwen, R. "A Dynamic Noise Filter." *JAES,* February 1971.
Burwen, R. "110 dB Dynamic Range for Tape."
Audio Magazine, June 1971.
Burwen, R. "Design of a Noise Eliminator System."
JAES, December 1971.
Burwen, R. "A Dynamic Noise Filter for Mastering."
Audio Magazine, June 1972.
Dolby, R. "An Audio Noise Reduction System."
JAES, October 1967.
Dolby, R. "Audio Noise Reduction: Some Practical Aspects."
Audio Magazine, June 1968 & July 1968 (2 parts).

Duncan, Rosenberg & Hoffman. "Design Criteria of a Universal Compandor for the Elimination of Audible Noise in Tape, Disc, and Broadcast Systems." *JAES*, October 1975.

Taylor, R. *Noise.* Penguin Books, 1970.

Glossary

A WEIGHTING – see **Weighting, "A"**.

A-B'ING – Comparing two programs, by frequently switching from one to the other.

ACETATE – see **Cellulose Acetate**.

ACOUSTIC BAFFLE – see **Baffle, Acoustic**.

ACOUSTIC CENTER – In a loudspeaker, the point at which a sound wave appears to originate.

ACOUSTIC DELAY LINE – see **Delay Line, Acoustic**.

ACOUSTIC INTENSITY – see **Intensity, Acoustic**.

ACOUSTIC LENS – A high frequency speaker attachment system, designed to provide a wide radiation angle.

ACOUSTIC PHASE CANCELLATION – see **Phase Cancellation**.

ACOUSTIC POWER – see **Power, Acoustic**.

ACOUSTIC SUSPENSION SYTEM – A sealed loudspeaker cabinet, in which the enclosed volume of air acts as an acoustic resistance to the speaker cone.

ACTIVE DEVICE – A network or circuit capable of supplying a power or voltage gain, as for example, an amplifier.

ALIGNMENT – The adjustment of a device to bring it into conformance with published specifications. See **Azimuth Alignment**.

ALIGNMENT TAPE – see **Test Tape**.

AMBIENT NOISE – see **Noise, Ambient**.

ANECHOIC CHAMBER – A room designed to provide a reflection-free environment, for testing microphones, loudspeakers, and other devices.

ASPERITY NOISE – see **Noise, Asperity**.

ATTACK TIME – The time it takes for the gain of a signal processing device to change in response to the input signal level.

ATTENUATION PAD – A resistive network inserted in a microphone or other line to lower the level by a specified number of decibels.

AUTO-LOCATOR – A trade name of the MCI Company, to describe

their tape transport control system.

AZIMUTH – The angular relationship between the head gap and the tape path.

AZIMUTH ALIGNMENT – The mechanical adjustment of the record or playback head to bring it into proper alignment (90°) with the tape path.

B WEIGHTING – see **Weighting, "B"**.

BACK COATING – A thin coating applied to the back of a magnetic recording tape, generally to reduce both slippage and the build-up of static charges.

BACK PLATE – The fixed rear element in the capacitor/diaphragm of a condenser (capacitor) microphone.

BAFFLE, ACOUSTIC – Any partition, designed to be an acoustic obstruction to the passage of sound waves.

BAFFLE, FOLDED – A speaker cabinet that is completely open at the rear. So-called because it is formed by folding over the sides of an open baffle. See **Horn, Folded**.

BAFFLE, INFINITE – Theoretically, a baffle so large that sounds originating on either side of it never reach the opposite side. A practical example would be a speaker mounted in an opening in a wall.

BAFFLE, OPEN – Simply a flat partition, of less than infinite dimension, in which a hole has been cut for mounting a speaker.

BALANCE – The relative level of two or more instruments, signal paths, or recorded tracks.

BALANCING – Adjusting the relative levels of instruments or recorded tracks.

BALANCED LINE – A line consisting of two conductors plus a shield. With respect to ground, the conductors are at equal potential, but opposite polarity. See **Unbalanced Line**.

BALLISTICS – A property of a meter movement, referring to its ability to precisely respond to the envelope of the signal being measured.

BAND PASS FILTER – see **Filter, Band Pass**.

BAND REJECT FILTER – see **Filter, Band Reject**.

BANDWIDTH – The arithmetic difference between the upper and lower cut-off frequencies of an audio system.

BASE – In magnetic recording tape, the plastic or other film upon which the magnetic oxide is coated.

BASIC TRACKS – In multi-track recording, those tracks that are recorded first. In general, the rhythm tracks (guitars, bass, drums, et al).

BASS REFLEX ENCLOSURE – A loudspeaker enclosure, with an open port cut into the front baffle. Also called a vented enclosure.

BI-AMPLIFICATION – The process of separating the audio bandwidth in two, with a separate amplifier for low and high frequencies.

BI-DIRECTIONAL MICROPHONE – A microphone that is sensitive to front- and rear-originating sounds, and relatively insensitive to side-originating sounds. Also called a Figure-8 microphone, after the shape of its polar pattern.

BIAS – A very high frequency current applied to the record head to linearize the transfer characteristic of magnetic recording tape.

BIAS BEATS – An audio frequency signal that may be created if two slightly different bias frequencies are combined. The audio frequency is the arithmetic difference between the bias frequencies.

BIAS FREQUENCY – The frequency of the applied bias signal. Generally, about 150,000 to 180,000 Hz.

BIAS OSCILLATOR – A fixed frequency oscillator built into the tape recorder to supply the bias current.

BIAS TRAP – A filter designed to block the bias frequency, thus preventing it from overloading the record or playback amplifiers in a tape recorder.

BINDER – The medium in which magnetic particles are suspended to form the oxide coating in magnetic recording tape.

BINAURAL RECORDING – A recording technique using two omni-directional microphones; one each on either side of an acoustic baffle designed to simulate the characteristics of a listener's head. For optimum results, the recording must be monitored over headphones.

BLUMLEIN PAIR – Any two microphones, arranged for a stereophonic pickup, according to the methods developed by Alan Dower Blumlein c.1930.

BOUNCING TRACKS – The technique of transferring several previously recorded tracks to a single unused track on the same tape. The previously recorded tracks may then be erased and re-used.

BREATHING – An audible rising and falling of background noise that may become objectionable when using a compressor. Also called pumping.

BULK ERASER – A strong electro-magnet, used to erase an entire roll of tape at once. See **Degausser**.

BUS – A common signal line, or junction, at which the outputs of several signal paths may be combined. (Frequently mis-spelled as Buss).

BUS SELECTOR SWITCH – A multi-position switch, which permits a signal path to be routed to one or more buses.

C WEIGHTING – see **Weighting, "C"**.

C.C.I.R. – *Comite Consultatif International Radio* (International Radio Consultive Committee).

CANCELLATION – The severe attenuation that occurs when two identical signals of opposite polarity are combined.

CAPACITANCE – An opposition to a change in voltage.

CAPACITOR – An electronic component that opposes a change in voltage. Parallel conductors in a signal line may take on the properties of a capacitor, thereby attenuating high frequencies.

CAPACITOR LOUDSPEAKER – see **Loudspeaker, Electrostatic**.

CAPACITOR MICROPHONE – see **Microphone, Capacitor**.

CAPSTAN – On a tape recorder, the motor-driven spindle that drives the tape past the heads.

CAPSTAN IDLER – The rubber coated wheel that forces the tape against the capstan when the tape recorder is in the play mode. Also called a pinch roller or puck.

CAPSTAN MOTOR – The motor that drives the capstan. The capstan is often the extended shaft of the capstan motor.

CARDIOID MICROPHONE – see **Microphone, Cardioid**.

CATHODE RAY OSCILLOSCOPE – A test instrument, providing a visual display of the waveform being measured.

CELLULOSE ACETATE – A plastic film, used as a base material in the production of magnetic recording tape.

CENTER, ACOUSTIC – see **Acoustic Center**.

CENTER FREQUENCY – In a peaking equalizer, the frequency at which maximum boost (or attenuation) occurs.

CENTER TAP – The electrical center of a transformer winding.

CENTER TAP, ARTIFICIAL – When two identical precision resistors are wired in series across a transformer winding, the point at which the resistors are joined together becomes the electrical equivalent of the actual center tap.

CLOSE MIKING – The technique of placing microphones extremely close to the instruments they are picking up, thereby eliminating almost all but the direct sound of the instrument(s).

CLOSED LOOP TAPE PATH — A tape transport system in which the tape passes through two capstan/capstan idler systems; one on each side of the head assembly. Called an Isoloop system by the 3M Company.

COCKTAIL PARTY EFFECT — The ability of the brain to pick out one conversation from many going on simultaneously.

COERCIVITY — The field strength required to bring a saturated tape to complete erasure. Coercivity is abbreviated as H_c, and is measured in oersteds.

COHERENCE — The instantaneous polarity relationship between two complex sound waves.

COHERENT SIGNALS — Two complex waveforms that are — most of the time — of the same polarity.

COINCIDENT MICROPHONES — Two or more microphones on the same vertical axis. A stereo microphone.

COLORATION — A distortion in frequency response, usually associated with off-axis signals picked up by a cardioid microphone.

COMBINING AMPLIFIER — An amplifier at which the outputs of two or more signal paths are mixed together, to feed a single track of a tape recorder.

COMBINING NETWORK — A resistive network at which the outputs of two or more signal paths are mixed together, to feed a single track of a tape recorder.

COMPANDER — A contraction of COMpressor/exPANDER, often used in describing the action of a noise reduction system.

COMPLEMENTARY SIGNAL PROCESSING — A signal processing technique, in which some processing is done before recording, with equal-and-opposite (complementary) processing during playback. Well known examples are noise reduction systems and tape recorder pre-and post-emphasis. See **Non-Complementary Signal Processing**.

COMPOSITE EQUALIZATION — see **Equalization, Composite**.

COMPRESSION DRIVER — A loudspeaker transducer with a relatively narrow throat, designed for maximum efficiency coupling with a horn assembly.

COMPRESSION RATIO — In a compressor, the ratio of dB change in input level to dB change in output level.

COMPRESSION THRESHOLD — see **Threshold, Compression**.

COMPRESSOR — An amplifier whose gain decreases as its input level is increased.

COMPRESSOR, PROGRAM – A compressor that acts on an entire program, rather than on a single instrument or track.

COMPRESSOR, VOICE-OVER – A speech-actuated compressor, in which an announcer's voice automatically drops the level of the regular program. Often used in broadcasting and paging systems.

CONDENSATION – The instantaneous crowding together of air particles during the positive-going half cycle of a sound wave. The opposite of rarefaction.

CONDENSER LOUDSPEAKER – see **Loudspeaker, Electrostatic.**

CONDENSER MICROPHONE – see **Microphone, Condenser.**

CONE – The diaphragm of a moving coil loudspeaker.

CONSOLE, RECORDING – The enclosure containing the various input, output, signal routing, and monitoring controls required for recording.

CONTACT MICROPHONE – A microphone which is directly attached to an instrument. Generally, it responds to the mechanical vibrations of the instrument to which it is attached.

COTTAGE LOAF MICROPHONE – A super- or hyper-cardioid microphone.

COUPLING – The transfer of energy from one system to another. Often used to describe the interface between a loudspeaker and the surrounding air.

CRITICAL DISTANCE – The distance from a sound source at which the level of the direct and the reverberant field are equal.

CROSSOVER FREQUENCY – The single frequency at which both sides of a crossover network are down 3dB.

CROSSOVER NETWORK – A one input/two (or more) output network, in which the audio bandwidth is separated into two (or more) bands. Frequently used with multi-speaker systems.

CROSSOVER NETWORK PHASE SHIFT – see **Phase Shift, Crossover Network.**

CROSSTALK – In a signal path, the unwanted detection of a signal from an adjacent signal path.

CUE SYSTEM – That part of the console, plus associated circuitry, by which the engineer may route a headphone monitor feed to musicians in the studio. Also known as foldback.

CURRENT – The rate of flow of electricity, measured in amperes.

CUT SWITCH – An on-off switch in a signal path which interrupts the signal flow. Commonly found in each input module on a recording console.

CUT-OFF FILTER – see **Filter, Cut-off.**

CUT-OFF FREQUENCY – In a high- or low-pass filter, the frequency at which the output level has fallen by 3 dB.

CYCLES PER SECOND – The number of complete oscillations of a vibrating object, per second. The unit by which frequency is measured. Also called hertz, abbreviated Hz.

DAMPING – Acoustical, electrical, or mechanical opposition to a moving system, as in a speaker voice coil assembly.

dB – see **Decibel.**

DEAD – Description of a sound in which reverberant information is severely attenuated, or missing completely.

DECAY – The fall-off in amplitude when a force applied to a vibrating device is removed.

DECAY TIME – The time it takes for echoes and reverberation to die away.

DECIBEL – A unit of level equal to ten times the logarithm of the ratio of two powers.

For a power ratio, $N_{dB} = 10 \log (P_{out}/P_{in}) = 10 \log (P_a/P_b)$
For a voltage ratio, $N_{dB} = 20 \log (V_{out}/V_{in}) = 20 \log (V_a/V_b)$
In the second set of formulae, the subscript **a** represents a measured value, while the subscript **b** represents a standard reference level. Depending on the reference level used, the decibel symbol will be immediately followed by a letter, as;

dBA – An "A" weighted decibel level. See **Weighting, "A".**

dBB – A "B" weighted decibel level. See **Weighting, "B".**

dBC – A "C" weighted decibel level. See **Weighting, "C".**

dBm – A decibel level in which P_b in the formula above represents one milliwatt of power dissipated in a 600 ohm line. P_a must also be measured in a 600 ohm line.

dBV – A decibel voltage level, in which the reference, V_b, is 1.0 volt. A reference of 0.775 volts is also frequently used.

DECODING – The process of applying complementary signal processing to restore a signal to its normal state, as in the playback mode of a noise reduction system.

DE-ESSER – A compressor designed to minimize sibilants.

DEGAUSSER – A device for demagnetizing the heads and other surfaces on a magnetic tape recorder. See **Bulk Eraser.**

DELAY – The time interval between a direct signal and its echo(es).

DELAY LINE – Any device that introduces a time delay between its input and output.

DELAY LINE, ACOUSTIC – A delay line, in which the delay is accomplished acoustically, as in a long tube with a speaker at one end and a microphone at the other.

DELAY LINE, DIGITAL – A delay line, in which the delay is accomplished electronically, via an analog/digital and digital/analog conversion.

DEMAGNETIZATION – The erasure of a magnetic tape, or the degaussing of the tape recorder heads.

DEPTH PERCEPTION – The ability of the listener to perceive the apparent relative distances of various instruments in a recording (or live concert).

DIAPHRAGM – The moving membrane in a microphone or loudspeaker.

DIFFRACTION – The bending of a sound wave, as it passes over an obstacle. The angle of diffraction is a function of wavelength.

DIGITAL DELAY LINE – see **Delay Line, Digital.**

DIRECT OUTPUT – A console output, taken directly from an input module and bypassing the pan pots and bus selector switches.

DIRECT PICKUP – A transformer pickup of a musical instrument, in which the instrument's amplifier output is fed directly to the console, via a matching transformer.

DIRECT RADIATOR – see **Radiator, Direct.**

DIRECT SOUND – The sound that reaches the listener via a straight line path from the sound source. A sound with no echoes or reverberation. The sound heard from a transformer pickup.

DIRECTIONAL CHARACTERISTIC – The polar response of a transducer.

DISPERSION – The splitting of a complex sound wave into its various frequency components, as the sound wave passes from one medium to another.

DISPLACEMENT – The distance between the position of a moving object such as a speaker diaphragm, and its original position.

DISTANT MIKING – The placement of a microphone, or microphones, relatively far from the sound source, thus picking up a larger proportion of reflected sound.

DISTORTION – An unwanted change in a waveform as it passes through an electronic component, or, from one medium to another.

DISTORTION, HARMONIC – The appearance of harmonics of the applied input signal, as measured at the output of an electronic component.

DISTORTION, INTERMODULATION – Distortion in the form of unwanted frequencies corresponding to the sums and differences between various components of a complex waveform.

DISTORTION, PERCENT – The amount of distortion, measured as a percentage of the total waveform amplitude.

DISTORTION, THIRD HARMONIC – The presence of the third harmonic (3 x f) of an applied input signal, as measured at the output of an electronic component.

DISTORTION, TRANSIENT – Distortion produced when an audio system is unable to accurately reproduce a transient.

DOLBY TONE – A reference tone, recorded at the head of a Dolby encoded tape, for alignment purposes.

DOMAIN – 10^{18} molecules of ferric oxide; the smallest physical unit that may be considered a magnet.

DOUBLING – Mixing a slightly delayed signal with a direct signal, to simulate the effect of twice as many recorded instruments. Also, a deficiency of some speaker systems, in which low frequencies may be reproduced up one octave.

DRIFT – In a tape recorder, a long term deviation from the specified tape speed.

DRIVER, COMPRESSION – see **Compression Driver.**

DRONE CONE – A passive radiator.

DROP-OUT – On a magnetic recording tape, a momentary drop in output level, usually caused by an imperfection in the oxide coating.

DRY SOUND – A description of a sound which lacks reverberant information. The direct sound of a musical instrument.

DUAL DIAPHRAGM MICROPHONE – see **Microphone, Dual Diaphragm.**

DYNAMIC FILTER – see **Filter, Dynamic.**

DYNAMIC LOUDSPEAKER – see **Loudspeaker, Dynamic.**

DYNAMIC MICROPHONE – A moving coil or ribbon microphone. See **Microphone, Dynamic.**

DYNAMIC MOVING COIL MICROPHONE – see **Microphone, Moving Coil.**

DYNAMIC RANGE – In a musical instrument, a measure of the span between the quietest and loudest sounds it is capable of producing. In a tape recorder, the dB interval between the noise level and the level at which 3% distortion occurs.

DYNAMIC RIBBON MICROPHONE – see **Microphone, Ribbon.**

DYNAMIC SIGNAL PROCESSING DEVICE – A signal processing device whose operating parameters change as a reaction to the program content. For example, a compressor or expander. See **Static Signal Processing Device.**

DYNE – A unit of force. At the threshold of hearing, the acoustic force per unit area is 0.0002 dynes/cm^2.

ECHO – A repetition of a sound. One, or a few at most, repetitions of an audio signal.

ECHO, POST- – A signal routed to an echo send line from a point after the input fader. The position on the echo send switch which accomplishes this. An after-the-signal tape echo, caused by print-through.

ECHO, PRE- – A signal routed to an echo send line from a point before the input fader. The position on the echo send switch which accomplishes this. A before-the-signal tape echo, caused by print-through.

ECHO RETURN – The signal path and the associated controls that affect the signal returned from an artificial echo and/or reverberation system.

ECHO SEND – The signal path and the associated controls that affect the signal sent to an artificial echo and/or reverberation system.

ECHO TAPE – The tape used to create artificial echoes in a tape delay system.

EDIT SWITCH – On a tape recorder, a switch that puts the machine in the play mode, while the take up motor remains disabled. Thus, the segment of tape being played spills off the machine, and may be easily discarded.

EDITING – The process of cutting and splicing a magnetic tape to remove or rearrange certain segments. Producing a master tape by splicing together segments of several different takes.

EFFICIENCY – In an audio system, the ratio of power output to power input.

ELECTRET MICROPHONE – see **Microphone, Electret.**

ELECTRICAL PHASE CANCELLATION – see **Phase Cancellation.**

ELECTROSTATIC LOUDSPEAKER – see **Loudspeaker, Electrostatic.**

ELECTROSTATIC MICROPHONE – see **Microphone, Condenser.**

ELEVATED LEVEL TEST TAPE – see **Test Tape, Elevated Level.**

ENCLOSURE, BASS REFLEX – see **Bass Reflex Enclosure.**

ENCLOSURE, SEALED – see **Sealed Enclosure.**

ENCLOSURE, VENTED – see **Vented Enclosure.**

ENCODING – The application of some form of signal processing before recording, that will be removed via complementary processing (decoding) during playback.

ENERGY CONVERSION – The process of changing a signal from one form of energy to another, as in a loudspeaker, which converts electrical energy into acoustical energy.

ENERGY DISTRIBUTION CURVE – A graph of energy *vs.* frequency for a typical voice, musical instrument, or program.

ENERGY TRANSFER – The delivery of power from a generator to a load.

ENVELOPE – The overall shape of the waveform of a musical instrument.

EQUAL LOUDNESS CONTOURS – A series of graphs of sensitivity (of the ear) *vs.* frequency at various loudness levels. Also known as the Fletcher-Munson curves.

EQUALIZATION – Any intentional modification of an audio system's frequency response.

EQUALIZATION, COMPOSITE – The net frequency response of an audio system in which two or more sections of an equalizer are in use.

EQUALIZATION, PLAYBACK – Equalization applied in the playback circuit of a tape recorder to produce a flat frequency response.

EQUALIZATION, RECORD – Equalization applied in the record circuit of a tape recorder.

EQUALIZATION, ROOM – The practice of tailoring the frequency response of a signal delivered to a speaker to correct for certain frequency response anomalies created by the room.

EQUALIZER – Any signal processing device that is used to change the frequency response of the signal passing through it.

EQUALIZER, ACTIVE – An equalizer containing active components, such as vacuum tubes or transistors.

EQUALIZER, GRAPHIC – An equalizer with a series of slide controls, arranged so as to give a graphic representation of the resulting frequency response.

EQUALIZER, PARAMETRIC – An equalizer in which the frequency selector control is continuously variable over a wide range.

EQUALIZER, PASSIVE – An equalizer containing only passive components, such as resistors, capacitors and inductors.

EQUALIZER PHASE SHIFT – see **Phase Shift, Equalizer.**

EQUALIZER, SHELVING – An equalizer that supplies a constant amount of boost or attenuation at all frequencies beyond the equalizer's turnover frequency.

EQUIVALENT CIRCUIT – A network designed to duplicate the operating parameters of some other network. For example, a resistive/capacitive network may be used to simulate a microphone line, for testing purposes.

ERASE HEAD – see **Head, Erase.**

ERASE OSCILLATOR – A fixed frequency oscillator built into the tape recorder to supply erase current.

ERASER, BULK – see **Bulk Eraser.**

ERROR SIGNAL – A voltage that is proportional to the difference between an actual and a desired condition (as in a servo motor system). The error signal brings the system back to the desired operating condition.

EXPANDER – An amplifier whose gain decreases as its input level is decreased.

EXPANSION, PEAK – The use of an expander in a playback system to restore peaks that may have been compressed during recording. The peak expander may also be used to widen the dynamic range of programs that were not compressed earlier.

EXPANSION RATIO – In an expander, the ratio of dB change in input level to dB change in output level.

EXPANSION THRESHOLD – see **Threshold, Expansion.**

EXPONENT – A superscript placed to the right of a number, indicating the power to which the number is to be raised. In the expression, $9^3 = 729$, the superscript 3 is the exponent.

FADE-OUT – Ending a recording by lowering the level, generally as the musicians play the last few measures over and over.

FADER – A variable level control in a signal path. Sometimes called a mixer.

FADER, MASTER – A single fader, which regulates the level of all tracks being recorded.

FEEDBACK – The return of some portion of an output signal to the system's input.

FEEDBACK, ACOUSTIC – An audible howl or squeal, produced when a portion of a speaker's output is picked up by a nearby microphone and fed back to the speaker.

FERRIC OXIDE – see **Gamma Ferric Oxide.**

FIFTH – A musical interval of five diatonic degrees. The interval between a fundamental frequency and its third harmonic is equal to an octave plus a fifth.

FIGURE-8 MICROPHONE – see **Microphone, Figure-8.**

FILTER – An equalizer designed to attenuate certain frequencies, or bands of frequencies.

FILTER, BAND PASS – A filter that attenuates above and below a desired bandwidth.

FILTER, BAND REJECT – A filter that attenuates a desired bandwidth, while passing frequencies above and below that bandwidth.

FILTER, CUT-OFF – A filter that sharply attenuates frequencies beyond a specified frequency.

FILTER, DYNAMIC – A filter whose bandwidth changes in response to the program level.

FILTER, FLUTTER – see **Flutter Filter.**

FILTER, HIGH FREQUENCY – A filter that attenuates high frequencies.

FILTER, HIGH PASS – A filter that passes high frequencies, while attenuating those below a specified frequency.

FILTER, LOW FREQUENCY – A filter that attenuates low frequencies.

FILTER, LOW PASS – A filter that passes low frequencies, while attenuating those above a specified frequency.

FILTER, NOTCH – A filter designed to attenuate a relatively narrow band of frequencies.

FILTER, PROXIMITY EFFECT – A filter built into a cardioid microphone to attenuate low frequencies when the microphone is used close-up.

FILTER, TELEPHONE – A narrow band pass filter, used to simulate the sound of a telephone transmission.

FLANGING – A variable comb filter effect, created by mixing a direct signal with the same signal slightly delayed. To create the effect, the delay time is continuously varied.

FLETCHER-MUNSON CURVES – The equal loudness contours.

FLUTTER – A high frequency speed variation of an audio signal, generally caused by irregularities in the tape path.

FLUTTER FILTER – A low friction surface, placed in the tape path, to minimize scrape flutter. Also called a scrape flutter filter.

FLUTTER, SCRAPE – Flutter caused by mechanical vibrations of the tape as it passes over various surfaces in the tape path.

FLUX – Magnetic lines of force.

FLUXIVITY – The measure of the flux density of a magnetic recording tape, per unit of track width.

FLUXIVITY, REFERENCE – A specified fluxivity, as recorded on a test tape.

FOLDBACK SYSTEM – A cue system.

FOLDED BAFFLE – see **Baffle, Folded.**

FOLDED HORN – see **Horn, Folded.**

FREE SPACE – A reflection-free environment, as in an anechoic chamber. Also called full space.

FREQUENCY – The number of vibrations per unit time, measured in hertz. (Cycles per second.)

FREQUENCY RESPONSE – A graph of amplitude *vs.* frequency.

FRINGING – A rise in low frequency response when a tape is reproduced by a playback head that is narrower than the record head that was used to produce the tape.

FULL SPACE – see **Free Space.**

FULL TRACK – A tape with a single track, recorded across its entire width.

FUNDAMENTAL – The primary frequency of vibration of a sound source.

GAIN-BEFORE-THRESHOLD – The dB gain of a compressor, when the input signal level is below threshold.

GAIN REDUCTION – In a compressor, the decrease in gain when the input signal level is above threshold.

GAIN RIDING – Manually adjusting the gain in a signal path in an effort to decrease dynamic range.

GAMMA FERRIC OXIDE – The type of ferric oxide compound that is used in the manufacture of magnetic recording tape.

GAP, HEAD – see **Head Gap.**

GAP SPACE – The gap dimension, measured in the direction of tape travel.

GAUSS – A unit of measurement of a tape's remanent magnetization.

GENERATION – A copy of a tape. The original recording is a first generation tape. A copy is a second generation; a copy made from the second generation tape is a third generation, and so on.

GOBO – A sound absorbing panel, used in the studio to acoustically separate one instrument from another.

GOLDEN SECTION – A ratio of room height-to-width-to-length, first recommended by the ancient Greeks. The Golden Section is 1:1.62:2.62.

GRAPHIC EQUALIZER – see **Equalizer, Graphic.**

GUARD BAND — The spacing between tracks on a multi-track tape or tape head.

HARMONIC — A whole number multiple of a fundamental frequency.

HEAD — On a tape recorder, the transducer used to apply and/or detect magnetic energy on the tape.

HEAD, ERASE — The head that is used to apply a gradually diminishing magnetic force to the tape, thus erasing it just prior to recording.

HEAD GAP — The space between pole pieces in a head.

HEAD LOSSES — Losses in frequency response that are a function of head design limitations.

HEAD, PLAYBACK — The head that is used to detect the tape's magnetic field.

HEAD, RECORD — The head that is used to apply a magnetic force to the tape.

HEAD SHIELD — A metal shield around the playback head, designed to protect it from stray magnetic fields.

HEAD, SYNC — The record head, when used for playback during Sel-Sync sessions.

HEADPHONE LEAKAGE — see **Leakage, Headphone**.

HEADROOM — In magnetic recording tape, the dB difference between standard operating level (+4 dBm) and the 3% distortion point.

HERTZ — Cycles per second. The unit of measurement of frequency.

HIGH FREQUENCY FILTER — see **Filter, High Frequency**.

HIGH OUTPUT TAPE — A high sensitivity tape.

HIGH PASS FILTER — see **Filter, High Pass**.

HISS — see **Tape Hiss**.

HORN — A speaker system, so-called because of its characteristic shape. The horn design provides an efficient coupling of the diaphragm to the surrounding air mass.

HORN, FOLDED — A speaker system in which the horn is folded over on itself to conserve space. See **Baffle, Folded**.

HORN LOADED SYSTEM — Any speaker system in which a horn is used.

HORN, MULTI-CELLULAR — A horn cluster, designed to provide a wide radiation angle.

HUB — The center of a tape reel, around which the tape is wound.

HYPER-CARDIOID MICROPHONE — see **Microphone, Hyper-cardioid**.

HYSTERESIS LOOP — A graph of magnetizing force *vs.* remanent magnetization.

IDLER, CAPSTAN — see **Capstan Idler.**

IMAGE SHIFT — An undesired change in the apparent location of a recorded sound source.

IMPACT NOISE — see **Noise, Impact.**

IMPEDANCE — The opposition of a circuit to the flow of alternating current. Impedance is the complex sum of resistance and reactance.

IMPEDANCE, HIGH — Generally, a circuit with an impedance of several thousand ohms or more.

IMPEDANCE, LOW — Generally, a circuit with an impedance of 600 ohms or less.

IMPEDANCE MATCHING TRANSFORMER — see **Transformer, Impedance Matching.**

INCOHERENT SIGNALS — Two complex waveforms that are — most of the time — of opposite polarity.

INDIRECT RADIATOR — see **Radiator, Indirect.**

INDUCTANCE — An opposition to a change in current.

INDUCTOR — An electronic component that opposes a change in current.

INERTANCE — The acoustical equivalent of inductance.

INFINITE BAFFLE — see **Baffle, Infinite.**

INSERTION GAIN/LOSS — A change in signal level, as a result of inserting an electronic component (amplifier, signal processing device, pad, etc.) in a line.

INTENSITY, ACOUSTIC — A measure of acoustic power per unit area. At the threshold of hearing, the acoustic intensity is 0.000000000001 watts/m^2.

INTERFACE — The proper inter-connection of two networks, components, or systems.

ISOLOOP — A registered trade name of the 3M Company, describing their closed loop tape path. See **Closed Loop Tape Path.**

ISOLATION — The acoustic (or electrical) separation of one sound source from another.

ISOLATION BOOTH — A small room, used to acoustically separate a soloist from the rest of the musical group being recorded at the same time.

JACK BAY — In a recording console or equipment rack, a strip of female input and ouput sockets, used in conjunction with patch cords for signal routing purposes.

JACK FIELD — A jack bay.

KEPEX – A trade name of Allison Research, Inc., to describe its KEyable Program EXpander.

KEYING INPUT – On a signal processing device, an input for a control input.

KEYING SIGNAL – A control signal, routed to the keying input.

KILO – A prefix, abbreviated k, for thousand. 10 kohms = ten thousand ohms.

LEADER TAPE – Non-magnetic tape, spliced between segments of magnetic tape, to visually indicate the beginning and end of the recording.

LEAKAGE – Extraneous sounds, picked up by a microphone. Generally used to describe the unwanted sound of one musical instrument as heard by a microphone in front of another instrument.

LEAKAGE, HEADPHONE – The transmission of sound, from a headphone to a nearby microphone.

LENS, ACOUSTIC – see **Acoustic Lens.**

LEVEL – The magnitude of a signal, expressed in decibels.

LEVEL SENSING CIRCUIT – Any circuit that converts an audio signal into a control voltage, which may be used to regulate the operating parameters of a signal processing device.

LIMITER – A compressor, whose output level remains constant, regardless of its input level. Generally, a compressor with a compression ratio of 10:1 or greater.

LIMITER, PROGRAM – see **Compressor, Program.**

LIMITING THRESHOLD – see **Threshold, Limiting.**

LINE – A transmission line, or, any signal path.

LINE, BALANCED – see **Balanced Line.**

LINE LEVEL – A signal whose level is at, or about, +4 dBm.

LINE MATCHING TRANSFORMER – An impedance matching transformer, used to match the impedance of one line to another.

LINE MICROPHONE – see **Microphone, Line.**

LINE PAD – An attenuation network, designed for insertion in a line.

LINE, 600 OHM – A transmission line with a characteristic impedance of 600 ohms.

LINE, UNBALANCED – see **Unbalanced Line.**

LIVE RECORDING – A recording made at a concert. Sometimes used to describe any recording that is done all at once, as opposed to a Sel-Sync session.

LOAD RESISTOR – A resistor placed across a line to meet impedance matching requirements. A resistor placed across the output terminals of an amplifier for testing purposes. The resistor takes the place of the normal load.

LOADING – Placing a load across a line. Often used to describe the effect on a circuit of a load that is equal to, or less than, the characteristic impedance of the line to which it is connected.

LOBES – The side and rear protrusions on some uni-directional polar patterns, denoting slight sensitivity increases at various off-axis angles. The front and rear segments of a bi-directional polar pattern.

LOG – A logarithm.

LOGARITHM – The logarithm of a number is that power to which 10 must be raised to equal the number. The logarithm of 1,000 is 3, since 10^3 = 1,000.

LOUDNESS – The subjective impression of the intensity of a sound.

LOUDSPEAKER – A transducer that converts electrical energy into acoustical energy.

LOUDSPEAKER, CAPACITOR – an electrostatic loudspeaker.

LOUDSPEAKER, CONDENSER – an electrostatic loudspeaker.

LOUDSPEAKER CONE – The diaphragm of a moving coil loudspeaker.

LOUDSPEAKER DAMPING – see **Damping.**

LOUDSPEAKER DIAPHRAGM – The moving membrane in a loudspeaker.

LOUDSPEAKER, DYNAMIC – A moving coil or ribbon loudspeaker.

LOUDSPEAKER, ELECTROSTATIC – A loudspeaker in which the diaphragm is one plate of a capacitor.

LOUDSPEAKER, MOVING COIL – A loudspeaker in which the diaphragm is attached to a voice coil suspended in a magnetic field.

LOUDSPEAKER POLAR PATTERN – see **Polar Pattern, Loudspeaker.**

LOUDSPEAKER RADIATION PATTERN – see **Polar Pattern, Loudspeaker.**

LOUDSPEAKER, RIBBON – A loudspeaker in which the diaphragm is a ribbon.

LOUDSPEAKER TRANSIENT RESPONSE – see **Transient Response.**

LOUDSPEAKER VOICE COIL – The moving coil to which the loudspeaker diaphragm is attached.

LOW FREQUENCY FILTER – see **Filter, Low Frequency.**

LOW PASS FILTER – see **Filter, Low Pass.**

M-S RECORDING – A coincident microphone technique, in which the M (middle) microphone is cardioid, pointing toward the middle of the orchestra, and the S (side) microphone is a Figure-8, with its dead sides on the same axis as the front of the cardioid.

MAGNETIC FIELD — The magnetic flux surrounding a magnet or a section of magnetic recording tape.

MAGNETIC FLUX — see **Flux.**

MAGNETIC RECORDING TAPE — A recording medium, consisting of magnetic particles, suspended in a binder, and coated on a plastic or other film base.

MASKING — The process by which a sound source becomes inaudible, due to the presence of some other sound source in the immediate area.

MASTER FADER — see **Fader, Master.**

MASTER TAPE — A completed tape, used in tape-to-disc transfer, or from which other tape copies are produced.

MATCHING TRANSFORMER — see **Transformer, Impedance. Matching.**

MATRIX — A transformer network, in which the outputs of an M-S microphone pair are combined additively and subtractively, to produce left and right output signals for stereo reproduction.

METER, PEAK READING — A meter whose ballistics allow it to closely follow the peaks in a program. Also called a peak program meter.

METER, SOUND LEVEL — A decibel-calibrated meter, used to measure sound pressure levels.

METER, VU — A meter calibrated to read volume units.

MICROBAR — A unit of pressure, equal to 1 dyne/cm^2.

MICROPHONE — A transducer that converts acoustical energy into electrical energy.

MICROPHONE, BI-DIRECTIONAL — A microphone with a bi-directional polar pattern. See **Polar Pattern, Bi-directional.**

MICROPHONE, BLUMLEIN PAIR — see **Blumlein Pair.**

MICROPHONE, CAPACITOR — A microphone in which the diaphragm is one plate of a capacitor.

MICROPHONE, CARDIOID — A microphone with a cardioid polar pattern. See **Polar Pattern, Cardioid.**

MICROPHONE, COINCIDENT — Two or more microphones on the same vertical axis. A stereo microphone.

MICROPHONE, CONDENSER — The popular name for a capacitor microphone.

MICROPHONE, CONTACT — see **Contact Microphone.**

MICROPHONE, DUAL DIAPHRAGM — A microphone with two

diaphragms. The second diaphragm may be electronically combined with the first to produce more than one polar pattern. In another type of dual diaphragm microphone, the two diaphragms are for high and low frequencies.

MICROPHONE, DUAL PATTERN — A microphone with two switchable polar patterns.

MICROPHONE, DYNAMIC — A moving coil or ribbon microphone.

MICROPHONE, ELECTRET — A microphone with a permanently charged capacitor/diaphragm.

MICROPHONE, ELECTROSTATIC — A capacitor microphone.

MICROPHONE, FIGURE-8 — A microphone with a bi-directional polar pattern. See **Polar Pattern, Bi-directional.**

MICROPHONE, HYPER-CARDIOID — A microphone with a hyper-cardioid polar pattern. See **Polar Pattern, Hyper-cardioid.**

MICROPHONE, LAVALIER — A microphone designed to be worn on a cord around the neck. Primarily used for announcers, talk shows, etc.

MICROPHONE LINE — Any line between a microphone and the first stage of amplification.

MICROPHONE, LINE — A highly directional microphone.

MICROPHONE/LINE SELECTOR SWITCH — On a recording console, a two position switch which allows any input module to be assigned to a microphone in the studio, or to a previously recorded track on a tape recorder.

MICROPHONE, MOVING COIL — A microphone in which the diaphragm is attached to a voice coil, suspended in a magnetic field.

MICROPHONE, MULTI-PATTERN — A microphone with more than two switchable polar patterns.

MICROPHONE, OMNI-DIRECTIONAL — A microphone with an omni-directional polar pattern. See **Polar Pattern, Omni-directional.**

MICROPHONE, PHASE SHIFT — A microphone whose directional characteristics are the result of acoustic phase shifts within the microphone. A uni-directional microphone.

MICROPHONE PREAMPLIFIER — In a recording console, the first stage of amplification, which raises microphone levels to line level. Also, the amplifier built into a condenser microphone.

MICROPHONE, PRESSURE — A microphone that responds to instantaneous variations in air pressure, caused by the sound wave in the vicinity of the microphone. An omni-directional microphone.

MICROPHONE, PRESSURE GRADIENT – A microphone that responds to the difference in acoustic pressure between the front and rear of the diaphragm. A bi-directional microphone.

MICROPHONE, RIBBON – A microphone in which the diaphragm is a ribbon.

MICROPHONE, SHOT-GUN – A highly directional microphone, so-called because of its characteristic appearance.

MICROPHONE, STEREO – A microphone with two separate transducing systems, built into one housing. The two outputs are kept separate, and are fed to two separate tracks on the tape recorder.

MICROPHONE, SUPER-CARDIOID – A microphone with a super-cardioid polar pattern. See **Polar Pattern, Super-cardioid**.

MICROPHONE, ULTRA-DIRECTIONAL – A microphone with an ultra-directional polar pattern. See **Polar Pattern, Ultra-directional**.

MICROPHONE, UNI-DIRECTIONAL – A microphone with a uni-directional polar pattern. See **Polar Pattern, Uni-directional**.

MICROPHONE VOLTAGE RATING – see **Open Circuit Voltage Rating**.

MIDDLE-SIDES RECORDING – see **M-S Recording**.

MIL – One thousandth of an inch.

MILLI – One thousandth.

MIXDOWN SESSION – A recording session, during which the many separate tracks of information on a multi-track tape are processed and combined (that is, mixed down) to form a two or four track program, which is then recorded on a second machine.

MIXER – see **Fader**.

MODULATION NOISE – see **Noise, Modulation**.

MONITOR – A loudspeaker in a control room or other listening area, so-called because its primary purpose is to monitor the recorded performance, signal transmission, etc.

MONOPHONIC – Pertaining to an audio system in which the entire program is heard from a single sound source.

MOTION SENSING – On a tape recorder, a system which prevents tape damage when the play button is depressed while the machine is in either rewind or fast forward. The motion sensing system brings the tape to a complete stop before going into the play mode.

MOVING COIL LOUDSPEAKER – see **Loudspeaker, Moving Coil**.

MOVING COIL MICROPHONE – see **Microphone, Moving Coil**.

MULTI-CELLULAR HORN – see **Horn, Multi-Cellular**.

MULTI-MICROPHONE TECHNIQUE – The practice of using many close up microphones, as opposed to a coincident pair, or similar stereo pickup.

MULTI-PATTERN MICROPHONE – see **Microphone, Multi-Pattern.**

MULTI-TRACK – Referring to a tape recorder, recording console, etc., in which there are more than two tracks of recorded information. Generally, Multi-Track implies eight or more tracks.

N.A.B. – National Association of Broadcasters.

NANOWEBER – A unit of magnetic flux. The flux density, or fluxivity, of a test tape is measured in nanowebers per meter.

NARROW BAND NOISE – see **Noise, Narrow Band.**

NECK – The narrow end of a horn, where it connects to the driver.

NETWORK, CROSSOVER – see **Crossover Network.**

NETWORK, WEIGHTING – see **Weighting Network.**

NEWTON – A unit of force. The sound pressure level at the threshold of hearing is 0.00002 newtons/m^2.

NOISE, AMBIENT – The long term noise within any environment, in the absence of extraneous sound sources.

NOISE, ASPERITY – Literally, roughness noise. An increase in noise level over a narrow bandwidth on either side of a recorded frequency.

NOISE, BACKGROUND – The noise level of the surrounding environment.

NOISE FILTER – A filter, such as a notch or cut-off filter, designed to filter out narrow band noise, or noise at either frequency extreme.

NOISE GATE – An expander, whose threshold is set to attenuate low level signals, such as leakage, rumble, etc.

NOISE, IMPACT – Noise that is a function of a mechanical contact with, or by, a moving object.

NOISE LEVEL – The amplitude of a noise. Usually refers to the decibel level of a steady state noise.

NOISE, MODULATION – Noise components across the entire audio bandwidth that are produced by any audio signal.

NOISE, NARROW BAND – Noise that is confined to, or measured across, a relatively narrow bandwidth.

NOISE, PINK – Wideband noise that maintains constant energy per octave.

NOISE, QUIESCENT – The noise of an audio system in a static condition; that is, with no applied signal.

NOISE REDUCTION SYSTEM – A signal processing system designed

466

to attenuate noise components within an audio system.

NOISE, RESIDUAL — The noise level of a tape, after it has been erased.

NOISE VOLTAGE — A noise measured on a voltage scale.

NOISE, WHITE — A wideband noise that contains equal energy at each frequency.

NOISE, WIDE BAND — Noise that is distributed over most, or all, of the audio bandwidth. See **Pink, White Noise.**

NON-COMPLEMENTARY SIGNAL PROCESSING — Signal processing that is done either before or after recording. See **Complementary Signal Processing.**

NOTCH FILTER — see **Filter, Notch.**

OCTAVE — The interval between any two frequencies, f_1 and f_2, when $f_2 = 2f_1$.

OERSTED — A unit of magnetic force, symbolized by the letter H.

OFF-AXIS — Not directly in front (of a microphone or loudspeaker, for example).

OFF-AXIS COLORATION — In a microphone, a deterioration in frequency response of sounds arriving from off-axis locations. In a loudspeaker, a deterioration in perceived frequency response when the listener is standing off-axis.

OHM — The unit of resistance to current flow.

OMNI-DIRECTIONAL MICROPHONE — A microphone that is equally sensitive to all sounds, regardless of the direction from which they arrive.

ON-AXIS — Directly in front (of a microphone or loudspeaker, for example).

OPEN BAFFLE — see **Baffle, Open.**

OPEN CIRCUIT VOLTAGE RATING — The output voltage of a microphone when it is not connected to a load, or, when the load is about twenty times the impedance of the microphone itself.

OPEN TRACKS — On a multi-track tape recorder, tracks that have not yet been used.

OPERATING LEVEL — The nominal level at which an audio system operates. See **Standard Operating Level.**

OSCILLATOR — A signal generator, whose output is a pure sine wave. Generally, the output frequency may be varied continuously, or in discrete steps, over the audio frequency bandwidth.

OSCILLATOR, BIAS — see **Bias Oscillator.**

OSCILLATOR, ERASE — see **Erase Oscillator.**

OSCILLATOR, VARI-SPEED – see **Vari-Speed Oscillator.**

OSCILLOSCOPE – see **Cathode Ray Oscilloscope.**

OUT TAKE – A take, or section of a take, that is to be removed or not used.

OVERDUBBING – Producing a recording by mixing previously recorded material with new material. The musicians listen to the previously recorded tape over headphones, while the old and new program material are recorded onto a second tape recorder.

OVERLOAD – The distortion that occurs when an applied signal exceeds the level at which the system will produce its maximum output level.

OVERTONE – A whole number multiple of a fundamental frequency.

OXIDE – In magnetic recording tape, a solution of magnetic particles suspended in a binder.

OXIDE, GAMMA FERRIC – see **Gamma Ferric Oxide.**

PAD – see **Attenuation Pad.**

PAN POT – A potentiometer used to vary the proportion of an audio signal routed to two or more locations.

PARAMETRIC EQUALIZER – see **Equalizer, Parametric.**

PASS BAND – The band of frequencies that are not attenuated by a filter.

PASSIVE DEVICE – A network or circuit containing only passive components, such as resistors, capacitors and inductors.

PASSIVE RADIATOR – see **Radiator, Passive.**

PATCH BAY – see **Jack Bay.**

PATCH CORD – A short length of cable, with a coaxial plug on each end, used for signal routing in a jack bay.

PATCH POINT – Any socket in a jack bay.

PATH LENGTH – The total point-to-point distance between a sound source and the listener.

PEAKS – The instantaneous high level transients of an audio signal.

PEAK PROGRAM METER – see **Meter, Peak Reading.**

PEAK READING METER – see **Meter, Peak Reading.**

PEAK EXPANSION – see **Expansion, Peak.**

PHANTOM POWER SUPPLY – see **Power Supply, Phantom.**

PHASE – The instantaneous relationship between two measured signals, when both are derived from a single, pure sine wave input. When the two outputs are always of the same polarity, the signals are said to be "in phase." When the outputs are always of opposite polarity, the signals are 180° out of phase, or "out of phase." Other polarity relationships are expressed as a number of degrees of phase shift. The word phase is often used to describe the relationship between complex waveforms.

PHASE CANCELLATION – The attenuation that occurs when two waveforms of equal frequency and opposite polarity are combined. The attenuation may be total when the waveforms are also of equal amplitude.

PHASE SHIFT – The angular displacement, measured in degrees, between two sine waves of the same frequency.

PHASE SHIFT, CROSSOVER NETWORK – The phase shift introduced by a crossover network.

PHASE SHIFT, EQUALIZER – The phase shift introduced in a signal path by the insertion of equalization.

PHASE SHIFT MICROPHONE – see **Microphone, Phase Shift.**

PHASING – A variable comb filter effect, created by mixing a direct signal with the same signal, passed through a phase shift network.

PHON – A unit of loudness level, related to the ear's subjective impression of signal strength. At 1,000 Hz, the phon rating corresponds to the measured sound level. At all other frequencies, a sound level which – to the listener – seems to be of the same loudness as the 1,000 Hz tone, is given the same phon rating, regardless of the actual measured sound level.

PINCH ROLLER – A capstan idler.

PINK NOISE – see **Noise, Pink.**

PLAYBACK EQUALIZATION – see **Equalization, Playback.**

PLAYBACK HEAD – see **Head, Playback.**

POINT SOURCE – Theoretically, a source of sound, of infinitely small dimension, located in free space.

POLAR PATTERN – A graph of a transducer's directional sensitivity, measured over a 360° circumference drawn around the transducer. See **Polar Pattern, Loudspeaker,** and **Polar Pattern, Microphone.**

POLAR PATTERN, BI-DIRECTIONAL – A polar pattern with axes of maximum sensitivity at 0° and 180°, and minimum sensitivity at 90° and 270°.

POLAR PATTERN, CARDIOID – A uni-directional polar pattern, with the axis of minimum sensitivity at 180°. The pattern is so-called because of its characteristic shape.

POLAR PATTERN, COTTAGE LOAF – A hyper- or super-cardioid polar pattern.

POLAR PATTERN, FIGURE-8 – A bi-directional polar pattern, so-called because of its characteristic shape.

POLAR PATTERN, LOUDSPEAKER – A graph of a loudspeaker's measured output level at various points on a 360° circumference drawn around the speaker.

POLAR PATTERN, HYPER-CARDIOID – A uni-directional polar pattern, slightly narrower than a regular cardioid pattern, and with a lobe in the rear. Axes of minimum sensitivity are at about 110° and 250°.

POLAR PATTERN, MICROPHONE – A graph of a microphone's relative output level for sound sources originating at various points on a 360° circumference drawn around the transducer.

POLAR PATTERN, OMNI-DIRECTIONAL – A circular polar pattern, indicating equal sensitivity (or measured output level) at all angles on a 360° circumference drawn around the transducer.

POLAR PATTERN, SUPER-CARDIOID – A uni-directional polar pattern, slightly narrower than a regular cardioid pattern, with a lobe in the rear that is somewhat wider than the one on a hyper-cardioid pattern. The axes of minimum sensitivity are at about 125° and 235°.

POLAR PATTERN, UNI-DIRECTIONAL – A polar pattern of a microphone that is most sensitive to sounds originating directly in front of it.

POLARITY – Referring to the positive or negative direction of an electrical or magnetic force.

POLARIZING VOLTAGE – The charging voltage applied to the capacitor/diaphragm of a condenser (capacitor) microphone.

POLYESTER – A plastic film, used as a base material in the production of magnetic recording tape.

POP FILTER – A wind screen.

PORT, SPEAKER – An opening in the front baffle of a loudspeaker cabinet.

PORTS, REAR- AND SIDE-ENTRY – Openings to the rear and side of a uni-directional microphone, allowing sound waves to reach the rear of the diaphragm.

POST-ECHO – see Echo, Post-.

POST-EMPHASIS – Playback equalization.

POTENTIOMETER – A network consisting of a resistor and a wiper arm. The resistance, measured from either end of the resistor to the wiper arm, is continuously variable, according to the position of the wiper arm.

POWER – Rate of flow of energy, developed by an acoustical or electrical system.

470

POWER, ACOUSTIC – The sound energy produced by a sound source.

POWER, ELECTRICAL – The electrical energy produced or dissipated in a circuit.

POWER SUPPLY – A circuit supplying d.c. power to an amplifier or other electronic system.

POWER SUPPLY, MICROPHONE – A circuit supplying d.c. power to a condenser (capacitor) microphone.

POWER SUPPLY, PHANTOM – A circuit that supplies d.c. powering to condenser microphones, using the same conductors as the audio signal.

PREAMPLIFIER – In an audio system, the first stage of amplification, usually designed to boost very low level signal to about line level.

PREAMPLIFIER, MICROPHONE – see **Microphone Preamplifier.**

PRE-ECHO – see **Echo, Pre-.**

PRE-EMPHASIS – Record equalization.

PRESENCE – An equalization boost in the middle or upper middle frequency range, often used to give a voice a more close-up effect.

PRESSURE GRADIENT MICROPHONE – see **Microphone, Pressure Gradient.**

PRESSURE LEVEL, SOUND – The acoustic pressure, expressed in decibels. The sound pressure level at the threshold of hearing is 0 dB SPL.

PRESSURE MICROPHONE – see **Microphone, Pressure.**

PRESSURE, SOUND – The acoustic pressure of a sound wave. The sound pressure at the threshold of hearing is 2×10^{-5} newtons/m^2.

PRINT-THROUGH – The transfer of a signal from one layer of magnetic tape to an adjacent layer.

PROGRAM COMPRESSOR – see **Compressor, Program.**

PROGRAM LIMITER – see **Compressor, Program.**

PROTECTION COPY – A copy of a master tape, generally filed as a protection against the damage or loss of the master tape.

PROXIMITY EFFECT – In a cardioid microphone, a rise in low frequency response when the microphone is used at very close working distances.

PSYCHOACOUSTICS – The study of the brain's perception of, and reaction to, all aspects of sound. (i.e., intensity, time of arrival differences, reverberation, et al.)

PUCK – see **Capstan Idler.**

PUMPING – see **Breathing.**

PUNCHING IN – The practice of recording a track, or tracks, in small segments, say one phrase at a time. So-called because the engineer spends so much time "punching" the record button.

PURE TONE – A single frequency sine wave, with no harmonics present.

Q – In a bandpass equalizer, the ratio of center frequency to bandwidth. $Q = \dfrac{fc}{\text{bandwidth}}$

QUIESCENT NOISE – see **Noise, Quiescent.**

RADIAN – The angle subtended by an arc that is equal in length to the radius of the circle of which it is a part. (Approximately 57.29°)

RADIATION PATTERN – The polar pattern of a loudspeaker.

RADIATOR, DIRECT – A loudspeaker diaphragm that is coupled directly to the surrounding air mass of the listening room.

RADIATOR, INDIRECT – A loudspeaker diaphragm that is coupled to the surrounding air mass by an acoustic impedance matching transformer; that is, a horn.

RADIATOR, PASSIVE – An unpowered loudspeaker cone, placed in the port of a vented enclosure system. Also called a drone cone, or a slave cone.

RAREFACTION – The instantaneous spreading apart of air particles during the negative going half cycle of a sound wave. The opposite of condensation.

RATIO, COMPRESSION – see **Compression Ratio.**

RATIO, EXPANSION – see **Expansion Ratio.**

RATIO, SIGNAL-TO-NOISE – see **Signal-to-Noise Ratio.**

REAR ENTRY PORT – see **Ports, Rear- and Side-Entry.**

RECORD EQUALIZATION – see **Equalization, Record.**

RECORD HEAD – see **Head, Record.**

RECORDING CONSOLE – see **Console, Recording.**

RECOVERY TIME – see **Release Time.**

REFERENCE FLUXIVITY – see **Fluxivity, Reference.**

REFERENCE LEVEL – A standard level, such as 0 VU, + 4 dBm, 0 dBV, to which other levels may be compared.

REFERENCE TONE – A single frequency tone, recorded at the head of a tape and used for alignment purposes when the tape is replayed at a later date.

REFLECTED SOUND – Sound waves that reach the listener after being reflected from one or more surfaces.

REFRACTION – The change of direction, or bending, of a sound wave as it passes from one medium to another.

REINFORCEMENT – An increase in amplitude when two sound waves combine additively.

RELEASE TIME – The time it takes for a signal processing device, such as a compressor or expander, to return to its normal gain-before-threshold, once the applied signal is removed or attenuated.

RELUCTANCE – Opposition to a magnetic force. Reluctance is analagous to resistance in a purely electrical circuit.

REMANENCE – The magnetization left on a tape when a magnetic force is removed. Remanence is measured in lines of flux per quarter inch of tape width. Also called remanent flux.

REMANENT FLUX – see **Remanence**.

REPRODUCING CHARACTERISTIC – The frequency response of the post-emphasis circuit in a tape recorder. The C.C.I.R. and the N.A.B. have both published recommended reproducing characteristics.

RESIDUAL MAGNETIZATION – The magnetization remaining in a magnetic material once an applied magnetic force is removed.

RESIDUAL NOISE – see **Noise, Residual**.

RESISTANCE – The opposition of a circuit to a flow of direct current. Resistance is measured in ohms, abbreviated Ω, and may be calculated from the formula, $R = E/I$.

RESISTOR – An electronic component that opposes current flow.

RESONANCE – The condition of a system when the applied frequency is equal to the natural frequency of vibration of the system.

RESONANCE, ROOM – A resonant condition that is a function of the dimensions of a room.

RESONANT PEAK – The increase in amplitude that occurs at the resonant frequency.

RETENTIVITY – A measure of a magnetic tape's flux density after a saturation-producing magnetic field has been withdrawn.

REVERBERATION – Many repetitions of an audio signal, becoming more closely spaced (denser) with time.

REVERBERATION SYSTEM – Any electronic or acoustical device used, to simulate the natural reverberation of a large concert hall, or to produce a reverberant effect.

RIBBON LOUDSPEAKER – see **Loudspeaker, Ribbon**.

RIBBON MICROPHONE – see **Microphone, Ribbon**.

ROOM ACOUSTICS – The properties of a room that affect the quality of a sound source in the room. (i.e., reverberation, resonance modes, etc.)

ROOM EQUALIZATION – see **Equalization, Room.**

ROOM MODES – Increases in amplitude at resonant frequencies that are a function of the dimensions of a room.

ROOM RESONANCE – see **Resonance, Room.**

ROOM RESONANCE MODES – see **Room Modes.**

ROOM SOUND – The distinctive acoustical characteristic of a particular room or concert hall. The characteristic ambient sound of a room or concert hall.

ROTATION POINT – The point at which the transfer characteristic of a compressor or expander intersects the unity gain curve.

RUMBLE – Unwanted low frequency signals that are a function of mechanical vibrations.

SATURATION – The condition of exceeding a tape's magnetic capacity.

SATURATION DISTORTION – The distortion created by driving a magnetic tape beyond its saturation point.

SATURATION POINT – The level, beyond which any further increase in applied signal strength will cause no further increase in fluxivity.

SCRAPE FLUTTER – see **Flutter, Scrape.**

SCRAPE FLUTTER FILTER – see **Flutter Filter.**

SEALED ENCLOSURE – A loudspeaker cabinet with no vents or ports, as in an acoustic suspension system.

SELF-ERASURE – The condition whereby a record head tends to partially erase a high level, high frequency signal as it is being recorded.

SEL-SYNC – A trade name of the Ampex Corporation used to describe the process of using the record head for playback of previously recorded tracks, while simultaneously recording new material on open tracks. Sel-Sync is an abbreviation of selective synchronization.

SELECTIVE SYNCHRONIZATION – see **Sel-Sync.**

SENSITIVITY – The acuity of the ear, or the response of a transducer, to various properties of a sound wave, such as frequency, level, angle of arrival, etc. On magnetic recording tape, an indication of the tape's relative output level, as compared to some specified reference tape.

SEPARATION – A measure of the degree of segregation of one signal from another.

SHELVING EQUALIZER – see **Equalizer, Shelving.**

SHIELD – Any device used to reduce the effects of spurious electrical or magnetic fields on a signal path or system.

SHIELDED CABLE – Any cable in which the conductors are protected by a surrounding braided or foil shielding.

SHOCK MOUNT – A suspension system which mechanically isolates a microphone from its stand or boom, thus protecting the microphone against mechanical vibrations.

SIBILANCE – A hissy type of distortion often produced by the presence of high energy level in words containing 's' sounds.

SIBILANT – A description of those consonants that are uttered with an 's' sound. (s, z, sh, zh, etc.)

SIDE CHAIN – A secondary signal path through which a signal may be processed before recombination with the primary signal path. As an example, the companding action in a Dolby Noise Reduction System takes place in the system's side chain.

SIDE-ENTRY PORT – see **Ports, Rear- and Side-Entry.**

SIGNAL FLOW CHART – A block diagram of a recording console or other audio system, showing the various possible signal paths through the system, but not detailing the actual electronic components making up each part of the system.

SIGNAL GENERATOR – A test instrument whose output may be one or another of the following; sine wave, square wave, sawtooth, ramp voltage, etc.

SIGNAL PROCESSING DEVICE – An audio system (equalizer, compressor, expander, et al) used to modify some characteristic of the signal passing through it.

SIGNAL ROUTING – The process of devising a signal path through a console or other audio system, using bus assignment switches, or patch cords.

SIGNAL-TO-NOISE RATIO – The ratio of the signal voltage to the noise voltage, usually expressed as the decibel difference between the signal level and the noise level.

SINE WAVE – The waveform of a single frequency.

SKEW – A deflection of a tape, as it passes over an improperly aligned head or tape guide.

SLAP-BACK – An audibly distracting echo from a reflective surface in a room.

SLATING – Recording of an announcement of the take number at the beginning of a recording.

SLAVE CONE – see **Radiator, Passive.**

SOLO SWITCH – On a recording console's input module, a switch that turns off the normal monitor system, and instead routes the appropriate input signal directly to the monitor.

SOUND LEVEL – see **Pressure Level, Sound.**

SOUND LEVEL METER – see **Meter, Sound Level.**

SOUND PRESSURE – see **Pressure, Sound.**

SOUND PRESSURE LEVEL – see **Pressure Level, Sound.**

SOUND SOURCE, IDEAL – Theoretically, a sound source in the form of a pulsating sphere of infinitely small dimension.

SOUND WAVE – The periodic variations in air pressure, radiating away from a sound source.

SOUND WAVE, SPHERICAL – The shape of a sound wave radiating away from an ideal sound source. Practical sound sources usually produce sound waves resembling a segment of a spherical sound wave.

SPECTRUM, FREQUENCY – A distribution of frequencies. For example, the frequencies within the audio bandwidth may be called the audio frequency spectrum.

SPHERICAL RADIATOR – An ideal sound source. See **Sound Source, Ideal.**

SPHERICAL SOUND WAVE – see **Sound Wave, Spherical.**

SPLICE – The point at which two pieces of magnetic tape are joined together, as in editing.

SPLICING BLOCK – A device used for positioning and holding down a section of magnetic tape while making splices.

SPLICING TAPE – An adhesive tape used for joining spliced tapes.

SPLIT FEED – Any network that enables a signal to be routed to two or more separate outputs.

SPRING REVERBERATION SYSTEM – An artificial reverberation system using springs to simulate the sound of natural reverberation.

STANDARD OPERATING LEVEL – A specified reference level. In recording applications, standard operating level is defined as 0 VU = + 4 dBm. In broadcasting, 0 VU = + 8 dBm.

STANDING WAVE – An apparently stationary waveform, created by a reflection back towards the sound source. At certain points along the standing wave path, the reflected and direct waves will always cancel, while at other fixed points the waves will reinforce each other.

STATIC SIGNAL PROCESSING DEVICE – A signal processing device whose operating parameters are not affected by the signal

passing through the device. See **Dynamic Signal Processing Device.**
STATIONARY WAVE – A standing wave.
STEEL PLATE REVERBERATION SYSTEM – An artificial
   reverberation system using a steel plate to simulate the sound
   of natural reverberation.
STERADIAN – The solid angle which, on a sphere, encloses a
   surface equal to the square of the radius of the sphere.
STEREO MICROPHONE – see **Microphone, Stereo.**
STEREOPHONIC – An audio system which reproduces spatial
   information, giving the listener the illusion of width and depth.
STEREOSONIC RECORDING – A stereo recording made with two
   bi-directional microphones whose axes are at $90°$ to each other.
   The microphones are usually aimed at the extreme right and left
   edges of the sound source to be recorded.
STRETCHED – Encoded, as in a noise reduction system.
SUB-MASTER – Any tape used in the production of a master tape.
   For example, if a master tape is an equalized (or otherwise
   processed) copy of an earlier tape, the earlier tape is called the
   sub-master.
SUPER-CARDIOID MICROPHONE – see **Microphone, Super-
cardioid.**
SUPPLY REEL – On a tape recorder, the reel from which tape winds,
   as it passes the head assembly.
SUPPLY REEL MOTOR – On a tape recorder, the motor that is
   used to supply hold-back tension to the tape on the supply reel,
   and to rewind the tape.
SWEETENING SESSION – A recording session during which strings,
   brass, chorus, etc. may be added to a previously recorded tape,
   usually containing basic rhythm tracks.
SYNC HEAD – The record head, when used as a playback head
   during a Sel-Sync session.
SYNC LEVEL – Pertaining to the output level of the sync head.
SYNC OUTPUT – The output of the sync head, in the Sel-Sync
   mode.
TAKE – An uninterrupted segment of a recording.
TAKE UP REEL – On a tape recorder, the reel on which tape is
   wound as it leaves the head assembly.
TAKE UP REEL MOTOR – On a tape recorder, the motor that is
   used, to supply take-up tension to the tape on the take-up reel
   and, for fast forward operation.
TALKBACK SYSTEM – The communication system by which

control room personnel may communicate with musicians in the studio, usually over the regular studio monitor system.

TANGENCY – The tangential relationship of the tape with the convex surface of the head, as measured at the location of the head gap.

TAPE DELAY SYSTEM – A delay system using an auxiliary tape recorder. The delay is a function of the tape transit time as it travels from the record head to the playback head.

TAPE HEADROOM – see **Headroom.**

TAPE, HIGH OUTPUT – see **High Output Tape.**

TAPE HISS – A low level, wide spectrum noise heard when a recorded tape is played back.

TAPE OVERLOAD – see **Overload** and **Saturation.**

TAPE SATURATION – see **Saturation.**

TAPE SENSITIVITY – see **Sensitivity.**

TELEPHONE FILTER – see **Filter, Telephone.**

TENSION, HOLD-BACK – The torque applied by the supply reel motor to keep the tape from freely spilling off the supply reel, and to maintain good tape-to-head contact.

TENSION, SUPPLY REEL – see **Tension, Hold-back.**

TENSION SWITCH – On a tape recorder, a two position switch which changes the torque applied by the reel motor(s).

TENSION, TAKE-UP – The torque applied by the take-up reel motor, to maintain a smooth wind as the tape leaves the capstan/capstan idler assembly.

TEST TAPE – A tape containing a series of test tones at a standard reference fluxivity. The test tape is used to verify the performance of the tape recorder's playback system.

TEST TAPE, ELEVATED LEVEL – A test tape with a higher-than-normal reference fluxivity. Such test tapes usually read about 3 dB higher than standard test tapes.

THIRD HARMONIC DISTORTION – see **Distortion, Third Harmonic.**

THRESHOLD, COMPRESSION – The level above which a compressor begins functioning.

THRESHOLD, EXPANSION – The level below which an expander begins functioning.

THRESHOLD, LIMITING – The level above which a limiter begins functioning.

THRESHOLD OF HEARING – The lowest level sound that an average listener with good hearing can detect.

THRESHOLD OF PAIN – The sound level at which the listener begins to experience physical pain.

THROAT – The opening at the narrow end of a horn, where it is attached to a compression driver. Also, the small diameter opening of a compression driver, where it is attached to a horn.

TIGHT SOUND – Subjective expression, describing the sound picked up by a microphone placed very close to an instrument.

TILT – A misalignment of a tape recorder head, around its vertical axis.

TIME DELAY SYSTEM – Any signal processing device, in which there is a time delay between input and output.

TRACKS – The recorded paths on a magnetic recording tape. See **Basic Tracks.**

TRACKING – The ability of a meter movement, or other dynamic device, to precisely follow the envelope of the applied waveform. The process of completing a recording session, track by track, as in a Sel-Sync session.

TRACKING ERROR – An unwanted error introduced in an audio system, when the output level or frequency response of the system deviates from the input signal.

TRANSDUCER – Any device which converts energy from one system to another. A loudspeaker is an electro-acoustical transducer.

TRANSFER CHARACTERISTIC – Any curve on a graph which is a plot of input *vs.* output.

TRANSFER CHARACTERISTIC, LINEAR – A transfer characteristic which may be drawn as a straight line.

TRANSFERRING TRACKS – see **Bouncing Tracks.**

TRANSFORMER – An electrical network consisting of two or more coils, used to couple one circuit to another.

TRANSFORMER, IMPEDANCE MATCHING – A transformer used to match the impedance of one line or network with another.

TRANSIENT – A relatively high amplitude, suddenly decaying, peak signal level.

TRANSIENT DISTORTION – see **Distortion, Transient.**

TRANSIENT RESPONSE – A measure of an audio system's ability to accurately reproduce transients.

TRANSPORT SYSTEM – In a tape recorder, the system of motors, tape guides, etc., used to move tape past the head assembly.

TURNOVER FREQUENCY – In a shelving equalizer, the frequency at which the equalizer begins to flatten out, or shelve. Defined as the frequency at which the level is 3 dB above (or below) the shelving level.

TWEETER – A high frequency loudspeaker.

ULTRA-DIRECTIONAL MICROPHONE – see **Microphone, Ultra-directional.**

UNBALANCED LINE – A line consisting of two conductors, one of which is at ground potential. The unbalanced line is often in the form of a single conductor-plus-shield, with the shield serving as the second conductor. See **Balanced Line.**

UNSTRETCHED – Decoded, as in a noise reduction system.

UNI-DIRECTIONAL MICROPHONE – A microphone that is most sensitive to front-originating sounds.

UNITY GAIN – A gain of x 1. That is, output level = input level.

VARI-SPEED OSCILLATOR – Any oscillator used to drive a tape recorder's capstan motor at various speeds, to effect pitch and tempo changes.

VARIABLE FREQUENCY OSCILLATOR – Any oscillator whose frequency may be varied, but usually used to describe a Vari-Speed Oscillator.

VELOCITY OF SOUND – The speed at which sound travels away from a sound source. The velocity of sound is 1,087 feet per second at a temperature of 32° f.

VENTED ENCLOSURE – A loudspeaker enclosure, with an open port cut into the front baffle. Also called a bass reflex enclosure.

VOICE COIL – The coil winding attached to the diaphragm of a dynamic microphone or loudspeaker.

VOICE-OVER COMPRESSOR – see **Compressor, Voice-over.**

VOLTAGE – The difference in potential between two points in an electrical circuit.

VOLTAGE RATING, MICROPHONE – see **Open Circuit Voltage Rating.**

VOLUME INDICATOR – see **Meter, VU.**

VOLUME UNIT – A unit of measurement related to the ear's subjective impression of program level or loudness.

WATT – A unit of power.

WAVE, STANDING – see **Standing Wave.**

WAVE, STATIONARY – see **Standing Wave.**

WAVEFORM – A graph of a signal's amplitude *vs.* time. The waveform of a pure tone is a sine wave.

WAVELENGTH – The length of one complete cycle of a sine wave.

WAVELENGTH RESPONSE – A graph of amplitude *vs.* wavelength.

WEBER – A unit of magnetic flux.

WEIGHTING – Filtering a frequency response, prior to measurement.

WEIGHTING, "A" – A filtering network, corresponding to the ear's sensitivity at 40 phons.

WEIGHTING, "B" – A filtering network, corresponding to the ear's sensitivity at 70 phons.

WEIGHTING, "C" – A filtering network, corresponding to the ear's sensitivity at 100 phons.

WEIGHTING NETWORK – A filter used for weighting a frequency response, prior to measurement.

WET SOUND – Subjective description of a sound with a high proportion of reverberation present.

WHITE NOISE – see **Noise, White.**

WIDE BAND NOISE – see **Noise, Wide Band.**

WIND SCREEN – An acoustically transparent filter, placed over a microphone to shield it from wind-induced vibration.

WOOFER – A low frequency loudspeaker.

WOW – A low frequency fluctuation in tape speed that results in an audible "wow", especially noticeable on sustained tones.

X AXIS – The horizontal axis on a graph or on a cathode ray oscilloscope.

X-Y RECORDING – A stereo recording made with two cardiod microphones located in the same vertical plane, with their axes about 90-135° to each other.

Y AXIS – The vertical axis on a graph or on a cathode ray oscilloscope.

Y CONNECTOR – Any 2:1 adapter placed in a line to permit a split feed.

Z AXIS – The horizontal axis on a graph or on a cathode ray oscilloscope.

ZERO REFERENCE LEVEL – see **Reference Level.**

Index

THE RECORDING STUDIO HANDBOOK

Release time
  compressor, 229
  expander, 236
Reluctance, 249
Remanence, 264
  and fluxivity, 296
Remanent flux, 264
Remanent magnetization, 253
Remote control
  of record/playback mode, 379
  of tape transport system, 294
Reproducing characteristic
  CCIR, 297
  NAB, 276-278
Residual magnetism, 251
Residual noise, 219, 313-314
Resonance
  loudspeaker, 159, 169
  room, 186-187
  peak, minimizing, 188
Resonant frequency, loudspeaker,
    159
Retentivity, 253, 263
Reverberation, 195
  chamber, acoustic, 203-204
  controls and signal paths in recording
      console, 351-352
  and decay, 198, 201
  definition, 193
  plate, 201
  spring system, 201, 203
  stereo, 204
  using, during recording, 385-386
Rewind switch, 289
Ribbon
  loudspeaker, 157
  microphone, 75
Roll-off switch, bass, microphone,
    111, 112
Room
  acoustics, 183-188, 195
  dimension ratios, 187
  equalization, 187-188
  modes, 186-187
  ratios, 187
  sound, effect of surfaces on, 184
Rotation point, 224-226
Rumble, building, 119

Safe mode, 379
Saturation, tape, 252
  vs. frequency, 271-272, 273

Scrape flutter, 291
  filter, 291
Sealed enclosure, 170
Seating plan, for recording, 384
Sel-sync process, 374-376
Self erasure, at high frequencies, 273,
    276
Sensitivity
  and bias, 261
  of ear, 59, 60
  microphone, 114
  switch, on recording console, 353, 354
  tape, 264-265
  tape, vs. bias level, 301
Separation
  microphone placement for
      maximum, 139-144
  with a figure-8 microphone, 140-141
  using isolation booths and goboes,
      141-144
Servo motor, 293
Shelving equalization, 207, 209, 212
Shield, head, 280
Shielded cable, 114-115
Shock mount, microphone, 122-124
Shot gun microphone, 97-99
Sibilants, minimizing, 232
Side chain, in Dolby Noise Reduction
    System, 328-329
Side-entry ports, microphone, 90-91
Signal flow diagrams—see Recording
    console signal flow diagrams
Signal flow path, summary of, 354
Signal processing devices
  acoustic delay line, 197
  compressors, 220-233
  digital delay line, 196-197
  dynamic complementary, 317-318
  dynamic non-complementary,
      317-318
  echo reverberation system, complete,
      205-206
  equalizers, 213-218
  expanders, 233-240
  filters, 214
  flangers, 241-244
  limiters, 220-233
  phasers, 241, 244
  in recording consoles, 342
  reverberation systems
    acoustic reverberation chambers,
      203-204

494